USING dBASE IV

BASICS FOR BUSINESS

USING dBASE IV

BASICS FOR BUSINESS

Mark Brownstein

John Wiley & Sons, Inc.
New York • Chichester • Brisbane • Toronto • Singapore

Publisher: Stephen Kippur
Editor: Therese A. Zak
Managing Editor: Ruth Greif
Editing, Design, and Production: G&H SOHO, Ltd.

Library of Congress Cataloging-in-Publication Data

Brownstein, Mark.
Using dBase IV: basics for business / Mark Brownstein.
p. cm.
Bibliography: p.
ISBN 0-471-61749-0
1. dBASE IV (Computer program) 2. Business—Data processing.
3. Data base management. I. Title. II. Title: Using dBase 4.
III. Title: Using dBase four.
HF5548.4.D243B76 1989 88-32282
650'.028'557565—dc19 CIP

Printed in the United States of America

89 90 10 9 8 7 6 5 4 3 2 1

Trademarks

Ashton-Tate, dBASE, dBASE II, dBASE III, Chart-Master, and Framework are registered trademarks, and dBASE III Plus, dBASE IV, Framework II, Framework III, and Rapid File are trademarks of Ashton-Tate Corp.

MultiMate, MultiMate Advantage, MultiMate Advantage II, and Advantage II are registered trademarks of Ashton-Tate Corp.

FoxBase and FoxBase Plus are trademarks of Fox Software, Inc.

Clipper is a trademark and Nantucket, Inc. is a registered trademark of Nantucket, Inc.

Lotus, 1-2-3, DIF, and VisiCalc are registered trademarks of Lotus Development Corp.

IBM, IBM PC, IBM PC/XT, and IBM PC/AT are registered trademarks of International Business Machines.

HotShot and HotShot Graphics are trademarks of SymSoft, Inc.

Microsoft Word, Microsoft, MultiPlan, Microsoft, MS-DOS, and Microsoft MultiPlan are registered trademarks of Microsoft Corp.

PFS, PFS File, PFS Professional File, and Professional File are trademarks of Software Publishing Co.

MailMerge is a registered trademark of MicroPro International.

For Vonnie, Charles, and Barbara.
Without you there would be no family.

And to all the people who use this book.

PREFACE

This is a book that had to be written. dBASE IV®, with its new, easy-to-use interface, opens the world of database design and management to a whole new generation of users.

Its predecessor programs—dBASE II® (for the PC and old CP/M computers) and dBASE III® and III+®—have sold millions of copies. But these earlier programs, which have dominated the PC database management market almost since their introduction, were hard to learn and hard to use. To design useful database systems, you had to go through the process of learning to write dBASE programs. If using a word processor was as difficult as using dBASE, millions more people would still be using their typewriters, and there would be millions fewer PCs in use today.

dBASE IV is targeted at two types of users. For the experienced user who is comfortable with programming dBASE, it has added significantly more functionality and improved speed of operation. It also includes automated design tools to write forms for data entry, report design and printing, labels and envelopes, design of form letters using merged text and data, a new Query By Example facility for analyzing data files, and an Applications Generator for automated application development.

But for the new user, it opens up a world of functionality that previously was available only to those users with the fortitude and aptitude to learn dBASE programming. The new user interface, via the Control Center, allows new users to do virtually all their data design and management tasks without writing a single line of program code.

The documentation provided by Ashton-Tate acknowledges the new ease-of-use features but scatters instructions for their use through a handful of manuals. This book was written as a single resource for users who want to do *real work* with dBASE IV without having to hunt for answers. It was also designed for experienced programmers who want to quickly master the elements of design built into the dBASE IV Control Center.

Acknowledgments

Although I wrote every word in this book, it wasn't a solitary effort. A number of people and products must be acknowledged for their role in actually creating the book you now hold in your hands.

This book was written using two Tandon computers—a Tandon PCA and a Tandon PAC 286 computer. Both machines performed extremely well. Special thanks go to Pat Meier of the Presentation Company, who arranged the loan of the PAC 286 and allowed me to bring my entire environment on a Data Pac and use her offices for writing during my week off from work.

The graphics and draft text were produced by a Panasonic Laser Partner printer. An AST Research RAMpage card was used in the PAC 286, but the early versions of dBASE IV used during the writing of the book were unable to make use of the expanded memory.

Graphics were captured and edited using two products: Inset and HotShot Graphics. My thanks to both companies for the use of their software.

In addition, I must thank the great people at InfoWorld who allowed me enough time to write this book. Your support means a lot to me.

And thanks also to my family, who put up with my strange hours, and got along with an absentee father and husband during the writing of this book.

Final acknowledgment goes to Bill Gladstone, my book agent, Teri Zak, Executive Editor at John Wiley, Alex Khalogli, technical editor of the manuscript, and Knox Richardson of Ashton-Tate, who provided me with prerelease copies of dBASE IV during the latter stages of its development. And a mention is due for the unnamed source of my original versions of dBASE IV—you know who you are.

Contents

USING dBASE IV
BASICS FOR BUSINESS

1 Installation and Setup

dBASE IV is designed to be easily installed on your system. In fact, it is designed to do most of the work for you.

After first looking at the directories on each disk, trying to get a feel for what files are on each disk, and trying to see how they differ from earlier versions, you may have the tendency to create subdirectories on your hard disk and copy files into it. *Don't.* The automatic installation routine provided with dBASE IV actually works very well, and still provides you with the capabilities needed to customize the program to most closely fit your needs. One reason the contents of the distribution disks cannot just be copied is that the installation program assembles an executable file that is required for the program to run.

To install dBASE IV first make backup copies of all the distribution disks that came with dBASE IV. The commands to make copies of your disks are simple and are outlined briefly here.

Make sure that the number of backup disks is equal to the number of disks that came with dBASE IV. Copy the labels from each dBASE IV disk (source disk) and affix the copies to the disk that you will be copying to (the target disk). Because dBASE IV will not be distributed on 1.2 MB floppy disks, 360 KB floppies are all you need. If dBASE IV is packaged on 3.5 inch disks, you will need 720 kilobyte target disks.

In a one-drive system, go to the DOS directory and

Type: *DISKCOPY A: B:* **ENTER**

Since the system does not detect a B: drive, it will prompt you to insert a disk in drive A: that will be written to as drive B:. On a two-drive system, in which both floppy drives use the same sized disks (two 5.25 or two 3.5 inch disks), go to the DOS directory and

Type: ***DISKCOPY* ENTER**

The system will automatically copy from one drive to the other, then prompt, asking if you want to make more copies. On a two-drive system with two dissimilar drives (for example, one 5.25 and one 3.5 inch drive), go to DOS and

Type: ***DISKCOPY A: A:* ENTER**

The system will prompt you to change disks after it has completed reading from, or writing to, the floppy disk.

Once all installation disks have been copied, enter the serial number on the disks and *put them in a safe place.* If something happens to your computer or the program, this will enable you to install dBASE IV after fixing the system problem.

To install dBASE IV, insert your copy of the *install* disk in drive A: and change to drive A:. To change to the A: drive,

Type: ***A:*ENTER**

Next,

Type: ***Install* ENTER**

The system will load a title screen, and then check to see if you have run the identification program. The identification program will ask for the serial number of your dBASE IV system disks and information about your business. This may require swapping a number of disks in and out of the drives.

Answer the system prompts to identify yourself to the system, and the system will prepare an executable system that will display your serial number and identifying data when you start dBASE IV on whichever system it is installed.

Press: **Ctrl-End**

when you have registered the dBASE IV disks.

Although dBASE IV is not copy protected, in installing from these disks your name will be seen when you boot the system. However, because the installation was done on backup disks, to change the identifying information, you may copy the Install and System 1 disks from your master disk set and reinstall the system with the new data. If the identification procedures had been performed on the original disks without backup, the identification on the dBASE IV system could not be changed.

Once the identification process has been completed, the system

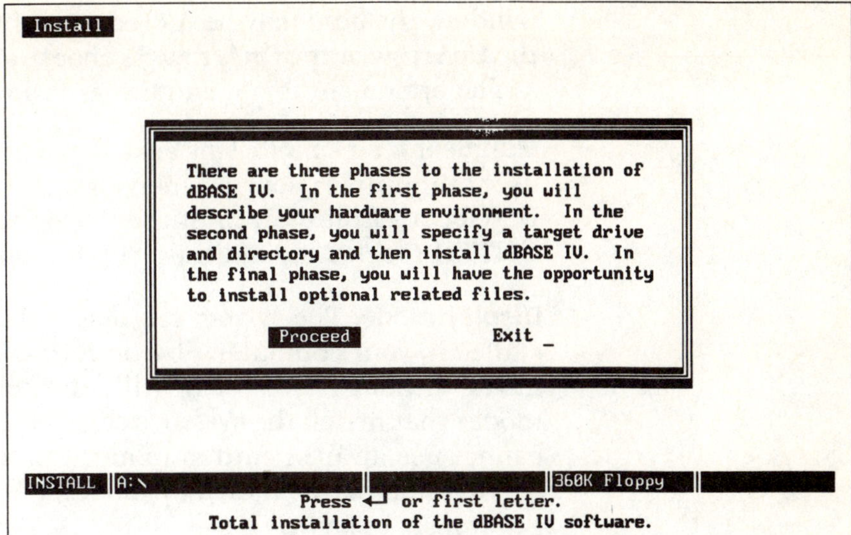

Figure 1-1

Phase 1 installation query.

will step through the phases of installation. The first screen will appear (Figure 1-1).

Press: *P*

to tell the system that you want to proceed with the installation. The Hardware Setup screen then appears (Figure 1-2). Within this

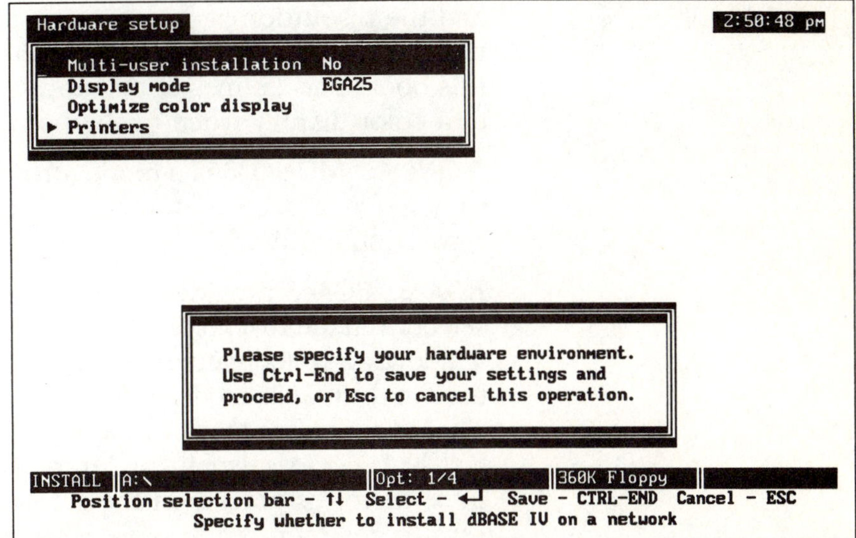

Figure 1-2

Hardware setup screen.

window, the bars may be moved to highlight each option using the **UpArrow** or the **DnArrow**. To choose an option, press **ENTER**.

The options in this menu are as follows:

Multiuser installation. This asks if you are installing for a single user or multiple users on a network, and may appear only in the Developer's Edition or multiuser versions of dBASE IV. Touching **ENTER** toggles the Multiuser option on and off.

Display mode. The system can detect the type of video card installed in your computer. Five options can be selected from this menu, although the system will later allow only those display modes that match the system's capabilities (in other words, you cannot use an EGA card in monochrome mode).

To switch between display modes,

Press: **ENTER**

to change to the next display mode.

The display options available in the initial release of dBASE IV are as follows:

Color: This option works with CGA adapters. It does not provide the higher resolutions available with EGA or high-resolution monochrome cards.

EGA25: The EGA25 mode provides 25 lines of text on an EGA screen. More colors can be used than with the Color option, and the resolution of the screen is higher. As a basic common denominator, this mode was used for the graphics in this book. The 25 lines of text approximate the appearance of a color display when printed out.

MONO43: MONO43 is a monochrome mode that produces 43 lines of text on monitors that can support the higher resolution required.

EGA43: EGA43 provides 43-line display and allows you to select from the 16-color EGA palette for display of text, boxes, windows, or other features on your screen. This palette is also used in the EGA25 mode. Both 43-line modes (mono and EGA) require a monitor that can accurately display the 43 lines of text. This mode is usually preferable to 25 line, because more information is placed on the screen at one time, and less scrolling is required to move through a database.

MONO: MONO is a 25-line, monochrome mode designed for monitors (or graphic cards) that are unable to display (or generate a display of) more than 25 lines.

Once the monitor and display type have been selected, move the cursor to the next option, Optimize color display.

Optimize color display. This option is used only with color displays. On some monitor/graphic card combinations, a high-speed scanning mode produced by the graphic card (usually a CGA adapter) creates the appearance of "snow" on the screen. This option tests the monitor/display adapter combination to determine the optimal scan rate.

To test the system, highlight "Optimize color display" and

Press: **ENTER**

(Figure 1-3). To perform the test,

Press: *P*

or

Press: **ENTER**

The system then produces a test screen (Figure 1-4).

Figure 1-3

Snow test selection screen.

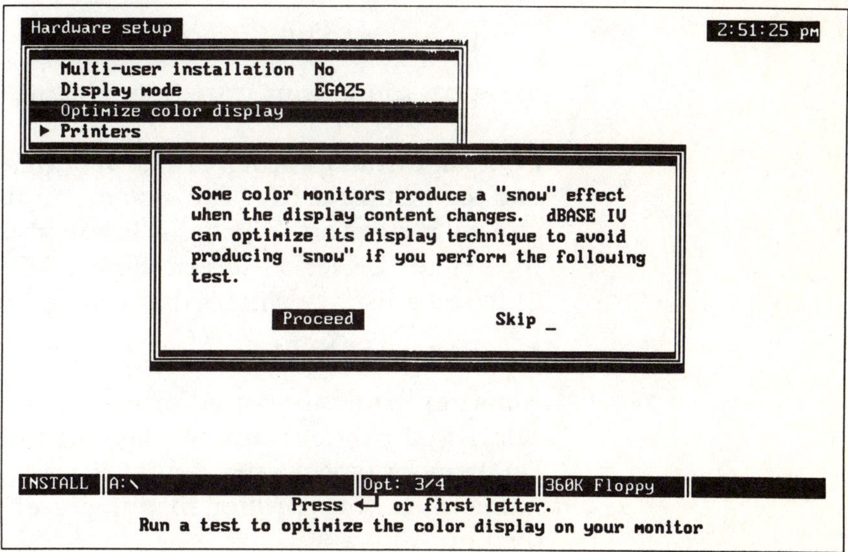

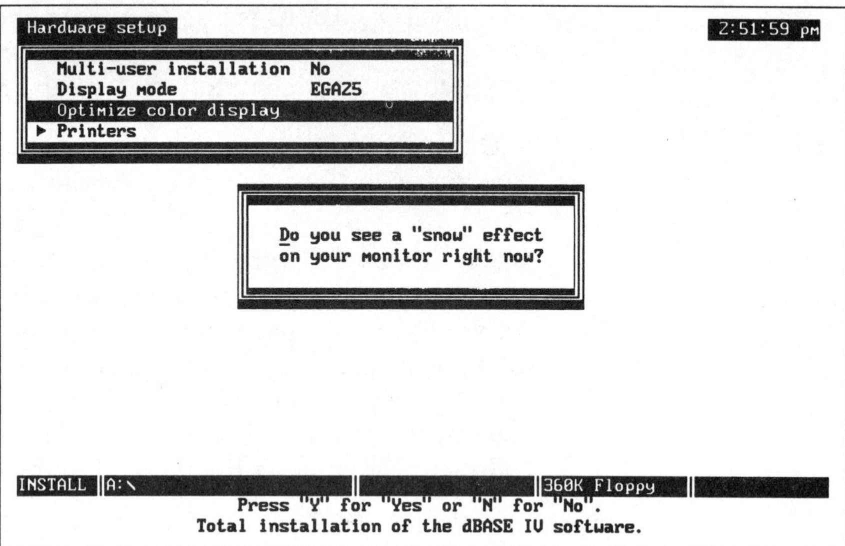

Figure 1-4

Snow test screen.

Press: *N*

if there is no snow, or

Press: *Y*

if there is a snow effect on the screen.

The system will thank you for testing your monitor/display card combination.

Press: **ENTER**

to return to the Hardware Setup menu.

Printers. Installation of a printer requires selection of the printer and the printer driver. The system can list printers for which it already has drivers. Highlight "Printers" and press **ENTER** to see the Printer Selection screen (Figure 1-5).

To see a list of printers that can be installed,

Press: **Shift-F1**

A partial list of supported printers appears on the window. To select your printer scroll through the list, using the **UpArrow** or **DnArrow**, or type the first few letters of the printer manufacturer name until your printer manufacturer's name is highlighted (Figure 1-6).

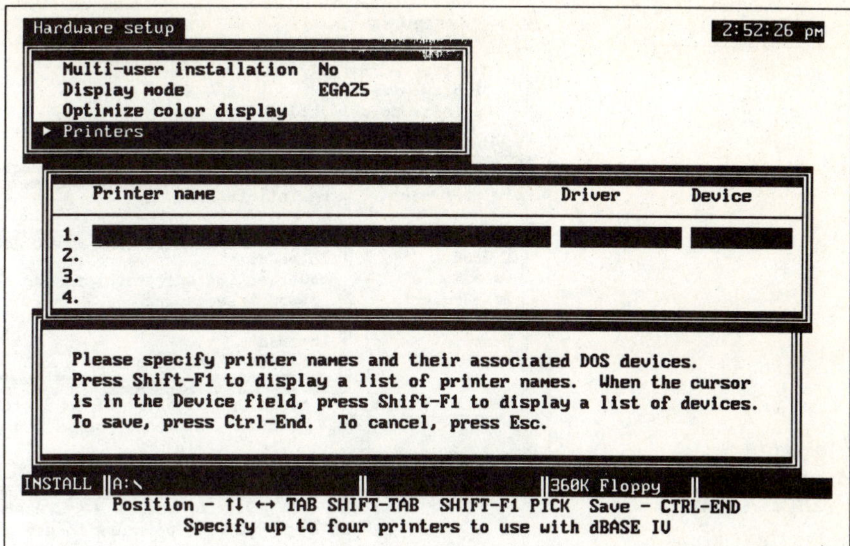

Figure 1-5

Printer selection screen.

Once a manufacturer has been selected, two other windows will appear, one showing the various printers supported and the second displaying the printer driver designed for that printer. The names of the printer manufacturers will scroll on the screen as you move through the list, as may be seen if you were trying to

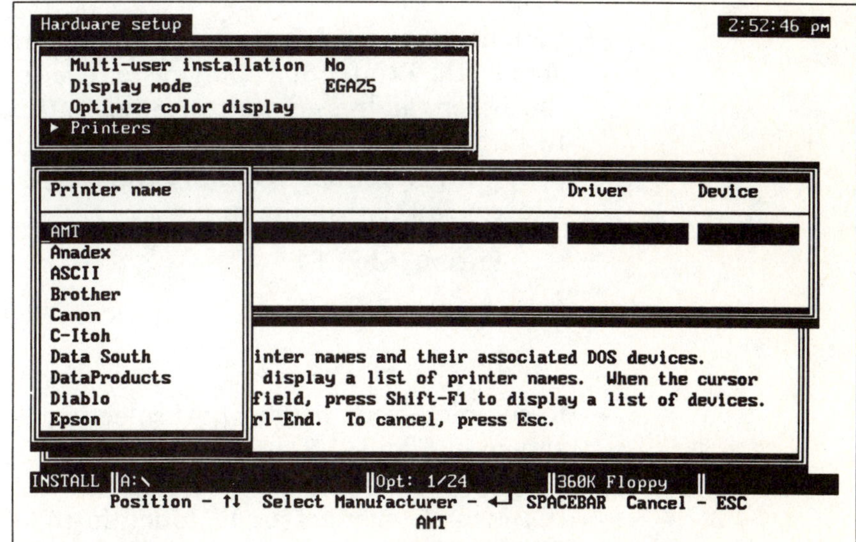

Figure 1-6

Printer selection menu.

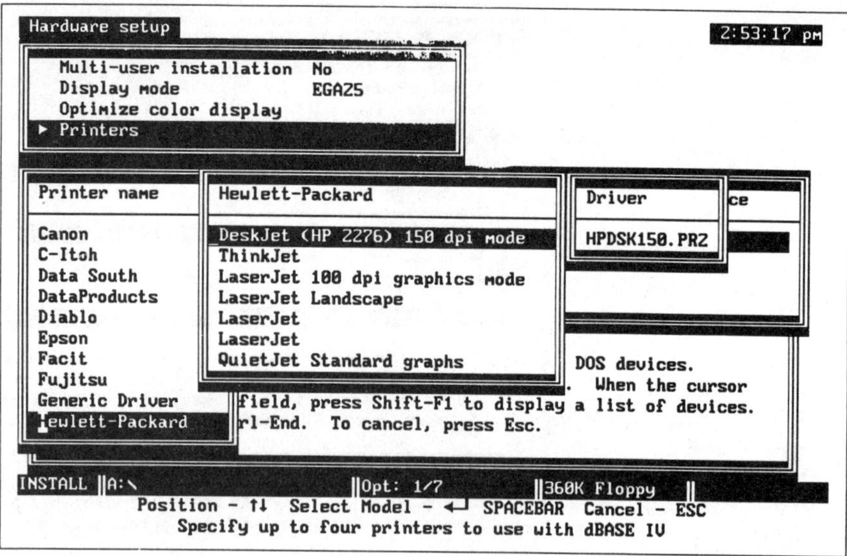

Figure 1-7

Printer/driver selection screen.

set up a Hewlett-Packard LaserJet printer. The screen will appear as shown in Figure 1-7 (if you were trying to set up a Hewlett-Packard printer).

Next, scroll through to the printer that you want to use. For most laserjet applications, select the 100 dpi mode. When the printer and driver that you wish to use are highlighted,

Press: **ENTER**

to transfer the printer name and driver name into the appropriate spot on the Printer Selection menu. The Device column asks how the system addresses your printer. Your printer will usually be LPT1, although in some cases a printer being used as a *serial* printer will be either COM1 or COM2. Type the appropriate device address in this column or

Press: **Shift-F1**

for a listing of the selectable devices. Highlight a device and

Press: **ENTER**

to complete your printer port selection. The device options are shown in Figure 1-8.

Two of the options may be somewhat unclear. The *spooler* option (which may not be included in the single-user version of dBASE IV) prints to a spooler, a device that stores data until the

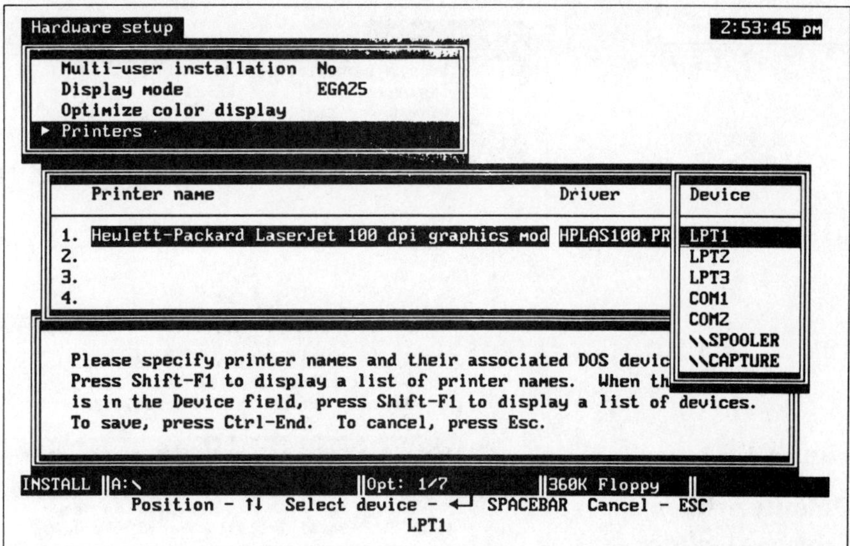

Figure 1-8

Device selection screen.

printer is ready to print. In many cases, this significantly speeds printing, because the system does not have to wait for the printer to catch up before sending data. For large print jobs, a large spooler can save a substantial amount of time. *\\capture* prints the printer commands to a file on disk. When you are ready to print the file produced by dBASE IV, you can then print the contents of the captured file. This may be useful for after-hours printing as part of a late night batch job. When printing to a file, your system becomes available quickly, because it will not have to wait for the printer to catch up before sending more data to the printer (in this case, a captured file).

In addition to the drivers selectable using the **Shift-F1** combination, drivers designed for Framework II or Framework III may be added by typing the name of the printer, the name of the driver, and the device number.

Once your printer(s) has been selected,

Press: **Ctrl-End**

for the Default Driver Selection menu (Figure 1-9), which allows you to select the default printer driver. This means that when the system is started and begins to print a report, the system will *assume* that the selected default printer is the one to which you are printing.

To select the default printer, move the highlight using the **Up-**

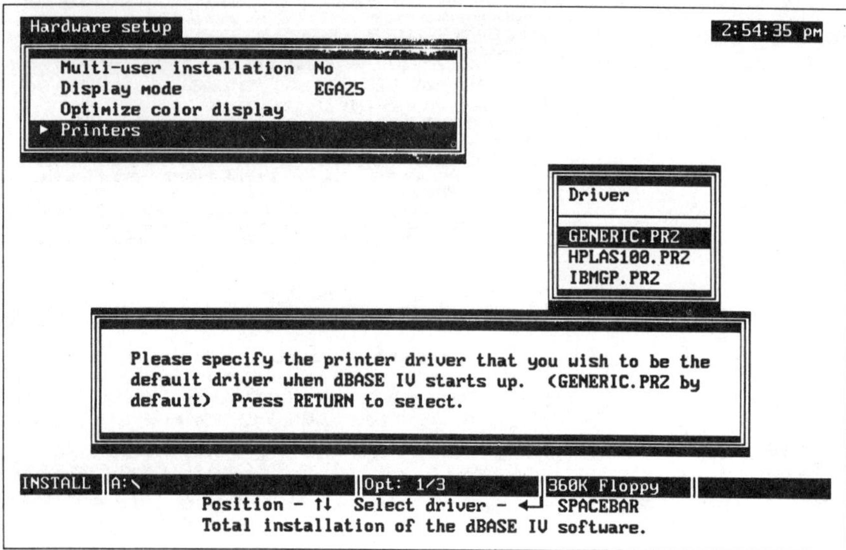

Figure 1-9

Default printer driver selection.

Arrow or **DnArrow** or type the first letter(s) of the driver you wish to use, and

Press: **ENTER**

This returns you to the Hardware Setup menu. Once your hardware options have been set, indicate that you wish to proceed with the next step in installation. To do this,

Press: **Ctrl-End**

The system brings up the next Installation menu (seen in Figure 1-10). In the middle of the screen, the system will indicate whether you are installing for a single user or multiple users on a network. If you wish to change this, or any of the hardware setup parameters,

Type: *M*

to modify the hardware setup. If you do not want to install the program now,

Type: *E*

to exit. If you wish to continue with the installation,

Type: *P*

or, making sure "Proceed" is highlighted,

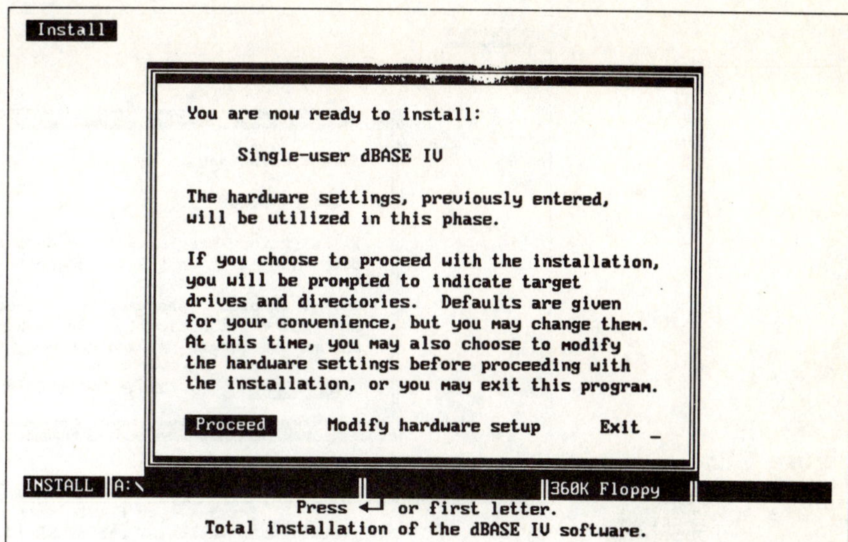

Figure 1-10

Install program menu.

Press: **ENTER**

The system next asks where you want to install dBASE IV. The default is C:\dBASE, as seen in Figure 1-11.

You may have to give this option some thought. If this is the first time you have installed dBASE on your disk, you can

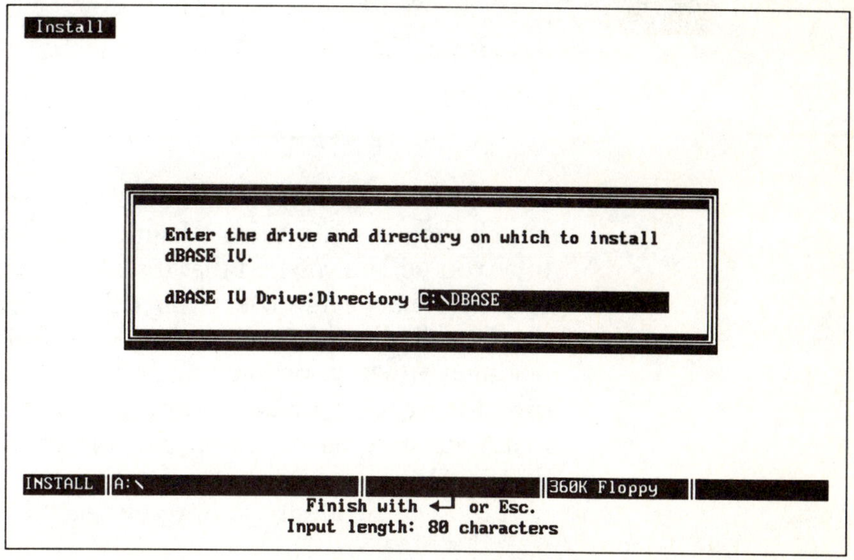

Figure 1-11

dBASE IV installation drive.

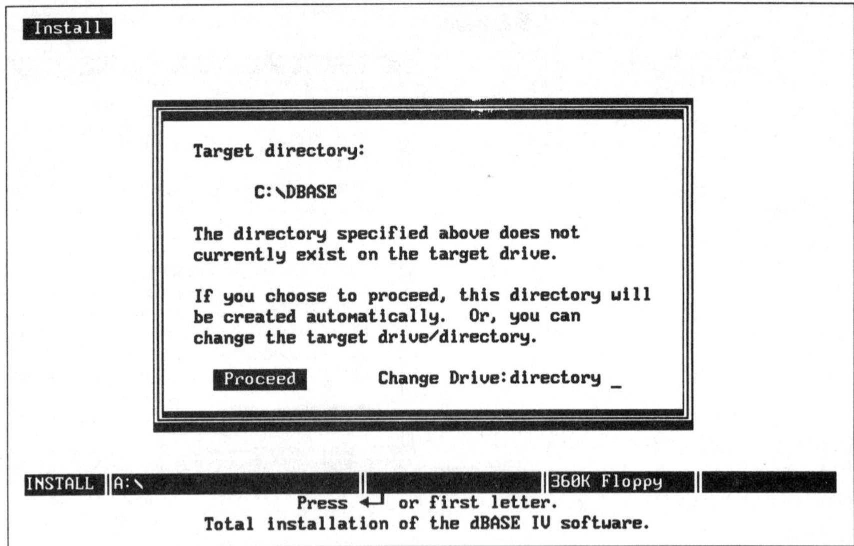

Figure 1-12

Create new directory screen.

Press: **ENTER**

to select the default drive and directory. If you do not have dBASE installed in the C:\dbase drive (or the drive you specified), the system will tell you that it will create a directory using the parameters you specified or accepted (Figure 1-12).

To allow the system to create a new directory and copy dBASE IV files into it,

Type: *p*

or, making sure that "Proceed" is highlighted,

Press: **ENTER**

On the other hand, if the system finds a drive and directory that match the ones you selected, and finds dBASE files in the directory, you will be warned that installing the program in this directory will overwrite the existing dBASE or may change the target drive or directory. The warning, seen in Figure 1-13, most often occurs if you have been using dBASE III or dBASE III+ in a subdirectory called dbase. Allowing the system to continue the installation removes the older version of dBASE and installs dBASE IV.

It may be prudent to copy your earlier dBASE program files

to another directory, in case you ever need to use dBASE III. (There are some minor incompatibilities between dBASE IV and earlier versions—particularly in memo fields. In addition, although Ashton-Tate has gone through extensive debugging on dBASE IV, dBASE III or dBASE III+ should be kept available as a backup. To copy the existing files, exit the Install menu and copy all .EXE and .OVL files into a new subdirectory.

Of course, dBASE IV could be installed to a new drive and/or directory. dBASE IV can read files in your dBASE III or dBASE III+ directories. It may be simpler to move the dBASE III files to another directory (or just retain your original disks) and move dBASE IV to the \dbase subdirectory. One final note: a copy protected version of dBASE III or dBASE III+ may have to be uninstalled, using the disks that were packed with the program. Simply moving files over may make dBASE III or dBASE III+ unusable.

Once your target drive and directory have been chosen,

Press: *P* (or, if "Proceed" is highlighted, press **ENTER**)

to begin installing the program disks. The system will also ask where you want to install the SQL files. If this is the first time you are installing dBASE IV, you will probably want to use the

Figure 1-13

Directory overwrite warning.

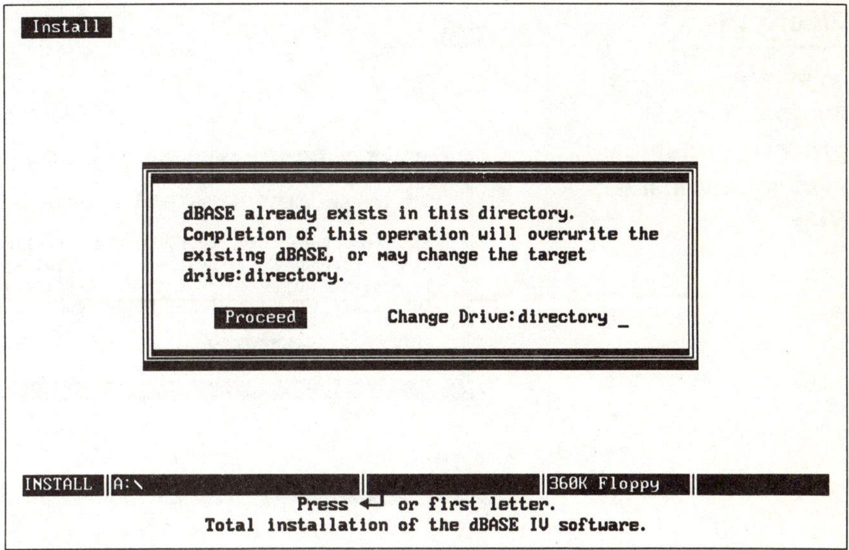

default directory that the system indicates. The system will prompt you to insert most of your other disks, while copying. When you install a new disk, make sure the drive door is closed and

Press: **ENTER**

to copy the next disk.

Once the system disks are installed, a window will appear on the screen indicating that the installation was successful. It will then ask if you wish to proceed to modify the **CONFIG.SYS** and AUTOEXEC.BAT files, and to copy sample files and the tutorial (Figure 1-14).

You may exit from the installation program if you do not want to use the sample files and tutorial included with the package. However, copying the sample files will enable you to work through the sample exercises described in Ashton-Tate documentation. The files are recorded into a new directory, as are the tutorial files, and can be easily removed from these files by using the **Del * . *** command and then deleting the subdirectory with the **RD** (remove directory) command.

For now, tell the system that you want to proceed with the installation. The next screen will ask if you want to modify the AUTOEXEC.BAT file in the root directory on your hard disk drive.

Figure 1-14

Successful completion, proceed to modify system and install files.

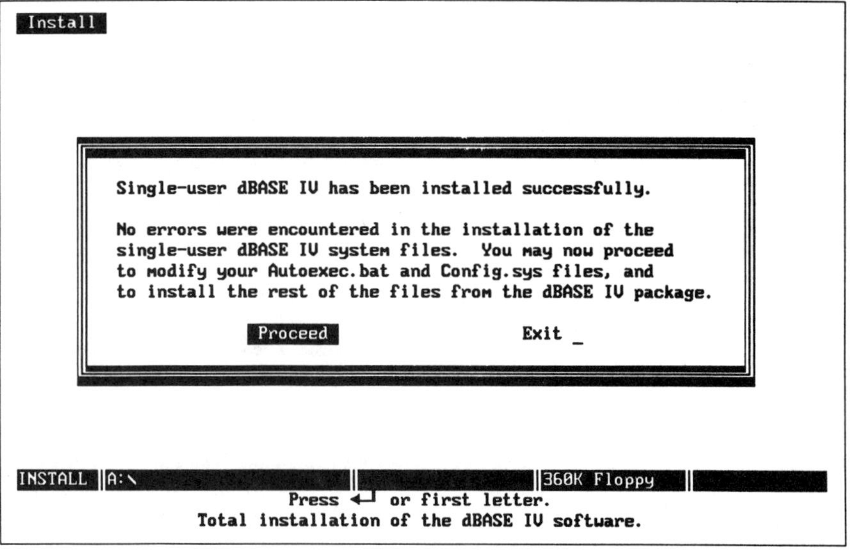

The AUTOEXEC.BAT file loads programs and defines paths (which the system goes through in looking for a particular file). Adding the path statement to your AUTOEXEC.BAT file does little harm, and it *will* tell the system that you have a subdirectory through which to search when trying to find a file. When you type the command to start dBASE IV from whichever directory you are in, the system will look in dBASE IV and execute the program.

This step may be skipped by highlighting "Skip" and pressing the **ENTER** key. To proceed with the AUTOEXEC.BAT modification, make sure that the highlight is on "Proceed" and

Press: **ENTER**

The next screen asks about updating the CONFIG.SYS file, which lets the system know how many files and buffers have been allocated to the system. (The system uses files and buffers to manage the flow of data through the system; in general, the more the better up to a point; by allowing the system to modify the CONFIG.SYS file, you will be setting the minimal number of buffers and files for the system to properly use dBASE IV.) The CONFIG.SYS file also loads device drivers, such as expanded memory drivers, mouse drivers, streaming tape drivers, and driver programs that allow the system to work properly with other installed hardware products.

The number of files and buffers is important in dBASE IV. If there are too few, the system will run dBASE IV either too slowly or not at all; if there are too many, there may not be adequate memory left to run dBASE IV, because it is a very large package and uses most of the available memory after DOS is loaded.

If you choose not to modify the files automatically, the CONFIG.SYS and AUTOEXEC.BAT files may be modified with a text editor. If you are a power user, you have probably allocated enough files and buffers for the system. If you do not know about CONFIG.SYS, you probably do not have enough allocated. The system should be allowed to modify your CONFIG.SYS file. Any changes can always be undone by a text editor.

Next, you have the option of copying your sample files. If you do not want to copy the files select Skip and press **ENTER**, or just

Type: ***S***

If you want to copy the files,

Press: **ENTER**

while "Proceed" is highlighted.

The system will ask you to accept a default subdirectory and drive for installing the files. Accept the new subdirectory path by pressing **ENTER**, or type in a new path. If the selected directory is not found on the disk, the system asks you to allow it to make a new subdirectory. If you prefer, you may specify a directory path by typing in the desired drive and path information.

The system will copy the sample files to the directory it sets up or the one you have selected. It next asks if you wish to copy the tutorial files. If you do, the system will use similar prompts to determine the disk drive and directory you wish to use. If you do not, tell the system to skip that process.

Once the sample and/or tutorial files are copied, or the step has been skipped, the system will prompt you to insert the Installation disk in the A: drive. Insert the disk, and

Press: **ENTER**

to tell the system that the disk is in the drive.

The system will copy DBSETUP.OVL and other files on the subdirectory onto which dBASE IV has been loaded and give you the option of exiting to DOS or transferring to DBSETUP. If you exit to DOS, you will be able to run dBASE IV as is. The program will run, but may not be optimized for your system or your particular preferences. However, if you wish, you may Exit to DOS and at a later time load DBSETUP from your dBASE IV subdirectory.

For the majority of users, the default settings should be adequate for most functions, so select Exit to DOS. (Actually, the setup performs more logically if you Exit to DOS and then run DBSETUP from within DBASE than it does if you do it during install, because during install, the system makes assumptions about your use of the A: drive for data storage. Therefore Exit to DOS and if you wish to make changes, do them from within the /DBASE directory.) To Exit to DOS,

Press: **ENTER**

The system brings you back to the A: drive, the drive that you were installing dBASE IV from. To change to the drive that dBASE IV was installed on (assuming drive C: for this example),

Type: ***C:* ENTER**

The system should now display [C:\DBASE] or C:\DBASE.

If it does not there may be two reasons for this. First, your system may not have been set up to display drive and path information. This is done using a text editor and modifying your AUTOEXEC.BAT file by adding the line

Prompt pg

if you want the display to look like C:\DBASE or by adding the line

Prompt [pg]

if you prefer [C:\DBASE].

By adding the prompt line, you tell the system to put the currently logged drive and directory (or path). This is a useful navigation tool, whether or not you will be using dBASE IV. The line can be added using any text editor, even the text editor dBASE IV. You may also use the prompt command as a DOS command. In fact, if your system is not displaying your current drive and path, try typing the *prompt* line now.

If the system tells you that it is not at the desired path for dBASE IV, use the change directory command. For example, if dBASE IV is installed on c:\dbase, you would

Type: ***cd c:\dbase* ENTER**

to change your directory. To load dBASE IV, simply

Type: ***dbase* ENTER**

You should see that the installation was successful and the program loads properly.

In Case of Problems Installing dBASE IV

The installation program for dBASE IV is fully automatic. However, on some systems the Installation screen appears and the system locks up. There may be ways to solve the problems that cause the system not to install.

The most likely problem is using too many system drivers in the CONFIG.SYS file, or loading too many memory resident programs in the AUTOEXEC.BAT file. Because of the design of the dBASE IV installation program, some system drivers or memory resident programs interfere with the installation.

To overcome these problems, first, copy your CONFIG.SYS files and AUTOEXEC.BAT file. To do this

Type: *COPY CONFIG.SYS CONFIG.DB4*

Type: *COPY AUTOEXEC.BAT AUTOEXEC.DB4*

The file extensions, .DB4, are your reminder that these are the *original* files that you have copied to be able to create empty CONFIG.SYS and AUTOEXEC.BAT files that allow loading of dBASE IV. Although a text editor may be used to create new CONFIG.SYS and AUTOEXEC.BAT files, it is probably as simple to use the COPY CON command editor provided with DOS.

NOTE: You will be making only the barest CONFIG.SYS file using the following commands. You should use the command **Type** ***CONFIG.DB4*** to list the contents of this file. If there are any drivers that *must be loaded* (such as special screen drivers) to start your system, write down the entire line used to invoke the driver. This will be copied to your loader CONFIG.SYS file later.

To make the new CONFIG.SYS file,

Type: *COPY CON CONFIG.SYS* **ENTER**

Type: *FILES=20* **ENTER**

Type: *Buffers=30* **ENTER**

(copy any device driver lines required for your system to boot properly).

Press: **F6** (or **CTRL-Z**)

Press: **ENTER**

A new CONFIG.SYS file will have been created.

To create your new AUTOEXEC.BAT, be certain that the original AUTOEXEC.BAT file has been backed up and

Type: *COPY CON AUTOEXEC.BAT* **ENTER**

Type: *PROMPT pg* **ENTER**

(It helps to have this path information displayed.)

Press: **F6** (or **Ctrl-Z**) **ENTER**

Press: **ENTER**

Once the CONFIG.SYS and AUTOEXEC.BAT files have been created, reboot your computer. (If you have a RAM disk, be certain to store the contents of the RAM disk before rebooting.)

Normally, the **CTRL-ALT-DEL** combination (pressing all three keys at once) resets the system so that you can install dBASE IV. In rare instances, there may be a device that is loaded that will not reset until you turn the power off and back on. If you reboot without turning power off, and you still cannot install dBASE IV, try turning the power off and then on to reboot the system.

A second reason for the failure to install dBASE IV is that there are not enough files and buffers to move the data from the floppy to the hard disk. The CONFIG.SYS file you created should overcome this problem.

Once dBASE IV has been successfully installed, you will probably want to restore your original CONFIG.SYS and AUTOEXEC.BAT files. First, however, you may wish to jot down the change that the install program has made to the AUTOEXEC.BAT and CONFIG.SYS files, so that you can make similar changes to the AUTOEXEC.DB4 and CONFIG.DB4 files.

To restore the files,

Type: *del config.sys* **ENTER**

Type: *ren config.db4 config.sys* **ENTER**

Type: *del autoexec.bat* **ENTER**

Type: *ren autoexec.db4 autoexec.bat* **ENTER**

Reboot the system, and it should behave exactly as it did before you installed dBASE IV.

Using a text editor (the one in dBASE IV can be used), you may wish to add the path information to your AUTOEXEC.BAT file, and consider modifying your FILES= and BUFFERS= lines to match those installed to your temporary CONFIG.SYS and AUTOEXEC.BAT files by the dBASE IV installation program.

Using DBSETUP

Although you may not need to use DBSETUP, it is helpful to know how to load it and to know a little about its options. DBSETUP is the program used to modify certain system parameters and to learn more about your system. It is useful if you have made changes to the system, and it can be used to reinstall dBASE IV.

To load DBSETUP, log onto the directory in which the DBSETUP program is located. In most cases, it will be C:\DBASE, the subdirectory that is set up when dBASE IV is installed.

Once in that directory,

Type: *DBSETUP* **ENTER**

You will see a title screen and a copyright notice.

Press: **ENTER**

to bring up the Setup menu (Figure 1-15). You will see five menu options, some available from within dBASE IV and others available only in DBSETUP. These options and the submenus are as follows.

Install. The Install option allows you to (1) modify your hardware setup, (2) install (or reinstall) dBASE IV, (3) transfer other files to

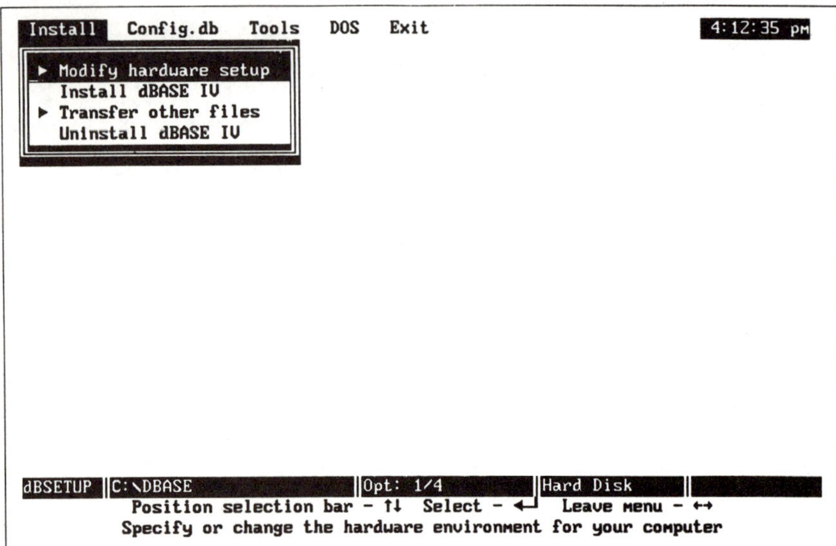

Figure 1-15

Setup menu from DBSETUP.

any directory you choose, or (4) uninstall dBASE IV from your system.

The first option is *Modify hardware setup.* This is basically the same menu that you used when you first installed dBASE IV. You may change the display modes and select new printers from within the Hardware menu.

The second option is *Install dBASE IV.* This can be used to install (reinstall) the program onto your hard disk drive.

Third, *Transfer other files* gives you a choice of files to transfer to your hard drive. These include the tutorial files, sample files, and AUTOEXEC.BAT and CONFIG.SYS files that the system prompted you to load during installation.

Finally, you may *Uninstall dBASE IV.* This option removes the program from your hard disk drive and removes the system files from your disk. Once you make the selection, the removal of the program is *very fast.* If you select this option, the program *will be removed,* and you cannot stop it. Be *very careful* before selecting this option.

CONFIG.DB. The CONFIG.DB file contains information that lets the system know how you want dBASE IV to look and act. When you start dBASE IV, it reads the CONFIG.DB file and is set up to use those features specified in the CONFIG.DB file.

Most of the options have been set up to meet the basic needs and style of the majority of dBASE IV users. When the CONFIG.DB file is modified, the changes will not be seen in the operation of the system until the *next time* you load dBASE IV.

This item gives you two choices: you can modify an existing CONFIG.DB file or create a new CONFIG.DB file. Whichever option you choose, the system brings up the CONFIG.DB modification menu (Figure 1-16).

Discussion of all the available options is beyond the scope of this chapter. You may feel free to make changes to the different options. You may move from column to column using the **LtArrow** or **RtArrow** keys, and from one line in a column to the next using the **UpArrow** or **DnArrow** keys.

When you exit, you have the option of saving your changes or exiting without changing them. After experimenting with the changes, you may wish to leave them as they originally were by choosing Abandon and exit (by typing **Alt-A**), or highlighting "Abandon and exit" and pressing **ENTER**.

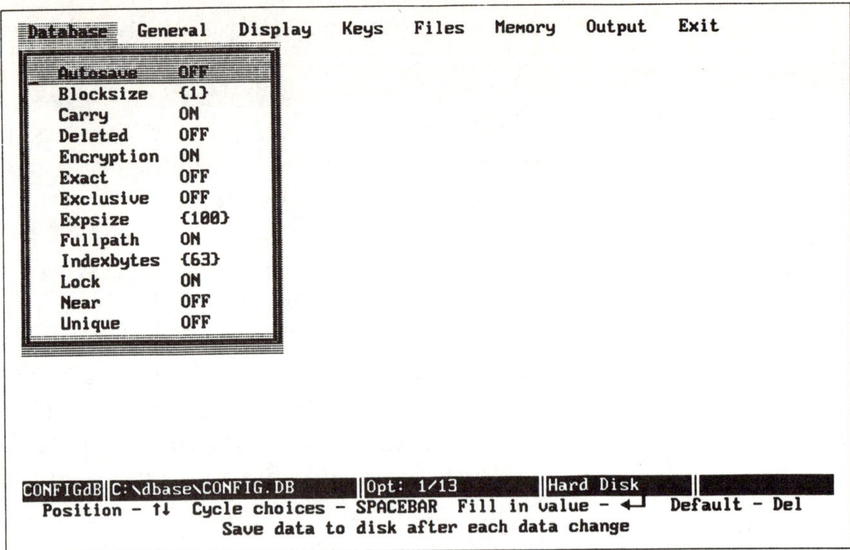

Figure 1-16

CONFIG.DB modification screen.

Tools. The tools are actually rather useful. Display disk usage supplies information about your current hard drive, for example, how much space was used, how much is left, and so on (Figure 1-17).

Test disk performance evaluates the speed of your hard drive for both reading and writing. It provides a useful performance

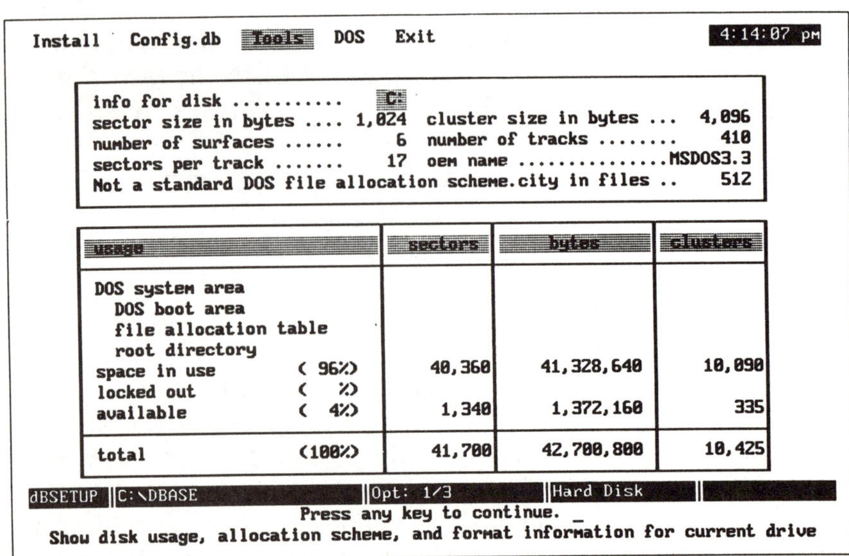

Figure 1-17

Disk usage screen.

record, although it probably will be more useful to systems designers than to most users.

Review system configuration tells you about your system and how it is currently set up. On a Tandon Pac 286 computer, the system reports various items of information (Figure 1-18).

DOS. The DOS menu provides three options: Perform DOS command, Go to DOS, and Set default drive:directory. The options are also available from within the dBASE IV Tools DOS menu that you will see in Chapter Two.

Perform DOS command allows you to type a DOS command without leaving the DBSETUP program. Typically, you would be entering commands that list directories or do other data management tasks. However, you may also be able to run programs using this method of DOS access.

You can also go to a DOS command shell by using the command *COMMAND.COM*. However, this provides essentially the same access as the next option, Go to DOS.

In addition, when you Go to DOS, the system reminds you that you are in a DOS shell. If you use Command.Com to go to DOS, you may forget that you were in a shell and could turn the system off (as if you were in DOS), losing any changes you may have made during your DBINSTAL session. In addition, changing a drive or

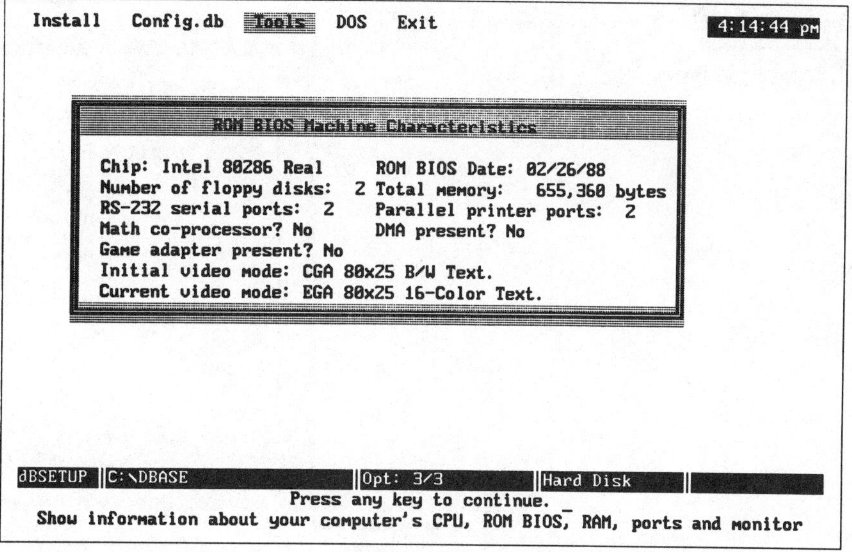

Figure 1-18

System configuration screen.

directory using Perform DOS command also changes the default drive and directory, as will be seen in the third option of the DOS menu screen.

Go to DOS brings you into a command shell, allowing you to use DOS for running programs, changing directories, or performing other tasks. Care should be taken *not* to load any memory resident programs from the DOS shell that is provided by dBASE IV or the DBINSTAL program, because the programs take up certain portions of memory. When you exit from DBINSTAL or dBASE IV, these programs may also be removed. At best, they may confuse the system; at worst, this could result in system lockup and possible loss of data.

If a number of DOS functions are to be performed, going to DOS rather than using the COMMAND.COM command is the best way to perform DOS commands. Again, any changes in drive or directory are reflected by a change in the setting for default drives and directories. When you select Set default drive:directory, the current default drive and directory are listed. To change to another drive, you must use Perform DOS command to change the drive. To change the drive and directory, you may type in the default drive and directory.

If you do not remember the name of the directory, once Set default drive:directory has been selected, you may press **Shft-F1**

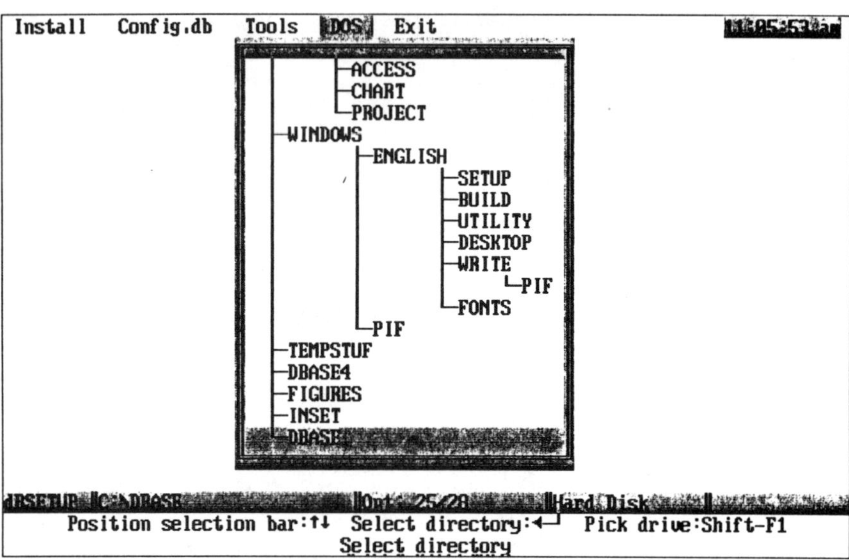

Figure 1-19

Directory tree.

to bring up a tree showing the directories and subdirectories on your currently logged hard disk (Figure 1-19). Move the highlight to the directory you want as default, and

Press: **ENTER**

to make that the default directory.

Exit. The Exit menu allows you to return to DOS. Changes you have made during this session will be saved, and you will be returned to DOS.

This chapter has provided the basics for the installation and setup of dBASE IV. Although many options and settings are available from within dBASE IV, the basic ones have been set by the system. Modifications can be made (through the Modify CONFIG.DB menu in DBSETUP or with dBASE IV's text editor), although these probably will not be required to successfully use dBASE IV.

Quick Tour/ Key Features

Starting dBASE IV is undoubtedly one of the simplest things you will do with the program. To start,

Type: *dbase* **ENTER**

If the program was configured as outlined in Chapter One, you will see the Title screen, followed by a screen asking you to accept the license to use the program. At this point, either touch the **ENTER** key or just wait, and the program will proceed to the *Control Center* screen.

NOTE: Starting dBASE IV can be made slightly simpler, using the two-key command, *DB* **ENTER**. To do this, first build a batch file that will type the command to start dBASE IV, *DBASE* **ENTER**, using any text editor you choose; it is easy to do this using the following DOS commands:

COPY CON DB.BAT **ENTER**

DBASE **ENTER**

F6

ENTER

Control Center

However you start the program, the system should bring you to the *Control Center* (Figure 2-1), which is the heart of your interface with dBASE IV. It has been described by Ashton-Tate as a non-procedural interface (NPI), which means that using it does not

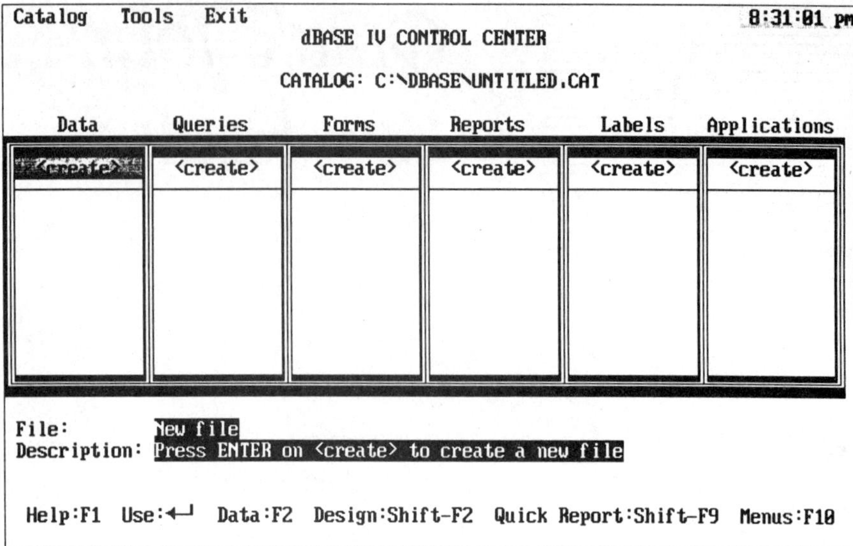

Figure 2-1

Control Center.

involve learning any specific procedures or programming languages to use dBASE IV.

The Control Center is a major departure from earlier versions of dBASE, because it provides most of what you need to build a complete database, design and print a variety of reports based on those data, and even design database applications without having to learn the dBASE programming language. Although you may want to learn to program in dBASE, or, in fact, may already be conversant with dBASE programming language, you will find that the Control Center will simplify your interactions with dBASE IV, and you may find yourself increasingly relying on it.

Help screens may pop up the first time you access many of the screens when using dBASE IV. Touching the **HOME** key will remove them.

If dBASE IV is loaded and you do not see the Control Center, your configuration file probably does not include the command necessary to bring it up when you start dBASE IV. Your screen (Figure 2-2) will be blank at the top, except for a dot and blinking cursor in the lower left corner, just above a solid line at the bottom of the screen. The dot is referred to as a dot prompt, signaling you to issue a command. In this case, to get to the Control Center,

Type: *Assist* **ENTER**

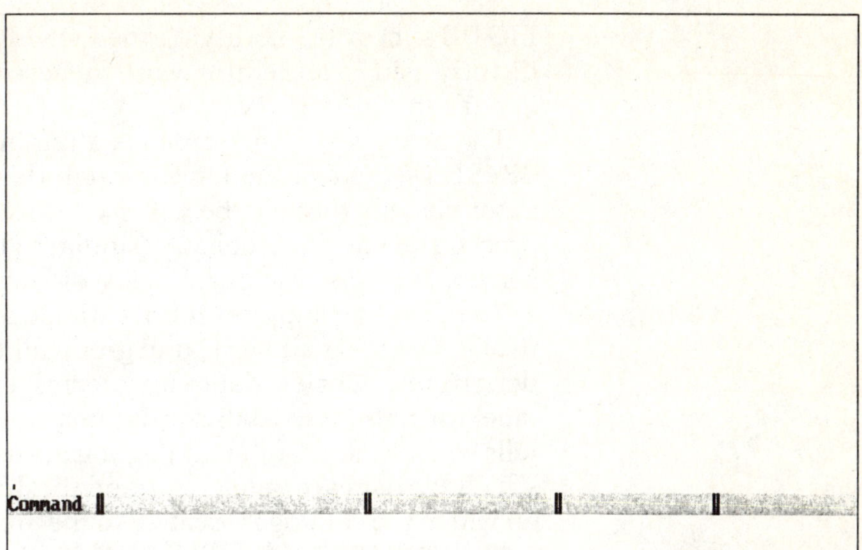

Figure 2-2

Blank screen with dot prompt.

Alternatively, you can touch the **F2** key, which, in a normally configured system, will type the assigned command (*Assist* **ENTER**). *Assist* is the command used to load the Control Center . Although the same command was used in dBASE III+ to load an interface referred to as the Assistant, the Control Center in dBASE IV bears little resemblance to the dBASE III+ Assistant, and is much more powerful and easier to use.

Assuming you are now in the Control Center, you will see the opening screen. The Control Center provides you with a good deal of information.

A Look at the Control Center

The *Menu Bar* and *Clock* are located at the top of the screen. The Menu Bar, on the top left side of the screen, offers three menu items: *Catalog, Tools,* and *Exit.* At the top right, the Clock gives you the current time.

One of the configuration options in the program is whether or not to display the clock. If your clock does not appear, it simply means that the program was not configured to show the clock on the screen. The clock can be turned on and off from within the DBSETUP program (which includes an option to modify the CON-

FIG.DB file) or by modifying the CONFIG.DB configuration file directly using a text editor, word processor, or the text editor that is built into dBASE IV.

The next line on the screen is a reminder that you are in the dBASE IV Control Center. Although this may seem redundant, other screens that can be accessed through the dBASE IV nonprocedural interface look very similar to the main Control Center screen, and this title bar helps avoid any possible confusion.

The next line supplies information about the *Catalog* you are using. A Catalog allows you to group all the database files, view definitions, queries, data entry forms, custom reports, printed label formats, and dBASE programs and applications. This line tells you the name of the catalog you are using, the disk drive from which the data are being read, and the directory or subdirectory on which the catalog is located. In the present example, a catalog called *CATALOG.CAT* on the *\DBASE* subdirectory of the *C*: drive is the one being used. Other catalogs may be selected using the *Catalog* menu at the top of the screen (more on this later).

The next area that dominates the screen is the *Work Space.* The top line of the work space tells you which options you have selected. Briefly, the following options are available: *Data,* used for database design and entry; *Queries,* used to tell the system what information you want to extract from the database file(s) selected; *Forms,* used to design special data entry and viewing forms that simplify the task of data entry and that allow the system to validate data as they are input and allow you to view the data in a particular format; *Reports,* which allow you to design the look of a report generated based on the data files and queries, and other instructions (such as totals or averages, for example) that you may include in your report specification; *Labels,* used to print mailing labels, file cards, rolodex cards, or envelopes using predefined sizes or formats and sizes that you prefer; and *Applications,* which actually consists of two options.

The *Applications* option provides access to the editor that is built into dBASE IV and that can be used to write or edit a new dBASE program or application. The second option allows you to use the Applications Generator to build an application that can be run by you or another user under dBASE IV or as a standalone application program using a runtime version of dBASE IV. A runtime program includes the program required to run an application, but does not include design and editing capabilities.

The next line tells you the name and location of the file that is currently highlighted in the Work Space. If you have attached a description of the file to the file, this description will be displayed on the next line.

The next lines provide a list of keys that can be used to quickly enter a database or functional area or to navigate on the screen. Only one line is shown in this example. This line can change, depending on what is being done within the Control Center. In general, when you are using dBASE IV, watching the bottom lines of the screen can provide information on what you can do with the currently selected option.

The Menu Bar

The *Menu Bar* provides three menu items, *Catalog, Tools,* and *Exit.* When any of the three items is selected, a screen drops down, showing the options available when using that item.

The options available in each pull down screen can be selected using either of two methods. First, pressing **F10** causes the drop down screen for the last called option to open. For example, if you last worked with the *Tools* screen, pressing **F10** will pop up the Tools options. However, the system normally defaults to the Catalog menu when you first start using dBASE IV.

Because this is the first time you have used dBASE IV in this work session, the **F10** key should pop up the *Catalog* menu (Figure 2-3). The second method for calling up a drop down menu for one of the selection items at the top of the screen is by holding down the **Alt** key and touching the first letter (for example, *E* for the Exit menu) of the option you want to see.

Once a menu item is opened, navigation from item to item, or within a menu item's options, is simple. The **Left Arrow** and **Right Arrow** keys (as well as the **F3** and **F4** keys) on your keyboard will move you from menu item to menu item. Items within an option screen may be selected by moving the highlight to the option desired (using the **Up Arrow** or **Dn Arrow** keys) and pressing **ENTER**, or by typing the first letter of the desired option.

dBASE IV may show more options than are available at this point in a program. The options that can be selected are highlighted on the screen; those options that are not currently

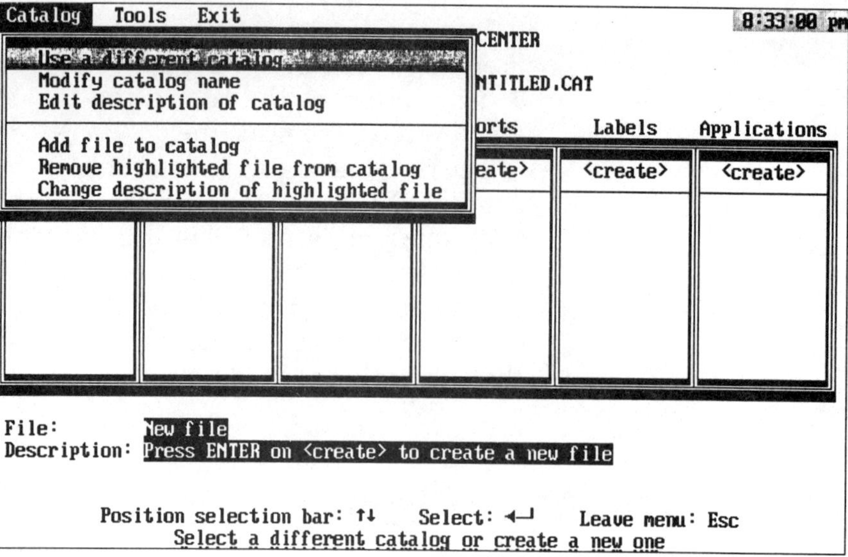

Figure 2-3

Catalog menu.

valid are shown in normal intensity characters. For example, in the Catalog option screen seen in Figure 2-3, only the first four lines are highlighted. The two options in dimmer characters are invalid because you have not highlighted a file in the current catalog. However, if your catalog has an item selected (other than <create>) in any of its option areas, all the options in Catalog will be highlighted.

Once you have called up a drop down menu, navigation and selection of a menu item or of another drop down menu is done as previously described.

Tools

The *Tools* menu offers a number of quite important capabilities.

Macros are a new feature that gives enhanced functionality and ease of use to your database sessions. This feature may be used to build up strings of keystrokes that will automatically be typed in for you by dBASE IV. For example, you can program a macro that will automatically load and execute a compiled dBASE program each time you touch the predefined key for that macro. If you wanted to automate printing a report, a macro assigned to a single key can call up the Reports menu, select the report format, and begin the print operation. More than 30 macros can be recorded. Function keys from **F2** to **F9**, and **F10** followed by an alphanumeric key, can all be assigned to a unique macro. **F1** through **F9** are already predefined when you load dBASE IV. Additional options such as appending keystrokes to an existing macro and pausing a macro's execution for user input enhance the power of the macro capabilities.

The *Import* feature allows you to bring data into dBASE IV from other database programs and from a number of spreadsheet programs. The Import options screen is shown in Figure 2-4. Note that dBASE IV can import data from RapidFile, dBASE II, Framework II, PFS:File, and Lotus 1-2-3, and dBASE III and III+ data, views, and catalogs can be used without any conversion by dBASE IV. In addition, an Append From menu, available from the Modify Database screen, allows you to use data from a number of other types of programs.

This import capability is important; it allows you to follow an upgrade path from a wide range of database management programs and spreadsheets. The list of databases and spreadsheets that can be imported into dBASE IV is actually much larger than the five in the Import menu, because most major database programs and spreadsheets can export files into one or more of the data formats that can be imported into dBASE IV.

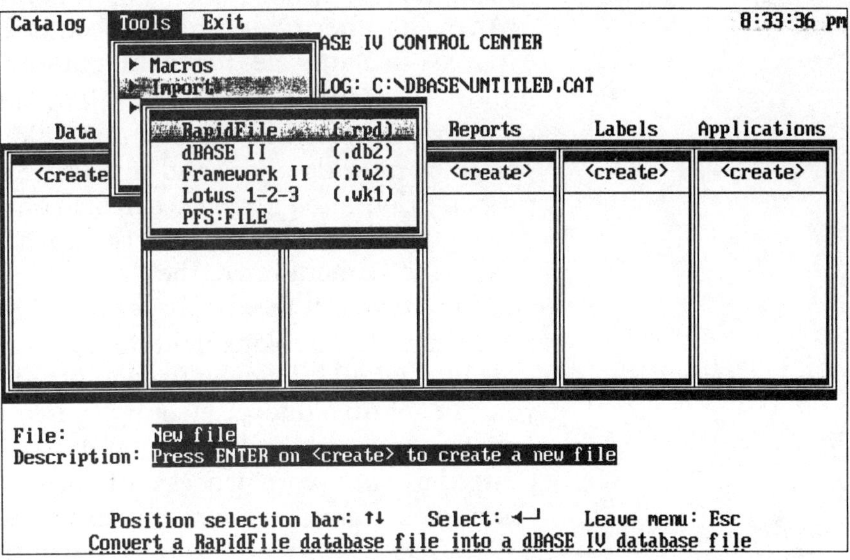

Figure 2-4

Import menu.

For example, if your company is using Quattro from Borland International or Microsoft Excel, you could import data into dBASE IV. Both programs (and many other spreadsheets, as well) produce industry standard worksheet files that are compatible with the .WK1 format. And, depending upon the database from which you are importing, dBASE IV may also import report forms, views, and other components of your other database structures.

The import utility is necessary to properly read the data structures you have created with other database management programs; you cannot just copy your data into the data directory of dBASE IV and expect to be able to use it. Although much of the data may appear to be saved in a format similar to that used by dBASE IV, the organization of the files, the location of field identifiers, and other characteristic aspects of the file format differ enough from dBASE IV to require the import utilities to make the conversion to dBASE IV. In addition, depending upon the database you have been using, field names, and possibly other aspects of your database, may not transfer from your former database to dBASE IV. For example, when importing a PFS:File database, field names are not transferred over—instead the fields are called FIELD 1, FIELD 2, etc.

One final note on importing files. dBASE IV is fully compatible with all files produced by dBASE III and dBASE III+ with one exception—the memo file structure in dBASE IV is no longer compatible with that used in earlier versions of dBASE.

An even richer *Export* menu, seen in Figure 2-5, allows you to export your database files to all databases from which you can import, in addition to Visicalc, Microsoft Multiplan SYLK files, and three different formats of text fields. Text fields can be imported by most database and spreadsheet programs. In addition, properly delimited text files can also be used by many word processing programs for mail merge operations.

As already mentioned, the *Append From* menu allows you to add data from all the databases listed in Import, in addition to fixed-length fields, blank delimited, and character delimited files.

Thus, dBASE IV can be used to build a large client database; you can set up a query selecting those clients with a particular profile, sort in zip code order, and produce a data file that can be used by your word processor to print customized letters to all the names that your query process selected.

The DOS utilities accessible from within the Tools menu pro-

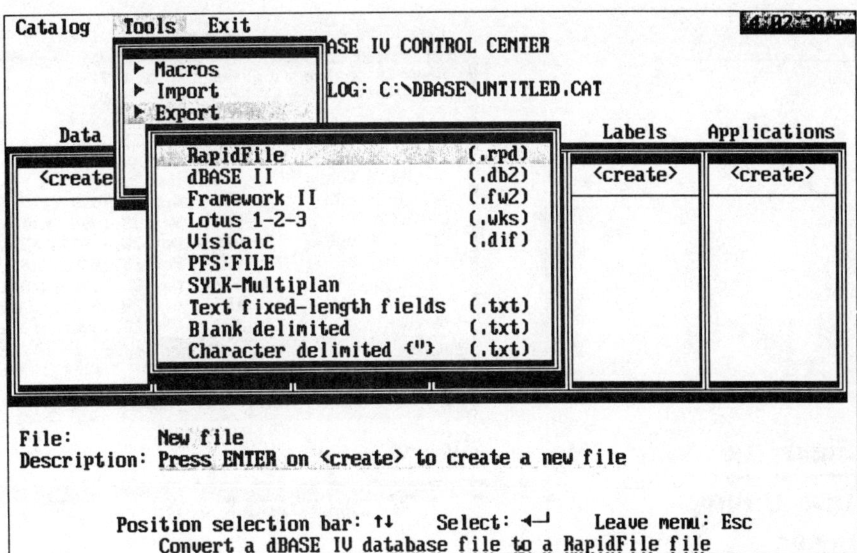

Figure 2-5

Export menu.

vide much information about the contents of your current directory, and can be used to find files anywhere in your system, in a different path, and on a different logical disk drive. In addition, the utilities provide excellent tools with which to manage your disk files. For example, you can tell the system to look for only executable programs or .dbf files. Or you may look for files that begin with the same letters—possibly your way of designating all the files in a particular database structure. You can mark these files for deletion, move them to other directories, copy them, rename them, and, depending on the file, even edit or view them. In addition, files can be sorted based on one of many criteria. The DOS Utilities menu is seen in Figure 2-6.

From within the DOS Utilities menu you can call up the DOS menu (Figure 2-7). This menu allows you to enter a single DOS command, go to a DOS shell, or change the default drive and directory for your dBASE files.

When you select the Perform DOS Command menu item, you may also load up a copy of the DOS shell by typing *COMMAND.COM*. This command loads the DOS command processor and is, in effect, another version of DOS. When you access DOS this way, however, you must be careful not to change or delete any of the files in use during your dBASE IV session, because the system cannot prevent you from making any changes to the files

```
DOS   Files   Sort   Mark   Operations   Exit                              4:17:27 pm
                              C:\DBASE
  Name/Extension       Size    Date & Time          Attrs      Space Used

  <parent>             <DIR>   Nov 29,1988  2:58p   ****
  SQLHOME              <DIR>   Nov 29,1988  2:58p   ****
  11166010 $ED             0   Nov 29,1988  4:15a   a***            4,096
  88956010 $VM             0   Nov 29,1988  4:15a   a***            4,096
  ASCII    PR2           680   Oct 20,1988 11:21a   a***            4,096
  CATALOG  CAT           607   Nov 29,1988  4:16a   a***            4,096
  CHRTMSTR DBO        38,996   Oct 20,1988 11:33a   a***           40,960
  CONFIG   DB            696   Nov 29,1988  4:05a   a***            4,096
  DBASE    EXE       146,432   Nov 29,1988  4:04a   a***          147,456
  DBASE1   HLP       247,155   Oct 20,1988 11:26a   a***          249,856
  DBASE1   OVL       349,120   Oct 20,1988 11:23a   a***          352,256

Total  <marked>             0 (  0 files)                               0
Total  <displayed>  2,840,406 ( 39 files)                       2,936,832

   Files: *.*                                           Sorted by: Name

DOS util ||C:\DBASE
          Position selection bar:↑↓   Mark file:←┘   Directories:F9
```

Figure 2-6

DOS Utilities menu.

from within the shell. If you do make changes, the system may be unable to load the changed files when you return to dBASE IV. The DOS command window is shown in Figure 2-8.

The next menu item in the Tools menu is *Protect data.* Protecting data ensures that only a user who knows the password required to load and run dBASE IV can load the program and work

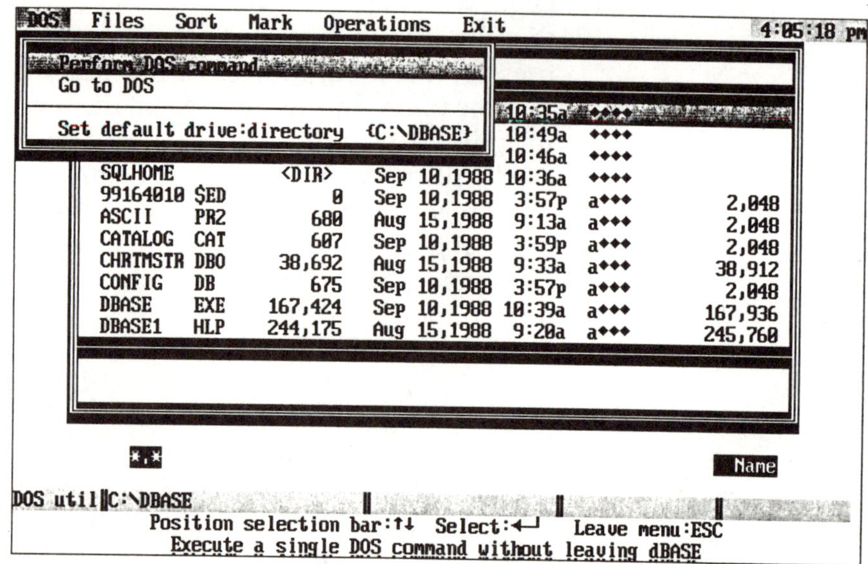

Figure 2-7

DOS menu.

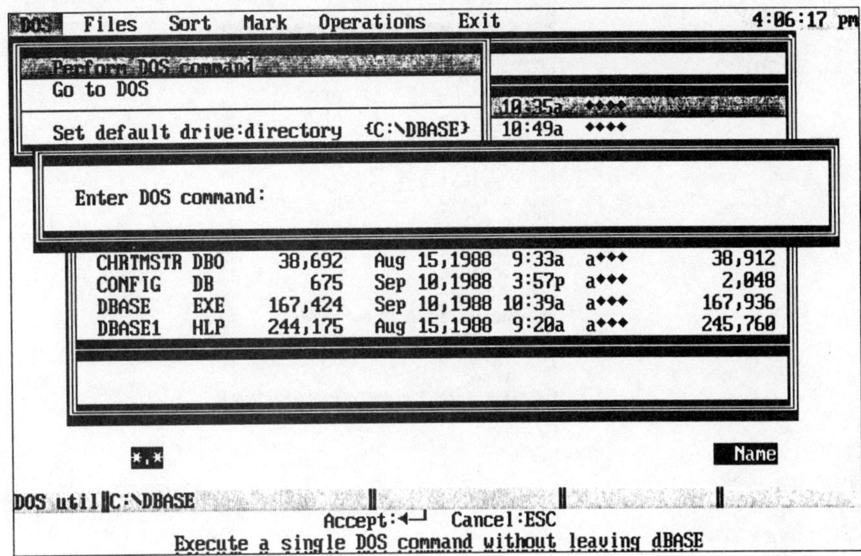

Figure 2-8

DOS command window.

with your data. This option should be used with great care. If you forget or misplace your password, you will be locked out of the program.

The final option in the Tools menu is *Settings*. When you select this option, a limited version of the setup screens seen in DBSETUP when the program was installed pops up. The options window appears in Figure 2-9.

You will notice that a brief description of what the highlighted option does appears at the bottom of your screen. The Display Options menu allows you to vary the colors that appear on screen when you use dBASE IV.

To return to the Work Area from the Menu Bar, touch the **Esc** key.

The Control Center was designed to allow you to interact with dBASE IV without having to go into the dot prompt mode and enter dBASE programming commands. To that end, the Control Center provides most of the information you need to determine which file you are using and which catalog is in use, and to design, evaluate, and produce reports based on a file or files in the catalog. You can even design and generate an application.

To get a brief overview of many of these features, a small database will be built here to demonstrate some of the key features of dBASE IV.

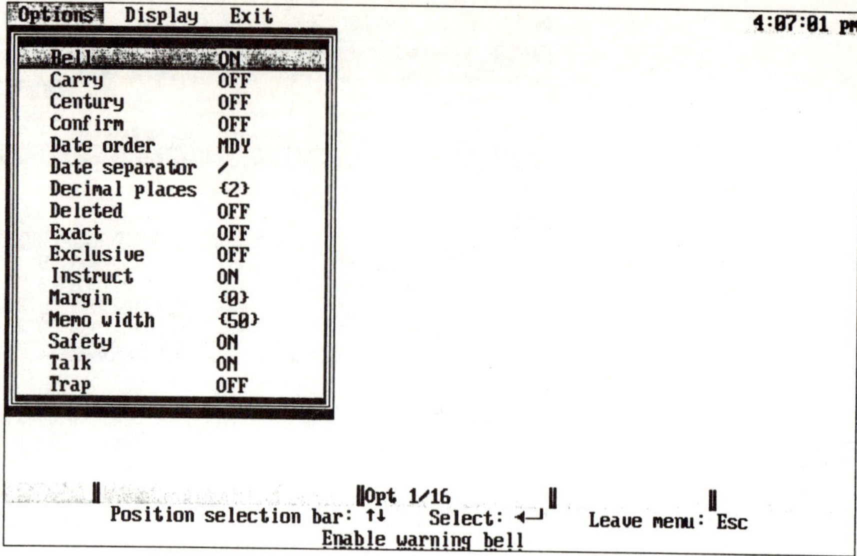

Figure 2-9

Settings menu.

First, we will start a new catalog called CH2 (for Chapter Two).

Press: **F10** (or **Alt-C**)

to call up the Catalog menu. Now,

Press: **u** (or **U**) (or press **ENTER** to accept the highlighted option, "Use a different catalog")

At the right of your screen, a selection window will pop up showing the subdirectories accessible from the current DBASE directory, and the catalog files you have already loaded onto your current directory.

Press: **DnArrow**

to move the highlight to <create> and touch the **ENTER** key to accept this option. You will then be asked for the name for the new catalog.

Type: *CH2* **ENTER**

The system automatically adds the .CAT extension for you. You should now have a screen with an empty Work Area (Figure 2-10).

Now, you will build a small database with employee names and birthdates. With <create> under the Data Bar, touch the **ENTER**

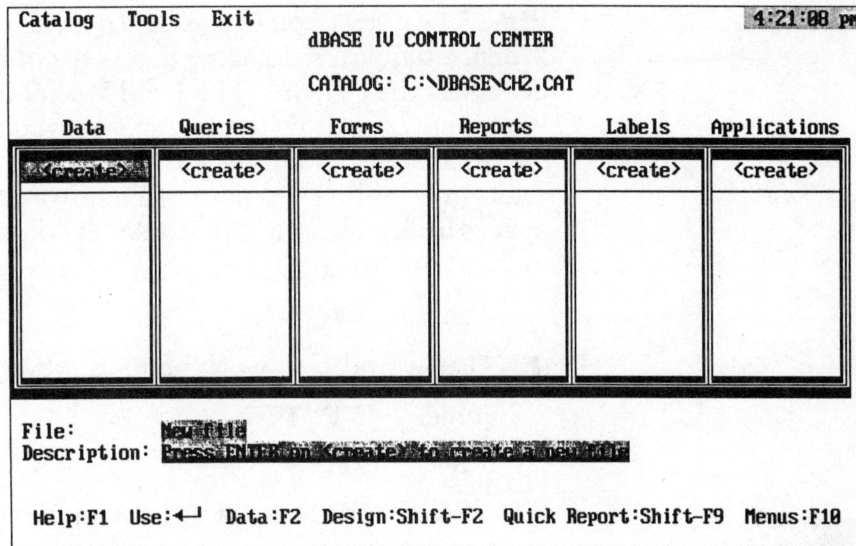

Figure 2-10

Empty CH2.CAT screen.

key. This brings you to the database design screen seen in Figure 2-11. This screen could also have been reached using the **Shift-F2** key combination.

For Field 1,

Type: *First_Name*

Figure 2-11

Database design screen.

Layout Organize Append Go To Exit 4:21:41 pm

Bytes remaining: 4000

Num	Field Name	Field Type	Width	Dec	Index
1		Character			N

Database C:\dbase\<NEW> Field 1/1

Enter the field name. Insert/Delete field:Ctrl-N/Ctrl-U

Field names begin with a letter and may contain letters, digits and underscores dBASE IV allows you to use field names up to 10 characters long. When you type a field name that is 10 characters long, the system advances the cursor to the Field type column. If you use a field name that is shorter than 10 spaces, you must press **ENTER** or **Tab** to advance from one entry option to the next. Note that an underline character separates First from Name—you cannot use spaces in a field name. The cursor is now at field type, which you do not wish to change.

Press: **Tab**

(**ENTER** would also work here) to move to Width.

Type: *15* **ENTER**

Press: **ENTER**

to accept *N* in the index field. This tells the system not to index on the first name.

You should be in line 2 on the data definition screen.

Type: *Last_Name* **ENTER**

Press: **Tab**

Give the field a width of 20 characters to accommodate long last names. Now, tell the system that you want to index the field by typing *Y* under the Index Bar.

The next field, Birth_Date, is a date field.

Type: *Birth_Date*

The highlight is now at the Field Type column. Touch the **Space Bar** to move the selector to "Date." The system automatically enters the appropriate number of spaces for a date field. Finally, type *Y* to identify this as an indexed field. The designed structure is shown in Figure 2-12. Now that the structure is defined, complete the design by pressing **ENTER.**

The system prompts "Save as:."

Type: *Births*

The screen will appear as shown in Figure 2-13.

Press: **ENTER**

to complete the name operation.

A window will pop onto the screen describing the structure of

```
Layout   Organize   Append   Go To   Exit                              4:22:18 pm
                                                        Bytes remaining:   3957
 Num | Field Name | Field Type | Width | Dec | Index
  1  | FIRST_NAME | Character  |  15   |     |   N
  2  | LAST_NAME  | Character  |  20   |     |   Y
  3  | BIRTH_DATE | Date       |   8   |     |   Y
  4  |            | Character  |       |     |   N

Database C:\dbase\<NEW>          Field 4/4
        Enter the field name. Insert/Delete field:Ctrl-N/Ctrl-U
Field names begin with a letter and may contain letters, digits and underscores
```

Figure 2-12

Database structure.

the database and indexed fields. At the bottom of the screen, the system asks if you want to "Input data records now? (Y/N)." The completed screen is shown in Figure 2-14.

Type: ***Y* ENTER**

and you will be in the Data entry screen.

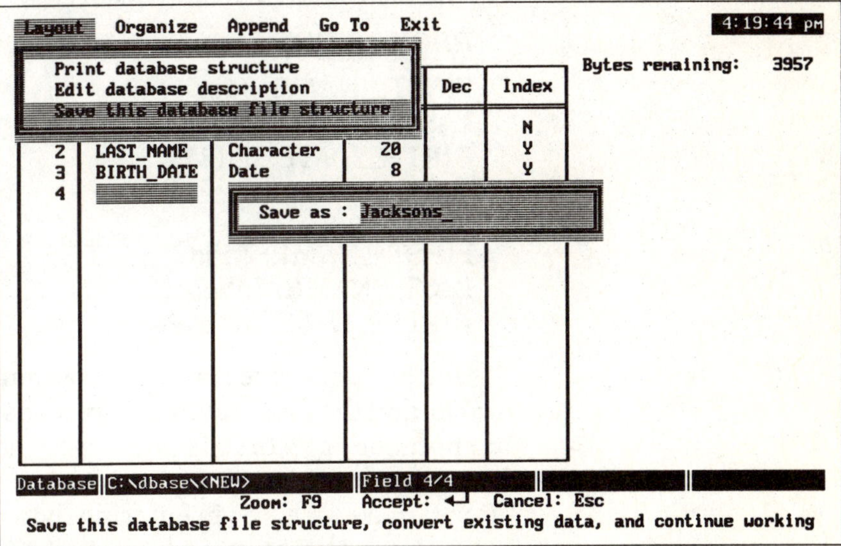

Figure 2-13

Design, with "Save as" prompt.

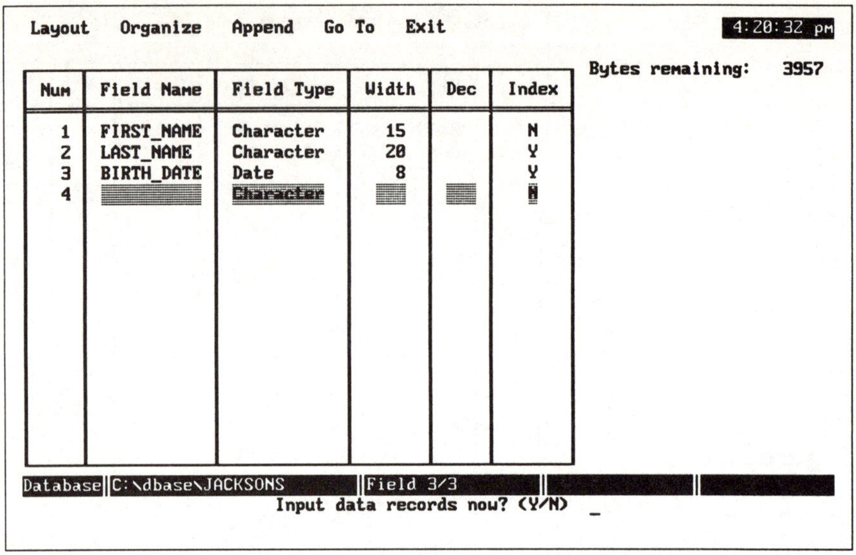

```
Layout   Organize   Append   Go To   Exit                          4:20:32 pm

                                                          Bytes remaining:   3957
 Num  Field Name   Field Type  Width  Dec  Index

  1   FIRST_NAME   Character     15         N
  2   LAST_NAME    Character     20         Y
  3   BIRTH_DATE   Date           8         Y
  4                Character                N

Database C:\dbase\JACKSONS          Field 3/3
                     Input data records now? (Y/N) _
```

Figure 2-14

Design, prompting for input.

For the purposes of this introduction, only two records will be entered. In future chapters, a larger database will be built.

Fill in the two records, using the following data. Use the **ENTER** key to move from one field to the next. Note that the system automatically moves from one completed field to the next. For example, after you complete the birthdate field in Record One, you will be moved to Record Two.

RECORD ONE

FIRST_NAME: Jack
LAST_NAME: Jackson
BIRTH_DATE: 051255

RECORD TWO:

FIRST_NAME: John
LAST_NAME: Johnson
BIRTH_DATE: 071648

At the bottom of the screen, the system will display the record number and the total number of records in the file. Note that the total number of records is one larger than the actual number of files.

If you make an error in entering data in an earlier record, you may go back to that record using the **PgUp** key.

Once you have completed entry of the two files, touch the **F2** key. This will bring you to the *Browse* screen (Figure 2-15). If your screen does not look like the one in the figure, the system may be showing only the last record entered. Pressing **PgUp** should correct this.

Now that the data structure has been determined and two entries have been made, you will quickly see some of the new features included in dBASE IV that will ease use of the program.

Press: **Alt-E**

to bring up the Exit menu.

There are two or three options in this menu, depending on whether you got to the Browse screen from the Database Design menu or directly from the Data column. The first option, "Exit," returns you to the Control Center . The second option, "Transfer to Query Design," transfers you to the Query Design screen. The Query Design screen is used to design the format for analyzing and retrieving the data in your data files or for creating a new data file. The third option, "Return to Data Design," returns you to the screen used to design or modify your database.

With "Exit" highlighted,

Press: **ENTER**

to return to the Control Center.

Figure 2-15

Browse screen.

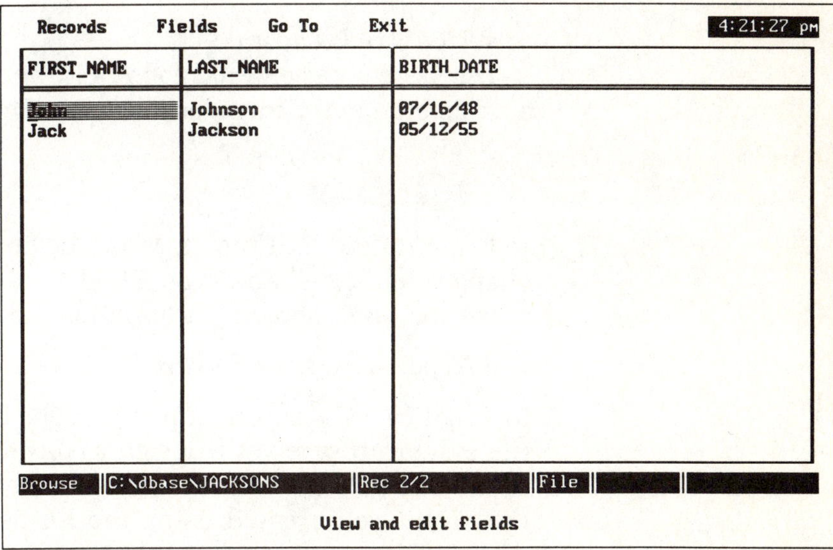

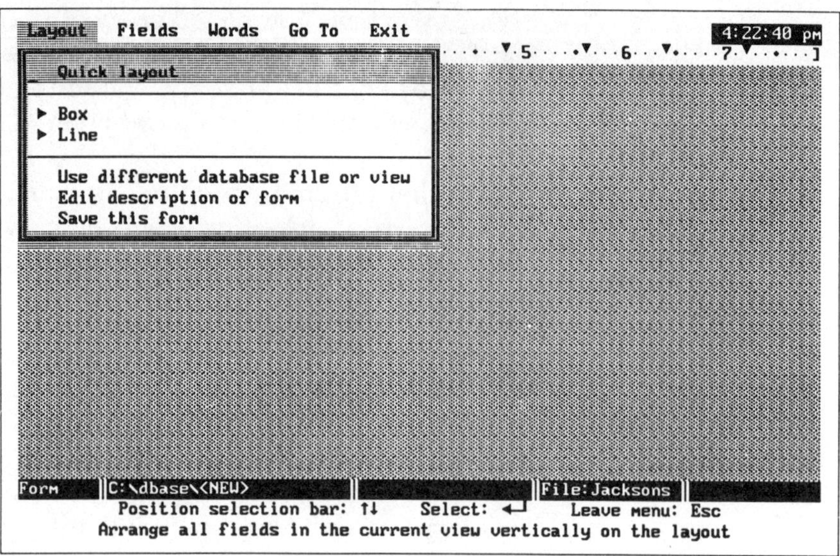

Figure 2-16

Layout menu.

dBASE IV allows you to quickly design custom data entry forms. To see a basic form, use the **RtArrow** to move the highlight to <create> in the *Forms* column.

Press: **ENTER** (or **Shift-F2**)

to bring you into the Layout screen (Figure 2-16).

Press: **ENTER**

to select *Quick Layout.*

The system has entered each field, and a data input area into a basic data entry form, as shown in Figure 2-17.

Next,

Type: **Alt-E**

to bring up the Exit menu. Move the cursor to highlight "Save changes and exit," and type **ENTER**. You will be prompted to name the input screen you have just designed.

Type: *Jacksons* **ENTER**

to identify this as the input screen. Pressing **ENTER** tells the system to save your design as JACKSONS.SCR. When you select this screen, you will be able to enter your data based on the layout you created using the forms generation facility in dBASE IV.

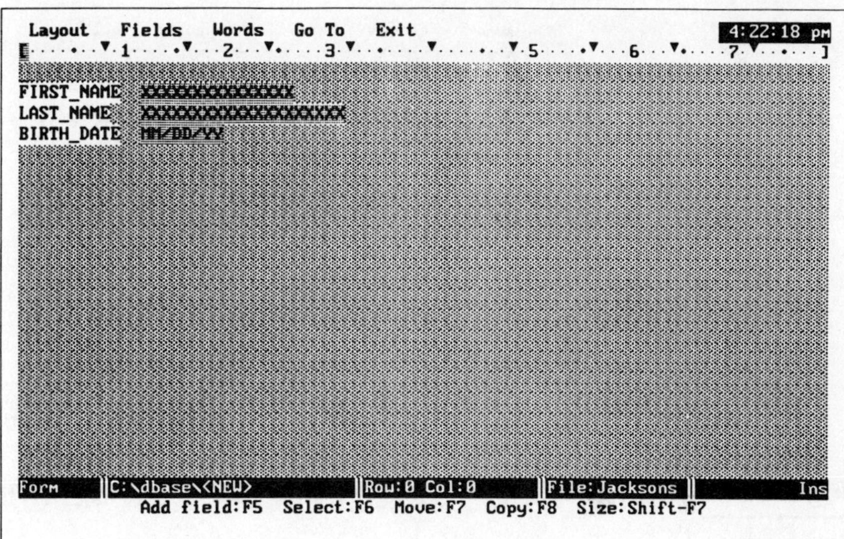

Figure 2-17

Data entry form.

The *Queries* portion of the Control Center uses a very powerful technique called *Query By Example.* This allows you to tell the system how you want it to retrieve data. Because no complicated commands have to be written, this facility is easier for new users to learn than the commands required in earlier versions of dBASE, and provides a good deal of power.

In this example, you want to find all employees who are named Jackson. Select <create> in the Queries column. The system displays a file skeleton at the top and a view skeleton (more on these in a later chapter) at the bottom of the screen. To tell the system to select all employees named Jackson, use the **Tab** key and move the highlight to the "Last_Name" column.

Type: *="Jackson"* **ENTER**

to define the condition you wish to select. (Note: be sure to enclose the text [Jackson] inside quotation marks.)

Your screen will appear as shown in Figure 2-18.

To quickly see the files that match the query condition,

Press: **F2**

The Browse screen will come up, showing only one record with a field that matched the desired parameters. Return to the Query design screen. To do this,

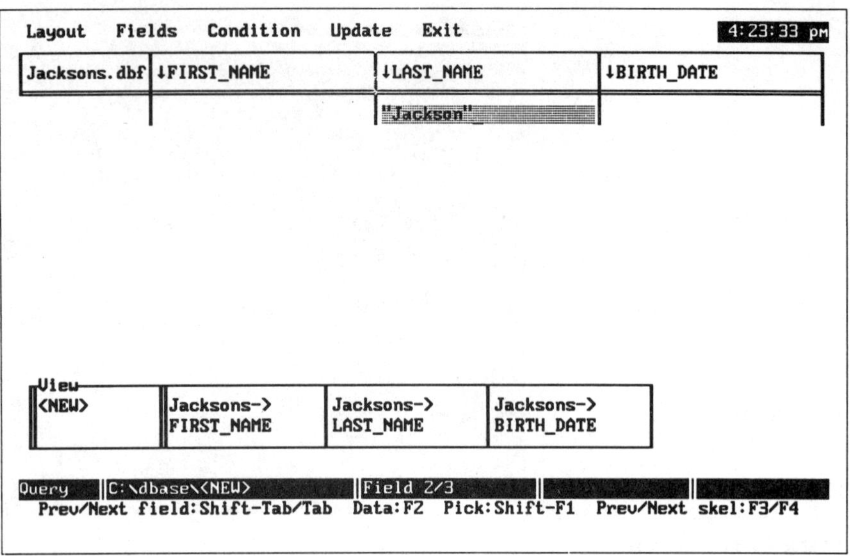

Figure 2-18

Query screen.

Type: **Alt-E**

to bring up the Exit menu. Next,

Press: *t*

to select "Transfer to query" design.

Type: **Alt-E**

then highlight and **ENTER** to select "Save changes and exit." Save the query form as Jacksons. The system will save your query as JACKSONS.QBE, as seen in the *File:* line of the Control Center screen.

To see how data extraction using a query works,

Press: **F2**

to display data that match the parameters of the search. The screen will quickly go through your entire database (in this case, two records) and select only those records that match your query.

You may want to verify that the query selects only those records desired. In this case, you can select the query by typing **ENTER**, and then select Modify query. Change the value of the operator from equal to (=) to not equal to (#) Jackson. There are two symbols that can be used for not equal to: the # (number symbol) and

< > (less than and greater than symbols next to each other) both represent inequality. If you set the condition, # "Jackson", the system will select all files in which the last name is *not* Jackson.

The other two columns that can be selected from within the Control Center are *Labels* and *Applications.* Labels allows you to design a print format for printing labels and envelopes in a variety of sizes. You can assign positions to desired fields, and define the dimensions of the labels as well as number of columns of labels on a sheet of paper.

The Applications menu provides two options. The first allows you to write or load the resident editor in dBASE and write a new or edit an existing dBASE program.

The second utility is a new addition to dBASE IV. The *Applications Generator* provides you with powerful tools for developing your own database applications. Such an application can be used with a runtime version of dBASE IV or a full copy of dBASE IV, and therefore the user does not have to learn to use dBASE IV. (A runtime version of dBASE IV provides the basic program but none of the programming or user interface capabilities of the full program—it is designed to allow you to execute a database program that you developed, but not to modify it.)

An application developed using the Applications Generator may have little resemblance to the dBASE IV interface. In fact, you can develop specific applications—such as an accounts payable or personnel management system—using the Applications Generator, and the ultimate user may need to see no dBASE IV windows or commands.

Many independent developers and consultants have created special applications programs using dBASE and runtime versions of the program and commercially marketed the special programs.

Special Keys from within Control Center

The function keys perform different functions depending on whether you are in the Control Center or at the dot prompt (programming) mode. From within the Control Center, the following keys perform the following functions:

Special Key	*Action Performed*
F1	Loads Help
F2	Displays data, toggles Browse/Edit
Shift F2	Brings up Design screen
F3	Moves one column left
F4	Moves one column right
F5	Brings up Field menu or selects a field
F6	Used to mark blocks for moving copy
F7	Used to place a moved block
F8	Used to place a copied block
F9	Zooms data entry window
Shift F-9	Generates a quick report
F10	Brings highlight to menu lines
Alt-C	Brings down Catalog menu
Alt-T	Brings down Tools menu
Alt-E	Brings down Exit menu
Ctrl-S	Moves left one column
Ctrl-D	Moves right one column
Ctrl-E	Moves up one line in column
Ctrl-X	Moves down one line in column (Note: **Ctrl-** commands are equivalent to WordStar commands)
Esc	Backs up one screen; exits to dot prompt
ENTER	Accepts highlighted option

Going to Dot Prompt

You can go to the dot prompt through the user interface that is common to all versions of dBASE. Although the Control Center is designed to assist you in doing many of the most important processes required to design, build, and evaluate data files, there may be times when you want to go into the original programming environment.

From within the Control Center you may exit to the dot prompt in two ways:

You may exit by touching the **Esc** key. The system will prompt you, asking you to verify that you want to abandon the current operation (Figure 2-19). Responding with *Y* will bring you to the dot prompt.

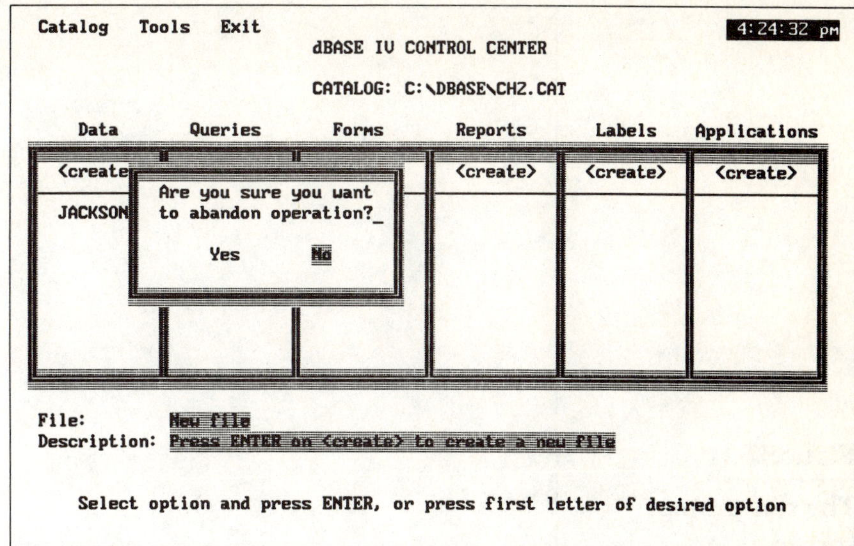

Figure 2-19

Abandon operation prompt.

The second method is from the Exit menu. The Exit menu may be accessed using the **F10** key and arrow keys to highlight the "Exit to dot prompt" prompt. It may also be accessed using the **Alt-E** key combination (Figure 2-20). Pressing **ENTER** returns you to the dot prompt.

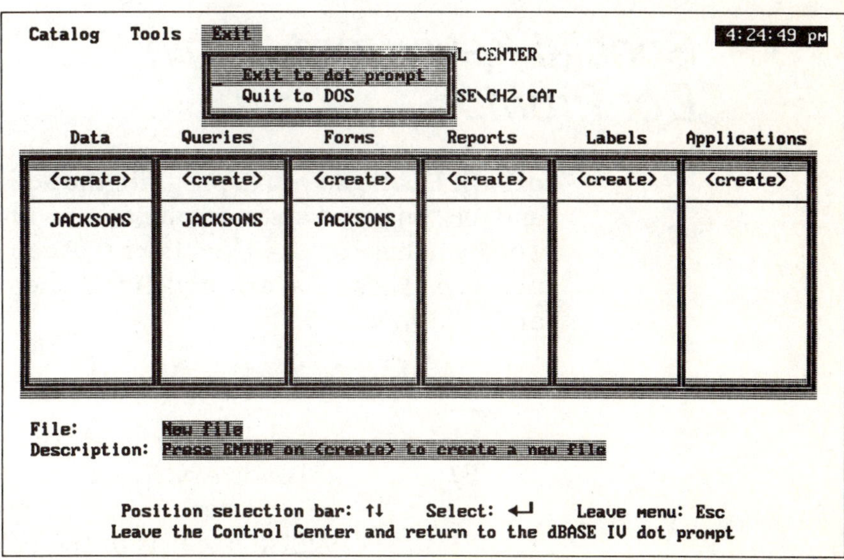

Figure 2-20

Exit to dot prompt.

Figure 2-21

The dot prompt screen.

The screen with the dot prompt appears as shown in Figure 2-21.

Yet another way to get to the dot prompt is to modify the CONFIG.DB file to *not* start the program at the Control Center. In the file CONFIG.DB, you will delete the line that says COMMAND=ASSIST.

Special Keys from within Dot Prompt

dBASE IV allows you to program the action of the function keys, and the function keys in combination with the **Ctrl** and **Shift** keys. Thus, you have up to 30 functions that can be assigned to the function keys. Those that are predefined when the program is shipped are as follows:

Key	*Function*
F1	Loads Help
F2	Loads Assist—brings you to the Control Center
F3	Lists records in the selected database file

Key	*Function*
F4	Gives a directory of database files in the current subdirectory; shows bytes used, date last used, and space remaining on disk (see Figure 2-22)
F5	Displays database structure
F6	Displays status of database, special keys
F7	Displays memory in use; use of memory variables, definitions stored, available system memory
F8	Display field names and contents in first record
F9	Append; brings up Data entry screen, allows new data to be entered after last record
F10	Brings up Data entry screen; starts at last record; allows you to edit data in database
UpArrow	Scrolls through last 20 commands, from last to first
DnArrow	Scrolls through last commands—reverse of order brought up by **UpArrow**; works only in combination with **UpArrow**

Figure 2-22

F4 (DIR) display.

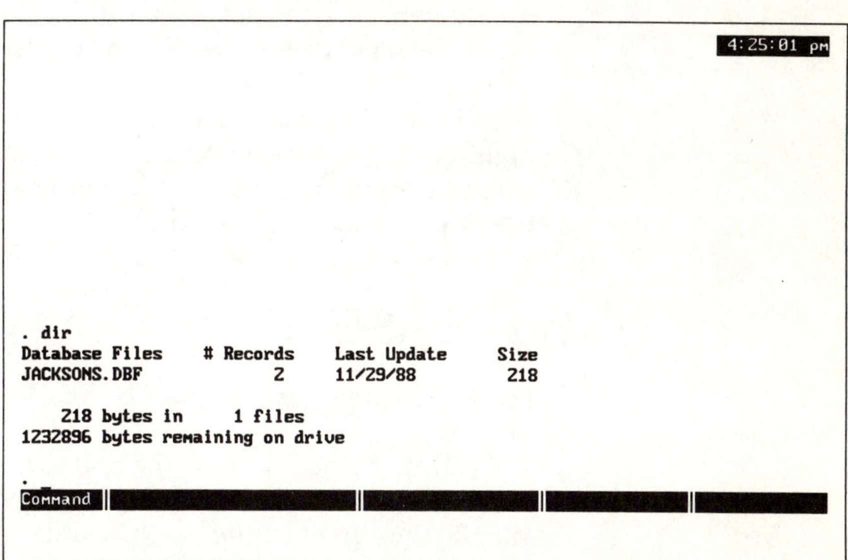

In addition, the function keys perform functions that are predefined by Ashton-Tate, and which you can redefine from within CONFIG.DB.

Returning to Control Center

As previously shown, you may return to the Control Center by typing *Assist* **ENTER**, or, assuming you have not redefined the function keys, by pressing **F2**.

Rapid File and Option Selection

Selection of files, fields, or other items in drop down menus has been simplified in dBASE IV. To select a file or field in such a menu, you need only type the first few characters in its name. The system will automatically move the highlight so that it is on the first item that matches the characters you typed.

For example, if you have two fields, *Salary* and *State,* you may select *Salary* by typing the letter *s.* Salary will be highlighted because it is the first match for the letter *s.* To select *State,* simply add the letter *t.* The first match for *st* will be state. It should be clear, then, that unless your files or fields all have names that use the same starting letters, any field or file (or other option that can be selected from a menu) can be selected by typing just a few letters.

You can, of course, continue using the arrow keys to move the highlight to the desired item. In either case, whether you use the arrows or type the letters of the item name, you still must press **ENTER** to accept the highlighted selection.

Quitting dBASE IV

There are three ways to quit dBASE IV—two right and one terribly wrong.

The first method is to use the Exit menu. This may be accessed by pressing **F10** and using the arrow keys to highlight the menu. Moving the cursor to *Quit to DOS* and pressing **ENTER** saves all files, views, queries, and other contents of the catalog that were used during the current session. You may also select the Exit menu using the **Alt-E** key combination. Again, use the arrow keys or type *Q* to escape back to DOS.

The second method for leaving dBASE IV is from the dot prompt. At the dot prompt,

Type: *quit* **ENTER**

The system will close all open files and return you to DOS.

When you quit to DOS using either of these two methods, dBASE IV stores all changes made during your current work session.

The third (*wrong*) method is any method of rebooting that goes outside of the above two. You will be able to leave the program, but it may result in loss of files. It may even corrupt any database files with which you were working and make them unusable. Leaving the program by this third method does not ensure that the required file pointers are recorded or that the files that must be closed are in fact closed. When you next load dBASE IV you may not be able to use the catalog or related files recorded during your last session.

Examples of the wrong method are turning the power off while using dBASE IV, which could do major damage to your catalog; or using the **Ctrl-Alt-Del** combination. dBASE IV is unable to trap the reset combination and prevent a reboot—so be careful not to use these combinations while using dBASE IV.

Although these are blatant errors, which are unlikely to be made by most computer users, there is one time when this type of error can be easily made—from within dBASE IV's DOS shell. The shell allows you to use DOS functions—and in one case does not make it apparent that you are still running dBASE IV. Thus, if you are working on a dBase session, go to the DOS shell, and then leave for a while, it is possible that you may return to the computer and *forget* that you are actually running DOS from inside a shell, rather than from within DOS. Thus, it is good practice to return to dBASE IV as quickly as possible after you have jumped to the DOS shell.

The purpose of this chapter was to provide a basic introduction to dBASE IV: its differences from earlier versions of dBASE, its main features, and a general introduction to navigation from within the Control Center. Future chapters explore the features of the program in further detail.

3 Building a Database

In Chapter Two, you saw how to quickly load dBASE IV and ran through a sample application, with a few stops to highlight key new features and such basics as function keys and navigation, and how to exit the program. This chapter presents detailed instructions for using a catalog and designing and building a database.

Catalog

The catalog contains all the database files, report forms, label forms, queries, indexes, and other files that you expect to use in a particular type of application. Your company may require many catalogs.

For example, the accounting department may have a catalog of vendors and products that are to be ordered from the vendors. In this catalog will be a database of vendor names, phone numbers, sales agents, products, and possibly a memo field with a historical record of problems or comments relating to experience with the vendor. A second database may include all the products that are on an authorized purchasing list, along with vendors providing the products, and, perhaps, pricing information. A third database may contain records of items ordered, price paid, and whether received by your company. Forms for filling in new vendor data or order information, or adding items to the approved product lists may be included in this catalog. In addition, report forms and predesigned queries may reside in the catalog and can be used to automate retrieval and reporting of ordering and vendor data.

A second catalog may be used for accounts payable. Similarly, this would have a vendor list data file, a database for logging and recording all orders placed and shipments received, and a database of all bills received and date paid. Forms for paying for invoiced items, summaries of weekly, monthly, and quarterly activity, and other accounts payable items could be included in this module.

It is important to note that within a catalog, a number of databases can be used concurrently. The data in identical fields may be related using a query that you design. For example, within the accounts payable catalog, you may wish to produce a report of all purchases that were received more than 30 days ago and have not yet been invoiced, and print out a list of the names, addresses, and items for which your company has not yet received a bill. Conversely, you may wish to print a list of vendors who have billed you for products that have not yet been received. Such reports will retrieve data from at least two of your database files.

In earlier versions of dBASE you were required to keep track of the database files, views, indexes, and other components of a catalog. dBASE IV does this for you.

You may have already deduced that multiple catalogs can use the same database and forms. When sharing a common database, be careful not to make changes to the structure of the data because it may alter the way other catalogs deal with it.

On the other hand, although you can copy a database, and use a different version in each catalog, this may not be a suitable option. For example, if you were to use a different vendor list in your accounts payable and your purchasing modules you may end up with different lists in each catalog. If someone in your company placed an order from a new vendor who was not entered into the accounts payable database, there may be problems getting payment for the items if the Accounts Payable vendor data are not upgraded. Thus, it is usually good practice to develop a core of data files that will be used for a variety of catalog functions. Reports, queries, labels, and fill-in forms that are unique to catalogs can, of course, be used.

Using the Catalog Menu

As described in Chapter Two, there are two ways to call up a menu from the menu bar. The first is to press **F10**. If you have just loaded dBASE IV, pressing **F10** will automatically pop down the Catalog menu. If you have been using dBASE IV for a while, the **F10** key will return you to whichever menu pull down you last used. In other words, if you previously used the Tools menu, pressing **F10** will bring this menu down.

Navigating from one menu to the next can be done with the arrow keys.

The second method for popping down the Catalog menu is to touch the **Alt-C** combination, that is, hold down the **Alt** key and press the **c** (or **C**) key (case of the C key does not matter here).

The Catalog menu is shown in Figure 3-1. Note that the menu is divided into two areas. The top portion has to do with catalog management—creating, renaming, and changing catalog descriptions, and changing to a different catalog. The bottom portion deals with assignment of files to a catalog and modifying a file description.

You may also notice that the bottom two lines, *Remove highlighted file from catalog* and *Change description of highlighted*

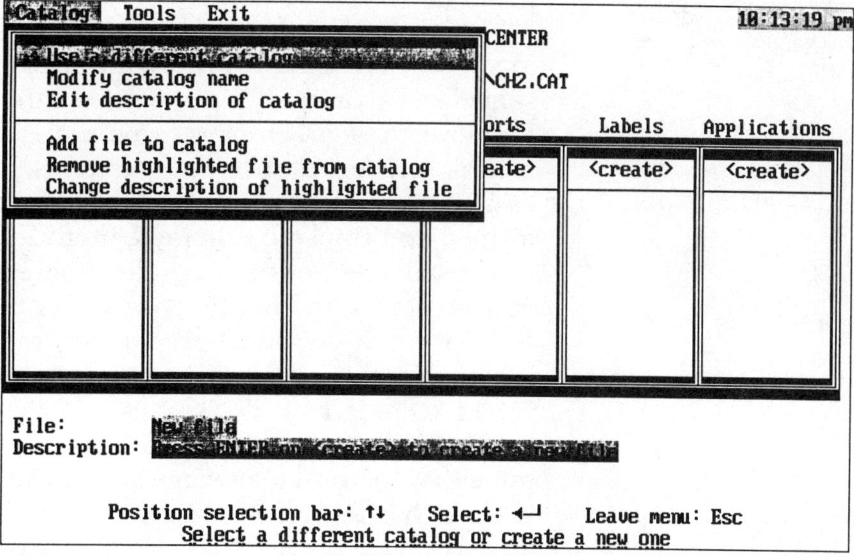

Figure 3-1

The Catalog menu.

file, may be a different color, or dimmer than the rest of the items. This is because unless you have told the system to use a particular file, the options are not valid, because you have not highlighted a file. dBASE IV will not highlight an option that is not valid.

If you created the catalog CH2.CAT in the last chapter, this catalog should now be showing as having been selected. If not, you may already have chosen to use a catalog that you were using in dBASE III+, or the system loaded the default catalog, UNTITLED.CAT.

A catalog can be thought of as the framework of your entire data management system. By developing a logical, modular structure—one from which you can hang all the required data structures and attach all the necessary data analysis, indexing, and output structures—a system that can be easily modified, you could save much time in the future.

Business is dynamic, and your company's needs may frequently change. Months or years from now you may have to modify your database structure—the time taken to develop a logical, easily understood data model can save many hours of confusion in the future. A system whose design is clear and easily understood can be easily modified and upgraded by others who were not involved in the original design and maintenance of your data system.

The example in this chapter is intended to provide some pointers in effective database design.

The catalog to be built is intended for use in a personnel department. Certainly, many different things are being done in a personnel department. Employees are hired. Employees are fired. Employees resign. Employees die. Equal employment compliance records and records of employee counselings are maintained. Occasionally employees are suspended. Employee transfers are performed and tracked. Employee anniversaries are followed, and ticklers are sent out for regular progress interviews. Employee marital status and tax filing records are changed and updated. Foreign employees must provide records of work eligibility. Virtually everything done in a company's personnel department involves keeping records.

In designing a personnel data system, it is important to determine how we want to manage the information and what we want to do with it. It is also necessary to take into account the existing forms that are being used by your department, because you have to determine whether or not these forms can be used to collect the raw data needed for your records, and whether or not the data on these forms can be moved to your new data system.

A personnel department would usually use a variety of forms. Most common would be employee applications, tax forms, and some type of internal employment information sheet. Therefore, the first form that you will probably want to create is an employee information form: this will contain all pertinent employee data—name, address, social security number, birthdate, hire date, employee number, licenses (if appropriate), withholding status, and possibly job title and department. Resident status may also be an important part of this file. If title and department are recorded, it may be useful to provide space for more than one entry: by setting up space for historic tracking of an employee's positions at your firm, you can easily determine information about promotion within the organization, and can quickly recover a history of the employee's various positions at the company.

A second set of records could track all job applications. This file will include the name, address, and phone number of all applicants. A confidential record of demographic group could be appended to the file. Access to this information can be restricted to authorized personnel only, and must be maintained in compliance with Equal Employment Opportunity Commission (EEOC) guidelines (names and addresses may not be permitted; however, outcome of the application, hire or no-hire, should, of course, be kept).

A third database of employee counselings may be kept. Again, access to this type of data can be password protected by a security feature available in dBASE IV. This data file will store, at a minimum, employee name, employee number (if applicable), department number, job title, type of counseling (correction, suspension, termination, commendation), and possibly a memo field for the initial counseling and a second memo field for follow-up. A tickler date for follow-up may also be included in this file.

Once the basic types of data files are determined, it is useful to determine what types of data input forms you want to use. These are the on-screen forms generated by dBASE IV, not the forms that are filled out by applicants, new hires, or counseling supervisors.

You will want an EEOC form that can be used to record ethnic background information and the outcome of the employment process, an employee information file with the data described above, and a basic counseling form. Each form can be easily designed using dBASE IV, once you have built your data files.

Now that you have conceptualized the types of data you want, at least initially, and have an idea of the kind of forms you need to complete to collect the information, it may be useful to think about the types of data that will have to be extracted. You can build your query now or later. But developing a general idea of the type of query you need, and testing with a small data sample, could expose problems that you may encounter after you have entered large amounts of data into your database structure.

You may also look into other aspects of your catalog. Types of indexing, and fields to be indexed on, should also be considered. Indexing will be explored later in this book.

In sum, it is important to be able to determine the structure of your catalog, the data files you need to build, the way the information will be used, and how you intend to print it out, *before* you design your catalog and forms. It is also often useful to design forms that are similar to those already in use in your organization. This will not only make it easier for input operators to transfer data into your database, but will also make it simpler to move data from earlier data forms.

The three data files you are concerned with here are

1. Employee data
2. EEOC data
3. Counseling data

Because the data in the above fields contain sensitive information, you will want to control access to it. That will be done using dBASE IV's *protect* capabilities. These files will be protected by assigning a password to the data from within the Tools menu.

Because these files will be protected, only a few, authorized employees will have access to them. However, there may be a number of legitimate uses for some of the data in these files. Therefore, you will want a fourth file of general employee data that contains information your company has decided should be available to employees without restriction.

We will now start a new catalog, called PERSONEL (dBASE IV is limited to eight-character catalog names—the word *personnel* is shortened to fit the eight-character limit).

To bring up the Catalog menu,

Press: **F10**

and move the arrow to highlight "Catalog" or

Type: **Alt-C**

You should now see the Catalog menu (as was shown in Figure 3-1). To create a new catalog, choose *Use a different catalog* by moving the highlight to that option (if it is not already there) and pressing **ENTER**. On the right side of your screen will be a list with the names of the files on your directory (Figure 3-2). Your current drive, directory, catalogs (with the *.CAT* extension), and subdirectories will appear in this box. If there are more catalogs or subdirectories than the window can display, you may scroll through the list of catalogs using the **UpArrow** or **DnArrow** on your keypad.

The File selection window is logically designed and easy to use. Although it is assumed that you are familiar with hard disk structure and understand the concepts of parent directories and subdirectories, these will be covered very briefly.

A hard disk may be organized in a number of ways. If you are using your computer only for database management, you may not want to create a separate directory for your database program and files. Your entire disk may be a database disk. However, even

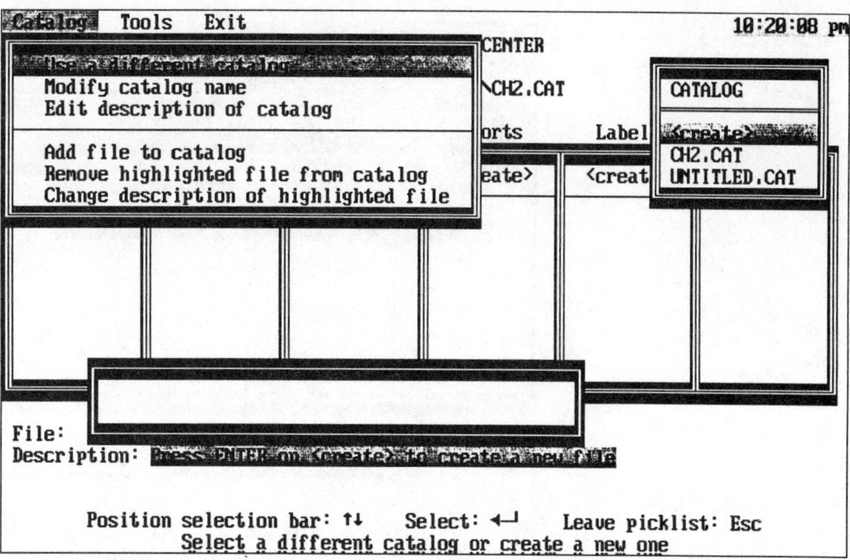

Figure 3-2

File selection from within catalog.

if all you are doing is database, you will probably want some simple method of finding particular categories of database development. For example, if you are planning to develop applications for a variety of clients, you would want to be able to set up a separate group of files for each of them.

In the dBASE IV setup, a number of subdirectories were created by the installation program. These included a subdirectory called \DBASE, the one you are now in, and a number of subdirectories of \DBASE—DBDATA, DBTUTOR, and SQLHOME.

In this case, the parent directory is the DOS root directory, which is the topmost directory on your disk, the one from which all first level subdirectories arise. Subdirectory names are listed below <create> and <parent> and are similarly bracketed. If your data files reside on your disk in their own subdirectory of the root, that is, not as subdirectories of \DBASE, you will have to select <parent>, which will then show all the available directories on your hard drive. You may then select the appropriate subdirectory.

When you find an existing catalog you wish to use, use the **UpArrow** or **DnArrow** key to move the highlight, and touch the **ENTER** key to select the catalog. In this case, however, you want to make a new catalog, called PERSONEL, and want to keep it on the \DBASE subdirectory. Move the highlight to <create>, and

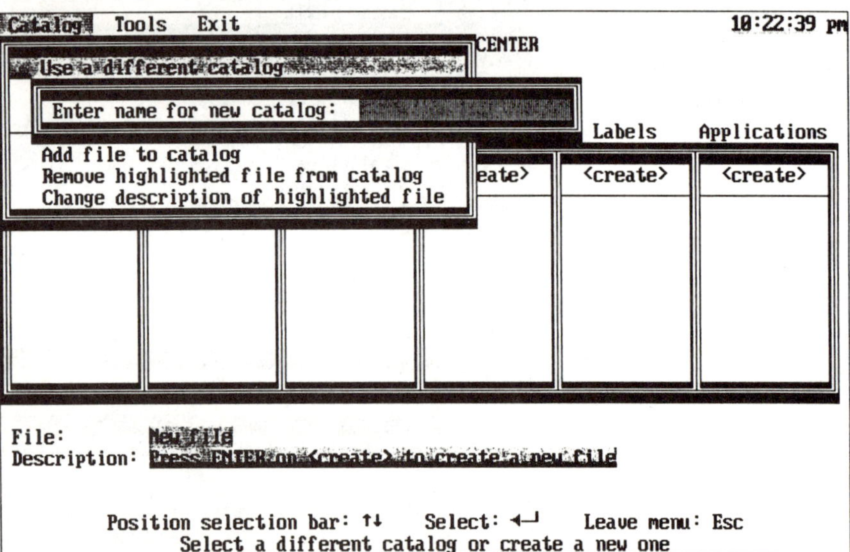

Figure 3-3

Catalog name prompt.

touch **ENTER**. The system will prompt for the name of the catalog, as seen in Figure 3-3.

Type: ***PERSONEL* ENTER**

Although you could have typed the extension *.CAT*, this was not necessary; dBASE IV automatically does that for you. On the screen, the catalog information line shows that you now are using a catalog called PERSONEL.CAT, located on the C:\DBASE subdirectory. And the catalog is currently empty.

Changing a Catalog Name

Changing a catalog name is simple in dBASE IV. Pop down the Catalog menu and select *Modify catalog name*, then press **ENTER**. The system prompts you for the new name to be given to the catalog. When you press **ENTER**, the catalog will be renamed. All attached files, views, forms, and the like will remain attached.

Describing a Catalog

Because you may be designing a number of different catalogs, and many may have similar sounding names or functions, it is important to prepare a description of each. For example, you are developing an overall personnel catalog to be used by your company's main personnel department. However, major departments in your company as well as branch locations handle their own personnel functions. Systems would have to be developed so that each of these departments could manage their own record keeping.

Thus, you may end up with a number of catalogs as follows: PERSNLWP (for the word processing department), PERSNLDP (for the data processing department), PERSNLAD (for administration), PERSNLPU (for purchasing), and perhaps a number of other PERSNL** catalogs. To avoid confusion, descriptions of each catalog are useful.

To edit a description of this catalog, pop up the Catalog menu and highlight "Edit description of catalog," then press **ENTER** (see Figure 3-4).

Type: *Main Personnel database* **ENTER**

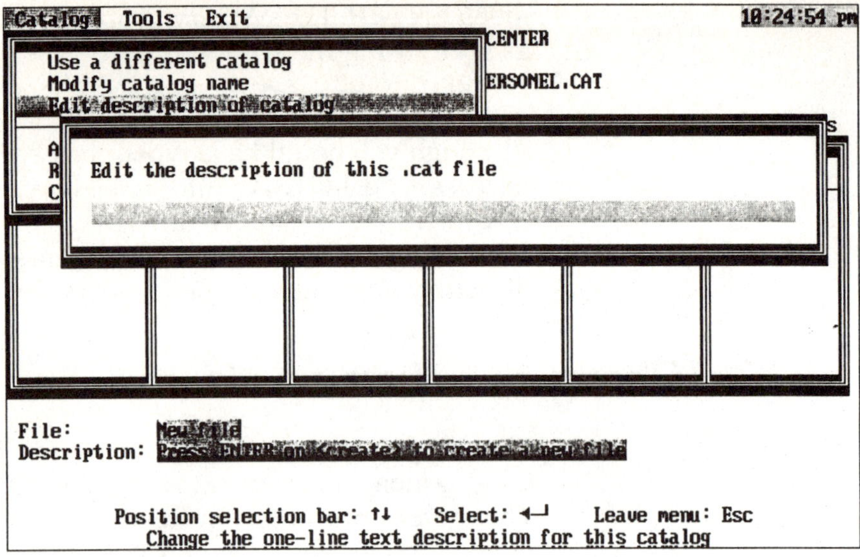

Figure 3-4

Edit catalog description.

In the future, to see the description of a desired catalog, you may select the catalog, then choose *Edit description of catalog* to see the information about the catalog selected.

You now have a new catalog that is empty.

In the last chapter, you created a data file called JACKSONS. We will use that basic data file, rename it, and add many data fields to demonstrate the method of using existing data files, editing existing files, and saving new database files.

First, make sure that the highlight is in the Data column. Next, pop up the Catalog menu and move the cursor to *Add file to catalog*. A File selection window similar to that for using a different catalog will pop onto the screen. In this window, seen in Figure 3-5, only the directory structure and database files (using the suffix .DBF) are shown. If the highlight was in a different column, the window will show the directory structure and the files appropriate to that column. For example, if the highlight was under the Queries column, all files ending with the extension .QBE and .QBO will be shown.

Note that if your query uses a specific data file, and if you first add the query to the catalog and then select *Modify query*, the system will load the related file(s) as well as the query into the catalog. This method may be used to quickly load a number of files that are associated to a query.

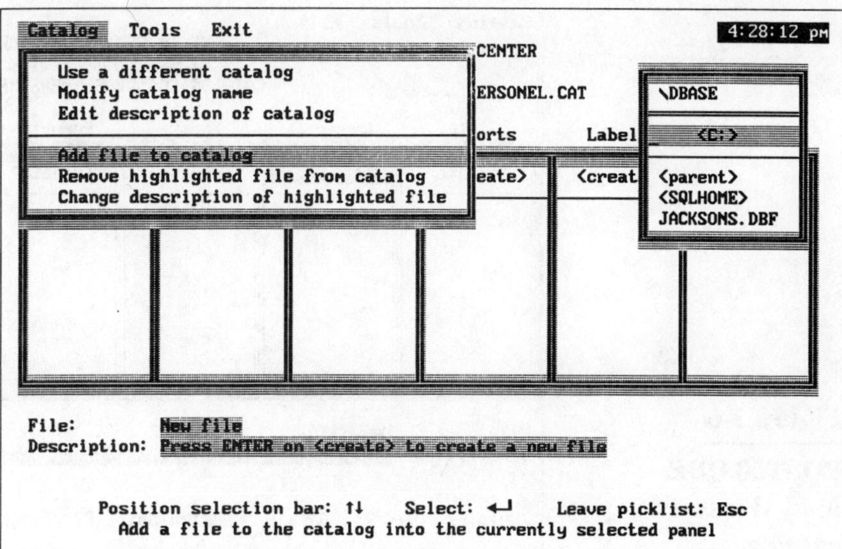

Figure 3-5

File selection window.

To see how this works, touch the **Esc** key to return to the work area. Move the cursor to the Queries column and bring down the Catalog menu. Select *Add file to query* and touch the **ENTER** key. Select JACKSONS.QBE and touch the **ENTER** key. The system will prompt for a description of this file. For now, leave the description blank, and press **ENTER** to load the file into the catalog (Figure 3-6). You will see that there are no data files loaded into the catalog. Now, highlight "JACKSONS" and touch **ENTER**. Select Modify query and press **ENTER** (or type *m* to automatically select and load the query). The query will then be loaded into the system (Figure 3-7). Press **Esc** to leave the Query menu, and you will see that the related data file has been added to the Data column.

Interestingly, you may view the data in the selected file without transferring it into the catalog if you go into the Queries menu, select your query, and choose the Display data option. After you finish viewing (or even adding to) the data, you can escape out of the file and the catalog will still not contain the data file that you used.

However, for the purposes of this chapter, the file will be loaded from the Data column. At this point, then, we must remove the query and data file from the catalog to show how the data file is usually loaded.

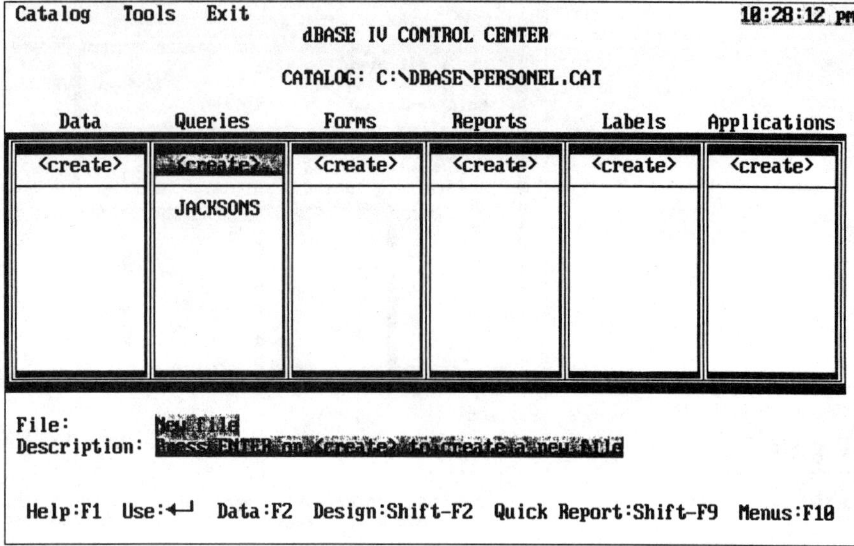

Figure 3-6

POST50.QBE loaded into catalog.

Highlight "JACKSONS" and pull down the Catalog menu. Select *Remove highlighted file from catalog* either by highlighting it and touching **ENTER** or by touching the *r* key. The system will ask you to confirm that you want to remove the file from the catalog, as seen in Figure 3-8. Tell the system *Yes* by touching the *y* key,

Figure 3-7

Query design for POST50.

```
Layout   Fields   Condition   Update   Exit                          10:29:48 pm
Births.dbf | ↓FIRST_NAME        | ↓LAST_NAME        | ↓BIRTH_DATE
           |                    | ="Jackson"        |

View
Jacksons   | Births->           | Births->          | Births->
           | FIRST_NAME         | LAST_NAME         | BIRTH_DATE

Query   C:\dbase\JACKSONS        Field 2/3
 Prev/Next field:Shift-Tab/Tab  Data:F2  Pick:Shift-F1  Prev/Next skel:F3/F4
```

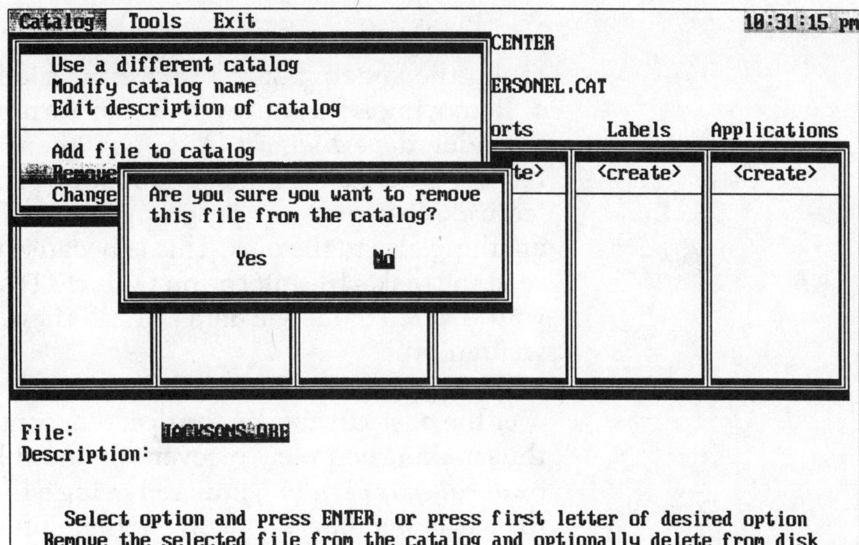

Figure 3-8

Remove from catalog prompt.

or moving the highlight to "YES" and pressing **ENTER**. The system will then ask if you want to remove the file from the disk, as seen in Figure 3-9. If you tell the system to do this, the file will be deleted from the disk; in nearly all cases you *never* want to do this. For now, however, do not remove the query from the disk, just remove it from the catalog.

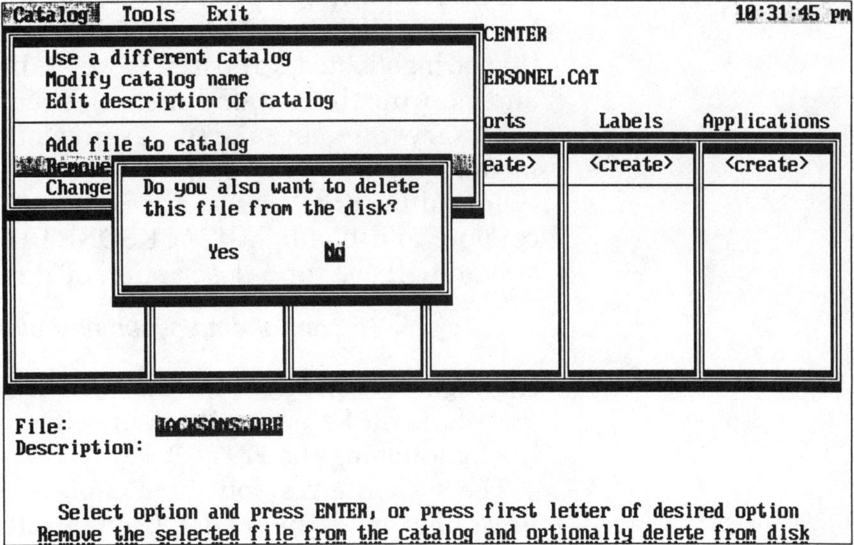

Figure 3-9

Remove from disk prompt.

Press: *n*

to tell the system not to remove the file from the disk.

Removing a file, query, or other form from the disk must be considered *permanent*. Although there are utilities that can recover a deleted file, these cannot be considered completely effective. Most recovery programs work only if you do not write anything else to the disk. This is because file recovery programs read the disk's file allocation table (FAT) and find the location of your deleted data. The data are still there, unless they have been written over.

When you quit dBASE IV, the program may write other data over the physical area on the disk that contained your deleted file, thus making complete recovery impossible. Therefore, you must be *absolutely certain* before removing a file from the disk. Unless the file is well backed up on another subdirectory, another disk, or a tape backup, you may risk complete loss of the file.

Once you have deleted the file from the catalog, but not the disk, you will notice that any associated files loaded as part of the query will still remain in the catalog. Although there is a ripple effect when you modify a loaded query, with the related data files added to the catalog, dBASE IV does not provide for deletion of related files when you remove a query, form, report form, or other individual file.

Thus, to remove a related data file, you must do so with each file individually. For now, remove JACKSONS from the catalog, but not the disk (it will be added later). (To remove a file, it must first be highlighted. To do this, move the highlight to "JACKSONS" and pop up the Catalog menu.) Then go through the steps necessary to remove the file, as previously done in the Catalog menu.

To add JACKSONS, select the Catalog menu, select Add file to catalog, and highlight "JACKSONS.DBF." Press **ENTER**. The system will ask for a description of the file,

Type: *Record of employees and birthdates* **ENTER**

Highlight the "JACKSONS" data file. You will notice the description of the file below the Work Area (Figure 3-10). Now, select the file by touching the **ENTER** key.

The system gives you three choices: *Use File, Modify structure/order,* and *Display data*. Use File tells the system that this is

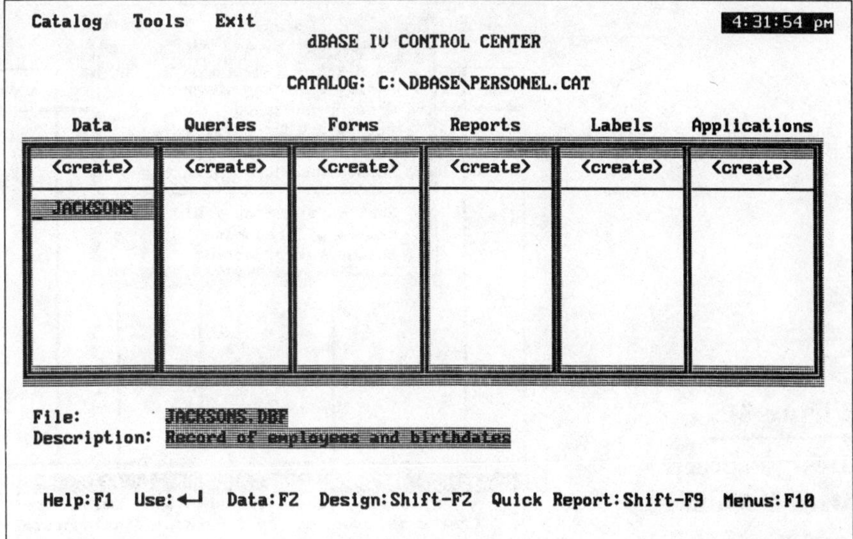

Figure 3-10

Control Center with file description.

the database file with which you want subsequent queries, forms, reports, labels, or applications to work. If you pop up the Data, Edit, or Browse screens (using the **F2** key), you will be viewing or modifying the data from this file.

Selecting Display data brings up either the Edit or the Browse screen (depending on which you were last in). Normally, the Browse screen, which lets you see the records in tabular form, is popped up using this command.

For now, however, you want to Modify structure/order of your data.

> Type: *m* (or highlight "Modify structure/order" and press **ENTER**)

Normally, your Design screen will come up with the Organize menu already popped down, as seen in Figure 3-11. (The Design screen could also have been brought up by pressing **SHIFT-F2**).

You will go through the options available later. For now, you will work on the layout for your file.

You should have three fields completed, a FIRST_NAME field, a LAST_NAME field, and a BIRTH_DATE field. Next, add HIRE_DATE, a date field that will show date hired. To remove the Organize menu from your screen,

> Press: **Esc**

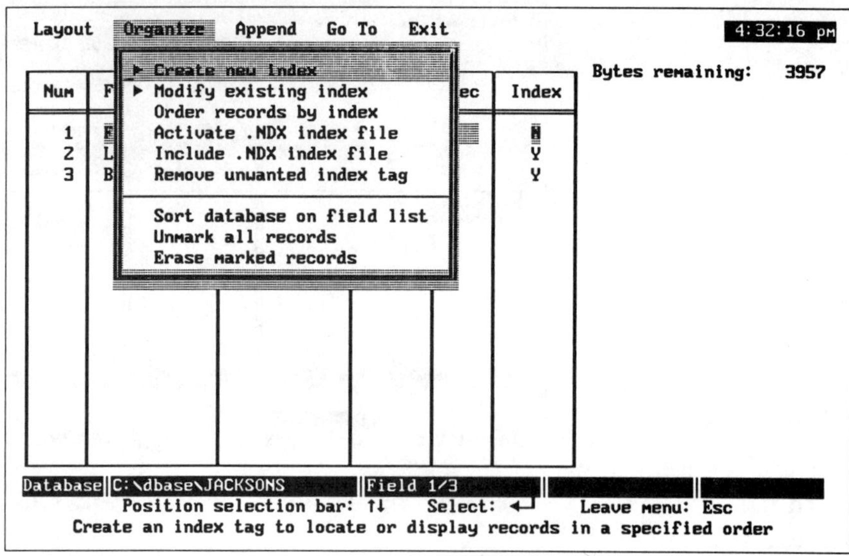

Figure 3-11

Design screen with Organize menu.

Next, to add a new field, use the **DnArrow** to move the highlight to line number 4.

Type: *HIRE_DATE* **ENTER**

The system will move you to the Field Type column. At this point it is important to understand the different field types that dBASE IV supports.

Touching the **Space Bar** toggles from one field to the next. The types of permitted fields are as follows:

Character: The character field type contains alphanumeric characters. Typical character data include names, addresses, and other alphanumeric information. Phone numbers and zip codes can also be included in character fields if you have no plans to perform any calculations using those numbers.

When you set up the system, you may still tell the system how to verify data in a particular field. Thus, for example, if you wished to describe telephone numbers as an alphanumeric, rather than a numeric, field, you would be able to tell the system to accept only numbers and no letters when the number is input. Although you will not be able to perform calculations on numeric data that are placed into an alphanumeric field, you can at least ensure that the data entered match the proper format. (Note: from the dot prompt, there is a command that can be used to convert an ASCII [alphanumeric] character to a numeric character, but this use is beyond the scope of this book.)

Numeric: A numeric field is, obviously, made up of numbers. The system will not accept any characters other than the + or − sign or the decimal point (or comma, depending on how you set the system to accept decimals). Bracketed values can also be used to represent negative numbers. The number of decimal places is specified in the fifth column, Dec.

Float: Floating point numbers are a new addition to dBASE IV. The difference between *numeric* and *float* fields requires some explaining.

A floating point number does not have a fixed number of decimal places. Thus, if you were to divide 10 by 3, for example, you would get 3. with as many 3s carried out as the system can handle. Multiply that number by 3, and you will get 9. with as many 9s as the system can handle. Thus, with floating point mathematics, the number of decimal places "floats" to fill the maximum number of places required to arrive at an answer.

Earlier versions of dBase used floating point math as the only method of calculation of numeric fields. Even if you defined a field as having two decimal places, the mathematics would be floating point, with rounding to two places after a calculation was completed.

With the addition of a floating point field, the numeric field has changed. Numeric fields are now evaluated, still using the computer's floating point processor, but as if calculations were actually being performed using fixed-decimal point math.

For many types of operations the differences may be insignificant. However, in dealing with many calculations, floating point math may introduce numeric artifacts that affect your final numbers. Since floating point calculations are a computer's way of approximating correct answers (computers *do not* divide the way we were taught in school), many results are extremely close approximations of the correct answers. If you were to do many calculations, the effects of the slight differences between the actual and the calculated (floating point) result could become magnified and produce errors in your final results.

In addition, dBASE IV has added a number of sophisticated financial, mathematical, and statistical functions. For large databases, requiring many calculations, the same calculations may produce different results, depending on whether you defined your fields as floating or numeric. In addition, for certain types of files, if you define your dBASE III numeric fields as numeric in dBASE IV, the dBASE IV numeric field results may differ from those in dBASE III.

A value for a numeric field that is calculated in earlier versions of dBASE may be different than one calculated by dBASE IV. If you are converting earlier dBASE files to dBASE IV, and numeric consistency between versions is important, numeric fields from dBASE III and dBASE III+ should be redefined as floating point numeric fields.

One further comment regarding floating point numeric versus numeric. A database designed for floating point fields is not downward compatible with earlier versions of dBASE. Thus, if upgrading to dBASE IV is not made throughout the company, and you have developed data files that include floating point fields, such data fields may be incompatible with dBASE II, III, or III+.

Date: The date field is automatically defined as eight characters. During setup you can tell the system the format you want to use for dates (for example, MM/DD/YY or YY/MM/DD). During data entry, the system automatically checks that all entries are numeric. It does not evaluate whether or not they make sense (for example, the date 02/31/88 would be accepted, although obviously incorrect).

Logical: Logical fields are fields that can be answered *Yes* or *No* or true or false. By definition, a logical field is only one character wide. Examples of logical fields include the following: Male? (Y/N), Female? (Y/N), U.S. Citizen? (Y/N), Completed Orientation? (Y/N).

Memo: Memo fields are fields that contain text. The text in a memo field is stored with each record. You cannot operate on memos. For example, you cannot write a query that looks into memo fields and retrieves all records containing the word Alabama.

Memos can be written using the text editor that is built into dBASE IV or a text editor of your choice. However, this choice is also limited by the available memory left after loading dBASE IV. In early versions of dBASE IV there was not enough memory to load many popular word processing programs.

Memo fields may also contain recurring text passages. At a later date, you may be able to prepare a file that can be merged into a word processed document. For example, you may wish to send a personalized letter to all employees hired after January 1 of this year. The letter would use the name and address fields, the hire date, and the contents of one or more memo fields to prepare the text of the letter (for example, one field may include text that either thanks the employee for completing orientation, or that gives the employee a 30 day limit for doing so).

One important point regarding memo fields. The memo file format in dBASE IV is different from that used in earlier versions of dBASE. Thus, although dBASE IV is almost fully compatible with earlier versions, memos created in earlier versions of dBASE cannot be imported for use by dBASE IV. Similarly, memo fields produced by dBASE IV will not work in earlier dBase versions.

Once you have typed the HIRE__DATE field name and pressed **Tab** or **ENTER**, you will be prompted for field type. Touch the **Space Bar** until Date is in the column, and press **Tab** or **ENTER**. The system will automatically fill in the width as eight characters. Tell the system that you want to index this field.

NOTE: When specifying field types, you may either toggle the **Space Bar** to go from one field type to the next, or you may type the first letter of each type to automatically complete the name, and move you to the next appropriate field (Character, Numeric, and Float will toggle you to Width; the others move you to Index).

Width is self-explanatory. It is a specification of the maximum width allowed for data to be entered into a certain field. When setting field widths, it is important to have a good idea of the maximum width you will actually need. If you had a last name field defined as 10 letters, and had last names that were 15 letters long, you would be able to enter only the first 10 letters of the last name. Having a field width that is too short can cause problems because of the necessary truncation of data. However, if you allowed for 30 letters, when the data in your fields normally hit a maximum of 15, you would waste disk storage space and processing time as a result of the overly large field. A general rule for something as variable as last names and street addresses is to estimate the largest possible entry, and add a small cushion, maybe 5 to 10 characters, depending on the variability of data.

This is what happens to an overly large field. When you define your data file, dBASE IV automatically allocates a selected width to all records. Each record will have that much space allocated, regardless of the number of characters actually input into a field. Thus, if your Last Name field is 25 characters wide, and the maximum width of last names in your database is 15 characters, you may be allocating 10 more spaces than necessary for *each* record. If your file has 1000 records, you'll be using 10,000 more characters storage than you need to for that database.

The problem is compounded when it comes time to run queries or otherwise process your data. When dBASE processes a query, it looks at the entire contents of a field, whether it is filled with characters or blank spaces. Checking each space in a field takes processor time. The wider a field, the longer it takes to read. For two databases that are identical, except that one has larger fields than necessary, you can expect a measurable time saving in running queries on the more efficiently designed database.

One approach to keep data fields small is the use of abbreviations that are commonly accepted in your business, although working with abbreviations can get quite messy. In theory, you can standardize certain commonly used abbreviations and can use the abbreviations as entries in data fields. However, unless your company *truly standardizes* on specific abbreviations, erroneous reporting may result. It is important that every person who will input data or update your data files conform to the approved abbreviations and proprietary language. For example, assume that you were purchasing apples. If the item on your purchase order was alternately listed as Apple, Apples, or

Gravenstines, and you wanted to produce a report on all apples ordered, the system would prepare a summary report on APPLES, but would not include the items called Apple or Gravenstine.

An additional point should be made about field width. Going into an existing data structure and shortening a field may result in losing part of the data that has already been put into the database. For example, if you were to change the Last_Name field from 20 to 10 characters, all names already entered into your database would be shortened to 10 characters. Before you save your changes, the system asks you to confirm the changes, because they may result in loss of data.

Similarly, if you were to widen a field into which data have already been entered, you may end up with records that have truncated data that look as if they were not completely typed in. For example, if you had originally designated a width of 10 characters for City Name, the city of Los Angeles would be entered into your file as *Los Angele.* Because the name of the city is longer than your field width, you will, in most cases, know that it is Los Angeles. However, if you were to spot the problem after thousands of entries have been made into the database, and were to increase the field width from 10 to 20 characters, you may have many entries for *Los Angele* (*not* Los Angeles). With a familiar city like Los Angeles this may not be a problem (you will be able to catch the occurrences of this type and correct them when you increase your field width), but for other, less-well known cities, in addition to other field types in which the data entered in a record are not easily recognized as truncated, you may end up with field entries that look correct, but as a result of their original truncation and the existence of blank spaces following them, are not.

For example, take the name Brownstein. If only five spaces had been allowed for last name, the record would show it as *Brown.* Extending the width to 12 spaces would still show the name as *Brown,* as it was originally entered when only five characters were used in the field, because the system would have no way of knowing that the name was not complete when initially input. Thus, it is important to allow enough width (but not too much) when designing your data structure, and to spot and correct any truncated data as soon as possible after you have extended the field's width.

Another item worth mentioning concerns field deletion. If you were to redesign a data form, the system allows you to remove a field from your database structure. If you allow the system to do this, you will lose all the data in the deleted fields in any records that used those fields. If you are planning any major changes to a data structure, it may be prudent to copy the data structure to a new name, and to make changes to the new structure, rather than your original.

The Dec column asks you to set the number of decimal places to be used in your numeric or floating data. In other words, how many digits do you want to the *right* of the decimal place? For dollars and cents calculations, you would probably want two places. If you were dealing in many units, you may want to use three or four decimal places and round down to two later, if fractional cents were important when working with the product you are buying or selling.

Finally, the *Index* column asks if you want the current field to be indexed by dBASE IV. Marking a field an indexed field tells the system to go through your database and create a new file containing the record numbers in the indexed order. When you then elect to use an indexed file, the system will display your records in the indexed order, rather than in the order in which they were entered in the system.

Indexed fields provide you with a certain amount of power for organizing and viewing your records. For example, you may want to set up an index that sorts all employees by ZIP code, so that you can take advantage of bulk rate mailings that require ZIP code sorts. Another sort may be alphabetically by department, so that you can distribute letters or memos through internal departmental channels without having to physically sort the memos after they are printed. Defining a field as indexed gives you the functionality to develop a variety of indexing schemes.

You can set up new indexing orders using the Organize menu. In fact, this is the menu that is brought up when you first bring up the Design menu for an existing database. You will see how to use it in a later chapter.

Once this is done, the system will move you to line 5 (the next empty line) of your database design form. Because this form is designed to provide most of the information needed to manage your personnel records, you will be creating many fields.

Complete the design, adding those fields listed in Figure 3-12.

Layout Organize Append Go To Exit 10:52:41 pm

Bytes remaining: 3831

Num	Field Name	Field Type	Width	Dec	Index
3	BIRTH_DATE	Date	8		Y
4	HIRE_DATE	Date	8		Y
5	HOME_ADDR	Character	30		N
6	APT_NUMBER	Character	6		N
7	CITY	Character	20		N
8	STATE	Character	2		Y
9	ZIP_CODE	Numeric	5	0	Y
10	MOTHER_MN	Character	20		N
11	SS_NUMBER	Character	11		N
12	USCITIZEN	Logical	1		N
13	EMP_NUMBER	Numeric	4	0	N
14	DEPT_NUMB	Numeric	4	0	Y
15	SALARY_GRD	Character	4		Y
16	HISTORY	Memo	10		N
17	UNION_MBR	Logical	1		N

Database C:\dbase\BIRTHS Field 12/17

Enter the field name. Insert/Delete field:Ctrl-N/Ctrl-U

Field names begin with a letter and may contain letters, digits and underscores

Figure 3-12

Completed database form.

A few descriptions of some of the fields follow:

Field 10: MOTHER_MN is for the mother's maiden name, useful to verify identification when an employee calls in for information.

Field 11: SS_NUMBER is for social security number. You will tell the system to accept only numbers when you design an input/viewing form for this database.

Field 16: HISTORY is a memo field. The intent of the field is to record pertinent comments relating to the person's employment. These may be anecdotal records, or may be a history of departmental assignments and transfers.

Once all 17 fields have been filled in, you will be brought to field 18, a blank field ready to be input. Touch the **ENTER** key, and the system will warn you that you have made changes to your prior database structure and ask if you really want to save the changes, as seen in Figure 3-13. Once you have completed the data design process, you have two choices. You can accept the changes, applying them to the existing data structure, or you may save them with a new name.

To accept the changes, applying them to the current data structure, JACKSONS.dbf, touch the **ENTER** key or type *Y* to change

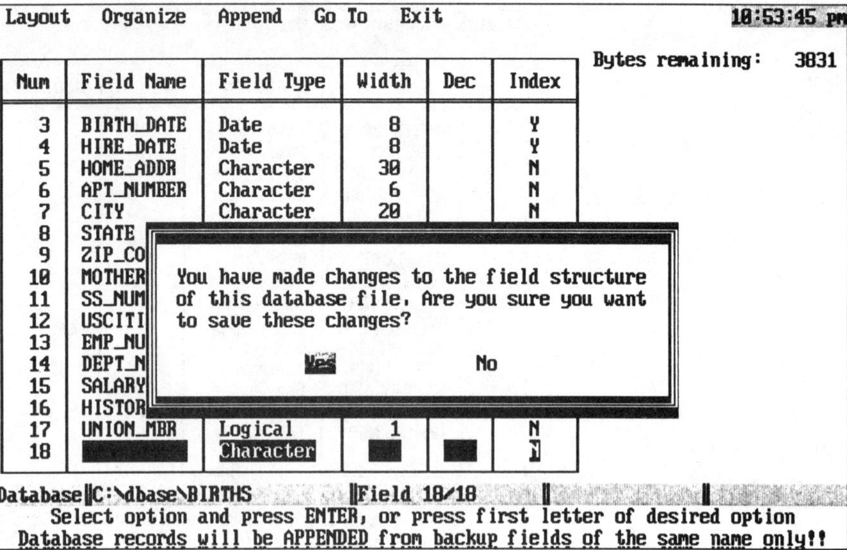

Figure 3-13

Field change prompt.

the existing data structure (but do not do this now—you will save this design with a new name). The system will go through an indexing process, changing the currently entered files to conform to the new structure, and changing file pointers for each defined index structure. When it is completed, it will return you to the Control Center.

Alternatively, you could have given the structure a new name. To do this, type *n* at the prompt, or touch the **Esc** key, bringing you back to the Design screen. From there, go to the *Layout* box. (Do this by touching the **F10** key and using the cursor arrows to move to the Layout box, or type **Alt-1**.)

Move the highlight to *Save this database file structure* using the arrow keys, and press **ENTER**, or touch the *S* key to select that option. A *Save as:* window will pop up, prompting you to keep the current name, or give the database a new name (Figure 3-14).

Rename the database *Personel*. The system will automatically apply the .dbf extension. It will then build the index structures, index the contents of the database, and copy the database's contents into the new database.

You should be aware of the naming conventions used in dBASE. dBASE IV allows you to use up to eight letters or numbers for naming a database. It does not allow special characters other than the underline (_) character, and does not allow you to begin a

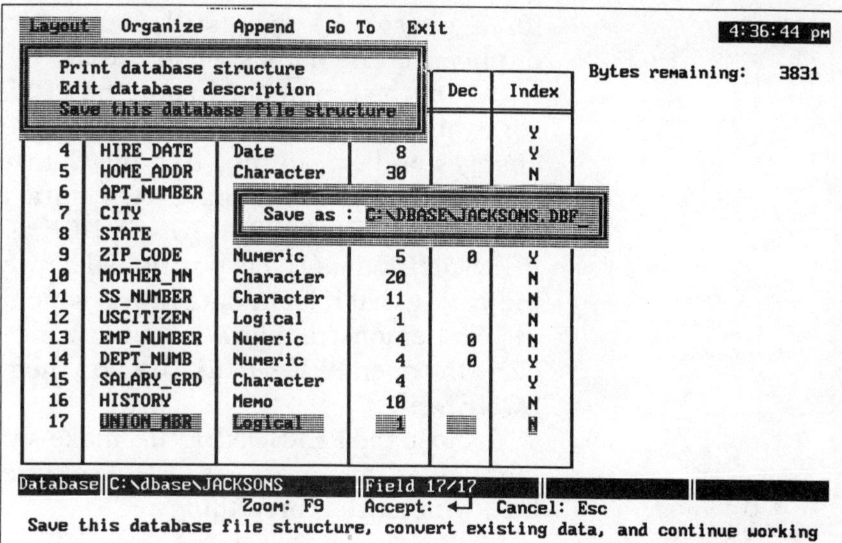

Figure 3-14

Save as screen, for renaming a database structure.

name with a number. Aside from these restrictions, you are free to give your file any name you wish.

It is advisable, however, to try to make your file names intuitively simple, so that you, or someone else who may be using your data files, can understand what the contents of the file(s) are. It is also advisable to avoid using names that sound as if they belong to other programs. For example, although you may be able to call a data file COMMAND, or DBIV, or even LOTUS123, to do so would probably result in confusion for you and whoever else uses your data files. At worst, it could confuse other programs that look for files with that name.

You should also be careful to give your files unique names; if you were to try to design another database named PERSONEL.DBF, the system should prompt you with an error message indicating there already is a data file by that name in the current subdirectory, and asking if you still want to use this file name.

However, if you were to build a new data file called PERSONEL.DBF and place it in a different subdirectory, the system would not detect the duplicate file names, and you would end up with two data files with the same name. Although this may not be a catastrophic problem, particularly if the files are in directories that are never used simultaneously (for example, one may be for a client in the plumbing business, and the other may be for a physician), it is still good practice to guard against duplicating file names on your disk.

Pop up the Exit menu (using the **F10** key and moving the cursor to highlight the "Edit" menu, or by pressing **Alt-E**). Select Save changes and exit to return to the Control Center.

At this point, you have two data files in your catalog, JACKSONS.DBF and PERSONEL.DBF, as seen in Figure 3-15. The PERSONEL data file is positioned above the bar in the column, indicating that it is the data file on which you are currently working. To demonstrate how to select a file on which to work, first close the open PERSONEL file, and then reopen the closed PERSONEL file.

To close the PERSONEL file, make sure that "PERSONEL" is highlighted, and press **ENTER**. The system brings up a Decision box, which asks three things:

1. *Close file:* This asks if you want to close this file. If you do, any forms, reports, queries, or applications you select will not use the data in this file.
2. *Modify structure/order:* This prompt asks if you want to change the design of your data file, or if you want to change the field order within the data file. Selecting this option brings you to the Data design screen with which you worked earlier in this chapter.

Figure 3-15

Control Center showing two data files.

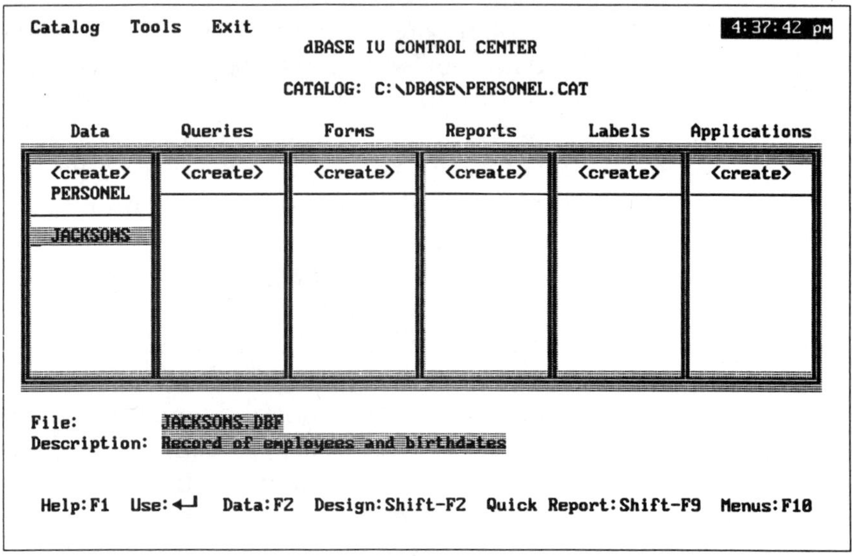

```
Catalog   Tools   Exit                                                    4:37:42 pm
                              dBASE IV CONTROL CENTER

                         CATALOG: C:\DBASE\PERSONEL.CAT

   Data        Queries       Forms        Reports       Labels      Applications
 <create>     <create>     <create>      <create>      <create>      <create>
 PERSONEL

 JACKSONS

File:         JACKSONS.DBF
Description:  Record of employees and birthdates

 Help:F1  Use:←┘  Data:F2  Design:Shift-F2  Quick Report:Shift-F9  Menus:F10
```

3. *Display data:* This option lets you see the data in your data file. When selected, it will bring you to either the Browse or the Edit screen (depending on which screen you used last). These data will not include any fancy formatting that has been produced using the form design capabilities of the Forms menu.

Each of the three options may be selected by highlighting and pressing **ENTER**, or by typing the letter of the option. For now, because you are choosing to close the file, make that selection. You will see that PERSONEL dropped below the line in the Control Center, showing that it is no longer an open file.

Next, select PERSONEL. Because it is not an open file, the options change slightly. Instead of the *Close file* option, you now have the *Use file* option. This loads the file as the active file. Any other tasks that are performed will be done using the currently open file.

There are faster ways to close one file and open another. Simply highlight the file that you wish to open, and press **F2**. The system will close the open file, open the highlighted file, and display the data on your screen. The only drawback to this method is that the system reads in the data file and displays data. If you do not need to see the data, and do not want to have to bother to **Esc** out of the Browse or Edit screen, the simplest way to close one file and open another is to highlight the name of the file you wish to open, touch **ENTER**, and select Use file. The old file will be closed and your selected file will be opened.

Now that you have constructed your general data file, PERSONEL, there are still three more that you want to build, an EEOC file (for equal employment opportunity data), a counseling file (to track employee reviews and counseling data), and a general employee data file that would be available to all employees.

The EMP__DATA file that you will build is an example of how you can use an existing file to create a new data file. With the PERSONEL data file loaded, go to Modify Data by typing **Shift-F2** or by touching the **ENTER** key and selecting the Modify option. Because you have already entered the data you will want in the EMP__DATA file, you need only delete and reorder the data in that file, then store the changed file with the new name, EMP__DATA.

The fields that you want to keep in this file are FIRST__NAME, LAST__NAME, HIRE__DATE, EMP__NUMBER, and

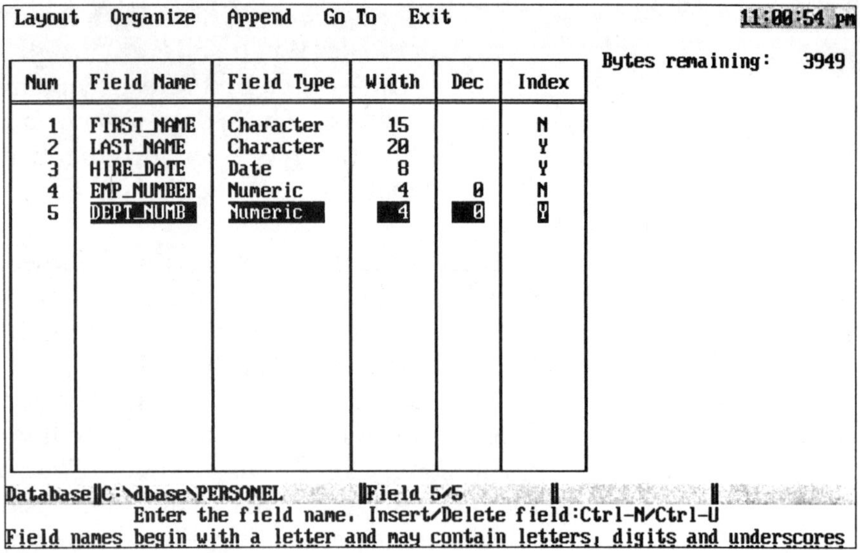

Layout Organize Append Go To Exit 11:00:54 pm

Bytes remaining: 3949

Num	Field Name	Field Type	Width	Dec	Index
1	FIRST_NAME	Character	15		N
2	LAST_NAME	Character	20		Y
3	HIRE_DATE	Date	8		Y
4	EMP_NUMBER	Numeric	4	0	N
5	DEPT_NUMB	Numeric	4	0	Y

Database C:\dbase\PERSONEL Field 5/5

Enter the field name. Insert/Delete field:Ctrl-N/Ctrl-U

Field names begin with a letter and may contain letters, digits and underscores

Figure 3-16

PERSONEL after deletions.

DEPT_NUMBER; you will also want to add a field for the employee's office phone number, calling this field OFF_PHONE.

You must delete the fields that are not needed in this data file. To delete a field, move the cursor to highlight the field that you want to delete, and press **Ctrl-U** (or **Ctrl-u**). Do this with all the fields that you do not want to retain in this database. Your data design will appear as shown in Figure 3-16 after you have made all the required deletions.

Next, you want to add the OFF_PHONE field between EMP_NUMBER and DEPT_NUMB. To insert this field, move the highlight to line 5 (highlighting the DEPT_NUMBER data field line) and

Press: **Ctrl-N** (or **Ctrl-n**)

All fields below the space in which you are inserting your field will have dropped down one line. You now have an empty field, as seen in Figure 3-17.

Type: *OFF_PHONE* ***ENTER***

Next, leave the field as a character field, because you will not do any analysis of the phone number. Allow seven spaces for this field, and do not index it. The width of the phone number field

```
Layout   Organize   Append   Go To   Exit                        11:01:59 pm
                                                   Bytes remaining:   3949
 Num | Field Name | Field Type | Width | Dec | Index
   1   FIRST_NAME   Character     15            N
   2   LAST_NAME    Character     20            Y
   3   HIRE_DATE    Date           8            Y
   4   EMP_NUMBER   Numeric        4      0     N
   5                Character                   N
   6   DEPT_NUMB    Numeric        4      0     Y

Database C:\dbase\PERSONEL          Field 5/6
          Enter the field name. Insert/Delete field:Ctrl-N/Ctrl-U
Field names begin with a letter and may contain letters, digits and underscores
```

Figure 3-17

Adding a blank field.

depends on the type of number you are using—for example, if all phones are in house, you may need to use only a four number extension.

In this instance, if you want to allow outside callers to be able to direct dial the employee, you may add three characters for area code. You may also wish to leave a character space for the hyphen that separates the prefix from the rest of the phone number.

When you have completed designing this file, bring up the Layout menu, and select Save this database file structure. Name it EMP__DATA. The system will go through the process of developing an index of your file and will build a database using the files from your source data file, PERSONEL (Figure 3-18). You should also notice that the name of the data file, as shown in the information line at the bottom of the screen, has been changed to match the new data file, which you just named.

You still have two more forms to build. Using PERSONEL as a master model, build EEOC.DBF and COUNSEL.DBF as shown in Figures 3-19 and 3-20.

One more thing needs to be said about building data structures based on earlier data files. In later chapters you will be performing queries relating the data in one file with the data in one or more other files. For example, you may want to prepare a file of

```
Layout   Organize   Append   Go To   Exit                           11:03:36 pm

                                                  Bytes remaining:   3942
 Num | Field Name  | Field Type | Width | Dec | Index
   1 | FIRST_NAME  | Character  |  15   |     |   N
   2 | LAST_NAME   | Character  |  20   |     |   Y
   3 | HIRE_DATE   | Date       |   8   |     |   Y
   4 | EMP_NUMBER  | Numeric    |   4   |  0  |   N
   5 | OFF_PHONE   | Character  |   7   |     |   N
   6 | DEPT_NUMB   | Numeric    |   4   |  0  |   Y
   7 |             | Character  |       |     |   N

Database C:\dbase\EMP_DATA          Field 7/7
          Enter the field name. Insert/Delete field:Ctrl-N/Ctrl-U
Field names begin with a letter and may contain letters, digits and underscores
```

Figure 3-18

The EMP_DATA data file structure.

names and office phone numbers for all employees who have not been counseled in 1988. To do this, you will have to relate data in the COUNSEL.DBF file, which contains the name and counseling date information, with the EMP__DATA file, which contains the name and office number of the employee(s). For the common

Figure 3-19

EEOC.DBF data file structure.

```
Layout   Organize   Append   Go To   Exit                           11:07:28 pm

                                                  Bytes remaining:   3933
 Num | Field Name  | Field Type | Width | Dec | Index
   1 | FIRST_NAME  | Character  |  15   |     |   N
   2 | LAST_NAME   | Character  |  20   |     |   Y
   3 | BIRTH_DATE  | Date       |   8   |     |   Y
   4 | HIRED       | Logical    |   1   |     |   N
   5 | HIRE_DATE   | Date       |   8   |     |   Y
   6 | SS_NUMBER   | Character  |  11   |     |   N
   7 | US_CITIZEN  | Logical    |   1   |     |   N
   8 | UNION_MBR   | Logical    |   1   |     |   N
   9 | ETHNIC_GRP  | Character  |   2   |     |   Y

Database C:\dbase\EEOC              Field 9/9
          Enter the field name. Insert/Delete field:Ctrl-N/Ctrl-U
Field names begin with a letter and may contain letters, digits and underscores
```

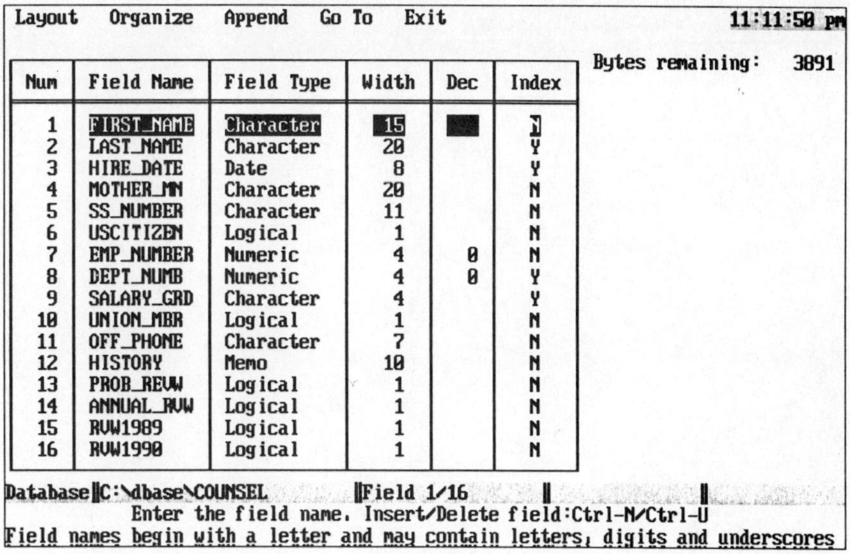

Layout Organize Append Go To Exit 11:11:50 pm

Bytes remaining: 3891

Num	Field Name	Field Type	Width	Dec	Index
1	FIRST_NAME	Character	15		Y
2	LAST_NAME	Character	20		Y
3	HIRE_DATE	Date	8		Y
4	MOTHER_MN	Character	20		N
5	SS_NUMBER	Character	11		N
6	USCITIZEN	Logical	1		N
7	EMP_NUMBER	Numeric	4	0	N
8	DEPT_NUMB	Numeric	4	0	Y
9	SALARY_GRD	Character	4		Y
10	UNION_MBR	Logical	1		N
11	OFF_PHONE	Character	7		N
12	HISTORY	Memo	10		N
13	PROB_REVW	Logical	1		N
14	ANNUAL_RVW	Logical	1		N
15	RVW1989	Logical	1		N
16	RVW1990	Logical	1		N

Database C:\dbase\COUNSEL Field 1/16

Enter the field name. Insert/Delete field:Ctrl-N/Ctrl-U

Field names begin with a letter and may contain letters, digits and underscores

Figure 3-20

COUNSEL.DBF data file structure.

fields to match (the name and department fields), the names and field widths used in each file should match, although the query facility will allow you to relate two fields even if they are not given the same names.

This chapter has provided the basics for designing your data files. In future chapters, you will learn how to design attractive, and often more useful, data entry and output forms, how to organize the data in your files, and how to work with indexing and sorting the data in your data files.

4 Fine-Tuning a Database

Chapter Three showed how to design a data system. The system included a Catalog, which contained a number of data files. The files were all related, in that they shared a number of common data fields.

In addition, each data file performed a different task: one stored much of the information required to keep track of a company's employees and was restricted to viewing or modification only by authorized employees; a second featured a subset of the first, which was available to all employees having access to the data; yet another was used to compile data to satisfy Equal Employment Opportunity Commission guidelines.

As they stand, the data structures can be used by those persons authorized to input or evaluate data. However, dBASE IV provides you with additional tools designed to improve the usability and ease the input and viewing of the data.

The Forms menu provides tools to custom design data input and display forms so that your data appear as they would on a specially designed, preprinted report form. In this chapter, you will see how to design and use such custom, fine-tuned forms.

In addition, dBASE IV provides you with the ability to index and sort records. It also allows you to append your current data files with records recorded in other dBase files or from other data sources.

This chapter and later chapters provide you with instruction in using these features. Importing data from other sources is covered in a later chapter, so the topic will receive only minimal coverage here.

A data input form is often the primary interface between users and their data. It may look like the data form used to define the

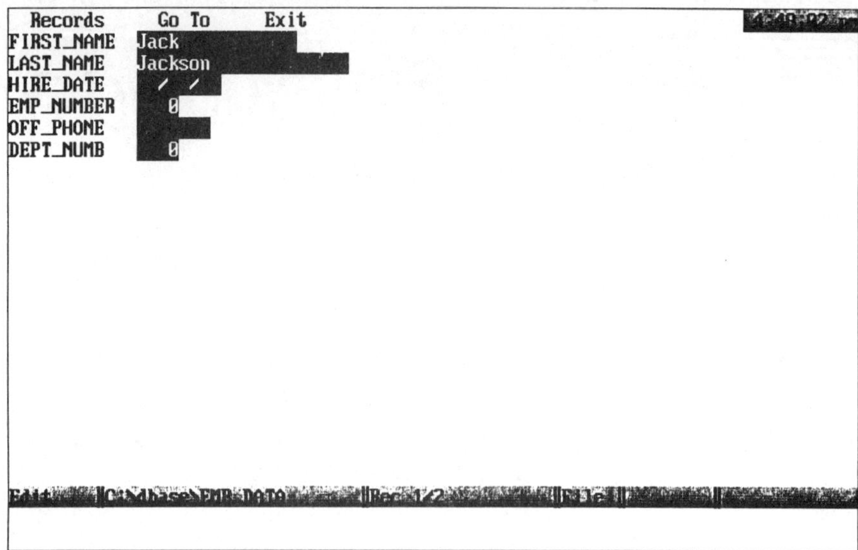

Figure 4-1

Basic data form.

data, as seen for the EMP__DATA.DBF file in Figure 4-1, or alternatively, the data may be displayed on a form similar to the one shown in Figure 4-2. Although the data structure is the same, the appearance is substantially changed. The second form is more interesting in appearance, and may even be easier to use. The form was designed using the components of the Forms menu.

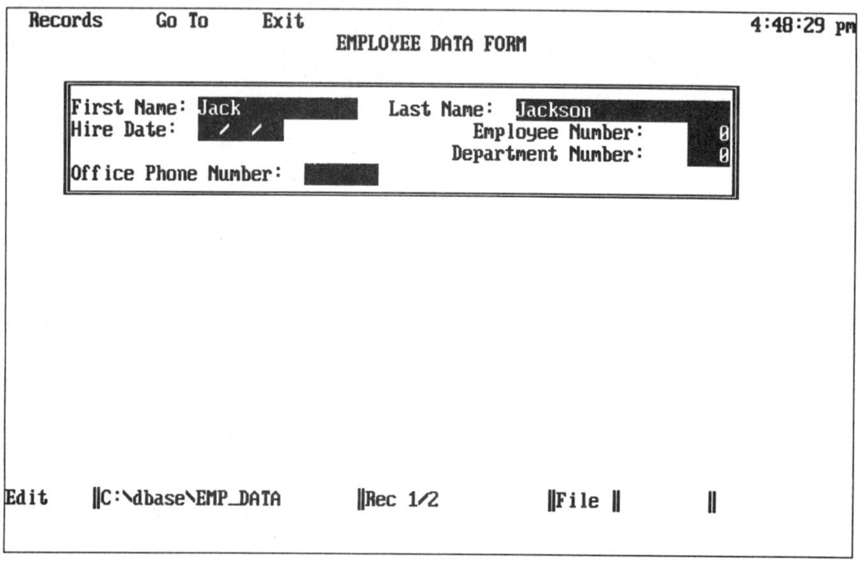

Figure 4-2

Same data structure, with newly designed form.

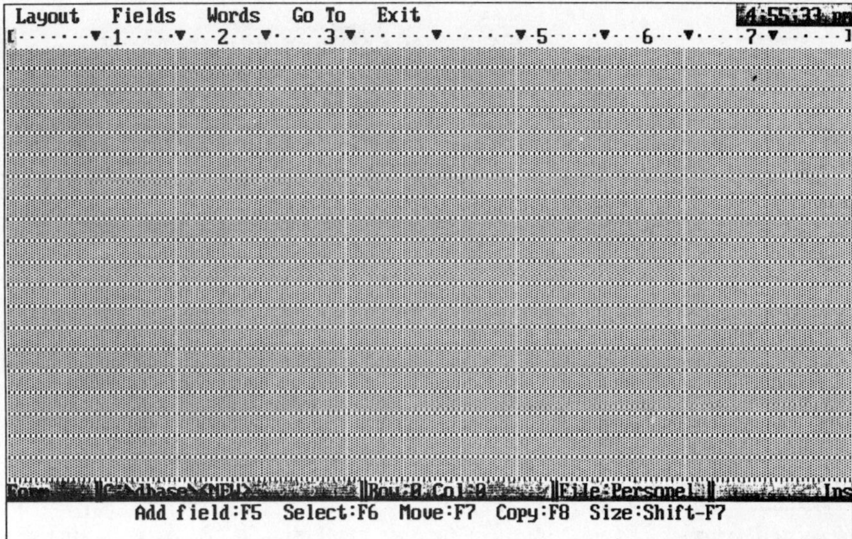

Figure 4-3

Forms Design menu.

In this chapter you will create a form for data entry to be used with the PERSONEL.DBF data file. Open PERSONEL.DBF by highlighting that data file and touching the **ENTER** key, followed by the *u* key to tell the system that you want to use the data file.

Next, move to the Forms menu. Select the <create> option in the Forms menu by highlighting the line with <create> and touching **ENTER**, or pressing **Shift-F2** with <create> highlighted. The Forms Design menu will appear. This menu provides you with five pull down menu categories. Each will be dealt with in more detail as you redesign the form for PERSONEL. The Forms Design menu appears as shown in Figure 4-3.

The Layout menu, shown in Figure 4-4, provides you with a number of options for designing your form. You will use many of these options in this chapter. The Quick layout option places the data on the work surface, referred to by Ashton-Tate as the *Blackboard,* in a pattern that matches that of the data file. Once Quick layout has been selected, your screen will appear as shown in Figure 4-5. This initial view will resemble the Edit form when you choose Browse/Edit from the Data column in the Control Center.

The screen provides you with a good deal of information. At the top, the menu line indicates the menu options that are provided by the program. Below that line is a *Ruler line,* which can

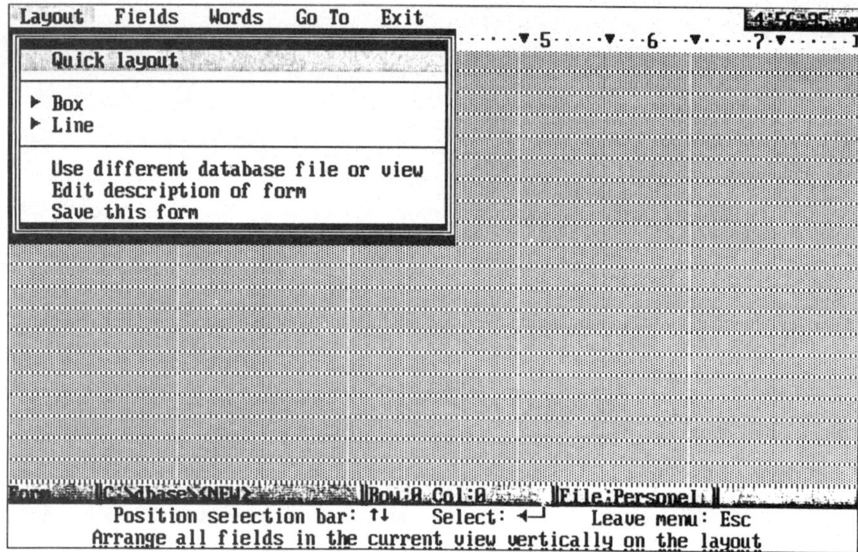

Figure 4-4

Layout menu.

be turned on and off by going into the *Words* menu and touching the **ENTER** key when the "Hide ruler" option is highlighted. Below the ruler is the area referred to as the Blackboard. This is the area in which your form is actually designed. Just below the Blackboard is a line that tells you that you are in the Form menu, the name of the form you are editing, the row and column

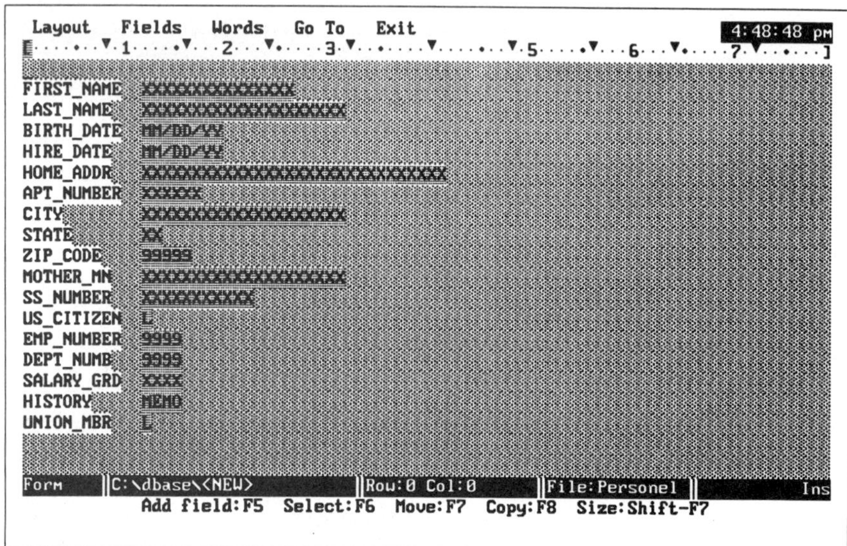

Figure 4-5

Quick layout for PERSONEL.DBF.

position of your cursor, the name of your data file, and the status of your **NumLock, CapsLock,** and **Ins** keys. If the features of the keys are on, the word Caps, Num, or Ins will appear in the rightmost box on this bar. Below the bar is a line of options for modifying or adding data. Below this line prompts for further actions may appear, depending upon the function you have called up.

To make this page look more interesting, you may want to group information into more logical sets of data. For example, personal data, such as name and home address, may be grouped together in one section, whereas data more relevant to work, including citizenship data, social security number, employee number, and hire date, can be grouped in a different portion of the form. It is also likely that such a grouping may be easier to use for data input because it probably more closely matches the arrangement of data on the employee's application for employment.

Ideally, you want to move the fields and data into the most logically placed position on the form. Later, you will separate data frames using lines or boxes. Further, if you are using a color monitor, you may even use different colors to further differentiate the sections in the data form.

To move or copy a field, you must first select it. To do so, move the cursor to the beginning (or end) of the field or fields that you wish to move and press **F6**. In this case, you want to move the LAST_NAME field onto the same line as the FIRST_NAME field. In fact, you want to put LAST_NAME before FIRST_NAME. Before doing this, though, give yourself a few lines of space for the name of the form and a box around your data.

Move the cursor to the top of the page, and press the **ENTER** key three times. The entire data form will slide down. Now, move the highlight to the first letter of FIRST_NAME, and press **F6**. The system prompts you to complete your selection with the **ENTER** key.

To select the entire field, you may move the cursor using the arrow keys or, using a shortcut provided by dBASE IV, the **End** key. If you are selecting a highlighted data field (but not text outside of the data field), you may also select the entire field by pressing **ENTER**. To move to the end of a field, you may use the **End** key. Moving to the beginning of a field is done with the **Home** key.

When you have highlighted the FIRST_NAME text and field,

Press: **ENTER**

Now the entire field may be manipulated. Touch the **F7** key to tell the system that you want to move the selected field.

By pressing the **Tab** key or using the arrow key, move the white highlight until it is at the tab stop just before the 5 inch mark on the ruler. The ruler is located at the top of the screen, between the blackboard area and the menu line. The inverted triangles indicate tab stops; the numbers indicate number of inches in from the left margin.

You will notice a marker on the ruler line that moves as you move the marked area. In addition, a highlight the same size as your marked area moves along with the cursor indicator. This white highlight indicates the position of your field after you have moved it. When the highlight has been moved to the location shown in Figure 4-6, touch the **Enter** key to complete the move. Your field will now appear in the same spot as highlighted on the blackboard, as seen in Figure 4-7.

Other ways to move fields and style your letters will be discussed later in this chapter. Complete the move by touching the **Esc** key. The highlight will disappear, with only the first character of the field highlighted.

As presently laid out, the form will begin printing at the left margin. Normally, you would not want to do this, because many

Figure 4-6

Location to move field.

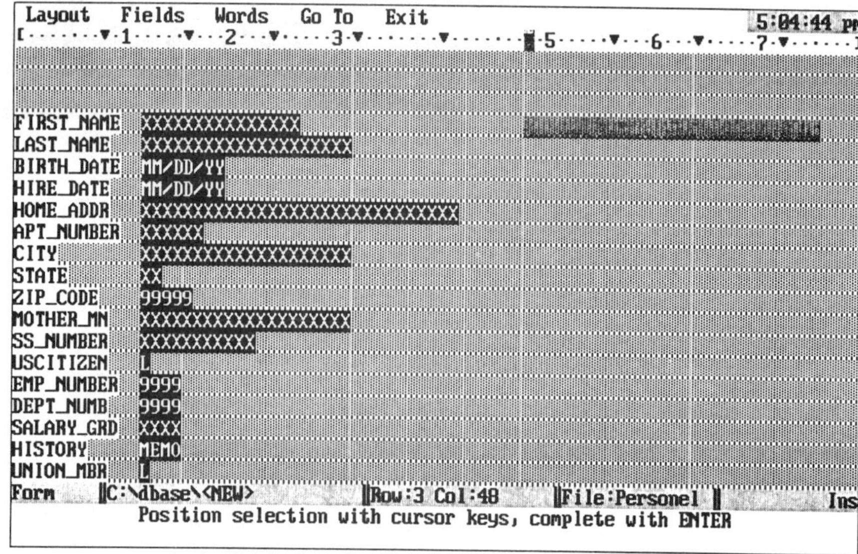

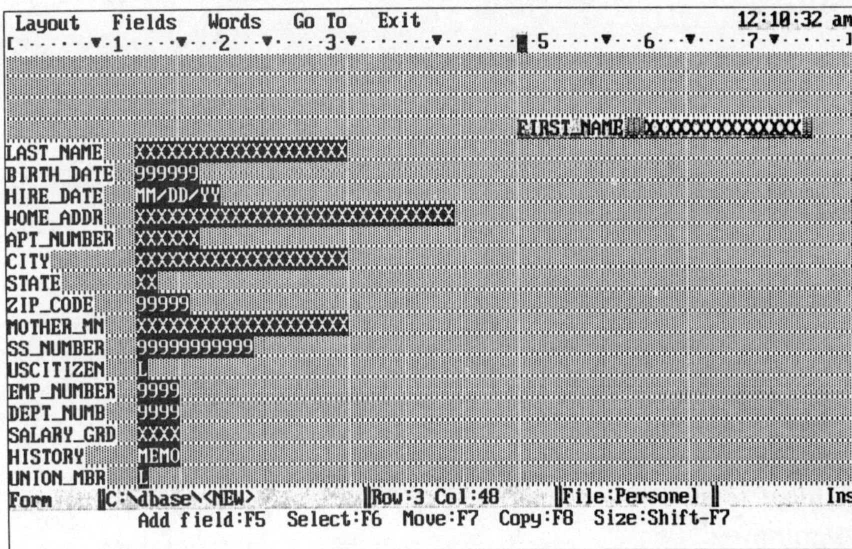

Figure 4-7

Moved FIRST_NAME field.

printers are unable to print starting at the left margin and you may lose a few characters when the form is printed. Further, not all photocopiers can copy to the edge of a sheet of paper. And, finally, a form that starts printing right at the edge of a page "just doesn't look right."

You will now move the rest of the fields in one block, indenting the entire body of the file. To do this, move the cursor to the *L* in LAST_NAME. This can be done quickly by moving the cursor down one line and pressing the **Home** key. Next, press **F6** to activate the Block function, and press the **DnArrow** three times, until the highlight moves to the *H* in HOME_ADDR. Because this is the widest entry, extending the highlight to the end of this field and bringing it down to include the rest of the form is the fastest way to highlight all the fields.

Press the **End** key to extend the highlight to the end of the field (Figure 4-8).

Next, to quickly select the rest of the form, touch the **PgDn** key. The highlight will fill the rest of the page.

> NOTE: if you had fields that extended below the bottom of this screen, you would have to continue using the **DnArrow** key to move the highlight farther down.

```
Layout   Fields   Words   Go To   Exit                                5:05:49 pm
                                             FIRST_NAME   XXXXXXXXXXXXXXX
LAST_NAME   XXXXXXXXXXXXXXXXXXXX
BIRTH_DATE  MM/DD/YY
HIRE_DATE   MM/DD/YY
HOME_ADDR   XXXXXXXXXXXXXXXXXXXXXXXXXXXXXX
APT_NUMBER  XXXXXX
CITY        XXXXXXXXXXXXXXXXXXXX
STATE       XX
ZIP_CODE    99999
MOTHER_MN   XXXXXXXXXXXXXXXXXXXX
SS_NUMBER   XXXXXXXXXXX
USCITIZEN   L
EMP_NUMBER  9999
DEPT_NUMB   9999
SALARY_GRD  XXXX
HISTORY     MEMO
UNION_MBR   L
Form   ║C:\dbase\<NEW>        ║Row:7 Col:42     ║File:Personel ║          Ins
                    Complete selection with ENTER
```

Figure 4-8

Widest field highlighted.

Touch the **ENTER** key to complete selecting the area on which you want to work (Figure 4-9).

Now, press the **F7** key to tell the system that you want to move the highlighted block. You will see that the top of the box begins at the bottom of the selected field. If you chose to leave the box

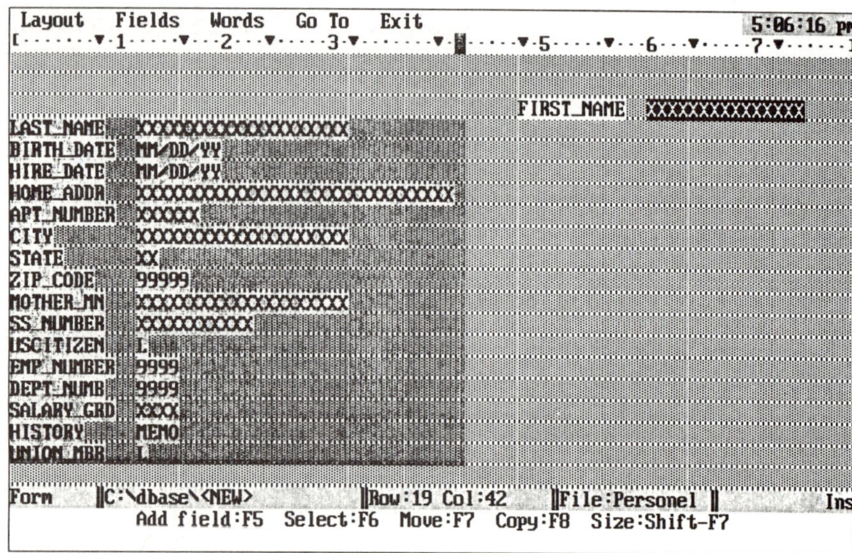

Figure 4-9

Highlighted file area.

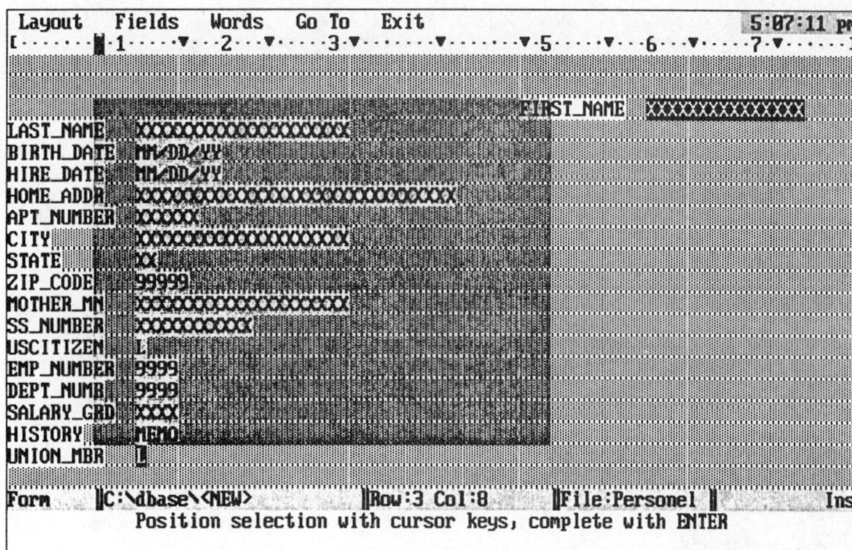

Figure 4-10

Block in desired position.

there, all the data will be printed at the bottom and roughly the center of the page. To move the highlighted area to the top of the page, touch the **PgUp** and the **Home** keys. Next, move the highlighted area down three lines by using the **DnArrow** arrow key. (The **ENTER** key cannot be used to add spaces here, because it is used to indicate that you have completed moving your highlighted area.)

Next, push the **Tab** key once to move the highlight in 0.8 inch. Note that the highlight slightly overlaps the FIRST_NAME field. However, remember that the highlight indicates the width of the widest field, and that the LAST_NAME field, which will share the line with FIRST_NAME, is not as wide (Figure 4-10).

Press **ENTER** to indicate that you have completed your move. At the bottom of the screen, the system will ask if you want to delete covered text and fields. This prompt tells you that the block has been moved into areas that cover existing fields. If you allow the move to occur, it will mean that any area under the marked block will be deleted when the block is moved.

Press: *y*

to remove the highlight (Figure 4-11).

You will notice that because the highlighted block overlapped into the FIRST_NAME field, and you told the system to delete

```
Layout   Fields   Words   Go To   Exit                                   5:07:41 pm
[·······▮·1·····▼···2···▼·····3·▼········▼········▼·5·····▼···6···▼·····7·▼······]

   LAST_NAME   XXXXXXXXXXXXXXXXXXXX                ST_NAME   XXXXXXXXXXXXXXX
   BIRTH_DATE  MM/DD/YY
   HIRE_DATE   MM/DD/YY
   HOME_ADDR   XXXXXXXXXXXXXXXXXXXXXXXXXXXXXX
   APT_NUMBER  XXXXXX
   CITY        XXXXXXXXXXXXXXXXXXXX
   STATE       XX
   ZIP_CODE    99999
   MOTHER_MN   XXXXXXXXXXXXXXXXXXXX
   SS_NUMBER   XXXXXXXXXXX
   USCITIZEN   L
   EMP_NUMBER  9999
   DEPT_NUMB   9999
   SALARY_GRD  XXXX
   HISTORY     MEMO
   UNION_MBR   L

Form   ‖C:\dbase\<NEW>          ‖Row:3 Col:8      ‖File:Personel ‖            Ins
         Add field:F5  Select:F6  Move:F7  Copy:F8  Size:Shift-F7
```

Figure 4-11

Moved fields.

the area of overlap, the first three letters of FIRST__NAME were deleted. To fix this, hit the **Tab** key until the marker is at the tab marker at 4.8 inches and type the missing letters, *FIR*.

In actual practice, of course, you could have moved the entire form, then shuffled the position of the fields. Next, move the address information below the name line (Figure 4-12). You will note

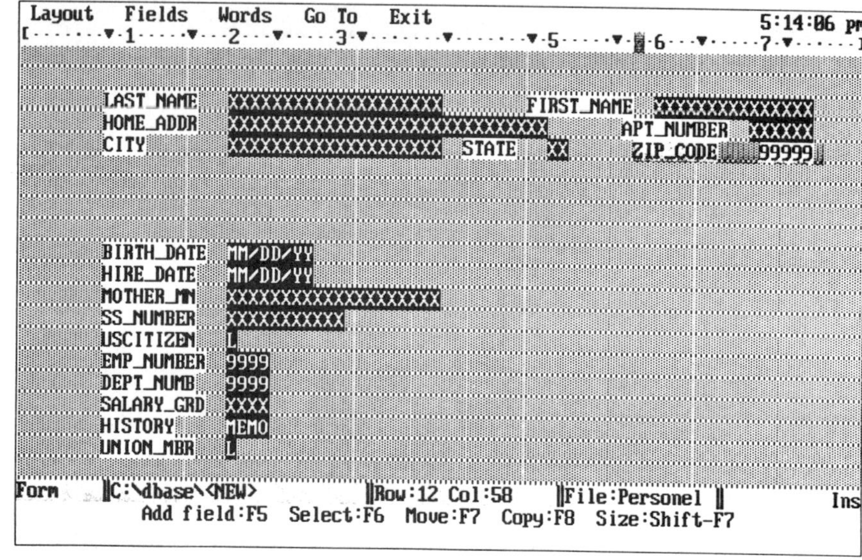

Figure 4-12

Name and address fields as they will appear on form.

that the space between STATE and the data fields is less than that provided by Quick layout. When Quick layout lays out your form, it assumes 10 spaces per field, and adds two spaces between the data fields and the data. For a short data description like STATE, this often results in too many spaces between the field name and the actual data field. This space was reduced by marking and then moving the data field.

> Note: The **F6** key allows you to make a variety of selections. The first time you press the key, it tells the system you will be marking a block that you wish to move, copy, or delete. If you use the **PgUp** or **PgDn** keys, the highlight will be moved from the cursor position to the top or bottom of the screen. Pressing the **End** key will move to the end of the text/field characters on the current line. The **Home** key will move the highlight to the first character at the left margin.
>
> In addition, pressing the **F6** key a second time will mark the entire line on which the cursor is placed. If you were to press **F6** a third time, the entire screen would be highlighted. Pressing the **ENTER** key completes your selection of the highlighted area. The repeated **F6**, in addition to the other special keys, allows you to rapidly select areas of your screen for modification.

Because you had to add spaces to make room for the HOME_ADDR, APT_NUMBER, CITY, STATE, and ZIP_CODE fields, you ended up with blank lines where the fields were. To remove these blank lines, type **^Y**.

This address area will be separated as one input area on the field. A second area will include further identifying data, and a third will include employee information. Now, move the fields so that they match the identifying information area in Figure 4-13. Be sure to leave five lines between the name and address block and the identification information. Now add a block for employment information, as seen in Figure 4-14.

Once the basic form is laid out, you can do many things to fine tune the appearance of the form. First, make the address fields more readable by changing the field names into upper and lower case characters and changing the underline to a blank. This is done by overtyping the current field name. Field names can be typed over. The areas that will be occupied by field data should not be typed over. The data areas will be explored later; for now,

```
Layout  Fields  Words  Go To  Exit                              5:17:33 pm
[·······▮·1·····▼···2···▼·····3·▼·······▼·······▼·5·····▼···6···▼·····7·▼·····]
        HOME_ADDR   XXXXXXXXXXXXXXXXXXXXXXXXXXXXXX        APT_NUMBER  XXXXXX
        CITY        XXXXXXXXXXXXXXXXXXXX  STATE  XX        ZIP_CODE    99999

        BIRTH_DATE  MM/DD/YY          SS_NUMBER    XXXXXXXXXXX
        MOTHER_MN   XXXXXXXXXXXXXXXXXXXX

        HIRE_DATE   MM/DD/YY

        USCITIZEN   L
        EMP_NUMBER  9999
        DEPT_NUMB   9999
        SALARY_GRD  XXXX
        HISTORY     MEMO
        UNION_MBR   L
Form    ‖C:\dbase\<NEW>       ‖Row:23 Col:8      ‖File:Personel ‖          Ins
           Add field:F5  Select:F6  Move:F7  Copy:F8  Size:Shift-F7
```

Figure 4-13

Identification information.

design the text areas of the form, and then work on data description and validation.

Ins is a toggled key. You can turn the Insert function on or off by touching the **Ins** key. Its status appears at the bottom of the screen in the box at the lower right.

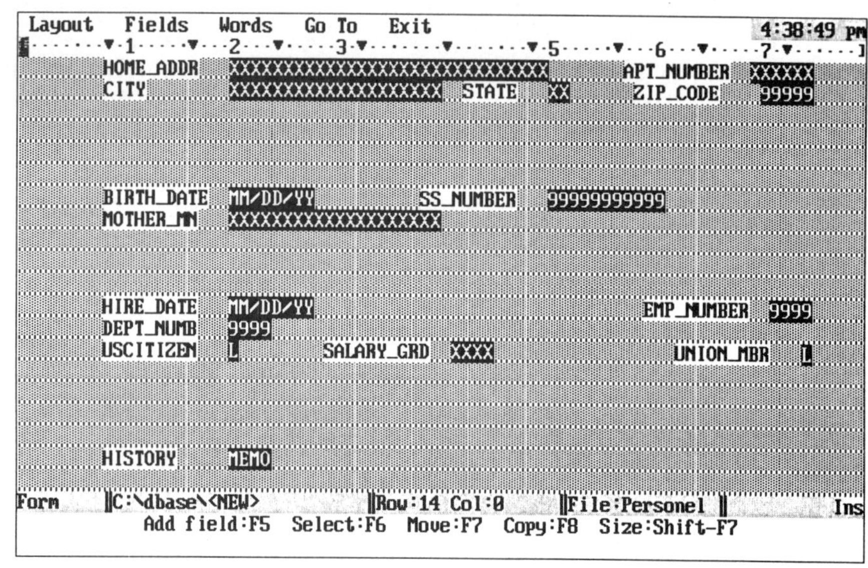

Figure 4-14

Employment information block.

When Insert is selected, anything you type pushes the rest of the text on the line to the right. This is useful when you are typing a field identifier and a name is not yet on your form. If you begin typing with two spaces before the data field location, the system will push the data field to the right as you type, and you will end up with a data field properly spaced to the right of your data identifier.

When the insert mode is not active, however, everything you type replaces the contents of the existing identifier. This also pushes the data entry fields to the right, as well as replacing the text in the description field. The completed form, seen in Figure 4-15, includes some field descriptors that are longer than their abbreviated names in the data file. These were typed in, starting farther to the left of the actual data fields, allowing enough space for the entire name to be input. You will notice that the space between the field description and the data field uses the pattern background of the blackboard, rather than the black of a blank space. Extra spaces that may be added when you type in the field names can be removed with the **Del** key. As you will see later, you may not want to delete the extra spaces if you plan to add colored backgrounds to your designed data fields. A space receives the selected color, whereas a blank area does not.

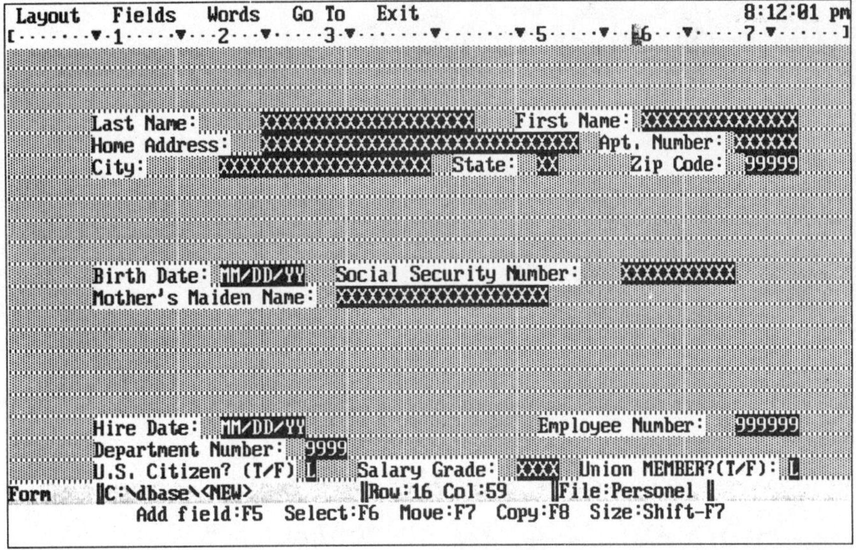

Figure 4-15

Typed field names.

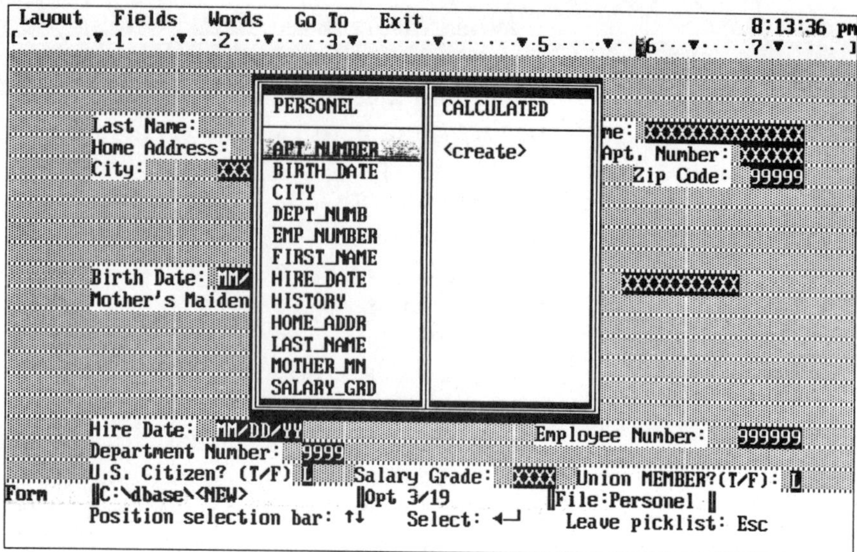

Figure 4-16

Field addition window.

Fields can be easily added using the **F5** key. In this example, we will add, and then remove, a field to see how it is done. To add a field, move the cursor to the position on the form at which the field is to be added. In this case, move to the first tab position on the first line. (Use **PgUp**, **Home**, and **Tab** keys to find the appropriate position.) Now,

Press: **F5**

A window for adding a field will drop down, showing the fields in your data file and allowing you to create a calculated field (Figure 4-16). A calculated field is one that is used as part of your form but is not part of your originally defined data.

For example, if you were designing an order entry and invoicing database, you may have a Units_Ordered field and a Unit_Cost field. A calculated field, possibly called TOTAL, will calculate the product of Units_Ordered and Unit_Cost. In this example, however, no such calculated field makes sense. For the purposes of demonstrating how to add a field, highlight and accept LAST_NAME by pressing **ENTER**. A set of options, as seen in Figure 4-17, will appear. These options will be discussed shortly.

Press: **Ctrl-End**

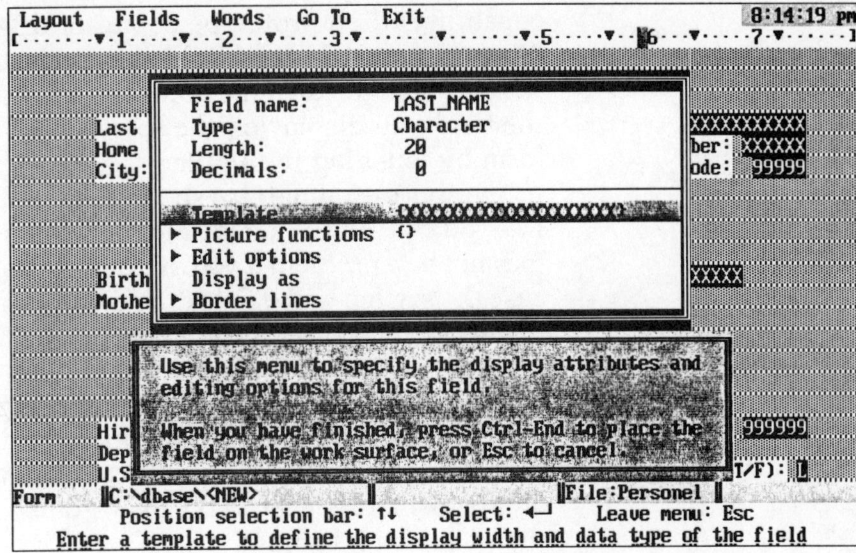

Figure 4-17

Field options.

to add the field. The system drops the data block onto the screen, as shown in Figure 4-18.

You could, of course, have designed the layout of your entire screen using the **F5** key to add the fields where you wanted them. (In fact, I rebuilt this screen many times using the **F5** Add Field

Figure 4-18

Data field added.

```
Layout  Fields  Words  Go To  Exit                              8:16:22 pm
XXXXXXXXXXXXXXXXXXXX

Last Name:     XXXXXXXXXXXXXXXXXXXX  First Name: XXXXXXXXXXXXXXX
Home Address:  XXXXXXXXXXXXXXXXXXXXXXXXXXXXXX  Apt, Number: XXXXXX
City:      XXXXXXXXXXXXXXXXXXXX  State: XX      Zip Code: 99999

Birth Date: MM/DD/YY  Social Security Number:    XXXXXXXXXXX
Mother's Maiden Name:  XXXXXXXXXXXXXXXXXXXX

Hire Date: MM/DD/YY                         Employee Number: 999999
Department Number: 9999
U.S. Citizen? (T/F) L  Salary Grade: XXXX  Union MEMBER?(T/F): L
Form   C:\dbase\<NEW>     Row:0 Col:28     File:Personel
       Add field:F5  Select:F6  Move:F7  Copy:F8  Size:Shift-F7
```

capability when prototype copies of dBASE IV blew up.) Now, move the cursor into the field that you just added. The entire field will be highlighted. At the bottom of the screen, information about the field will display on the screen. Delete this field from your form by touching the **Del** key.

The above example also shows a potential problem with dBASE IV—you can put the same field on a single form many times. This may not be a problem if you are *viewing data* in the form, in which case the system will display the data from the data field for your record in each place where you call for it. However, if you are designing a data entry form, you will have to define the field as one that cannot be edited. If you are using the Add field options, you may select the Edit Options menu and indicate that this field cannot be edited for all appearances of this field after its first time on the form. It is best to try to avoid using the same field more than once on a form.

One field has still not been completed on this form, the HISTORY field. This is a memo field. It will contain text that you record using dBASE IV's text editor, or another word processor that you designated when you set up dBASE IV. Being a memo field, HISTORY is different from the other fields you have designed. This is because, although the system indicated a width of 10 characters, you can actually have the contents of a large text file in a memo file.

What happens when you set up a memo field is that the system writes a pointer, indicating where the actual text that will be used in that field is to be read from and written to. The pointer automatically records the location of your associated text file, which may be as large as 64 kilobytes.

The form setup for a memo field allows you to define a window for the text to be input or viewed. In its present form, the word *MEMO* appears, indicating that memo text will be used. However, you must define how the memo text is to appear. To see how this is done, press **PgDn** until HISTORY appears at the top of the screen, with an open blackboard below it. Move the cursor to highlight the word "MEMO" and press **F5**. The Data definition window will appear.

The system gives you two options. You may display the memo text as an open window, which allows you to read the memo text on your form. When this option is selected, a window is drawn onto your data form. Data from the memo file will be placed in the window when you view or edit your file.

A second way to display the memo text is with a marker. With a marker, the word Memo is displayed on the data form during your design process and when you browse or edit your files. When this is selected, you will be required to perform a special key sequence (**Ctrl-Home**) to load and view the memo file. When viewing or editing data, the memo text will appear, beginning at the location of the text marker if you cursor into the marker using the **F4** key (while in Browse) or move to the marker and press **Ctrl-Home.**

If you choose to define a text window, you should next define the outline for the window. This is discussed along with the field description options a little later in this chapter.

> Note: the top line of any data form is normally used to display user prompts. The prompts *Record, Go To,* and *Exit* provide the user with tools to move through the database. For the prompts to appear the top line of your form must be blank. Entering data onto the first line will remove the space for these prompts. If you were designing a system in which you *did not* want the user to see these prompts, beginning your form with text or lines on the top line of the form will hide the user prompts. It is important to note, however, that the functionality afforded by the menu line is still there—that to access the features of the menu line, the user would hit the quick-keys required to bring the menu up (**Alt-R, Alt G,** or **Alt-E**) or the **F10** key. As a rule, however, it is good practice to leave the top line of your form blank so that the menu options will display.

Now that the data fields have been laid out, and names attached, you can explore some more sophisticated design features. Because you have created blocks of related data, it would be well to label and delineate the separate blocks.

dBASE IV allows you to draw lines and boxes on your forms. You have the option of single or double lines, or a text character (instead of the hyphen or bar). Selection of the style for your lines or boxes is done from the Layout menu.

You should be careful when drawing your boxes—if you draw a box over text and later move the text, you will be left with a hole. Thus, it is a good idea to place your fields first, then draw your lines and boxes. Determining where you want to place your boxes is also important. If you add or delete lines to move the text, your text, but not the box overlaying it, will move. Your once neatly enclosed text can therefore end up outside the box.

However, moving a box is simple. Move the cursor so that it is on top of a line on the box. Next,

Press: **F6**

to highlight the box.

Press: **ENTER**

to select the box. Next,

Press: **F7**

to tell the system that you want to move the box. Reposition the box to the location at which you want it and

Press: **ENTER**

You will be building lines and boxes to separate the various elements of your design. The final form will look something like Figures 4-19 and 4-20.

You will note that lines have been added to position the boxes

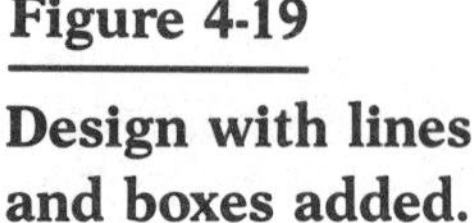

Figure 4-19

Design with lines and boxes added.

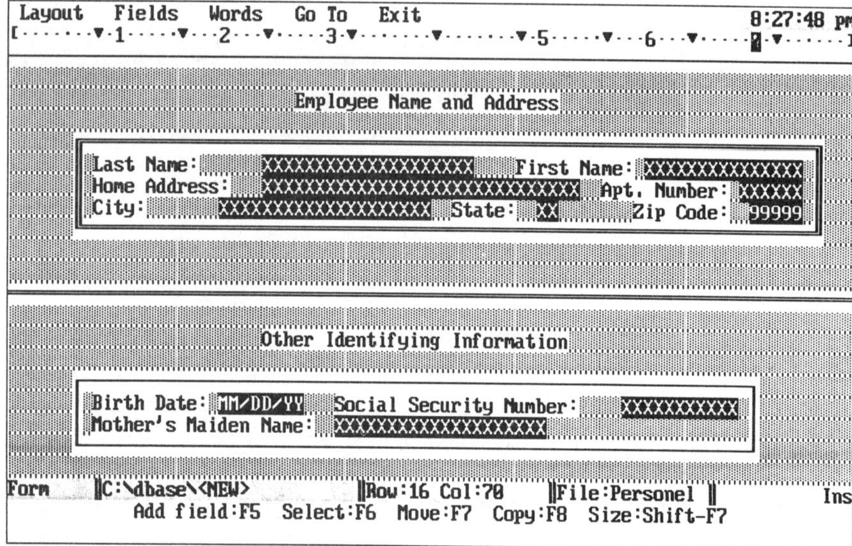

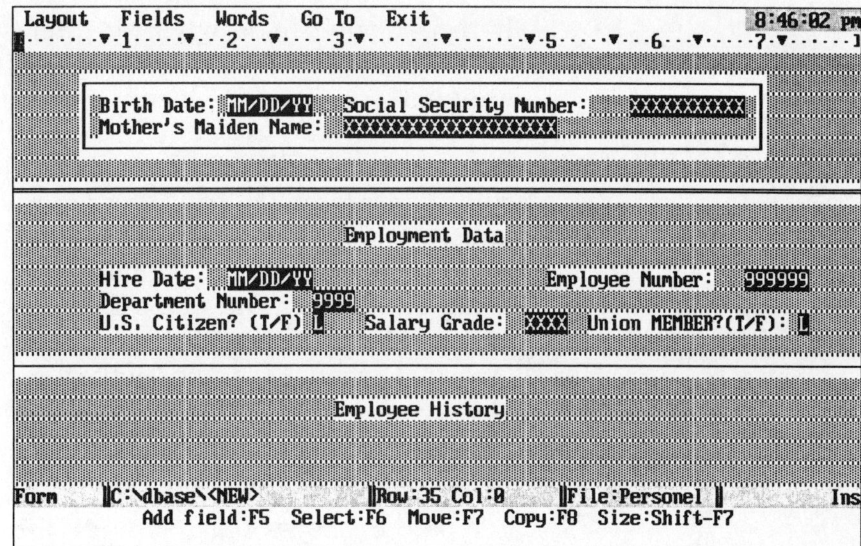

Figure 4-20

Second part of design.

and section headings. In addition, you will see samples of boxes and lines using single- and double-line format.

Line and box drawing with dBASE IV is simple. First, call up the *Layout* menu, and select either *Box* or *Line*. From there, select *Single Line, Double Line,* or *Using specified character.* If you want to use a character for drawing the lines, the system will prompt you to indicate the character for drawing the box.

Once the type of box or line is selected, move the cursor to the point at which you want to start the line or box and touch **ENTER**. Next, move the cursor with the arrow keys, stopping at the point at which you want to end your line or box, then touch the **ENTER** key to finish the line or box.

The line draw function is something of a misnomer. In addition to just drawing horizontal or vertical lines, you may use the line drawing function in much the same manner as an Etch-A-Sketch; that is, you are drawing with vertical and horizontal segments. Any horizontal movement places a small horizontal line; a vertical movement places a vertical line. You may back up over a line segment and can easily do staircase patterns. You can also draw boxes around irregularly shaped data fields.

Boxes can be deleted by moving the cursor anywhere on the box and pressing the **Del** key.

In theory, you can design some interesting data entry effects using the line drawing capabilities of dBASE IV.

Although you have graphically matched most of what would have been considerably more difficult in terms of design with earlier versions of dBASE, there are still other capabilities that should be explored. Notice the properly centered headings in Figures 4-19 and 4-20. The design of these headings was effortless and can be done without calculation.

Using the *Words* menu, you can modify the appearance of the words and of marked areas on your screen (Figure 4-21). This menu allows you to change the color of the foreground and background of your text or other selected fields. It also provides you with a number of text formatting possibilities. To see how this works, go to the second line of your form and

Type: *Employee Data Form* **ENTER**

Next, call up the Words menu.

The **Display** option allows you to modify the text and the background color. To use this option, select the text or area that you wish to modify, and then load the Words menu.

In this example, you will be reversing the normal appearance of your text. On screen (and on paper) the heading *Employee Data Form* will appear opposite what the rest of the text appears like.

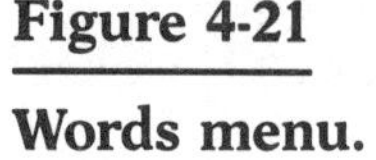

Figure 4-21

Words menu.

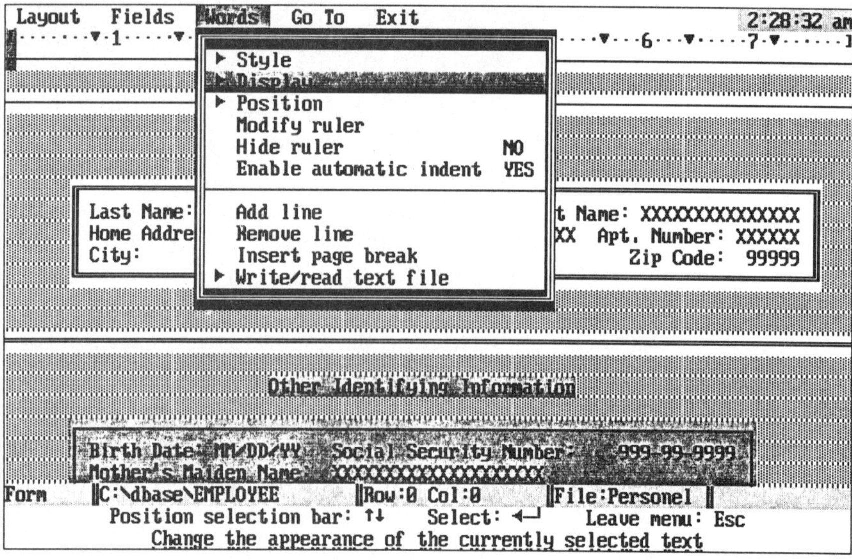

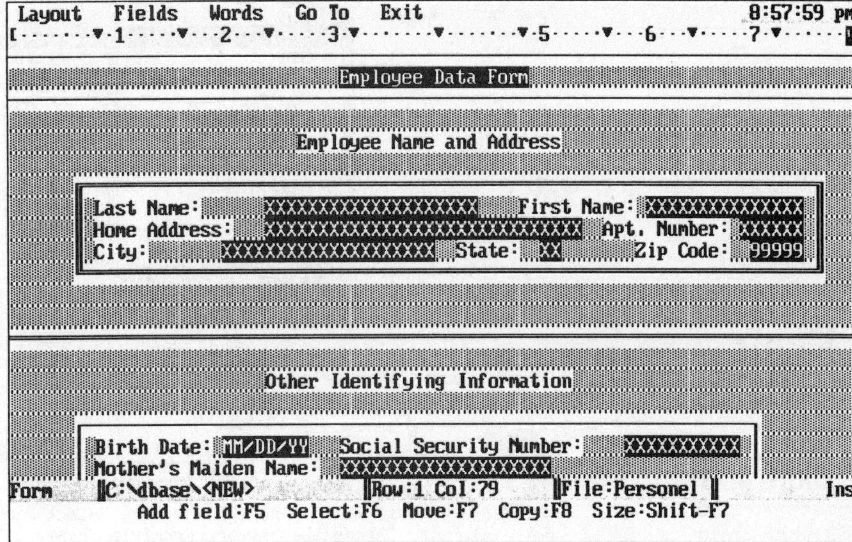

Figure 4-22

Line with inverted header.

On screen, the characters are white on a black background (Figure 4-22). To accomplish this look, select the line of text, using the **F6** key to tell the system that you want to select an area for modification, and using the arrow or other keys to highlight the text to be modified. One simple way to mark the text is to place the text at the margin. At the last character, press **F6**, then the **Home** key, which brings the highlight from the last character to the beginning of the line. Pressing **ENTER** then marks the desired text.

Next, go to the Words menu. Finally, select Display.

A Color menu will appear on the screen (Figure 4-23). This menu can be somewhat confusing. On one side of the menu, a solid bar sits on the line showing the color selected for the foreground (or background, depending on which side the bar is located), and on the other side, an arrow points to the color selected for the background (or foreground) text. Using the **UpArrow** or **DnArrow** keys, you may move the bar to change the colors of the foreground (or background). The **LeftArrow** and **RightArrow** keys move the selection bar between the background and foreground columns.

The color combination selected for your highlighted area is the one at which the arrow points. As you move the color selection bar, you can see the changes made by watching the text at which the arrow points. With a little practice, the principle of operation becomes obvious, although it can be somewhat confusing at first.

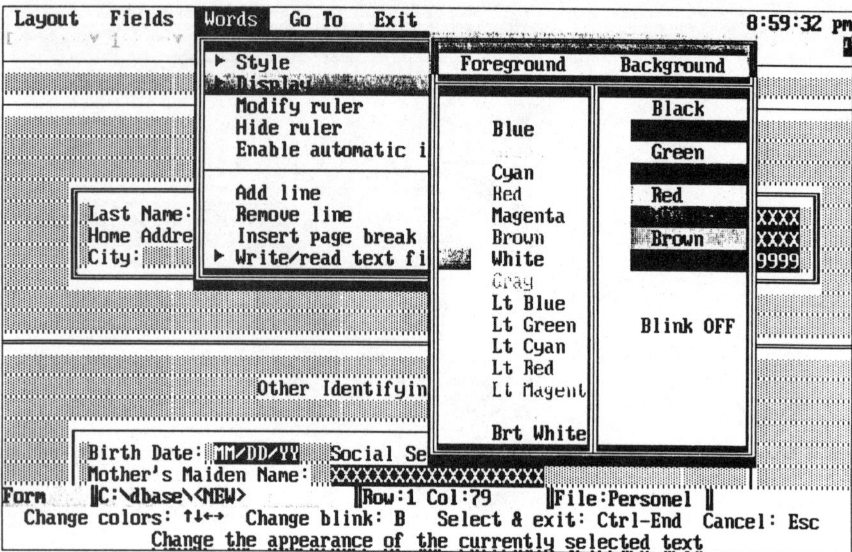

Figure 4-23

Color menu.

The main thing to remember is that the solid bar is used to select the new color for background or foreground, and the arrow previews how the selected combination will look. If you are using a monochrome display, your range of choices will be smaller, although the method of choosing a combination of intensities remains the same.

To match the color combination selected for this example, that is, black text with a white background, make sure that the color bar is in the *Foreground* column (if not, the **LtArrow** or **RtArrow** will put it there), and press the **UpArrow** or **DnArrow** to move the highlight to the top of the display. You will not be able to read the word Black because the arrow indicates that the background is also black, and with the same color for foreground and background, your text disappears. You can, however, see the color of your foreground text by looking at the text against the other background colors in the *Background* column.

Next, press the **RtArrow** or **LtArrow** to move the pointer to the Background column. The arrow in the display will move to the Foreground column. Now, move the cursor down (or up) until the bar is next to White. You will notice that the bar and the arrow point to displays with the same appearance. To accept this combination,

Type: **Ctrl-End**

The Display selection screen will clear, and you will return to the display selected before you made the color selection.

To see the selected text approximately as it will appear on the form,

Press: **Esc**

Text can be automatically placed at the left margin, right margin, or center of the screen using the Words menu. After selecting the text you wish to place on your line (using the **F6** and other keys), select the Words menu. Next, select Position. This menu gives you three options: *Left, Center,* and *Right.* Typing the first letter of the desired position, or moving the highlight to the line with the position name you want, and pressing **ENTER** tells the system to complete the placement of the text.

Blanks and spaces will now be discussed.

As you built this form, you undoubtedly noticed that areas in which you typed text or entered spaces were shown on screen with a black background. If you deleted those spaces using the **Del** key, the background hatching was restored to the screen.

What does this mean and why is it important? If you were simply planning to use white (or cyan, depending on how you set up the colors for your system) text on a black (or blue) background for your display, the difference between blanks and spaces would not be significant. Field names will appear on your forms with white (or cyan) characters on a black (or blue) background, and fields will appear white (or cyan) with black (or blue) characters (Figure 4-24). However, using the Display options, you may produce more colorful, interesting forms. The use of color or variable backgrounds on monochrome screens can be valuable for data input.

For example, a different color may highlight a different type of field. With the current form as an example, the design for such a form using color has the Employee Name and Address fields using bright white foreground and blue background, and Other Identifying Information using bright white foreground and red background. Although the colors cannot be seen on the pages of this book, the different backgrounds still make the differences apparent, as seen in Figure 4-25.

When data on such a form are being viewed or updated, the color cues can quickly indicate which type of data area is being used.

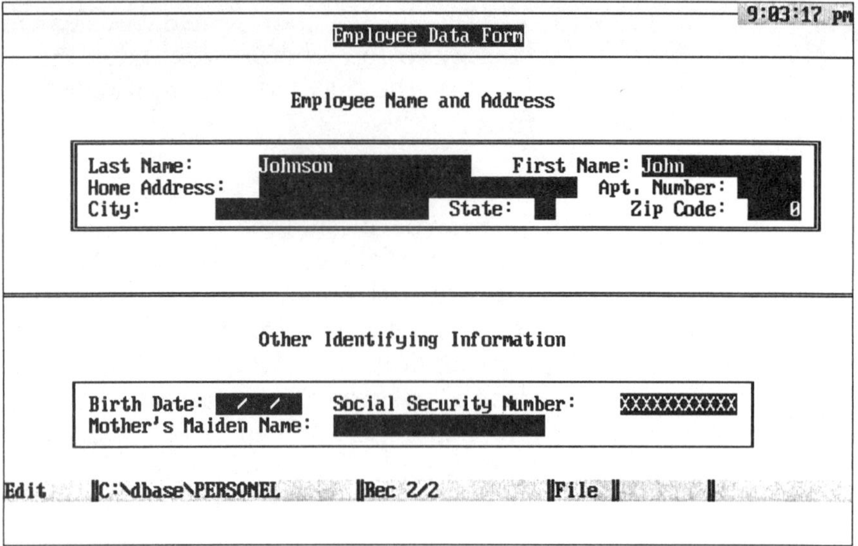

Figure 4-24

Display form with standard display settings.

In another instance, in which there are many lines of data, one on top of the other, in lists or other structures, using lines or bars of color makes it easier for readers to find their place on a crowded sheet.

When it comes to using color backgrounds (or different inten-

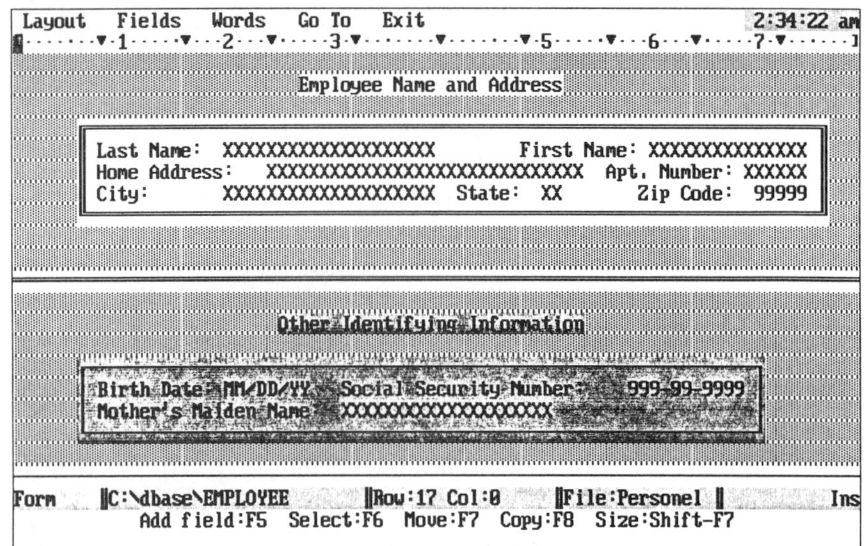

Figure 4-25

Fields with colored backgrounds.

sity backgrounds on a monochrome system), the difference between blanks and spaces becomes important. When your form is displayed, any blank areas are shown with a black background (if this is how you set the default background for your system). Areas that are occupied by spaces will be seen with a colored background if you placed color on the selected area.

Figure 4-26 used spaces between entries on the design to indicate that the background should appear in the selected background color. In Figure 4-24, the areas between fields are blanks (on the design form, they appear as the background hatched area). As you can see, most displays look best when spaces, rather than blanks, fill a line or separate fields.

It may also be useful to note that the character attributes stay with the text, and that boxes are directly overlaid on the form and do not move if you make changes in your form. To quickly see this, return to the top of the form and touch the **ENTER** key a few times. The text lines will move, but the boxes will remain in their preset position. Boxes can be easily moved, however. To move a box, position the cursor onto a line on the box, and press **F6 ENTER** to select the box. Press **F7** to select the *Move* command, and, using your cursor keys, position the box in its new location, pressing **ENTER** to complete the move.

Before going further, save the form to avoid making any per-

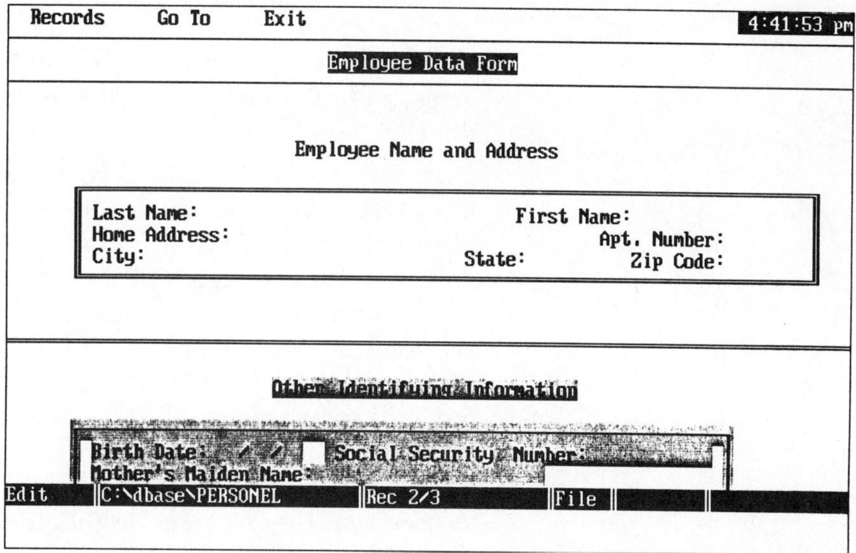

Figure 4-26

Display with blanks between fields.

manent changes in the next section. To do this, go to the Layout menu and select the *Save this form* option, retaining the name EMPLOYEE.

The Menus and How to Use Them

The Layout Menu

The basic features of the Layout menu have already been used to build the application designed so far in this book. However, the major facets of this menu are briefly explored here.

Quick layout: Selecting Quick layout places all the fields on your screen, with each field on its own line. The fields can therefore be quickly placed on a blank form. This option is useful for laying out a basic data entry form; the layout of anything more complicated will probably be uninteresting. Quick layout is most useful for transferring the fields from a data design onto a basic form for modification by the user or form designer.

One other point should be made here: Quick layout begins your form at the top of the page. In this position, the user prompts that normally appear at the top menu line will not be visible when the form is used to edit or view your data. Unless you want to hide the menu line, it is usually best to insert a blank line between the top of the form and the first field.

Box: The Box option allows you to select from two different line styles. When selected, you can draw a box around any desired field or block of fields. A single line or double line may be used for design of the box.

Boxes should be the *last* item added to a form, because they are not locked to any particular fields. This means that if you add or delete a line on your form, the text enclosed by the box will move, although the box will remain where it was placed. The net result is that the text that was included in your box will no longer fit properly inside the box. It is useful to note that a box can be highlighted and moved so that it again fits around the field names or text, as just described.

Line: The Line option also provides you with the choice of single or double lines. As stated earlier, this option works in a manner similar to an Etch-A-Sketch toy. You can use the option to draw vertical or horizontal lines. A line is placed wherever you move the cursor.

Thus, crude graphics can be drawn by placing vertical or horizontal lines in desired positions. It is also useful to remember that deleting drawn lines requires deletion of *each* line segment—you cannot highlight a line in the same way you can highlight a box, and then delete it.

Use different database file or view: This option allows you to select a different file in your catalog to which the constructed form will be applied. When selected, your screen will show the database files in your currently selected catalog and a description of the highlighted file, as seen in Figure 4-27.

If you wish to use the same form for different data files or to modify a form so that it could be used for data entry or retrieval in another data file, this option can be used to attach the new file. If fields on your form do not exist in the data file, the system will pop up a window listing the field(s)

Figure 4-27

Use different database file or view file selection screen.

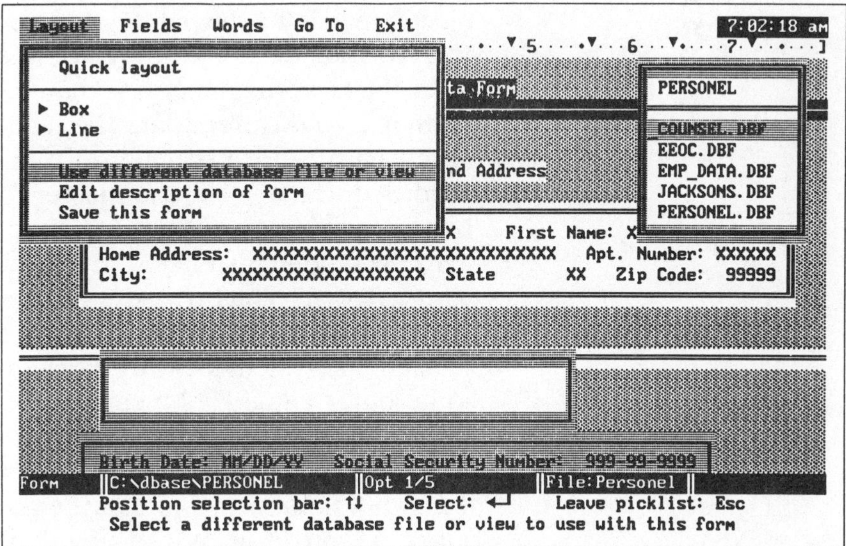

that are used on the form, but not included in the attached data file. You should be careful to remove the extraneous fields from your form, or to go back to your data file and add the appropriate fields.

Once the file is attached and your form modified (if necessary), you should save your form with a new name appropriate to the data file to which it is attached.

Edit description of form: This option allows you to write a description of the form. The description appears on the description line of the Control Center when the form name is highlighted. The current form will now be described.

Highlight "Edit description of form" and

Press: **ENTER**

(or from within the Layout menu, type *e* to select this option). For the description

Type: ***Data entry screen for Personnel database*** **ENTER**

The description will be attached to the form when it is saved.

Save this form: This option can be used in a number of instances. Because the other save option, *Save changes and exit,* saves the form and returns you to Control Center , this is the option to use if you wish to rename the form, or if you wish to save your design while you are designing it.

In the first instance, you may be modifying a "master" form to fit a different data file. The modified form must be saved with a different name from the "master" that you modified—otherwise, the master form will be overwritten by the form that you just designed.

In the second instance, you may be designing a long, complicated form. The form stays in system memory until it is saved. If something happens to the system during your design session (the system locks up, power to the computer fails, or some other catastrophe causes the system to cough), any work done during that session that was not saved could be irretrievably lost. Although this may not happen often, in fact it may never happen, it is always a good idea to regularly save a form as you design it to ensure that your work is preserved.

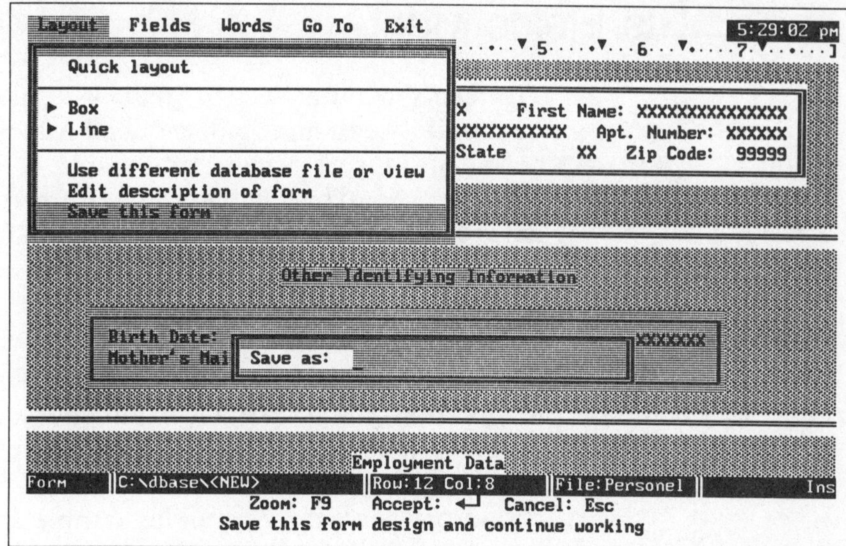

Figure 4-28

Save this form prompt.

When this option is selected, the current name of the form is presented in a window on screen, as seen in Figure 4-28.

You may accept the current name for your file by pressing **ENTER**. If you wish to rename your file, you may type any name up to eight letters in length, starting the form name with a number, and avoiding the use of punctuation marks. You do not have to type the *.SCR* extension for the new file name; the system automatically adds that for you.

Once you name your form, dBASE IV's form generator takes over, creating code that describes your form. Once your form has been saved, you may exit from the Form design screen. To do this, you may use the Exit menu or

Type: **Esc**

The system will ask if you wish to abandon the operation. If you answer *Y* (for yes), the system will return you to the Control Center without saving any of the changes you have made since you last saved your file. If you are sure you have saved your form design exactly as you wish to have it, you may exit using the **Esc** key. Do not, however, routinely exit using **Esc**. Because your changes are not saved, you may one day use the key after having made, but not saved, changes in your form, and therefore lose them.

The Fields Menu

The *Fields* menu, as seen in Figure 4-29, allows you to add, remove, or modify fields that will be used in your form. You may also define and insert a memory variable. A memory variable, most commonly used by database programmers, refers to a field whose data may change from record to record. The value of that variable is used in report generation or in analysis of the contents of a database.

About Fields and Field Validation. Two of the field options in this menu allow you to define certain characteristics of your fields. These options allow you to tell the system how to process the data that are being entered into each field and to verify that the type of data are correct. As a simple example, the system will not allow you to type *abcdef* in a date field—it will look instead only for numbers. As another example, a logical field cannot be filled in with an *X* or *W* (only with *Y* [for yes], *N* [for no], *T* [for true], or *F* [for false]).

A number of the routines used by both add field and modify field are the same in each option. There is a broad range of options provided for field management and definition. Because field

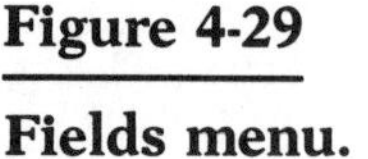

Figure 4-29

Fields menu.

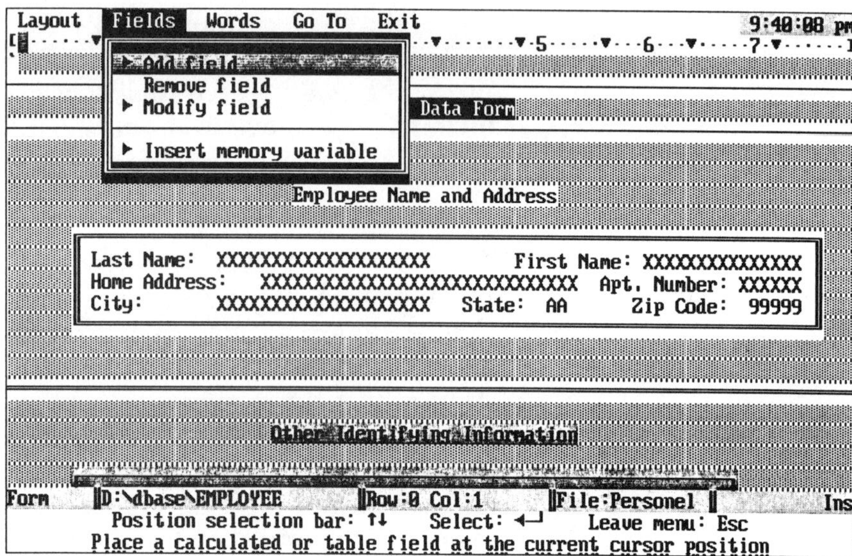

validation and definition are important parts of form design and data entry, many of the capabilities for field definition are described and illustrated in this chapter.

The functions performed by *Add field* and *modify field* are very similar. In *add field*, you are selecting a field from the field list that is created by the data file you have attached to the form. In *modify field*, you select a field that is already placed on the form and refers to a field in the attached data file.

The basic procedures, once you select either option, are to (1) select a field to modify, (2) make your changes, and (3) tell the system that you are through with your changes, and to record the changes, returning you to the Design screen.

There is another difference between *Modify field* and *Add field*. When you modify a field, the system brings up a list of fields that have already been attached to a form. *Add field* provides the option of creating calculated fields.

Let's modify a field to demonstrate some of the field management and definition functions provided by dBASE IV. Select *Modify field*. To do this,

Type: *m*

or move the highlight to "modify field," and

Press: **ENTER**

A window with the names of all the fields in your data file will appear on the screen. At the bottom of the screen, information about the highlighted field is displayed (Figure 4-30).

You will want to designate the way the SS_NUMBER (social security number) field is completed. To quickly select this field,

Type: *s*

The highlight will be on "SALARY_GRD." Recall that when you type letters to select a field, the first match is highlighted. In this case, SALARY_GRD was the first field that matched the single character, *S*. Although it is just as simple to press the down arrow to move the highlight to SS_NUMBER,

Type: *s*

to move the highlight to SS_NUMBER. Now,

Press: **ENTER**

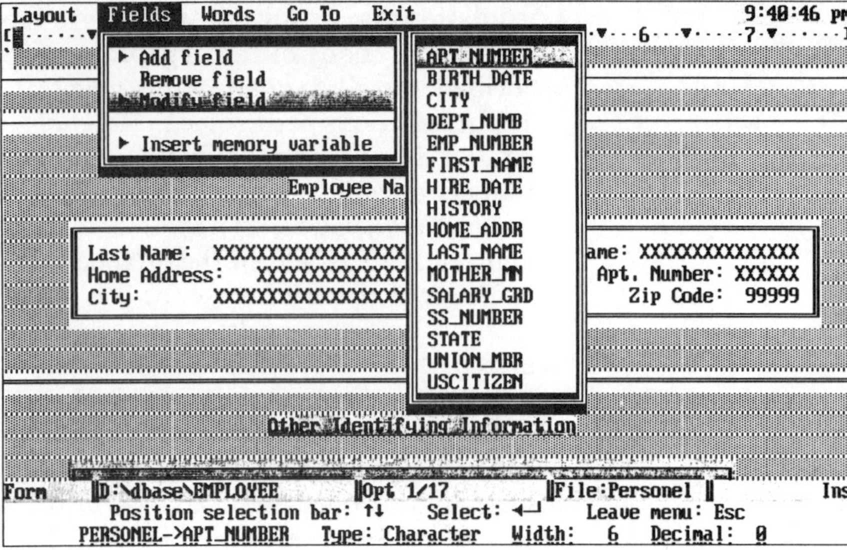

Figure 4-30

Field Selection window.

to select the highlighted field. The Field Definition menu will pop onto the screen (Figure 4-31).

Text in the windows is either highlighted or dim. The top half of the window provides information about the field that has been selected. At the bottom are options for display and definition of

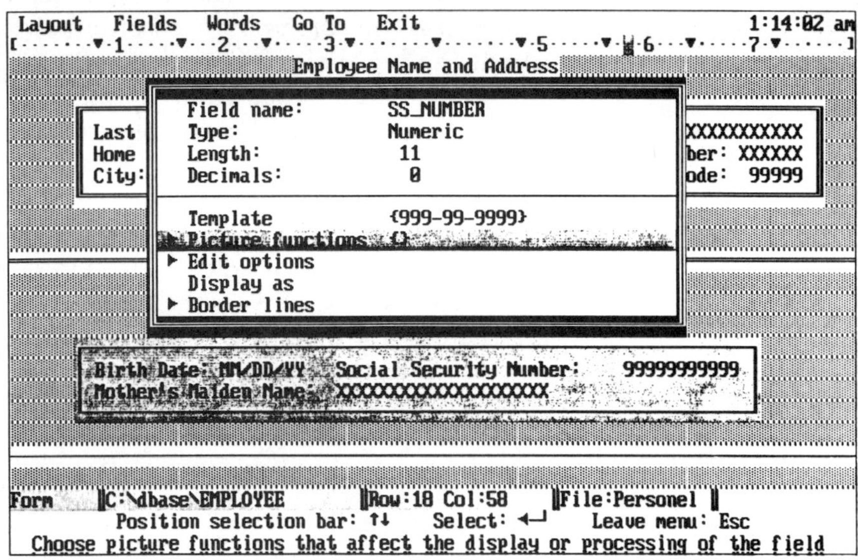

Figure 4-31

Field Modification window.

the field selected. Highlighted text displays options that are available to you at this time.

Template: The template defines the way your data must be entered. When Template is selected, a template option window appears below the Character input options window, as seen in Figure 4-32.

The input symbols are fairly straightforward. If you choose not to change the template, which now shows all *X*s, any character will be allowed. In this case, however, you are working with a social security number. You will notice that, for logical fields, you have the option of accepting only *T* (for true) or *F* (for false), or for additionally accepting *Y* (for yes) or *N* (for no). In some cases, as with the USCITIZEN and UNION_MBR fields, *Y* or *N* makes more sense than *T* or *F*. The template options allow you to select the appropriate type of acceptable responses.

You want to develop a template that accepts only numbers for the Social Security Number field. In addition, you would like hyphens to separate the three blocks of numbers in a social security number. You have two options to describe this field. You may use *#* or *9* to tell the system to accept numbers (digits) and not accept alphabetic characters. However, *#* also

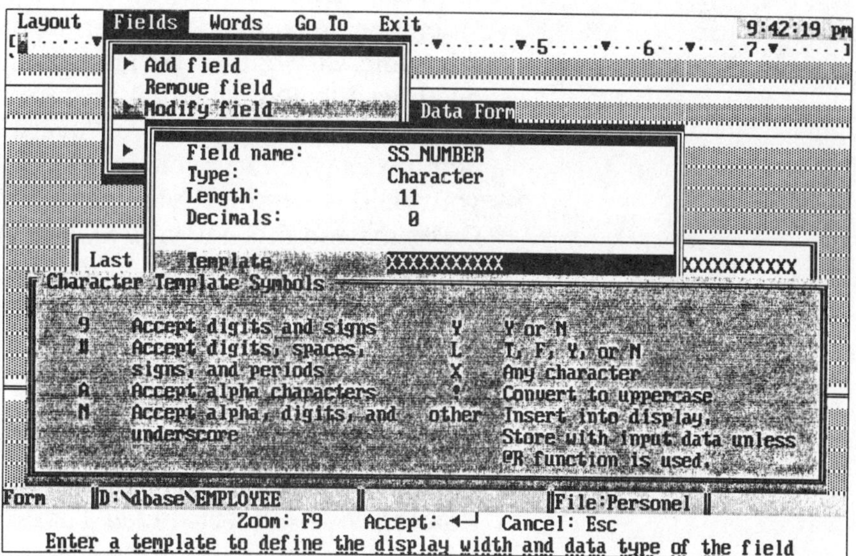

Figure 4-32

Character input options window.

accepts spaces, signs, and periods. Choosing *9* allows only digits and signs; because social security numbers do not include spaces or periods, the correct descriptor of numeric input is *9*.

Move the cursor to Template and

Press: **ENTER**

to load the Template definition window.

Type: ***999-99-9999***

to tell the system to accept only numbers, and to automatically input a hyphen in the indicated location. To accept this template,

Touch: **ENTER**

You will be back at the Fields menu.

Template design may take more planning than anticipated. For example, you might expect to use the A character (any alpha character) input symbol as your template for the LAST_NAME field. This would work well in most cases, preventing the erroneous typing of numbers in this field. However, it would also prevent use of punctuation marks. If you were to have records on people with hyphenated last names, such names *could not be entered* with this template in place. Therefore, when using a template, you must consider the *exceptions*, if any, that may make the template unusable. City names are another area in which the use of an alpha only template may require some careful consideration. This template will be useful only if there are no employees who live in cities with hyphenated names; but if your field is too small, you may want to be able to type 1000 Oaks, instead of Thousand Oaks (CA).

Picture Functions: The term *Picture Function* is a carryover from earlier versions of dBASE. These functions tell the system how you want it to display the contents of your field on screen, how it is to be printed at print time, or if the field is a multiple choice field, if you are working with a non-numeric field.

A second set of picture functions is used for numeric or floating point numeric fields. These functions also deal with on-screen display and printed display, and also, quite logi-

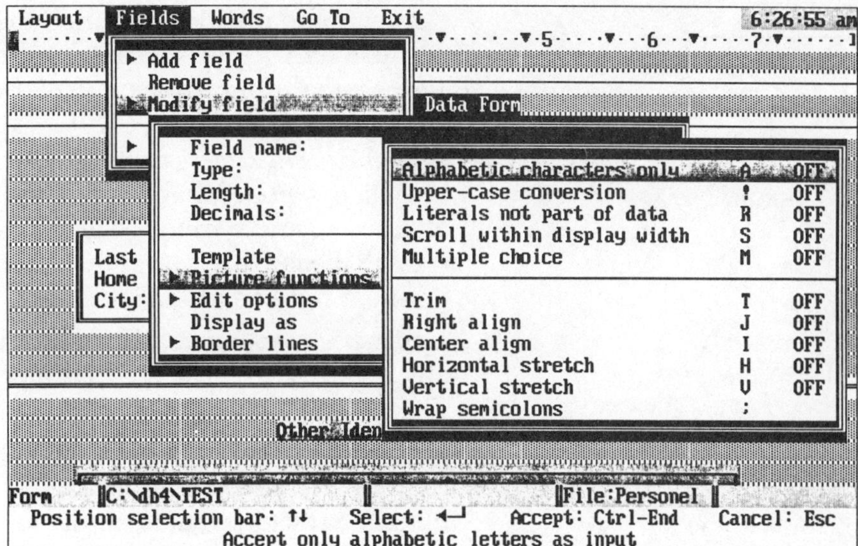

Figure 4-33

Picture Functions menu, character fields.

cally, include options for the way the values in the fields are handled.

The Picture Functions menu for character-based fields is shown in Figure 4-33. The Picture Functions menu for numeric fields is shown in Figure 4-34. Picture Functions are not available for memo or logical fields.

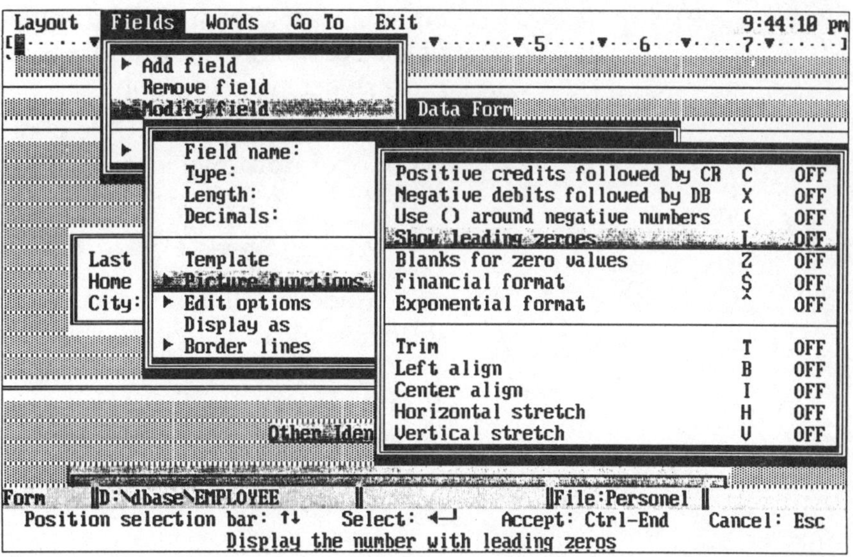

Figure 4-34

Picture Functions menu, numeric fields.

Returning to the Picture functions window for character fields, you will see that a variety of options are given. With the exception of multiple choice, these are toggled on and off using the **Space Bar**.

Alphabetic characters only: When selected, the system will not accept nonalphabetic characters, such as numeric characters and symbols. There is some redundancy here, though, because the template function also allows you to define a field as alphabetic only.

Uppercase conversion: When selected, this option converts any lowercase character to uppercase.

Literals not part of data: Characters that you have included in your template, such as the hyphen in the SS_NUMBER field or the dollar sign in a salary field, are considered literal characters, that is, characters that are automatically assigned by the system and cannot be modified. When this option is selected, the literal character will display on screen and be printed, but will not be counted as part of the data.

Scroll within display width: If your data field is large, you may want to be able to use cursor controls to move (scroll) through a field to view the data in the field. For example, you may have designed your form with 10 spaces available to display addresses. When you get an address that is 20 characters wide, you will be able to scroll through the rest of the characters in the address within this window if you have selected this option.

Multiple choice: A multiple choice field allows the data input operator to select from a variety of optional entries for a field. To define multiple choice fields, first

Press: **Space Bar** (or **ENTER**)

A window will pop onto the screen asking for entry of the choice(s). To enter each choice, type the choice, followed by **ENTER**. The system will continue accepting multiple choice options until it receives an **ENTER** on a blank choice. For example, you may be managing data for a number of your company's locations. By entering the name of each location into a multiple choice field, you can predefine the appropriate field entries, which can be quickly selected during input.

The Picture Functions menu for numeric fields has options that are different from those for the character fields. However, the bottom half of the window, which contains display and formatting settings, is basically the same as the one for character fields, with a single exception to be discussed later.

The options at the top of the screen for numeric and floating point fields are as follows:

Positive credits followed by CR: This field, though not showing in the figure, is used for financial functions. When the value of the field is positive, selecting this option puts the letters *CR* after the value. This option is available when preparing a report or label.

Negative debits followed by DB: This is similar to the previously described option. When a negative value is encountered and this option is selected, the number is followed by the characters *DB*.

Use ( ) around negative values: When this option is selected, a negative number will be enclosed by parentheses.

The above three options are available only in reports and in display-only form fields. A display-only field is one that cannot be edited or modified by the user. This option is selectable as an Edit option.

Show leading zeroes: The default for this option is *OFF*. Depending on the way your field is defined, small values may be preceded by zeroes. For example, the numbers 12 and 0000012 are equivalent. Leading zeroes are most frequently encountered in calculated fields. For example, a field that subtracts *accounts payable*, with a value of 54321, from *total assets*, with a value of 54399, would yield a calculated value of 00078. When you set the option to Show leading zeroes, 00078 will appear as the value of the field. When the option is off, the displayed value will be 78. Another instance is with the use of small decimal amounts. If a field is a decimal value, .89, for example, the value will be displayed as 00.89 when Show leading zeroes is on, and will be seen as .89 when the option is off.

Blanks for zero values: This option is similar to Show leading zeroes. In this case, setting the option On uses blanks to represent zero values. The two options, *Blanks for zero values* and *Show leading zeroes*, are related, because they are used to define the way that zeroes are displayed.

Financial format: When selected, the number in this field will be displayed as dollars and cents. Two decimal places will be supported, and a dollar sign will precede the number displayed.

Exponential format: This is particularly useful for scientific applications or in fields in which large numbers are used. Use of the exponential form can reduce the required width of a display field. For example, the number 1,300,000 will be listed as 1.3E6 (this means 1.3 × 10 to the sixth power). The E in the displayed number means exponential; the number following the E is the current power of 10 that is assigned to the displayed figure.

Four of the next five menu items, which appear in the bottom half of the Picture functions window, are the same for both character fields and numeric fields. The only fields that are not the same are the left align and right align fields.

The field options perform as follows:

Trim: This option tells the system how to deal with spaces that extend beyond the field entry. For example, if your first name field allowed 15 characters, and a first name typed into the field took only four, what is to be done with the other 11 positions allocated to that field?

The answer to this question becomes important, particularly when the data in such a field are to be searched for, analyzed, or displayed. If you were to prepare a report that listed FIRST_NAME and LAST_NAME, a field entry that was not trimmed would use all the space allocated to it. For example, in a database file that assigns 15 spaces for first name and 20 for last name, an untrimmed printout of first name and last name, with a comma separating the fields, would appear like this (periods denote blank spaces):

JOHN..........,SMITH..............

With FIRST_NAME and LAST_NAME trimmed, the same information will appear like this:

JOHN,SMITH

Field trimming becomes important if you want to search through a large database or if you plan to create many data entries. The reason for this is that each character or space in a file is stored as a bit of data. For a name like John Smith, which is only 9 characters in length, 35 characters are required in an untrimmed field. Multiply this by hundreds or thousands of records, and you can easily see how the amount of disk space required to store an untrimmed file can significantly exceed that used by trimmed fields.

An untrimmed field can also contribute to slowing down the performance of dBASE IV. When you are doing a search for a particular entry or character string, the system reads through each database record until it finds the one you are seeking. Reading through blank spaces takes as long as reading through fields filled with characters. In simple terms, it takes longer to read through records that have not used trimmed fields than it does to read through a record whose fields have been trimmed.

The major key to deciding whether or not a field should be trimmed is deciding whether the data entered into that field *should* (or *can*) be trimmed. Obviously, SS_NUMBER should not be trimmed, because all social security numbers utilize the same number of digits and trimming such a number would not make sense.

Trimming is an option that is also used to design reports and labels. When a field is trimmed, the data in two or more adjoining fields are usually easier to read (and more logical) than if the data were untrimmed. The above example of first and last names would appear more readable (and logically spaced) when used in a letter if trimmed than if they were untrimmed. A Picture function allows activation of the trimming of a field.

Alignment options: Alignment options are used to tell the system how to deal with information that is not as wide as the field into which the data are entered. The options for display are different in numeric than in character fields because the default method for display is different.

Left align: This option is available only in the numeric Picture functions window. The reason for this is that the default setting for this is right alignment. This means that the numbers start at the right edge of the field and move to the left. When this option is selected, numbers begin at the left margin of the field and move to the right. In most cases, left alignment is the alignment of choice.

Right align: This option is available only for character fields. The reason for this is that the standard default is to left align the contents of the field, that is, to print or display the text in the field starting from the left edge of the field. Selecting right align moves the text to the right side of the field, with the last letter of the data entry at the right edge of the field described, and the first character somewhere between the right margin and the left side of the field.

Center align: Center align is an option available for both character and numeric fields. When this option is selected, the data are centered inside the area defined to display the field.

Note that only one alignment can be assigned. The system does not allow you to assign more than one alignment to a particular field, because this would make no sense to the system and could not properly be printed out. To confirm this, you may try to turn on both the Left align (or Right align) and the Center align options. You will see that only one alignment setting is permitted.

About stretch: The next two options, Horizontal stretch and Vertical stretch, deal with the way dBASE IV displays data that are longer than the template designed for the field. Both types of stretch are related only to appearance when printed. They primarily relate to memo fields but could also apply to numeric fields in which totals exceed the length of the field template.

Horizontal stretch: Horizontal stretch allows characters that exceed the defined field width to continue to be printed. In essence, the field template is stretched horizontally across a page. This capability is useful for mail merge documents, in which text may be combined with data in a field, resulting in a text string that is much larger than that included in a field definition.

Vertical stretch: Vertical stretch is a different way of dealing with text or data that extend beyond the defined width of the field. In this case, a column is created that is the same width as the defined field. For example, if you define a field as 20 spaces wide, and 80 columns of text are to be printed in that field, you will end up with a column that is 20 characters wide and 4 lines high. The text at the end of each line is wrapped to the next line during printing if Vertical stretch is selected.

Edit options: The Edit options selection defines whether or not (and when) the contents of the field can be edited (Figure 4-35).

The Edit options are as follows:

Editing allowed: This option tells the system whether or not the data in the field can be modified by the user. In conjunction with the next option, you may define *when* the field may be edited. If you select *no*, you will be unable to address any of the other options in this window.

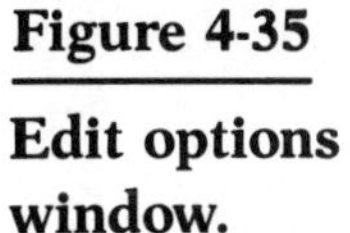

Figure 4-35

Edit options window.

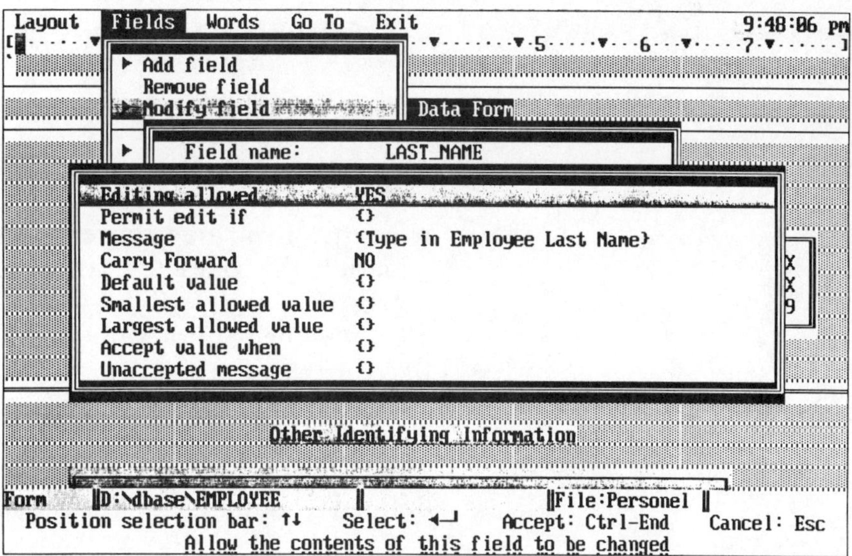

Permit edit if: This option allows you to tell the system when it is to allow the user to move the cursor into the field and edit the contents of the field. To use this option, you have to be able to state a logical condition that must be met before the system will allow the user to edit the contents of the field.

The actual syntax for such a logical statement is *Fieldname operator value*, in which fieldname refers to the contents of a selected field, operator is the test for equality, and value is the value to which you are comparing the contents of the field.

For example, if you wanted to enter collection data only for accounts that were over 90 days past due, you would create a field or fields for the data that is used by the collections department. Each such field would be set to check the value of a DAYSLATE field. If the value is greater than 89, editing of the various collection fields could be entered or modified. Such an equality statement for the test would look like this:

```
DAYSLATE>89
```

An alternative, yet essentially equivalent, statement could have been DAYSLATE=>89. The equality operators most commonly used are as follows:

>	Greater than
<	Less than
=	Equal to
<>	Not equal to
#	Not equal to
<=	Less than or equal to
=>	Greater than or equal to

Note that if you are using character strings to validate an equation, the character string must be put into quotation marks. For example, if you want to make a database of people *not named* Smith, your equality statement would look like this:

```
LAST_NAME<>"SMITH"
```

The system would then allow you to edit the fields that are defined as editable only if the last name is not Smith.

Numbers cannot be operated on in a character field. Thus, if you wanted to choose people whose zip codes were larger than 90000, you would normally be unable to unless you had set up the field as a numeric field. Thus, the expression ZIP_CODE>89999 would be invalid in a character field. The expression ZIP_CODE>"89999" would be correct, but cannot normally be treated as a number.

Note that a command that can be used to convert the contents of a character field to a number will allow you to treat the contents of a character field as numeric, although you would have to go into a programming mode to make this definition.

Equality statements can also be linked together, using a series of logical links. Two of the most frequently used logical links are .AND. and .OR. The two links must be preceded and followed by a dot. Their functions are fairly straightforward.

The following linked statements demonstrate the operation of the logical links:

```
LAST_NAME="SMITH".AND.
FIRST_NAME="JOHN"
```

The above expression allows editing for any record in which the first and last names were John Smith. Editing would not be permitted for any records other than those for John Smith.

```
LAST_NAME="SMITH" .OR.
FIRST_NAME="JOHN"
```

In this case, editing would be permitted for any person whose last name was *smith* and for anyone whose first name was *john*, as well as all people named John Smith.

Thus, the AND operator means that all conditions defined by the link must be satisfied if editing would be allowed. The OR operator allows editing if either of the conditions linked by the OR expression is true.

You can access the field names, logical operators, and functions by pressing the **Shift-F1** key combination. To select a fieldname, operator, or function, move the bar to the appropriate column and move the highlight to the appropriate item (or type the first character or characters so that dBASE IV can find a match).

Message: The Message option allows you to type a one-line message or instruction that appears at the bottom of the screen when the cursor is on this field. For example, a typical message for use with the social security number field might be something like "Type Social Security Number."

Carry Forward: The Carry forward option copies the value of the field in the previous record into the current field. This is useful in instances in which the contents of a field do not frequently change. For example, your company may typically make payroll entries department by department. To simplify data entry, you would have to type the department code number on only one record. All subsequent records will carry over the department number from the previous record. A new department number would have to be typed in only when the input operator has completed records for one department and goes on to another department.

Default value: The Default value is a value that is entered by the system whenever a new record is created. For example, if your company is located in California, you can set the system to use CA as the default entry for STATE.

Smallest allowed value: This field specifies the smallest numeric value allowed in this field.

Largest allowed value: This field specifies the largest numeric value allowed in this field.

In addition, when an entry falls outside the range specified by Smallest allowed value and Largest allowed value, the system prompts the user with the acceptable range.

Accept value when: This value assigns conditions that must be met for the entry to be accepted. This setting usually relates to the actual entry in the field, whereas Permit edit if usually relates to conditions that must be met in other fields in the data file. For example, a California company may want to build a database of employees who live outside of California. In this case, a condition like STATE< >"CA" would define the condition that must be satisfied if the entry is to be accepted.

However, this option contains a potential trap. The system will accept only data entries that meet the parameters you describe when you set up the form. If a user attempts to enter a value that does not meet the conditions you defined, the record cannot be saved. The only way to escape from the form is to type in a correct value or to **Esc** from data entry, which loses the information in the current record.

You should be certain that you do not want a record on any but those matching the parameters specified in this instance.

You may set up an "escape" value when you design your form. Such a value allows your data entry operators to continue editing. This would be done by adding an .OR. condition to your acceptable values. For example, if you were designing a database for employees in departments above 5555, you would set the statement to HIRE_DATE=> 5555. When the input operator comes to an employee in department 3333, the system would lock the user into this field until a correct value is received, unless he or she exits without saving the record. By adding an .OR. condition that the data operator uses if the true value is outside the acceptable range, the user can then add the record, although the field value is out of range. For example, if there is no department 99, you can use this value as the escape. The value required to accept data will then be HIRE_DATE=>5555.OR.=99. When you later attempt to evaluate your data, you can then exclude all records in which the value of this field =99.

Be careful to provide proper exclusion of incorrect values through the use of the Permit edit if option. Note also that this option works as new records are added to an existing database. It does not validate current data entries, which may be outside of the acceptable range.

Unaccepted message: In this option, you may enter a comment that is displayed at the bottom of the screen when an unacceptable entry is detected. An example may be in a field defined as alpha only. When a number is entered, the message, "Please type characters only" or "No numbers, stupid," or "Type 99 if value is not accepted" may be used as an error message when an unacceptable value is entered into the field.

The following two options are used for logical or memo fields.

Display as: This option allows you to define the way a memo field is displayed on your form. The two options are *Marker* and *Window*. A Marker displays the word *Memo* in the position at which the memo text will be printed or displayed on your form. It indicates that there may be text in this field, but the text will not display on screen and must be called up using the **Ctrl-Home** keys (or **F3** or **F4** keys).

A window can be defined for your field when you design your data entry/view form or your report form. When your window has been defined, memo text will be displayed within it. The window will scroll text that goes beyond the bottom border of your window. This is truly an on-screen window onto your text.

Border lines: The Border lines option allows you to select single lines, double lines, or a box using a specified character. One effective character for box drawing is the star (or asterisk), which can be selected from a window that appears on screen when this option is selected. The menu is seen in Figure 4-36.

Insert memory variable: This selection places a memory variable onto the form in the location at which the cursor is set. Memory variables can be thought of as placeholders that store the value or contents of a particular field, calculation, or the status of a system variable. The memory variable must have been defined before the form was used. The variable is defined from within the dot prompt or from a program. You will not be able to define a memory variable from within this form.

Once your options are made, they are accepted using the **Ctrl-End** key combination. If you try to escape from a menu without saving your changes, the system will ask if you really

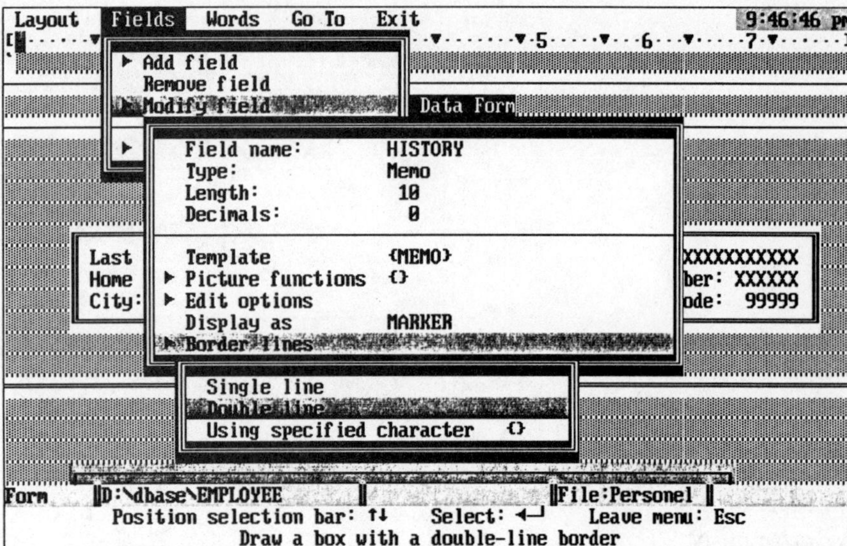

Figure 4-36

Character selection window.

want to *Cancel procedure?* (cancel changes made without saving them).

Add field, as mentioned earlier, is essentially the same as modify field, with one exception. You may create calculated fields from within the Add Field menu.

A calculated field performs a calculation based on entries made in another field or other fields on the form. For example, in an order processing data file, you may want a field that calculates a total cost for each item ordered—this will be the product of unit price and units ordered. You may also specify an operation to be performed on a single field (such as calculating sales tax).

Thus, for a stationer, one field may be CLIPBOX (the number of boxes of paper clips ordered), and a second field, CLIPPRICE (the per box price for paper clips). A calculated field, CLIPTOTAL, will show the total price for the current order of clips. The calculated field will be defined as follows:

CLIPTOTAL=CLIPBOX * CLIPPRICE

The * is the character used for multiplication. Although the reader should be familiar with mathematical operators

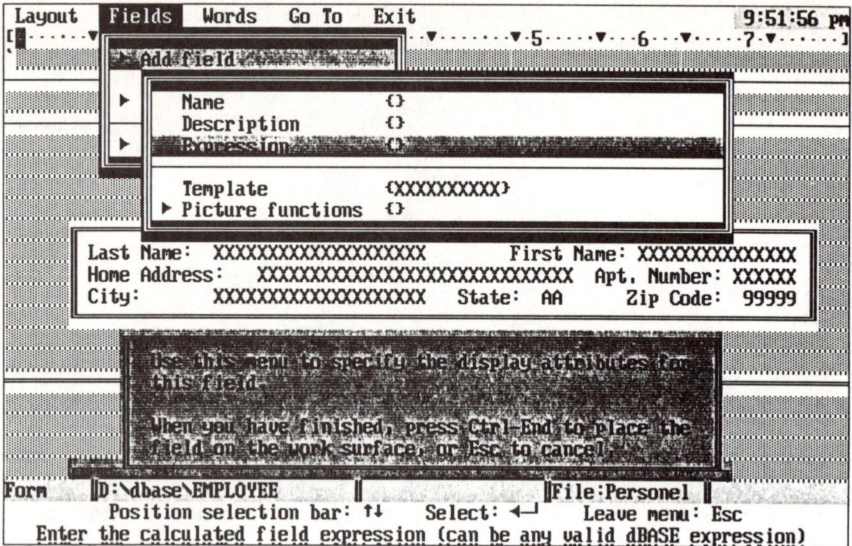

Figure 4-37

Calculated field definition window.

as used by computers, a quick review of less-than-intuitive operators is useful. The star (asterisk) (*) is used to denote multiplication. Two stars (**) indicate that a number is squared. The slash (/) is used to indicate division. Plus and minus are denoted by the traditional signs.

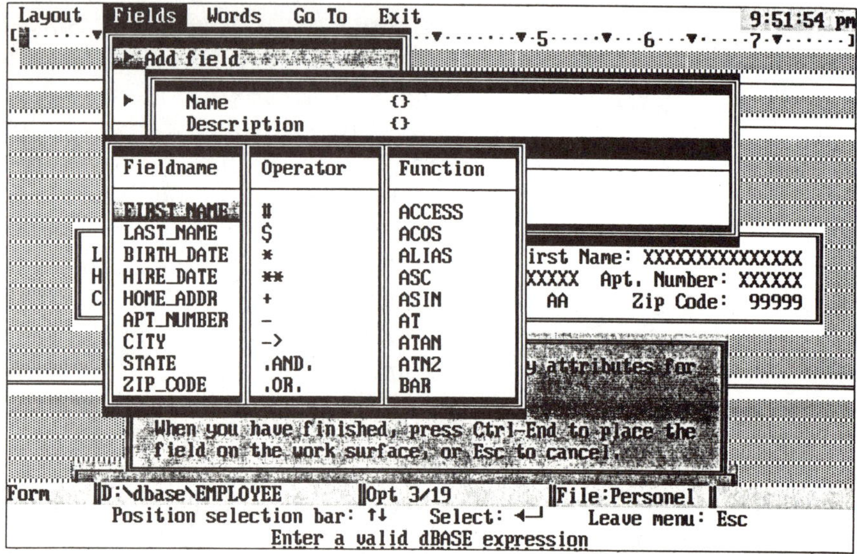

Figure 4-38

Expression Selection window.

In addition to traditional mathematical operators, a number of mathematical and scientific functions are also available. These may be seen from within the Calculated field design window by selecting *Expression* and touching **Shift-F1**. The Calculated field definition window is seen in Figure 4-37.

The options for selecting a fieldname, operator, and function for use in the calculated field expression are seen in Figure 4-38.

The other components, aside from the expression, are either self-explanatory or have been discussed previously and will not be further explained here.

The Words Menu

The Words menu, as seen earlier in this chapter, provides options for display and style of your text or for the form you are using. You already used the menu to modify the colors of your text and background. This menu is not only used in forms design, it is also used in report design, label design, memo field editing, and program and text file editing. Depending on which application invokes it, you may have a variety of functions that you can perform from within the menu.

These will be discussed in order here, although not all are available from within the Forms design function.

Style: This option is not available from within the Forms design function. It is used for print formatting, and is thus available in Reports design and Labels design functions.

Six text options are provided: Normal, Bold, Underline, Italic, Superscript, and Subscript. Only one style attribute may be assigned at a time. In addition to the predefined styles, you may also set up five additional styles. The configurable styles are defined by the user in the CONFIG.DB file. Printer control codes that are sent to the printer to start and stop the selected style are defined in the configuration file.

You may assign styles to selected text (by highlighting the text that you wish to style, then going to the Words, followed by selection of the Style option), or you may apply a style to text that is about to be typed by selecting the style, followed by the affected text.

Display: The Display option has already been explored. In this option you define the appearance of the foreground and background for your selected text or window areas.

Position: The Position option tells the system how to treat selected text. Text may be centered, or may be right or left positioned. Right positioning is not the same as right justification. In this type of positioning, the last character in the field is printed at the right margin of the selected field. The first characters are pushed to the left of the last characters, and may appear anywhere on the line—they normally will not begin at the left margin of the field.

Modify ruler: The Modify ruler option allows you to redefine the tab settings, margins, and paragraph indents. Selecting this option places the cursor on the ruler line. To indicate a new left margin, move the cursor to the desired position for the margin and type *[* (left bracket). To indicate the new right margin, position the cursor on the desired right margin and type *]* (right bracket).

A paragraph indent is used for the first line of text in a paragraph. To set an indent, position the cursor to the position for the indent and press # (the number sign or pound key).

Evenly spacing tab stops is accomplished with the = key. When the key is pressed, if you are using unequal tab stops or no tab stops, the system prompts for the number of spaces between tab stops. Once this number is entered, the system automatically places tab stops in the desired positions on the ruler line. The system counts spaces as tenths of an inch, and defaults to eight spaces (8/10 inch) for each tab stop on the ruler line. Settings are saved using the **Ctrl-End** key combination. An alternate way to save the ruler line is by touching **ENTER**, followed by the **DnArrow**.

Hide Ruler: The Hide ruler command removes the ruler from the top of the design form, although the settings remain in effect. A ruler is hidden so that you can get a better idea of how your form will look. In most cases, there is little reason to hide the ruler line.

Enable automatic indent: This option tells the system that whenever **ENTER** is pressed, the following line will be considered to be the first line in a new paragraph and will be indented. This option is not available from within Forms design.

Add line: The Add line option adds a line at the location of the cursor. In most cases, this option is extraneous, because the same function can be accomplished by typing **Ctrl-n**.

Remove line: As above, this option deletes the line on which the cursor is currently located. The same function can be performed using the **Ctrl-y** combination.

Insert page break: This option is also not available inside this function. However, it is useful for printed reports or labels, and when activated forces the printer to eject the current sheet of paper. Depending on the printer, the next page will either be loaded or the user will have to feed the paper into the machine (or a laser printer will eject the page and prepare to accept the text for the next page).

Write/read text file: This option actually gives you two choices.

Write selection to file allows you to take the highlighted text and write it to a file on disk. The saved file can then be imported into, or appended to, another data file or form design. If you have selected only one character (the one the cursor was sitting on when you went to the Words menu), the entire form layout or text will be written to a file.

Read text from file allows you to copy text from another file into your form at the location of the cursor. The data from the selected screen are transferred to your screen as if they were typed in.

The Go To Menu

The Go To menu is useful for quickly moving the cursor to a desired location (Figure 4-39).

The options perform as follows:

Go to line number: This option prompts you to indicate a line on the form. Once that number is selected, the cursor will be moved to that line.

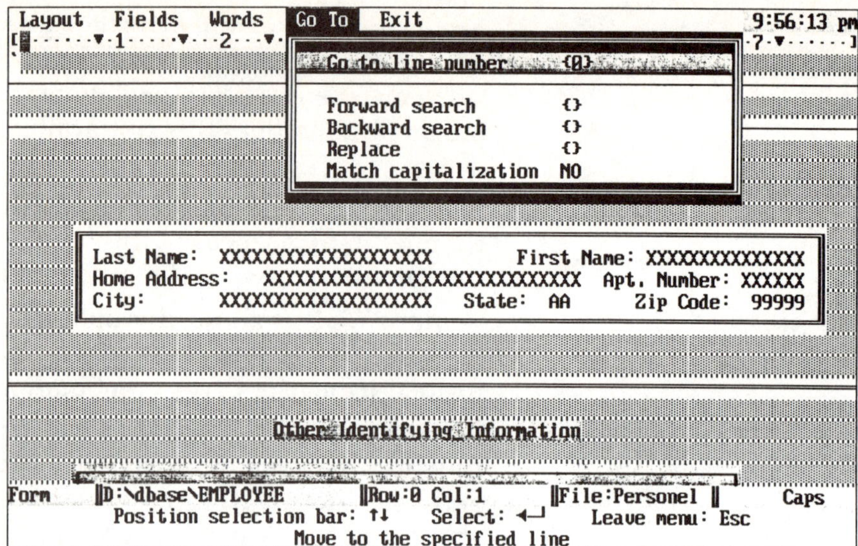

Figure 4-39

The Go To menu.

Forward search: The system prompts for a search string. When the string is selected, the system searches for the first match. Be careful not to use too short a string, or the cursor may stop in an area different from the one you had in mind. This search is from the top of the form down. If the field or data that you want to find are located *above* the cursor, this type of search will not find the first occurrence you are looking for. Thus, it is good practice to return to the top of form (using the **Home** key) before doing a forward search.

Backward search: A backward search is essentially the opposite of a forward search. This type of search is made from the cursor toward the beginning of the field. Again, if the string you are looking for occurs below the cursor, you will not find the desired string. For this reason, you probably will want to go to the end of your file (using the **End** key) before doing a backward search.

Replace: Replace replaces a selected string with a different text string. It is a top-down search. The function is actually a search and replace operation; it searches for the desired string and replaces it with a different string. When a match for the search field is found, the system asks if you wish to Replace the string as defined (respond by touching the *r* key), Skip the string and move to the next match (respond by touching the *s* key), All (replace all occurrences of the string without prompting by the system) (respond by touching the *a* key), or Quit the replace function (using the **Esc** key). After replacements have been completed, the system indicates how many replacements were made.

Match capitalization: When this option is on, the system looks for a character string that not only matches character for character, but that also matches case by case. For example, if you wanted to find the word *Name* on your form and set up the search for the word *name*, you would be able to find each occurrence of the word no matter how the case appeared (name, Name, NAME, or any combination of upper- and lowercase). If you selected Match capitalization, the current selection would find only matches that were all lowercase.

One other point should be made about capitalization. In Replace, the case of found characters will be preserved. Thus, if you were converting your form to Spanish, you may set up Replace to search for Last Name and replace it with Apellido (Spanish for last name). If the search finds the words *last name*, it would replace it with *apellido*. On the other hand, if it finds *Last Name*, the replacement would be *Apellido*. Similarly, if it found *LAST NAME*, the replacement would be *APELLIDO*.

The Exit Menu

The Exit menu gives you two options: to Save changes and exit or to Abandon changes and exit. Selecting either one gets you out of the form and back to the Control Center. If you choose to Save changes and exit, the form will be recompiled by the system (that is, the dBASE code describing your form will be generated), followed by an exit to the Control Center.

If you wish to Save changes and not exit, or to save your changes to a file with a different name, this function is accessible from the Layout menu.

If you choose to Abandon changes and exit, you will be returned to the Control Center with any changes made following your last save procedure ignored and lost from the system. You should be sure that you want to abandon changes and exit, because you will not be able to retrieve your changes and return to the form as it was before you exited.

You may also Abandon changes and exit using the **Esc** key. The system asks you to confirm that you want to abandon the operation before it returns you to the Control Center.

Before concluding this chapter, however, it would be useful to complete the design of your form. The bottom half of the form, left as it is, is plain and uninteresting. Add a box around the Employment Data section and give it an interesting background. A bright white foreground with a blue background is pleasing to many people. Use this combination if you are designing for a color system, or use an interesting foreground/background combination if you are using or designing for a monochrome system. The Employee History label is also given a color treatment—in this case bright white foreground and red background.

In addition to the more interesting foreground and background treatments, messages have been added to the fields (through the Fields-Modify Field-Edit options menu). Further, some changes in templates were also made, as listed below.

Field Name	*Message*
LAST_NAME	Type in employee last name
FIRST_NAME	Type in employee first name and initial
HOME_ADDR	Type street number and street name
APT_NUMBER	Type apartment or unit number
CITY	Type name of city here
STATE	Type state abbreviation here [Template: AA, Picture Functions: A!, Default value "CA" (may change, depending on state you are in)]
ZIP_CODE	Type five digit zip code (Template: 99999)
BIRTH_DATE	Type birth date here
SS_NUMBER	Type social security number here (Template: 999-99-9999)
MOTHER_MN	Type employee's mother's maiden name
HIRE_DATE	Type employee hire date

Field Name	*Message*
EMP_NUMB	Type employee number
DEPT_NUMB	Type department number here
USCITIZEN	Is the employee a U.S. Citizen? Y(es) or N(o) Note: Template changed to Y; field description changed to U.S. Citizen? (Y/N):
SALARY_GRD	Type employee's current salary grade
UNION_MBR	Is the employee a union member? Y(es) or N(o) Note: Template changed to Y; field description changed to union member? (Y/N):

Finally, save this version of the form, calling it PERSONEL.

The techniques described in this chapter are useful for designing effective forms to be used both for data entry and for viewing your data. In addition, many of the drop down menus that are used in other Control Center columns were described.

Data Entry and Modification

In previous chapters, you designed a database, built the forms for data entry and viewing, and described the validation and message system for data entry. This chapter discusses the methods used for data entry and modification of data that have already been entered.

The form that you designed in the last chapter will demonstrate the difference between the standard data entry screen normally provided by the system and the one that you custom designed. If you are not currently in dBASE IV, please start the program and select PERSONEL as the file on which you want to do data modification/addition.

To do this, type *pers* (actually, fewer letters were required to select file) and press the **ENTER** key. Alternatively, you may have moved the cursor to the file name (the **UpArrow** would have brought you to this file, because it is the last one in the catalog). You can then tell the system that you want to display the data.

A faster way to get to the Edit or Browse screens is by highlighting the file name (or typing the first letter[s] of the name until it is highlighted) and pressing **F2**.

Browse and Edit

The Browse screen and the Edit screen are selected using the **F2** key. The main difference between the two is that the Browse screen shows you a full page of records (the number of lines displayed varies, depending on the graphics mode selected). The edit mode shows you a single record.

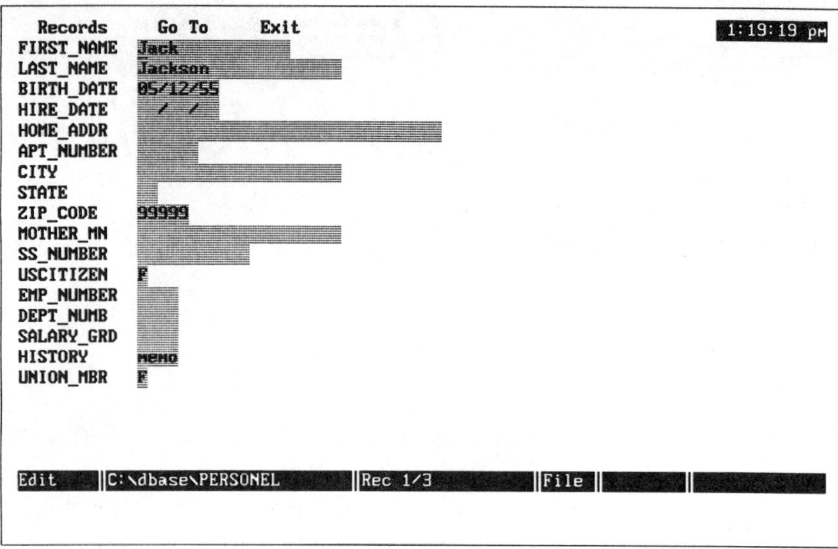

Figure 5-1

The Edit screen.

Data in both screens can be edited. The Edit screen, when selected from within the Data column, is a simple, relatively unformatted screen that matches that done by Quick layout from within Forms design. For this data file, the Edit screen will appear as shown in Figure 5-1.

The Browse screen, in which the two entries that were moved from the data file used to create PERSONEL are displayed, has each record on its own line, as seen in Figure 5-2.

The **F2** key toggles between Edit and Browse, and can be used in areas other than those called up by the Data and Forms menus. Navigation in each screen and the menu options will be discussed later. However, for now, you can use the **F2** key to see the difference between the two screens. Touch the **Esc** key to return you to the Control Center. Next, to see the difference in the standard Edit screen and the designed Edit form, move the cursor to the Forms column and highlight the "PERSONEL" form. Next,

Press: **F2**

to display the data. (You could also have pressed **ENTER** and selected Display data to bring you to the Edit screen.)

The top half of the Edit screen is shown in Figure 5-3. Again, to toggle between the Edit screen and the Browse screen, use the **F2** key.

```
Records     Fields     Go To     Exit                              1:19:42 pm

FIRST_NAME    LAST_NAME         BIRTH_DATE  HIRE_DATE  HOME_ADDR
Jack          Jackson           05/12/55     /  /
John          Johnson           07/16/48     /  /
                                  /  /       /  /

Browse  |C:\dbase\PERSONEL        |Rec 1/3          |File |
                          View and edit fields
```

Figure 5-2

The Browse screen.

One additional advantage to using a designed form is that the templates and prompts you have designed are applied to ease the input process and to monitor data integrity. To use a form, select it from the Forms column, then move the cursor back to the Data column and press **F2** to load your Edit (or Browse) screen.

```
Records     Go To     Exit                                  1:34:27 pm

                       Employee Data Form

                   Employee Name and Address

  Last Name:  Jackson                        First Name: Jack
  Home Address:                                 Apt. Number:
  City:                           State:          Zip Code:   99999

                  Other Identifying Information

  Birth Date: 05/12/55   Social Security Number:      -  -    0
  Mother's Maiden Name:

Edit    |C:\dbase\PERSONEL        |Rec 1/3          |File |
                     Type in Employee Last Name
```

Figure 5-3

The PERSONEL screen design for editing data.

For the purposes of this chapter, you will be working with the Edit window using the PERSONEL screen design but accessing data from the Forms column. The Browse screen is the same whether called from Data or Form.

Using the Edit Screen

Press: **Esc**

to move the cursor back to the Control Center. Next, move the cursor to the Forms column and highlight "PERSONEL."

Press: **F2**

to tell the system that you want to edit data. If the Browse screen appears, press **F2** a second time to bring up the Edit screen as seen in Figure 5-3.

The Edit screen provides a straightforward approach to data entry or modification. To enter the data, simply type the appropriate data in each field. Pressing the **ENTER** key or **Tab** key tells the system that you have completed entry into that field, and move you on to the next field. To move backward, the **Shft Tab** combination brings you to the previous field. In addition to **ENTER** and **Tab**, the **DnArrow** and **F4** keys move you into the next field, whereas the **UpArrow** and **F3** keys move you back one field at a time.

Within a field, the **Home** key brings you to the beginning of your field. The **End** key, as would be expected, brings you to the end of your defined field. This may not be of much value in short fields. However, if you are editing a long field, or a memo, the ability to quickly jump from the beginning to the end can be quite useful.

The **PgUp** key moves the display up one screen at a time, or to the previous record, if you are not already in the first record. The **PgDn** key brings you down one screen at a time, or to the next record if you are at the end of a record when you press the key.

Basically, the above keys, in addition to the required alphanumeric keys for data entry, are the ones that you will be using most while in data entry.

The Edit screen provides additional information about your record. An information line near the bottom of the screen indicates that you are currently in Edit mode. It tells you the name and path of the data file that your data are being read from or written into. It also gives you the record number, and how many records have already been entered. Further information includes key status. The box at the right of the line will show when Insert, CapsLock, or NumLock is active.

Edit and Browse

The Edit screen menu line provides three main selections, *Records*, *Go To*, and *Exit*. This line may not be visible if the designed form began on the top line of the Form design screen. If the menu lines are not shown, they may be made visible using the **F10** key or by pressing **Alt-R** (for the Records menu), **Alt-G** (for the Go To menu), or **Alt-E** (for the Exit menu). These three option boxes are your interface with the system for data entry and review.

At times you might not want the options visible to the casual (or nonexpert) user. In these instances you may intentionally design your form to cover these items; although they will still pop up when the right keys are pressed (the **Alt-** keys or the **F10** key), they will not be visible unless the right keystrokes are used.

Records

The Records menu provides you with options for modification of existing records or addition of new records. This menu is also available from within the Query function. Not all options in this menu are available at all times, and the selections may change as you are using them. The following discussions will illustrate the changes that appear from within the Records menu. When initially called up, the Records menu will appear as shown in Figure 5-4.

Starting from the top of the menu list, the options are as follows:

Undo change to record: This item is toggled on and off, depending on whether a change has been made to the record on which you are presently working. If you just entered the Edit screen and have not made any changes to the record,

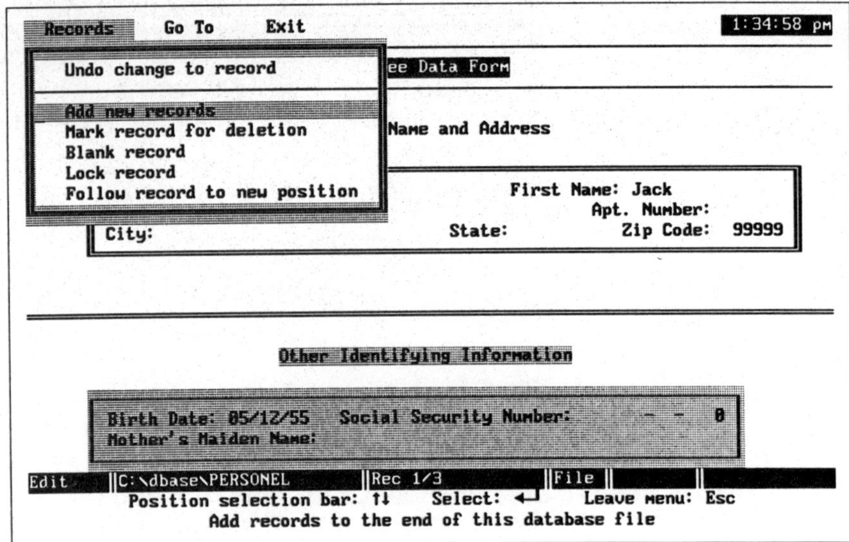

Figure 5-4

The Records menu.

this option should not be highlighted, and you will be unable to select it.

To see how it works,

Type: **Esc**

to bring you back to the Edit screen. You should be at the first record, the one for Jack Jackson. Using the **Tab,** the **F4** key, or the **DnArrow**, move to the Home Address field.

Type: *1234 Fifth Avenue*

Now, return to the Records screen. The option Undo change to record will be highlighted. Type *U* or move your cursor to the field and press **ENTER** to select the option. The address that has been added will be removed from the screen.

It is important to know *when* this works. The system will save any changes that you make *within* a single record. If you go from one record that you have changed to another record, you will be unable to undo the changes made to the previous record. Therefore, you should decide whether you want to retain changes made to a record either before you move to another record or when you are completing the data in the last field on a form, because once completed, the system automatically moves to the next record, saving your changes.

Additionally, it is useful to know that the system remembers changes made in each record, or following an Undo of changes made to the current record. Therefore, subsequent changes to a record can also be undone.

Add new records: The Add new records option moves the cursor to the end of your file. The cursor is placed in the same field in your new record as it is when you select the Add new records option. Thus, if you were at the last field in your record when you chose Add new records, your cursor may be placed in the last field in a new record, requiring you to move to the first field if you wanted to fill in the record in order from the top down. When selecting this option make sure your cursor is at the top of your current record to be certain that you are moved into the beginning of a blank record.

Mark record for deletion/Clear deletion mark: This selection is a toggled option. It can be used to remove (delete) a record from your database. However, it is useful to note that merely selecting the option for deletion *does not delete the record.*

To delete the record, you have to exit the Browse or Edit screen and return to the Database design screen, finally selecting the Organize menu and selecting an option to erase marked records. In other words, many steps must be taken to delete a file from your database—deletion of a record is not something that can be done casually (unless you choose Blank record, the next option; however, Blank record can be undone using the Undo changes option before moving to the next record).

Deleting a record completely removes it from your database. This is useful when you have many records to remove. Blanking a record effectively removes the data from the record but still leaves an empty record in your database.

By leaving blank records in your database you are, in effect, wasting time and space. For any process involving a search to locate data, the system will have to read through the blank record, even though it contains no data. The disk space used for a blank record is the same as that used for one filled with data, because dBASE IV allocates space for each record that represents the size of each field in the record—whether filled in or not.

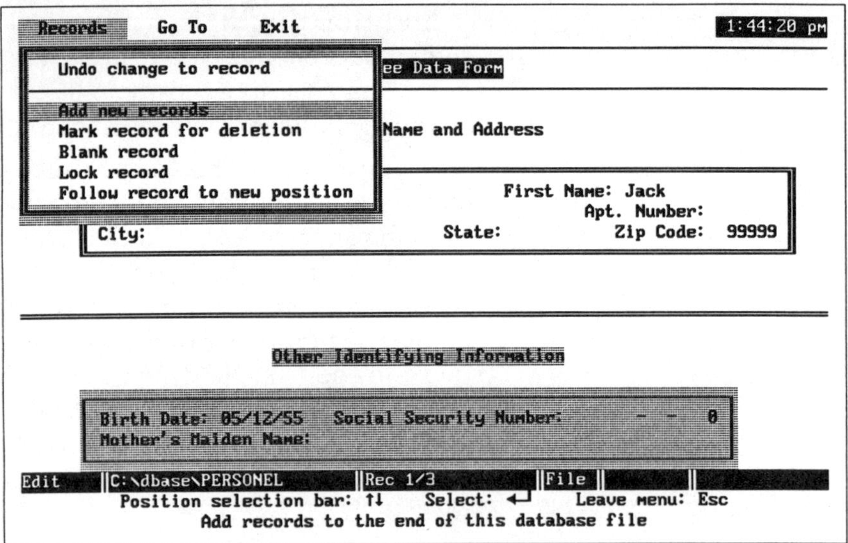

Figure 5-5

Mark record for deletion.

Thus, you may blank a record if you are going to put other data into the now blank record; if not, it is best to delete it.

As mentioned earlier, Mark record for deletion and Clear deletion mark are toggled fields. If a record is already marked for deletion, Clear deletion mark will appear in this position on your Records menu screen. On the other hand, if a record has not been marked for deletion, Mark record for deletion will appear. Mark record for deletion appears as it does on Figure 5-5. Figure 5-6 shows the toggle, Clear deletion mark.

To see how to delete a record, let's delete the first record in your database, the one for Jack Jackson.

First, be sure that you are in Record #1. Although you can get there from within the Edit menu, the fastest way is probably using the **Ctrl-PgUp** key combination (navigation keys will be presented shortly).

Press: **Alt-R**

or use the **F10** key and cursor to Records, if you are not already there. Next,

Type: *m*

to select Mark record for deletion.

Of course, you could also have moved the cursor to the Mark record for deletion option and selected it with the

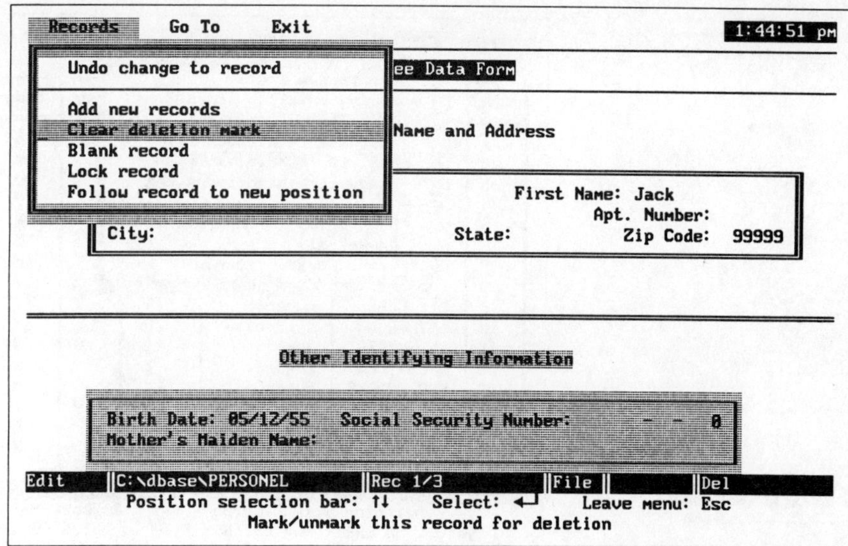

Figure 5-6

Clear deletion mark.

ENTER key. Typing the first letter for the option is faster, however.

Next, exit from this menu by selecting Exit from the menu line and then return to the Data column, and go into the Modify structure/order option for the current file. As with many operations in dBASE IV, this can be done in more than one way.

You can move the cursor to highlight "PERSONEL," press **ENTER**, and select Modify structure/order, or you can

Press: **Shift-F2**

The Modify structure/order screen normally comes up with the Organize menu active (Figure 5-7).

The last option, Erase marked records, tells the system to go through your database file and remove all records that are marked for deletion. In this case, only one record was marked for deletion. This command repacks your database, and is equivalent to the PACK command from the dot prompt.

Once this option is selected, the system goes through the database and removes the marked records. It then rebuilds the indexes that were specified when you designed your data structure, or one that was redefined prior to the reorganization of your file.

Sorting and indexing are discussed later in this book.

```
Layout  Organize  Append  Go To  Exit                          1:48:22 pm
                                                     Bytes remaining:   3831
 ▶ Create new index
 ▶ Modify existing index
   Order records by index
   Activate .NDX index file
   Include .NDX index file
   Remove unwanted index tag

   Sort database on field list
   Unmark all records
   Erase marked records

Num  F                                    ec   Index
 1   F                                          N
 2   L                                          Y
 3   B                                          Y
 4   H                                          Y
 5   H                                          N
 6   A                                          N
 7   C                                          N
 8   S                                          Y
 9   ZIP_CODE     Numeric       5     0         Y
10   MOTHER_MN    Character    20               N
11   SS_NUMBER    Numeric      11     0         N
12   USCITIZEN    Logical       1               N
13   EMP_NUMBER   Numeric       4     0         N
14   DEPT_NUMB    Numeric       4     0         Y
15   SALARY_GRD   Character     4               Y
16   HISTORY      Memo         10               N

Database  C:\dbase\PERSONEL          Field 1/17
     Position selection bar: ↑↓    Select: ◄┘     Leave menu: Esc
  Select an index tag or .NDX file by which to order this database file
```

Figure 5-7

Organize menu.

When you select Erase marked records, the system gives you *one last chance* to change your mind, as seen in Figure 5-8.

Type: *Y*

When you tell the system *Yes*, it will repack your database.

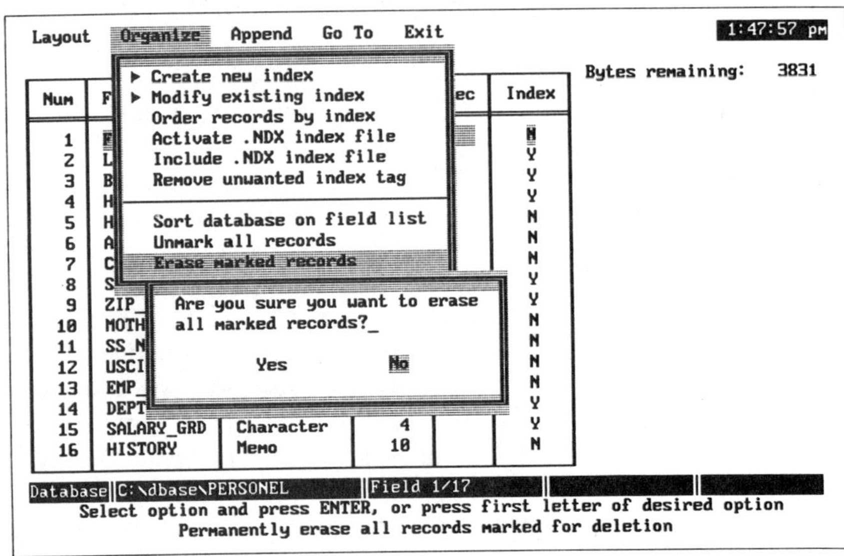

Figure 5-8

Last chance to cancel erasure of marked records.

A window will pop up on screen informing you of the progress it is making in repacking your data. Once completed, you will be brought back into the Design window.

Now, exit from the Design screen via the Exit menu. Tell the system to Save changes and exit when prompted, and you will be returned to the Control Center. Now, return to the Forms column, select the PERSONEL input file, and press **F2** to bring you back to the Edit screen. You will see that the first record is now that of John Johnson; the original record #1, Jack Jackson, has indeed been deleted from your database.

Now, bring up the Records menu by pressing **Alt-R**.

Blank record: This option has been discussed briefly. Basically, what this does is clear the contents of all the fields on the current record. It is an alternative to record deletion and may be useful in instances in which you wish to *both* remove a record and add a new one. Thus, in effect, you are erasing a slate, only to immediately refill it.

In fact, the analogy between a record and a blackboard or slate is an accurate one. Each record in a file can be thought of as a blackboard. And although the system does not prevent you from blanking any, or all, records in a file, doing so is inefficient unless new data are rewritten onto the now blank records. The reason, as indicated previously, is that dBASE IV has to look through all the blackboards to find files or perform its various functions. And it takes almost as long to read a blank board as it takes to read one filled with data. Thus, it is much more sensible to delete any records that will not contain new data than it is to leave blank records in a file.

A blanked record, and any data that are input onto such a record, can be unblanked; that is, the original record can be restored by using the Undo change to record command, as long as the following conditions are met.

First, you will not have moved to another record after blanking the current record. Second, you did not already Undo the change to the current record.

Although any data that existed prior to blanking of a record can be expected to be restorable using the Undo change to record option, it is always best to be *certain* before blanking a record that it should be blanked. Although Undo is a reliable option, if the Records menu is accessed with the **Alt-R** key combination, rather than using the **F10** key, you should operate under the assumption that once blanked, a record *cannot* be restored.

Lock record: The Lock record option relates primarily to use of a database file in a multiuser environment. When this option is selected, the system will not allow any other users to make changes to it while it is being edited by the current user.

In the current example, the name and data relating to an employee does not change very often—certainly not often enough to worry about more than one data operator making modifications to the file at once. But in a business that may be running an order entry database, it is likely that the orders for one day may be entered by many order entry operators. It is similarly likely that a customer may have placed many orders in a single day, or that a customer may have had a number of different departments simultaneously ordering different merchandise. Thus, the likelihood that more than one user may attempt to modify an order update file (or perhaps an accounts receivable file or automatic invoice generation file) simultaneously could be significant. In this case, if two or more operators were working on the same file at once, and neither knew that the other was making changes, it is possible that some changes to a file could be lost because of the collision between the two files.

When a record is locked, it prevents other users from making any changes to it until the record is saved (by moving to another record or exiting the Browse/Edit function). In a single-user environment, this option is of little importance, and appears on the Records menu only when a new record is being added. Once the record is stored, however, the option is no longer selectable.

Follow record to new position: dBASE IV is designed to automatically index files as they are entered. Indexing of a record, in essence, means that the record is placed in order, alphabetically or numerically, depending on the data type.

To best see how this works, in addition to viewing the extra menu options available in Browse, switch to the Browse screen. To do this

Press: **F2**

```
 Records    Fields    Go To    Exit                              4:57:15 pm
FIRST_NAME     LAST_NAME            BIRTH_DATE HIRE_DATE HOME_ADDR
John           Johnson              02/27/46   06/12/82  3712 Leimert Ave.
Samuel         Samuelson            01/24/11   12/12/25  3254 Centinela Blvd.
Robert         Robertson            07/12/50   01/14/80  4802 Santa Tomato
Alan           Alanovich            06/06/55   03/30/83  99112 Ventura Blvd.

Browse  C:\dbase\PERSONEL      Rec 1/4        File
                        View and edit fields
```

Figure 5-9

Browse screen.

You will see that the menu bar at the top of the screen also shows the Fields option. You should note that the format for Browse allows you to see many files on screen at one time. A few records have been added, as shown in Figure 5-9.

Please add the data and records, as shown in Figures 5-10 through 5-13. At this point, the records are all in the order

Figure 5-10

Johnson data.

```
 Records    Go To    Exit                                        4:39:45 pm
FIRST_NAME  John
LAST_NAME   Johnson
BIRTH_DATE  02/27/46
HIRE_DATE   06/12/82
HOME_ADDR   3712 Leimert Ave.
APT_NUMBER  17C
CITY        Santa Clara
STATE       CA
ZIP_CODE    90909
MOTHER_MN   Shapiro
SS_NUMBER     321428291
USCITIZEN   T
EMP_NUMBER  9811
DEPT_NUMB    128
SALARY_GRD  119
HISTORY     memo
UNION_MBR   T

Edit    C:\dbase\PERSONEL      Rec 1/5        File
```

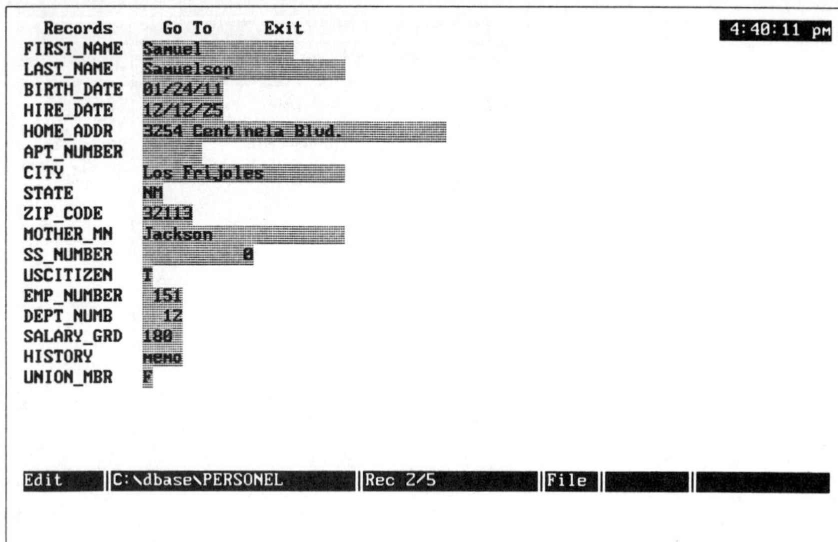

Figure 5-11

Samuelson data.

in which they were entered into the system, as can be seen by the order of the items in figure 5-10.

Although indexing is covered later, it is useful to see how these data can be indexed and how Follow record to new position works.

Figure 5-12

Robertson data.

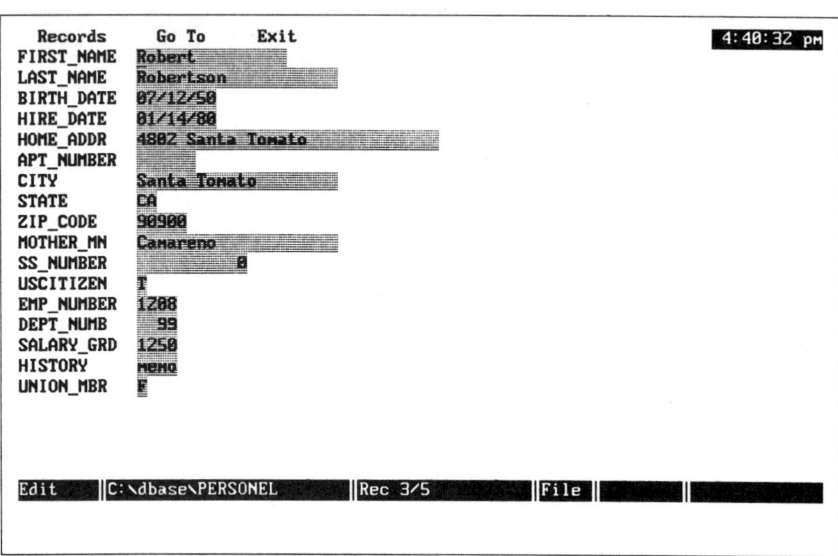

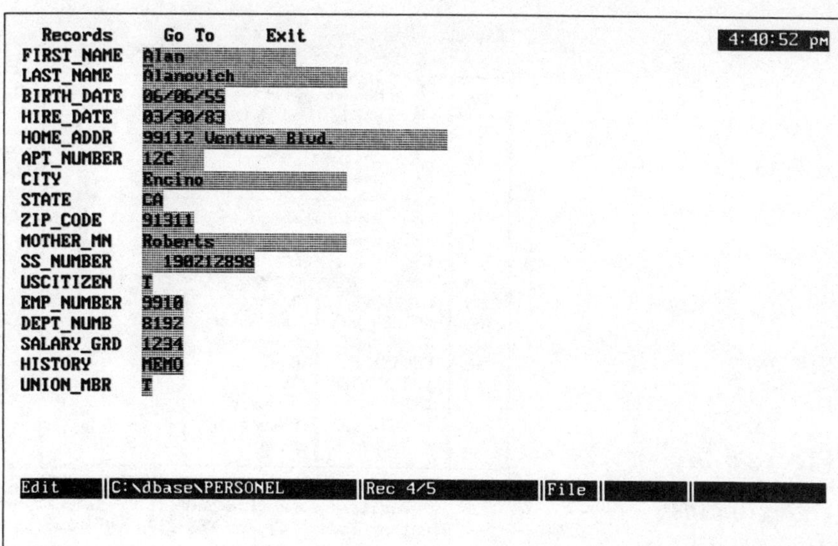

Figure 5-13

Alanovich data.

Exit from the Browse screen and return to the Data column in the Control Center. With "Personel" highlighted,

Press: **Shift-F2**

to go to the Modify database structure screen. Next, select Order records by index. This tells the system to put the records into order based on an index that you defined when you set up the system, or added later. Once this item is selected,

Type: *L*

to move the highlight to the "LAST_NAME" field. You could, of course, have moved the highlight to the field. By now, you are also familiar with selecting an option by typing the letters of that option. Your selected index should appear as shown in Figure 5-14.

Press: **ENTER**

to select this index, and the system will index the records in the database.

Now,

Press: **F2**

to go to the Browse/Edit window. If the screen shows the Edit

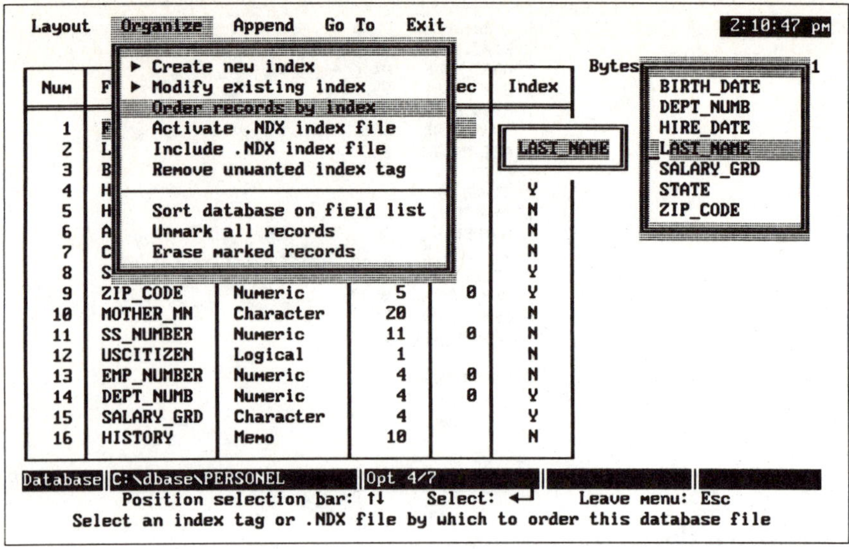

Figure 5-14

Index on last name field.

window, press **F2** again to bring up the Browse window (Figure 5-15).

You will notice that the last names are, indeed, in alphabetic rather than numeric order. By using the **UpArrow** and **DnArrow** keys, you can move from record to record. You

Figure 5-15

Data indexed by last name.

Records Fields Go To Exit 4:42:53 pm

FIRST_NAME	LAST_NAME	BIRTH_DATE	HIRE_DATE	HOME_ADDR
Alan	Alanovich	06/06/55	03/30/83	99112 Ventura Blvd.
John	Johnson	02/27/46	06/12/82	3712 Leimert Ave.
Robert	Robertson	07/12/50	01/14/80	4802 Santa Tomato
Samuel	Samuelson	01/24/11	12/12/25	3254 Centinela Blvd.

Browse C:\dbase\PERSONEL Rec 4/4 File

View and edit fields

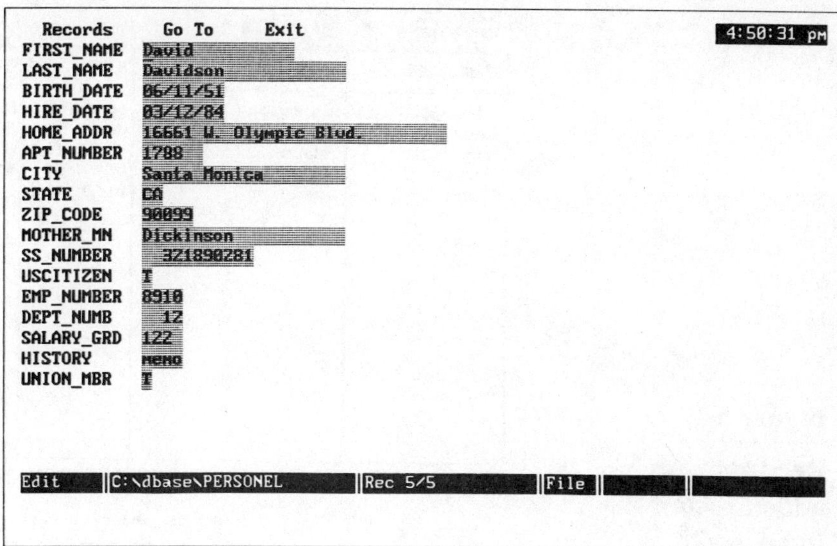

Figure 5-16

Davidson data.

should quickly notice that the number of the record, as indicated on the information line at the bottom of your screen, is unchanged—only the order in which the records are displayed has changed.

Now we return to what Follow record to new position does. Move the cursor to the line after Samuelson. The system will prompt = >Add new records?(Y/N).

Type: *Y*

to tell the system that you want to add records to your file. You will add a record for David Davidson. After you enter the data for each field, use the **Tab** or **ENTER** key to move to the next field. If you have made a mistake and want to go to a previous field, use the **F3** key. Enter the data, as shown in Figure 5-16.

Once you have completed entering the data for Davidson, the record should be placed in its correct position within the index, as seen in Figure 5-17.

This is what Follow record to new position does. The previous text described a long way to set up a rather simple concept. When this option is selected (and the default is *yes*), and you add or change a record, the *next* record will be the next one in the normal index order. For example, you may

Records Fields Go To Exit 5:01:32 pm

FIRST_NAME	LAST_NAME	BIRTH_DATE	HIRE_DATE	HOME_ADDR
Alan	Alanovich	06/06/55	03/30/83	99112 Ventura Blvd.
David	Davidson	06/11/51	03/12/84	16661 W. Olympic
John	Johnson	02/27/46	06/12/82	3712 Leimert Ave.
Robert	Robertson	07/12/50	01/14/80	4802 Santa Tomato
Samuel	Samuelson	01/24/11	12/12/25	3254 Centinela Blvd.

Browse | C:\dbase\PERSONEL | Rec 4/5 | File

View and edit fields

Figure 5-17

Records with added record in index order.

be typing in a list of new employees. You have already alphabetized the list of employees by last name and are going to be entering them into the database.

Following the entry of each record into the database, the system rebuilds the index. In a large database, this can be a time-consuming job, because it must realphabetize (or otherwise reorder) your indexed field. By moving the record to its new position, you are placing the next record *closer* to its correct position than you would be if you were merely placing it at the end of a data file. In most cases, it is preferable to leave this option selected as *yes*.

Fields

The Fields menu is available only from within the Browse screen. It allows you to control the way you will view the displayed fields and provides some control over how you will modify the contents of the fields. The four options are as follows:

Lock fields on left: This option is useful for browsing or editing files that have many fields—records that, when displayed on the Browse menu, are wider than the screen.

In the current example, for instance, you may want to up-

Records Fields Go To Exit 5:08:12 pm

FIRST_NAME	LAST_NAME	USCITIZEN	EMP_NUMBER	DEPT_NUMB	SALARY_GRD
Alan	Alanovich	T	9910	8192	1234
David	Davidson	T	8910	12	122
John	Johnson	T	9811	128	119
Robert	Robertson	T	1208	99	1250
Samuel	Samuelson	T	151	12	180

Browse | C:\dbase\PERSONEL | Rec 4/5 | File

View and edit fields

Figure 5-18

Browse with two fields locked on left.

date salary grades, following a number of promotions of employees in the company. To do this easily, it would be valuable if you could see the name of the employee on the screen, alongside the salary grade. You can easily see that pressing the **F4** key to move the SALARY_GRD field quickly moves both FIRST_NAME and LAST_NAME off the screen. However, when you use the Lock fields on left selection, you can easily get a screen that appears as shown in Figure 5-18.

A locked field, then, is one that does not move when you scroll the other fields in your data file. Setting up the locked fields in this example is easy. First, pop up the Fields menu using **Alt-F** or **F10** followed by **Alt-F** (or moving the cursor to the Fields menu). The Fields menu will pop up (Figure 5-19). Next, select Lock fields on left. This field should already be highlighted, so just

Press: **Enter**

The system will then ask for the number of fields you wish to remain stationary, as seen in Figure 5-19.

Type: ***2* ENTER**

The system will then lock the leftmost two fields, allowing you to scroll through the file with the locked fields staying

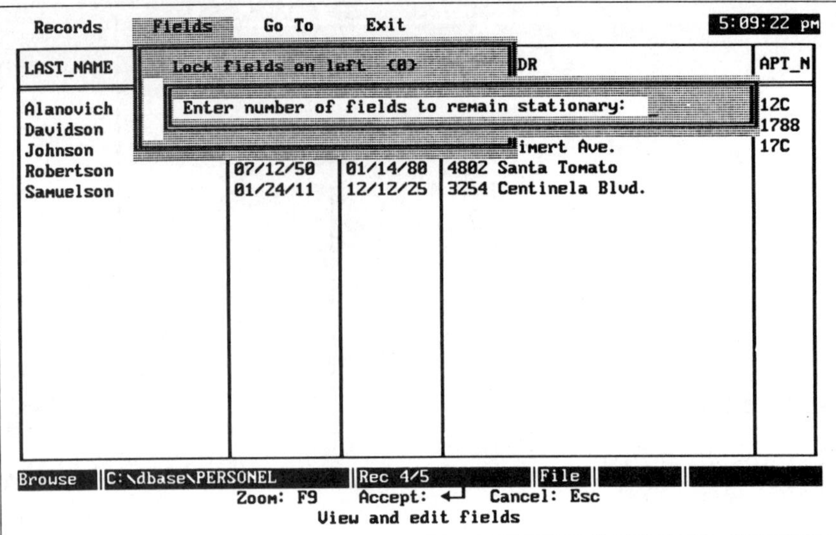

Figure 5-19

Prompt for number of fields to lock.

on screen. It is also useful to note that when you next pop up the Fields menu, the number of fields that are locked will appear to the right of the Lock fields on left prompt (Figure 5-20). Clearing or changing these values will cause the screen to be redrawn.

Note that the field locking applies to those fields that are

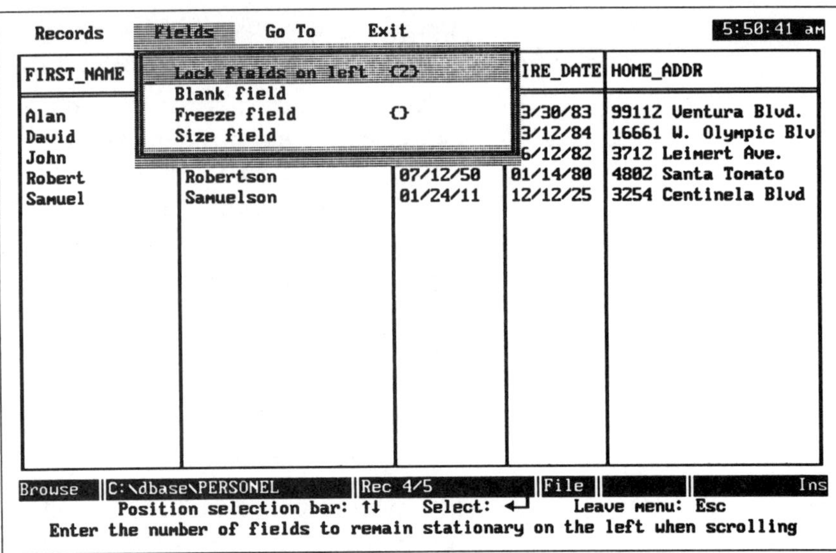

Figure 5-20

Number of locked fields appears when Fields menu is selected.

at the left side of your screen *when you invoke the lock fields* command. For example, if you scroll your screen to the right through enough fields so that LAST_NAME was the leftmost field, you can lock that field onto the screen without having to lock the FIRST_NAME field.

You can lock only adjoining fields, however. Thus, you cannot lock LAST_NAME, then scroll so that SS_NUMBER appears to the right of the LAST_NAME field, and attempt to lock both LAST_NAME and SS_NUMBER. The system will instead lock LAST_NAME and BIRTH_DATE, which is the next field in the database structure.

Proper ordering of fields in a data file is an important function, because it is through the database design that you can lock the most important fields together.

Blank field: A blank field is one in which the data have been blanked. In this field, whatever has been entered will be canceled by selecting this command. It can be restored to its original state using the Undo changes to record option in the Records menu. Be very careful, however, not to scroll up or down into a different record, because changes can be undone *only* if you have not moved out of a record being edited.

Freeze field: The Freeze field option allows you to edit the contents of only one field. When this is selected, the system will prompt for a field name, as seen in Figure 5-21.

Once a field is frozen, you may edit only that field—the system will not allow you to access the other fields to enter data. This is useful if you want to edit only a single field—in effect, you will be locking out all the other fields. Use of the **Tab** or **Shft-Tab** combination, or **F3** and **F4** keys, will move you from record to record only *within* that one field.

You can Lock fields on the left to display the name of the employee, for example, and freeze the field onto the one you will be updating. This allows you to quickly update the employee records to reflect correct employee salary codes.

Unfortunately, one option that was available in many other areas of dBASE IV has been excluded from Freeze field. You must know the field name *before* selecting Freeze field: the **Shft-F1** key combination will not bring up a listing of the fields in your data file.

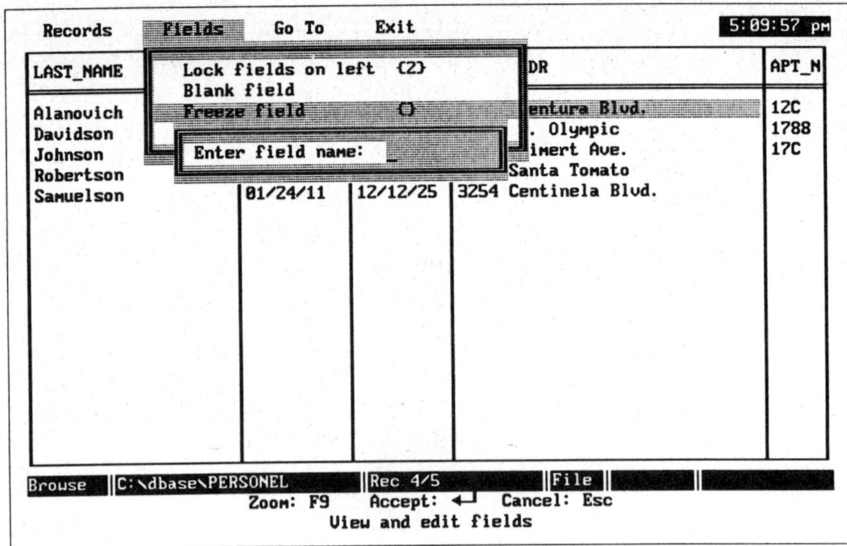

Figure 5-21

Prompt for name of field to freeze.

Size field: The Size field option lets you widen or contract the field as it is displayed on your Browse screen. The actual contents of the field are unaffected. This option can also be selected using **Shft-F7**.

When selected, the highlight moves to the current field. Moving the left and right arrows widens or contracts the field display. Pressing **Enter** completes the sizing process.

If you shorten the field display so that it is smaller than the contents of the display, you may use the right and left arrow keys to scroll through the contents of the field in the window. The window size cannot be made smaller than the field name.

Go To

The *Go To* menu is used to move the cursor to a record that you select, to search for a record, or to quickly jump through the records. It is available in both Edit and Browse (Figure 5-22).

The options are as follows:

Top record: The Top record is either the first record in your database or, if you are displaying an indexed record, the first

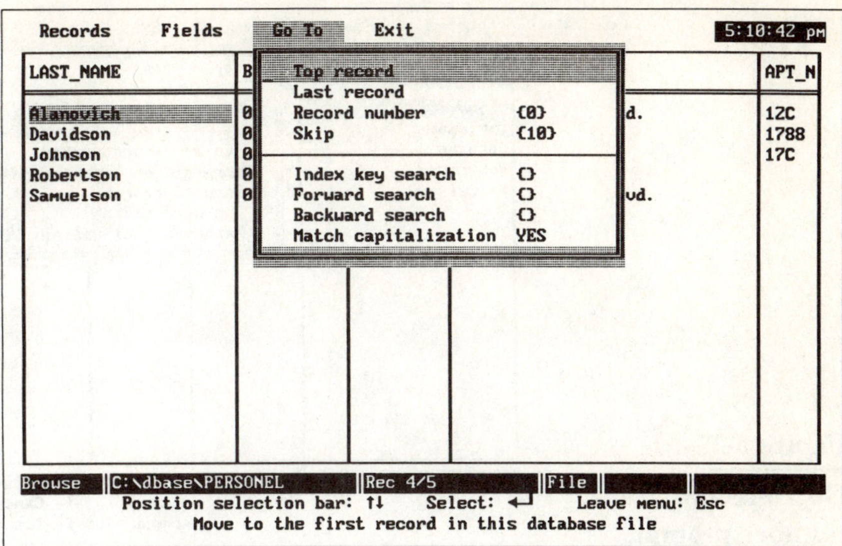

Figure 5-22

Go To menu.

record in your indexed file. For example, because you are indexing the current records on LAST_NAME, the top record is the one with the alphabetically first last name. In this case, the first indexed last name is Alanovich. If you select Top record, the cursor will move to Alanovich.

On the other hand, if the system was not indexed, your top record will be Record #1. The cursor will be placed in the same field that it was in when you invoked the Top record option.

Last record: Although it would have been more consistent to call this Bottom record, Ashton-Tate chose not to. Just as with Top record, this option moves you either to the last record in your indexed list or the last record entered. In other words, if you are viewing your data based on index order (in this case, indexed by last name), the last file in the index will be displayed. In this case, the last record is Samuelson, #2 of five records in the database. If you were not viewing an indexed file, record 5 would have been displayed.

Record number: If you know the record number of the field you are seeking, or want to go to an approximate position in your database, this option is useful. For example, if you have records for 2000 employees and want to find an employee whose last name began with *L*, you can take a file

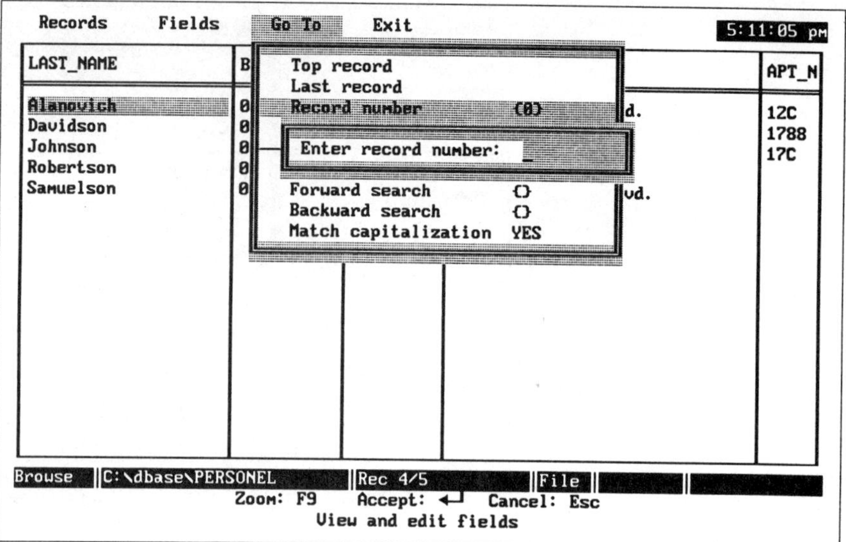

Figure 5-23

Go To record number prompt.

that is indexed by last name and aim for the approximate middle of the database, with a skip to Record number 1000. Moving up and down through the database or Browse windows should fairly rapidly find the employee whose name you were seeking. Of course, knowing the exact number of your target record will quickly move you to the record you are seeking.

When you select this option, a window (Figure 5-23) will ask for the record number you wish to locate. As with the other options, the cursor will remain in the field that called it.

Skip: The Skip option allows you to quickly skip through your files. For example, if you were still looking for the ubiquitous *L* entry, you may wish to narrow the search by skipping through your database.

Skip displays the records that come up after a skip. The default setting is 10. Thus, if you chose to skip from the first record, the next displayed record would be 11, the one after that would be 21, and so forth. Skipping by 100s in your 2000 record database will allow you to fairly rapidly narrow down the location of your missing file (if it is indexed on last name). When you select this option, you get a window asking for the number of records to skip, as shown in Figure 5-24.

In addition to forward searches, you can also perform

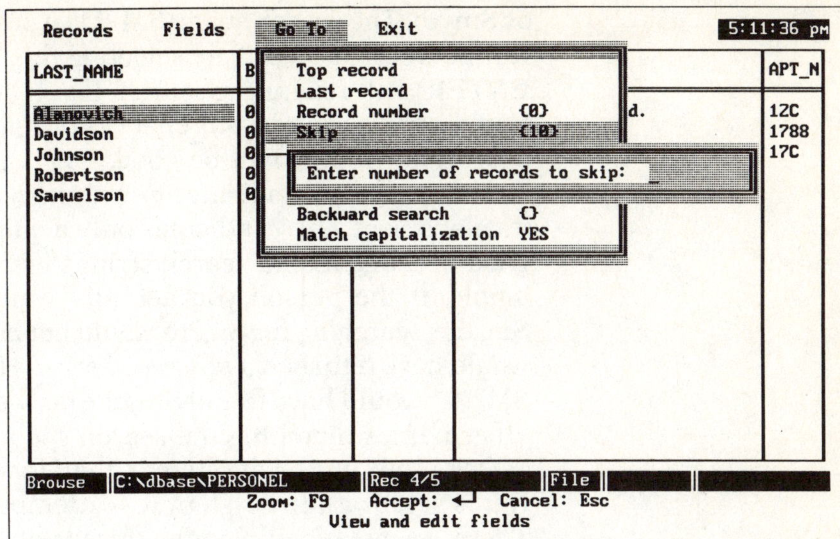

Figure 5-24

Skip numbers prompt.

backward searches. To do this, give the system a negative number to skip. Again, the system will bring up the record with the cursor in the field that originally called the Skip function.

Searches. Searches are part of the Go To menu. Although there are only three types of search, these should be explained further.

When the system searches for a match, it searches for exact matches to specified characters in the field that called for the search (or in the indexed field). However, there is more to it than this.

Searches can use wild cards and be set up to match or ignore capitalization. For example, to search for someone whose name sounded something like Smith (but was not Smith), you could use the * wildcard. The * is used in much the same way as it is in DOS, to represent any character string from that point to the end of the field.

Thus, in this example, you could enter the search instruction SM* to list everyone whose name begins with the letters SM. To narrow it down further, the ? can be used to indicate that any character in that position can be considered a match.

For example, you may not remember if the name was Smith

or Smyth. The search string SM?TH would return the first match for the field. Successively selecting this field (using **F10 ENTER ENTER**) will repeat the search. If you activate Browse once the first match is found, your chances of finding the *correct* name in a Browse window will be good.

Although the * indicates *any number* of characters following its placement, the ? indicates only a single character. It is often good practice to end search strings with an * character. For example, if the person you actually wanted to find was named Smythe, searching for Sm?th would not have matched Smythe and would have returned a *not found* error. However, using the string SM?th* would have found Smythe (as well as Smithson, and any other names matching the search spec).

One other important item is the *Match capitalization* option. If it is set to *yes*, the system will attempt to find an *exact* match. There are instances in which this is not always desirable. For example, your database may have names that mix upper- and lowercase. For example, last names such as DeKuyper or De Luca may be difficult to match unless you know the exact case. Because dBASE IV ignores spaces in a search, telling the system to ignore capitalization and search for deluka or dekuyper will return matches; the search would otherwise fail if you wanted the system to match capitalization.

The search options are as follows:

Index key search: This option is selectable only if you are using an indexed view of your data. When selected, the name of the index key appears, as shown in figure 5-25.

At the prompt, you type the contents of the search string, using whichever wildcards you may require. Once selected, the system will begin its search for the desired last name. The cursor will remain in whichever field it was located when you called for the indexed search.

Forward search: A forward search searches the contents of the current field, searching from the current record to the end of the database. If the database being viewed is not indexed, the search will be in numerical order, from the current to the last record. If the database is indexed, the search will be in index order, from the current record in the index to the last indexed record.

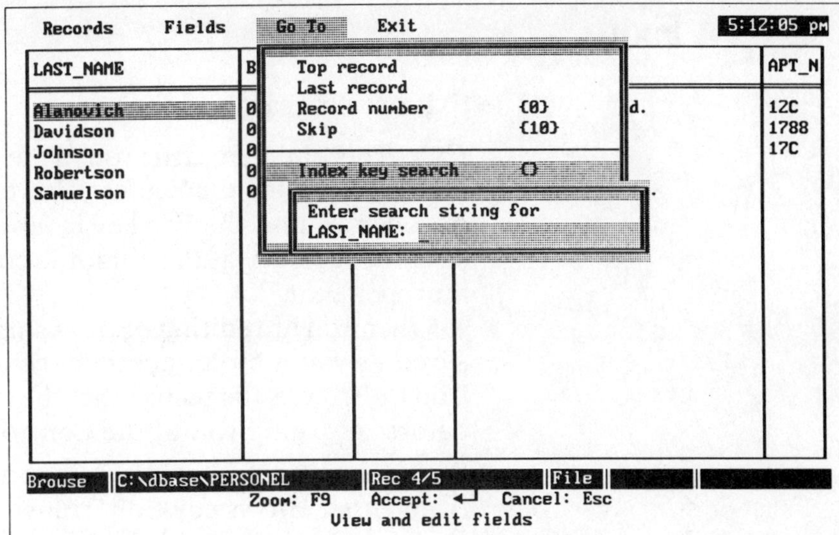

Figure 5-25

Index key search string prompt.

When this is selected (using the *f* key or by highlighting and selecting the option) a window will pop up, asking for the name of the search field. Once this is typed and the **Enter** key pressed, the system will begin its search.

It is often useful to remember, when doing a forward search, that the **Ctrl-PgUp** combination will bring you to the first record in your file, so that a forward search will search all records in the file.

Backward search: This is very similar to the Forward search, with the only difference being the direction. In this case, the search is toward the top of the database file. In an indexed database, the search will move toward the first file in the index. In a nonindexed view, the sort will be toward the first record entered.

The **Ctrl-PgDn** combination moves the cursor to the end of the file, if you want to search backwards through the entire database (or from deeper into the database) to find the targeted file.

Again, the search text or numbers apply to the *field* that you were in when you activated the search. You should be careful to ensure that the cursor is in the field you want searched *before* activating a search option.

Exit

The Exit option gives you choices:

Exit: This option returns you to the Control Center. You may also exit by using the **Esc** key. However, if the record you are on when you hit the **Esc** key is new, it will not be saved. To save the record that the cursor is currently on, you must do a proper Exit.

When you are editing or browsing records, each record is saved as you move to another record. When you exit from Edit or Browse, the record that the cursor is on will be saved before returning you to the Control Center.

Transfer to query design: This option, which is accessible from either Browse or Edit, transfers you to Query design. Query design is the method provided in dBASE IV for designing queries to analyze the data in your database.

In essence, the Query design capabilities allow you to extract from your files the data required to produce reports and evaluate your data. In earlier versions of dBASE, complex codes would often have to be generated to produce the data extraction and analysis that dBASE IV's Query facility provides.

Once you become comfortable with database design, data entry, and query development (by the time you finish this book), you may opt to go into this option directly from Edit or Browse, which explains why this option is available here.

Data Entry and Navigation

The Browse and Edit screens are the two areas that allow you to enter and edit your data. You have already seen the menu options available in both screens and should have an understanding of how both work.

The keys that are used to navigate through these screens are as follows:

Key	*Action*	*Comments*
F1	Help	Provides help for function highlighted

Key	*Action*	*Comments*
F2	Browse/Edit	Toggles between Browse and Edit
F3	Previous	Moves to a previous field; opens a memo field
Shft-Tab	Previous	Moves to the previous field
UpArrow	Previous	Moves to the previous field
F4	Next	Moves to the next field; opens a memo field (such as the History field in the current example)
Tab	Next	Moves to the next field
DnArrow	Next	Moves to the next field or record
F6	Extend select	Selects data or text written in a memo field
F7	Move	Moves text selected with **F6**
F8	Copy	Copies text selected with **F6**
F9	Zoom	Zooms memo to full screen; from within menu options, moves data input to a window at the bottom of the screen
F10	Menus	Brings the cursor to the menus
Return		Saves current field entry, moves to the next field
Esc		Leaves the record without saving it; leaves Browse without saving changes

Key	*Action*	*Comments*
Del		Deletes the character on which the cursor is currently positioned
Ins		Toggles insert mode on and off; when on, inserts characters as typed, pushing other characters to the right; when off, typed characters erase and overtype existing characters
Shft-PgUp		Moves to the top of the previous record
Shft-PgDn		Moves to top of next screen; in a multipage form, moves to next screen of form, rather than to the next record

Control key options in edit mode are as follows:

Key	*Comments*
Ctrl-RtArrow	Moves cursor to the end of current field, then to the first character of the next word
Ctrl-LtArrow	Moves cursor to the end of the previous field, then to the beginning of the previous field if pressed again

Key	*Comments*
Ctrl-PgDn	Moves to the last record
Ctrl-PgUp	Moves to the first record
Ctrl-Home	Moves into a memo field (opens the memo field)
Ctrl-End	In a memo field, saves changes and returns to the Edit mode
Ctrl-W	Same as **Ctrl-End**
Home	Moves to first character in the current field
End	Moves to the end of the current field

Control key options in browse mode are as follows:

Key	*Comments*
Ctrl-RtArrow	Moves cursor to the end of the current field; if pressed again, moves to the first character of the next field
Ctrl-LtArrow	Moves cursor to the last character of the previous field; if pressed again, moves to the first character of the previous field
Ctrl-PgDn	Moves to the last record
Ctrl-PgUp	Moves to the first record
Ctrl-Home	Moves into a memo

Key	*Comments*
	field (opens the Memo field)
Ctrl-End	If in a Memo field, saves changes and returns to Edit mode; if not in Memo, saves changes and returns to Control Center
Ctrl-W	Same as **Ctrl-End**
Home	Moves to the first field of the current record
End	Moves to the end of the current record

Adding Records to Your Database

There are a number of ways to add to your database. The first, of course, is using the Add new records option in the Records menu. This brings you to the bottom of your database file, where you can then add new records.

A second, very similar way is to finish editing the last record in your file. When you move the cursor beyond the last field, the system will ask you if you wish to add files to your database. Responding *Y* to the prompt allows files to be added.

A third way to append files is through the Modify Structure/Order menus accessible from the Data function. To see the options, Exit from your current database. To do this

Press: **F10** and move the cursor to the Exit menu (or type **Alt-E**)

Next,

Type: *e*

to exit. Then move the cursor to the Data column and select the PERSONEL database.

Press: **Shft-F2**

to select the file and to bring you into the Modify structure/order screen. Finally, move the cursor to the Append menu (Figure 5-26).

The Append menu gives you three options. Each of the options adds data at the end of your database file, that is, they append the data to your current database. The three Append options are as follows:

Enter records from keyboard: This option switches you from the Modify database screen to the Edit screen and brings you to the end of the database file. You can then begin adding files to your database.

Append records from dBASE file: Actually, this is something of a misnomer. This option allows you to append the contents of any dBASE III or dBASE IV database, or a PFS:File or PFS:Professional File database. When this is selected, the system displays a list of .DBF files in the current catalog. To bring in another data file, first list it in the currently logged directory. (Note: *This should be checked for PFS compatibility.*)

Copy records from non-dBASE file: This option allows you to import the contents of other files. Once this is selected,

Figure 5-26

The Append menu.

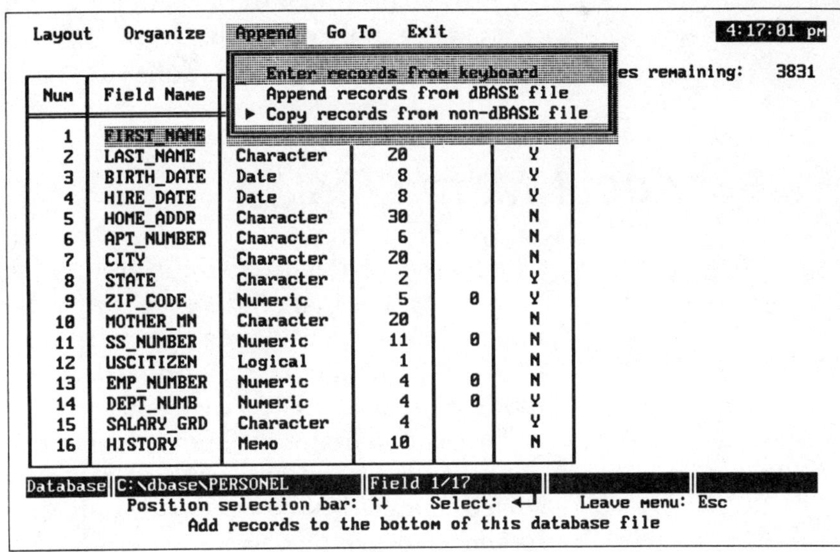

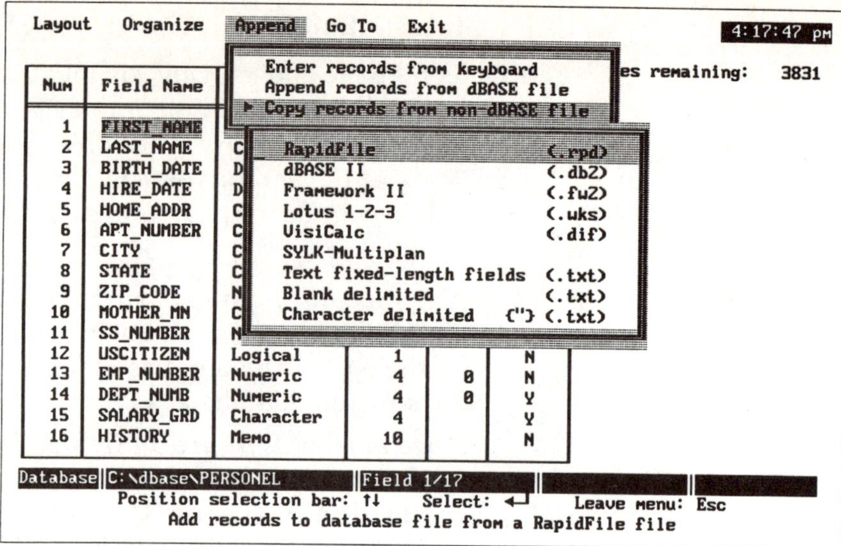

Figure 5-27

Non-dBASE files that can be appended to a dBASE file.

a list of files from which you can import appears on the screen (Figure 5-27).

When one of these file formats is selected, the system then brings up a directory so that you can choose the directory and file that you want to copy from and append to your data file. Once selected, the system reads the data and converts them (as much as possible) to dBASE IV format. Importing and exporting of the many different supported formats is discussed in the next chapter.

About Memo Fields

The memo field is treated differently from the rest of the available fields. The main difference is that the memo field is a flexible length field—you can open up a memo and dBASE IV's text editor appears on screen. From within the editor you can write, edit, or modify the data inside the field.

The second major difference is that the system does not do any analysis of the contents of this field. Whereas text fields can be sorted, scanned, and otherwise analyzed, and numeric fields can be summed, averaged, and sorted, Memo fields are text fields that cannot be modified during a query or during report or label generation.

Moving the cursor into a field using **F3** or **F4** keys opens the Edit window, from which you can type in your comments. A memo field that already contains text displays the word *memo* in uppercase characters.

To get into a memo field, highlight that field and

Press: **Ctrl-Home**

You could also have moved forward into the Memo window by pressing **F4** or backward into it by pressing **F3**. The window will open, allowing you to type your text. The Memo window, with a short sample message, is shown in Figure 5-28.

To return to your Browse or Edit screen,

Press: **Ctrl-End**

or select the Exit menu to save or abandon your changes and return to the Edit or Browse screen.

Editing is discussed in more detail later in this book.

In addition to the editor provided by dBASE IV, if you have enough memory in your system you may also use a more familiar word processor or text editor, as long as it can produce ASCII text.

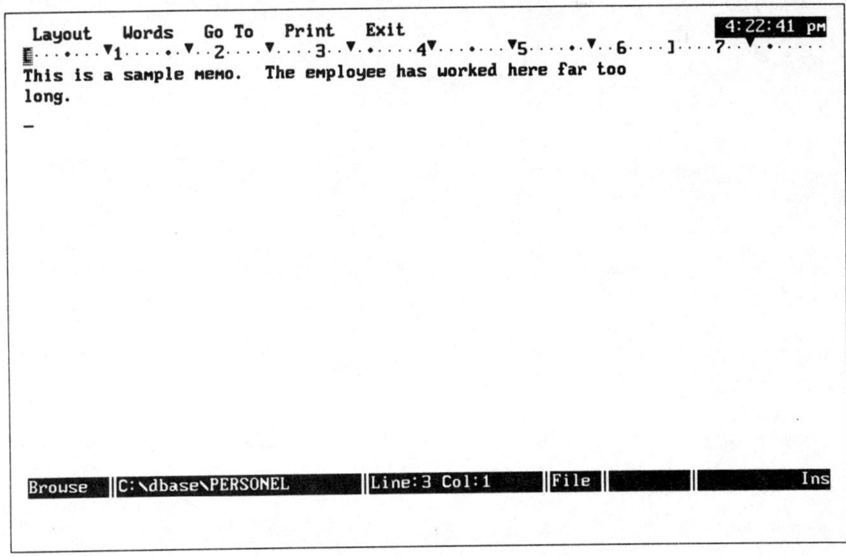

Figure 5-28

Memo window with a sample memo.

For the purposes of this book, however, the editor provided by dBASE IV should be more than adequate.

This chapter has explored the methods and tools for entering and editing data in your files. If you have been following the chapters in this book in order, you should now be able to design your data file, design the input and viewing form(s), and input and modify your data.

Future chapters cover more advanced topics, including sorting and indexing, importing and exporting with other file formats, and retrieving and reporting on desired data and relationships.

6 Data Import and Export

dBASE IV will undoubtedly be an upgrade for many current users of dBASE III and dBASE III+. This new version of the program, providing more power and speed and also providing a significant improvement in user interface, will undoubtedly attract users of other database programs as a result of its significant new capabilities.

However, many potential users may be concerned that the data they have already produced, in some cases databases they have been using for many years and in other cases databases they will continue to use, will have to be scrapped if they convert to dBASE IV.

In other cases, your company may have branches that use different database management systems. Concerns that databases built with and analyzed by dBASE IV will not be compatible with other software are, in a majority of cases, unjustified.

dBASE IV includes utilities that allow you to import or append data in a variety of formats from other databases, Lotus 1-2-3 compatible .WK1 and .WKS files, and from Framework; Ashton-Tate's package integrating word processing, spreadsheet, and database functions. In addition, files can also be appended from specially formatted files that can be created by most database and text processing programs. Thus, dBASE IV is capable of bringing in data from a vast majority of software (excluding recreational or other specialized types).

Export facilities included in dBASE IV also allow the data in a database, or selected data filtered by the program based on a variety of parameters, to be exported to other database programs, spreadsheets, Framework, or word processors. Data that are prepared by dBASE IV can be used to create the information needed for producing "mail merge" printed documents—letters or forms that combine standard text with contents of specific data fields for custom printed documents.

This chapter will explore methods for importing data into dBASE IV and exporting data from dBASE IV to other programs, and look at some of the exceptions and compatibility problems that may arise with some of the conversions.

dBASE IV Compatibility with dBASE III and dBASE III+

Files, views, and indexes created with dBASE III and dBASE III+ can be used by dBASE IV with virtually no changes. Data file structures, format, and .VUE files are the same in both dBASE III and dBASE IV.

However, other factors must be considered when trying to use dBASE III files with dBASE IV. The first is that dBASE IV has improved indexing capabilities. In dBASE IV, a list of index files can be used, rather than the 10 .NDX files that were supported by dBASE III. The ability to work with .NDX index files provides compatibility with dBASE III and dBASE III+. These files will continue to work with dBASE IV and become part of an .MDX file when imported into a catalog.

A second factor is that Memo fields have been changed in the current version of dBASE IV. Memo documents can be up to 64 kilobytes long. If you have a dBASE III+ file that is over 64 kilobytes long, it will be truncated by dBASE IV to 64 kilobytes.

In addition, dBASE IV uses a slightly different format for writing the Memo field. This makes Memo files created by dBASE IV incompatible with Memo files from earlier versions of dBASE.

File Formats Supported

dBASE IV supports a wide range of file formats. The degree of support varies depending on the menu you are in when you call for the import or export function. For example, when you call up the import function from within the Tools menu at the Control

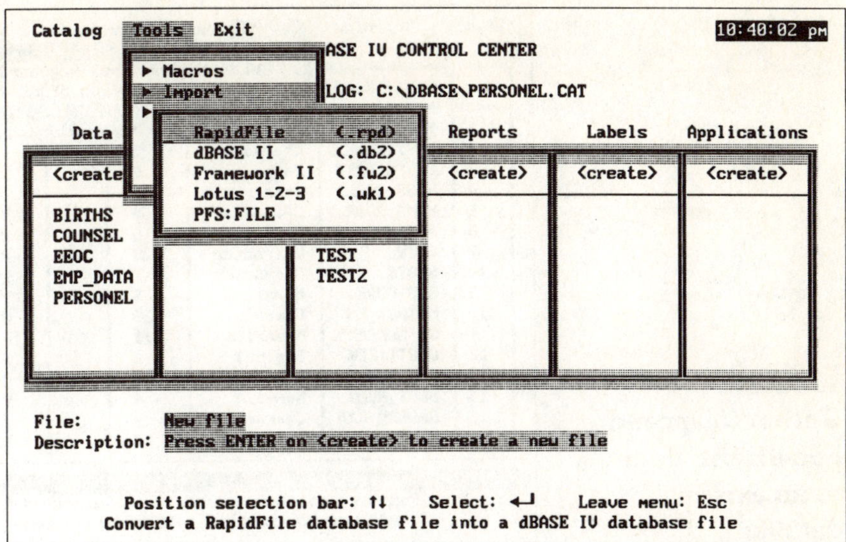

Figure 6-1

Import options from within Tools menu.

Center, you will see a list of Import options that includes only five types of import file formats, as seen in Figure 6-1.

To see those formats, return to the Control Center (if you are not already there) and bring down the *Tools* menu (using the **Alt-T** combination, or **F10** and the cursor keys to select the *Tools* menu). Next,

Type: **I**

to bring down the Import menu, which was seen in Figure 6-1.

A significantly larger list of import file formats supported can be used when appending data from other files to a dBASE IV data file. To see this list, escape from the Tools menu by pressing the **Esc** key twice. Next, move the cursor to the Data column and select the PERSONEL database by typing the first few letters from within the Data column, or by moving the cursor to PERSONEL. Next, tell the system that you wish to modify the database structure. To do this,

Type: **Shift F2**

An alternate way to select this function is to highlight the file and press the **ENTER** key, then select the *Modify structure/order* option.

The system will bring you into the Organize menu. Move the

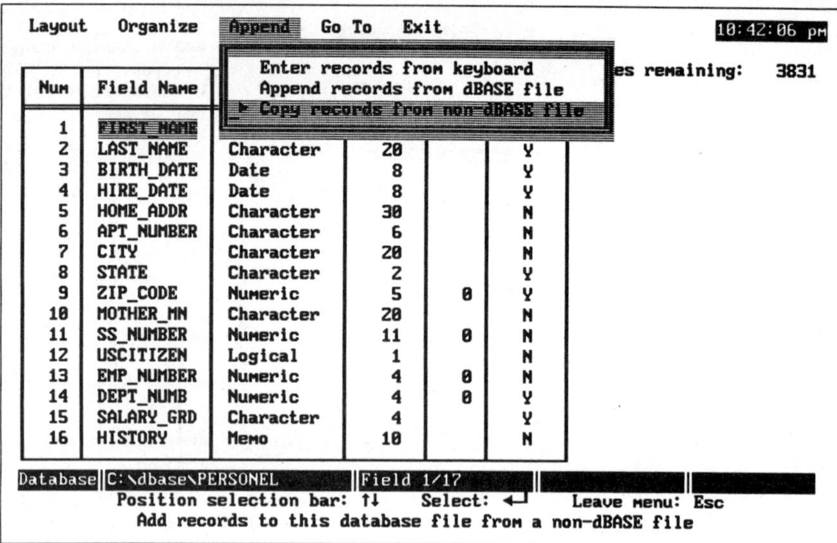

Figure 6-2

Option to append non-dBASE data to an existing database.

cursor to the Append menu panel and select *Copy records from non-dBASE file* (or highlight the option, then press **ENTER**). The screen will appear as shown in Figure 6-2 before you select this option.

When you select this option, a window showing the many different file formats supported for import will appear on screen. You will quickly see that many more formats are supported for appending to a file than for importing into a new database, as seen in Figure 6-3. The reason for this is very clear. When you wish to append a data file, you are copying data from another file into a database whose data structure is already defined.

The additional files that are supported consist of data that are relatively unstructured: in a delimited field or fixed-length field, the data are simply presented as a list, with a blank space, predefined character, or predetermined field length used to differentiate the data for one field from the data for the next. Such data files lack the information needed to tell the system anything in advance about the fields or field length; this makes it impossible to correctly import into a separate file (you must first know about the contents of the file before it can be imported).

If you wish to import a file that cannot be imported using the formats available from within the Tools–Import menu, you should

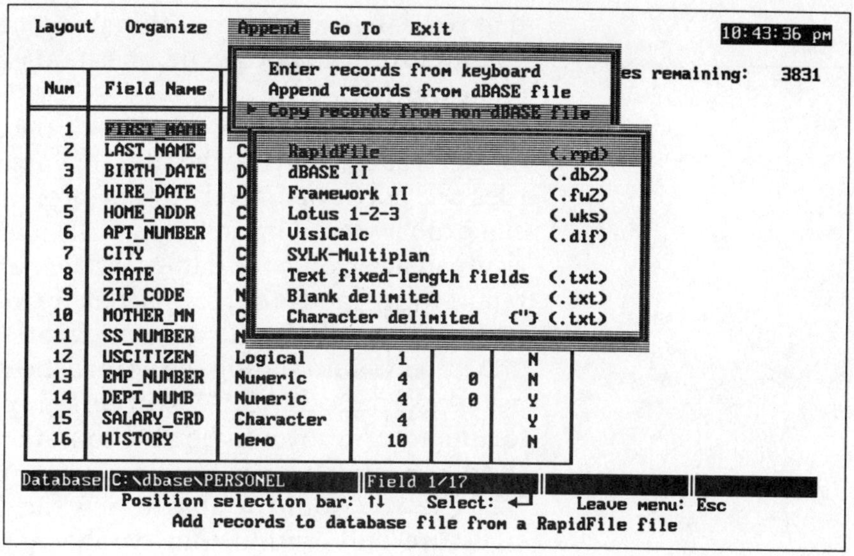

```
Layout  Organize  Append  Go To  Exit                              10:43:36 pm

                   Enter records from keyboard          es remaining:   3831
 Num  Field Name   Append records from dBASE file
                 ▸ Copy records from non-dBASE file
   1  FIRST_NAME
   2  LAST_NAME   C  RapidFile                 (.rpd)
   3  BIRTH_DATE  D  dBASE II                  (.db2)
   4  HIRE_DATE   D  Framework II              (.fw2)
   5  HOME_ADDR   C  Lotus 1-2-3               (.wks)
   6  APT_NUMBER  C  VisiCalc                  (.dif)
   7  CITY        C  SYLK-Multiplan
   8  STATE       C  Text fixed-length fields  (.txt)
   9  ZIP_CODE    N  Blank delimited           (.txt)
  10  MOTHER_MN   C  Character delimited  {"} (.txt)
  11  SS_NUMBER   N
  12  USCITIZEN   Logical      1        N
  13  EMP_NUMBER  Numeric      4    0   N
  14  DEPT_NUMB   Numeric      4    0   Y
  15  SALARY_GRD  Character    4        Y
  16  HISTORY     Memo        10        N

Database C:\dbase\PERSONEL    Field 1/17
   Position selection bar: ↑↓   Select: ◄┘    Leave menu: Esc
         Add records to database file from a RapidFile file
```

Figure 6-3

Window showing all supported file import formats.

first create a database structure that defines the fields in your data import file, and then import data into that structure.

The reasons such text files cannot be imported will be made clear when each file type is discussed.

Format Checking: A Methodology

Importing and exporting are conceptually very straightforward processes. When you import data, you are bringing data from another format into a dBASE IV file; when you export data, the data are being sent in a format that can be understood and used by another database, word processor, spreadsheet, or other program.

dBASE IV provides you with many features other than database management. If you were doing only data manipulation, you would need only one column in the Control Center—the Data column.

The methods for entering, viewing, and analyzing the data in your files and catalogs are set in specially designed files stored in the different functional columns (called Panels by Ashton-Tate) that you can access from within the Control Center. Ideally, when you import or export a file, these other files also get imported and exported.

dBASE IV represents the state of the art in database management. As such, many of the files that are associated with the data files are not supported by other programs. Thus, although you can export your data to Lotus 1-2-3, and manipulate the data in a spreadsheet, only the data and field names are exported. Views, report forms, and other forms that are in a catalog and associated with your database file are not exported by dBASE IV.

If, after manipulating the spreadsheet data, you wanted to import those data, dBASE IV will certainly allow you to do this. Unfortunately, you would be able to import only the data, and not the other catalog structures. Thus, if you were to import a Lotus 1-2-3 file, you would be able to view the data and modify the data structure only within that database. Unless you had already developed the forms, reports, labels, index files, and other files that can use the data in your imported data file, you would have to create these collateral files.

To explore what does and what does not get passed through imported and exported databases, and to better understand some of the different supported file structures, the following methodology will be used:

1. The PERSONEL file will be exported to each file format.
2. The Modify Structure screen will be accessed, and the structural design given the name of the previously exported structure.
3. The exported data will be imported back into the new structure and evaluated.

This actually sounds more difficult than it is. The first format, RapidFile, will illustrate the steps involved.

RapidFile (.rpd)

First, bring up the Export menu. To do this from the Control Center (if your cursor is not at the Control Center, **Esc** back to the Control Center),

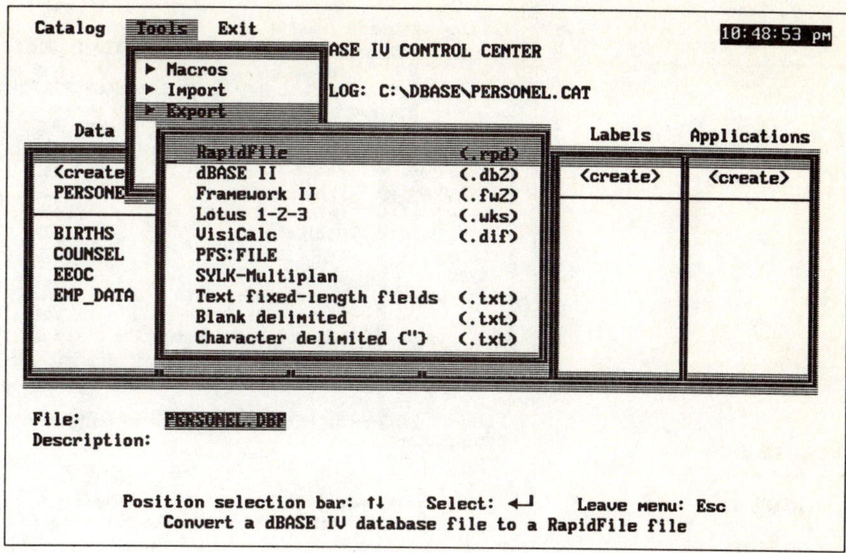

Figure 6-4

Export menu.

Type: **Alt-*e***

(Figure 6-4).

Next, select the RapidFile format. Because this is already highlighted,

Press: **ENTER**

(You could also have selected RapidFile by typing *r*.) A window with the names of the Catalog (at the top of the window) and all database files in the window will pop onto the screen. A description of each selected database file will appear slightly below the center of the screen (Figure 6-5).

Select PERSONEL and press **ENTER** to begin exporting the PERSONEL.DBF data file. A window will appear on screen, indicating that the file is being copied into RapidFile format.

NOTE: The exported file will be exported to the current subdirectory on your disk. To use it in RapidFile, copy it to the RapidFile subdirectory. If you already have a file with the name you wish to give your exported file, you will be prompted to Cancel or Overwrite the existing file. In this case, be certain to move a previously copied file onto another subdirectory or to rename the file to avoid loss of data.

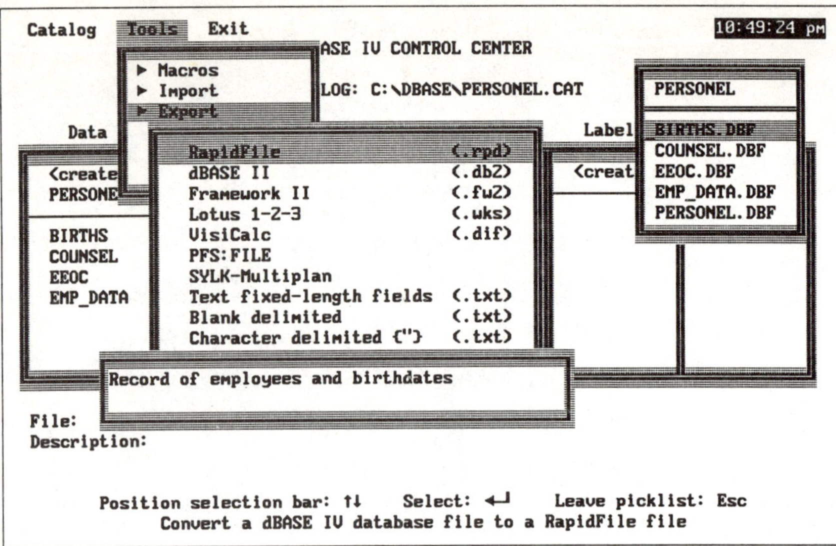

Figure 6-5

Export file selection screen.

Next, you will set up a new file structure into which to import the RapidFile records. To do this, select PERSONEL and

Type: **Shift-F2**

The Modify screen will appear, with the field definitions for PERSONEL already there. The Organize menu will be on screen. Using the keyboard arrows, select the Layout menu.

Next, select Save this database file structure. To do this,

Type: ***S* ENTER**

or use the arrow keys to move the highlight to the option and

Press: **ENTER**

dBASE IV will then bring in a window, asking you to name the database file. The default name is that of the currently loaded structure (Figure 6-6).

Using the backspace keys, delete the name of the current file, PERSONEL.DBF. Then

Type: ***RFILE* ENTER**

to create a new database structure named RFILE. All the records in PERSONEL.DBF will be copied into RFILE.DBF, and all

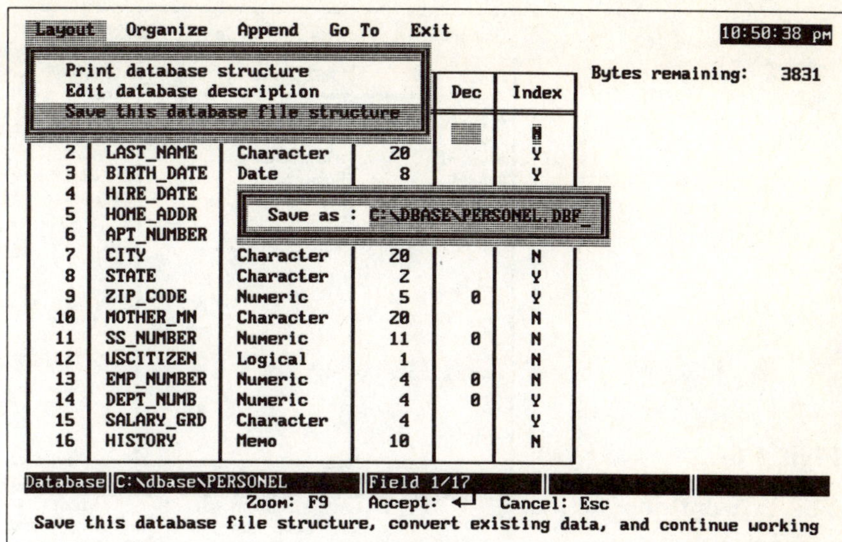

Figure 6-6

Save as screen for renaming your database structure.

records will be reindexed. It is not necessary for you to type the .DBF file extension—dBASE IV automatically does that for you.

To see that the records in the PERSONEL.DBF file have been copied into RFILE.DBF, press the **F2** key. The Browse screen will show the five records.

Next, return to the Database Design menu. To do this,

Type: **Alt-e**

to bring up the Exit menu. The screen will give you three options, as seen in Figure 6-7. Select the Return to Database Design option and press **ENTER**.

You will be brought back to the Database Design screen. Next, using the cursor, move to the Append menu.

Select the Copy records from non-dBASE file option, using the up or down arrow keys, and

Press: **ENTER**

to bring up the File Import Format menu, as seen earlier in Figure 6-3. The RapidFile format should already be highlighted—if not move the highlight to this format.

Press: **ENTER**

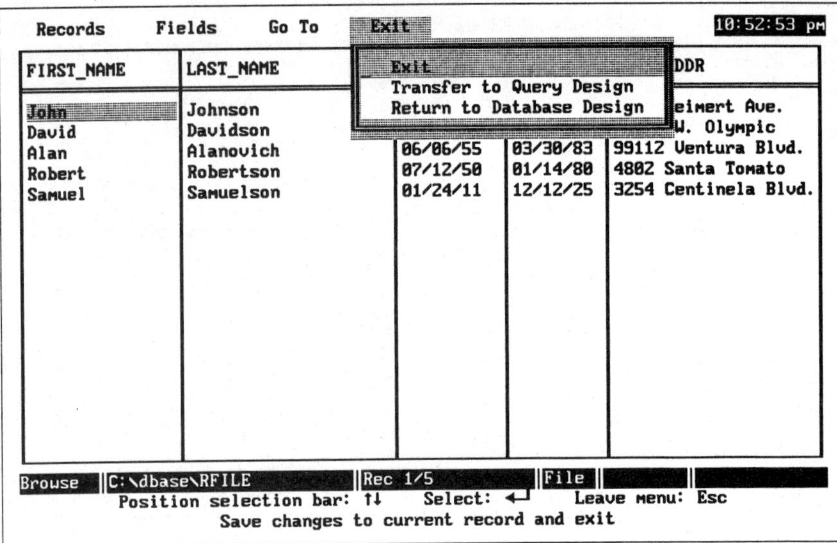

Figure 6-7

The exit options screen.

The system will bring up a file selection window. The window should show available directories, and files with the appropriate extension from which to append your file (Figure 6-8).

The name of the current subdirectory appears at the top of the window. Below this, the current disk drive is listed. If you wish to select a file from another drive, move the cursor to highlight

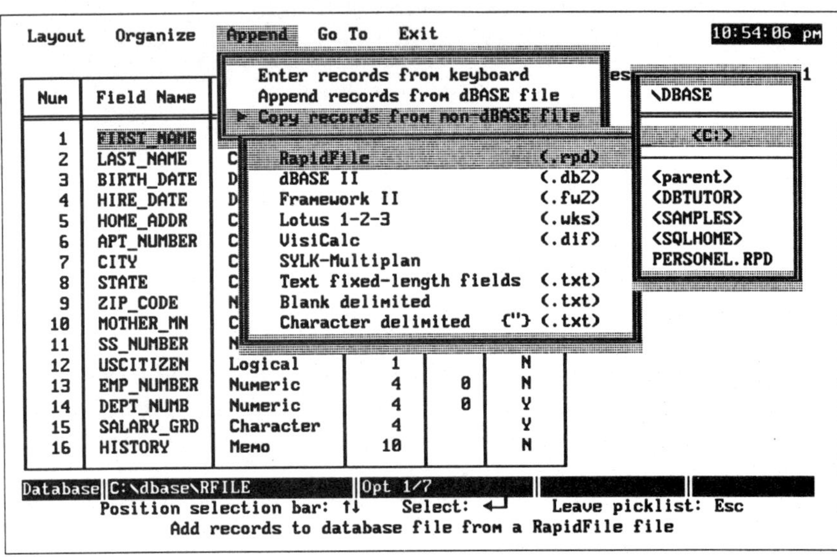

Figure 6-8

Import file selection window.

the letter of the current drive, in this case **<C:>**, and a list of all available drives will appear in a new window to the left of the file window. You can then move the cursor to highlight the desired drive, and select that drive using the **ENTER** key.

For now, we will assume that you wish to use the currently logged drive. Below the drive designator, a selector for the parent directory and the names of all subdirectories will appear. Below the subdirectories will be the list of all files having the .RPD (RapidFile) data extension. The system will show only those importable files.

Select PERSONEL.RPD, the RapidFile data file you created when you exported the PERSONEL.DBF file to RapidFile.

Press: **ENTER**

to import the data file and append it to your existing RFILE.DBF database. The system will then read the files and add them to your current database. To view the new database,

Press: **F2**

You will be returned to the Browse or Edit menu, depending on which menu was on your screen when you last used the Browse/Edit menu. You will probably also be at a blank record, the last record in your file. Use the **F2** key to return to the Browse menu if the Edit menu is on screen, then

Press: **PgUp**

to bring the original and imported files on to the screen. The Browse screen is seen in Figure 6-9.

The top five records are those that you created when you built the PERSONEL.DBF file. The bottom five are the ones that were imported from the RapidFile format. It should be clear that date fields are supported by RapidFile, although early versions of dBASE IV did not import dates from RapidFile.

Scrolling through the Browse screen will indicate that in addition to the date fields, the Memo fields are also not supported.

> *About Date Fields*: Date fields are handled somewhat differently from other fields, because they must conform to a specific format for month, day, and year. To export to the spreadsheet-based (Lotus, MultiPlan, VisiCalc) and delimited forms, or to import from these types of files, *both* files must use the same format for dates (normally an eight-character

Records Fields Go To Exit 6:42:15 am

FIRST_NAME	LAST_NAME	BIRTH_DATE	HIRE_DATE	HOME_ADDR
John	Johnson	02/27/46	06/12/82	3712 Leimert Ave.
Samuel	Samuelson	01/24/11	12/12/25	3254 Centinela Blvd
Robert	Robertson	07/12/50	01/14/80	4802 Santa Tomato
Alan	Alanovich	06/06/55	03/30/83	99112 Ventura Blvd.
David	Davidson	06/11/51	03/12/84	16661 W. Olympic Blv
John	Johnson	02/27/46	06/12/82	3712 Leimert Ave.
Samuel	Samuelson	01/24/11	12/12/25	3254 Centinela Blvd
Robert	Robertson	07/12/50	01/14/80	4802 Santa Tomato
Alan	Alanovich	06/06/55	03/30/83	99112 Ventura Blvd.
David	Davidson	06/11/51	03/12/84	16661 W. Olympic Blv

Browse C:\dbase\RFILE Rec 10/10 File Ins

View and edit fields

Figure 6-9

Browse screen with original and imported records.

wide field with MMDDYYYY format, in which MM is the two number month, DD is the two number day, and YYYY is the four figure year).

Export files will create a new date field in the above format. This should be kept in mind when using the date field in your other program. Similarly, when importing or appending from such a file, the date must be in the above format so that it can be used by dBASE IV.

About Spreadsheets: Spreadsheets handle data somewhat differently than databases. They are set up to work in terms of rows and columns. dBASE IV's import and export facilities are designed with the assumption that columns refer to individual fields and rows correspond to individual records. To get an idea of how this orientation appears on your spreadsheet, look at the Browse screen, which presents data in the same way.

If your spreadsheet takes a different approach, using a new column for each record and a row for each field (a highly illogical method; because most databases will have many more records than fields, you could end up with a spreadsheet two miles long), you will have to convert the spreadsheet, if possible, so that it matches the format required by dBASE IV.

About Size Limitations: Although dBASE IV can handle significantly larger files than earlier versions, there are still important limitations, in terms of file size for import, export, and appending from, that must be observed.

dBASE IV allows up to 255 fields in a record. Each field may be up to, but no larger than, 255 characters. When importing PFS:Professional File data, dBASE IV also treats headings and comments as fields, which could reduce the actual number of data fields available from PFS:Professional File.

Now that RapidFile has been explored, the other formats will be described, and special instructions, in addition to losses in data format, will be discussed briefly.

dBASE II (.db2)

dBASE II, the forerunner of dBASE III, dBASE III+, and the current dBASE IV, is not fully compatible with dBASE IV files. The problem it presents is basically a simple one: it also creates files with the .dbf extension. To dBASE IV, this makes such files *look like* they are dBASE IV or the compatible dBASE III files, which they are not.

Attempting to import a dBASE II file without using the translation procedure will result in lost data, and possibly worse problems. To prepare a dBASE II file for import, change the .dbf extension to .db2. Doing this is simple, and can be done if you wish to import from your current drive. Assuming that your original dBASE II files are on a subdirectory on drive C: called DBASE II, and that dBASE IV is installed in a subdirectory on drive C: called DBASE, and further assuming that a file called TEST.DBF was to be imported from the DBASE subdirectory, the DOS command to move and rename the TEST.DBF file is as follows:

COPY C:\DBASE II\TEST.DBF C:\DBASE\TEST.DB2

NOTE: Using the Control Center, you may be unable to append your file from a dBASE II file because of an error in the coding for the automatic execution of the command. This is a bug that should be fixed well in advance of the product's shipment. If not, one method of appending the file is to go to the dot prompt, once the correct target file is selected as the open file, and type the following command: *APPEND FROM FILENAME.DB2 type DBASE II*, in which FILENAME.DB2 is the name of the dBASE II file that you wish to import and append to your file.

Although dBASE IV will import most of your fields, it has trouble with date fields. In addition, memo fields are also not supported by dBASE IV. Forms, views, and indexes created by dBASE II are not converted by the conversion program.

A database that is exported to dBASE II will be given a .db2 extension. If you plan to use this exported database file from within dBASE II, you must rename it, giving it the .dbf extension. The command to do this, assuming that you have created a file called PERSONEL.DB2, is as follows:

REN PERSONEL.DB2 PERSONEL.DBF

Before doing this, however, check the directory in which the newly renamed file will be written to ensure that you are not overwriting an existing dBASE II file. You may also copy and rename the file in another directory. If you wish to move the PERSONEL.DB2 file from a subdirectory called DBASE to one called DBII, the command to copy and rename your directory is as follows:

COPY PERSONEL.DB2 C:\DB2\PERSONEL.DBF

The above syntax assumes that you are copying from the current subdirectory; otherwise the command syntax for the source file is C:\DBASE\PERSONEL.DB2. And, of course, it is assumed that both directories are on the C: drive.

Framework II, Framework III (.FW2)

Framework II does not support date fields. In this example, hire date and birth date are not exported to Framework II. The fields are undefined in Framework II and thus cannot be imported from Framework.

Lotus 1-2-3 (.WKS), (.WK1)

Lotus 1-2-3, like Ashton-Tate's dBASE III+ and undoubtedly dBASE IV, is a standard application program. As the standard for PC-based spreadsheet programs, its impact on the industry is more pervasive than its sales figures indicate.

Once Lotus 1-2-3 became a standard, developers of competitive spreadsheet products quickly realized that to compete, the file structures for their spreadsheets had to be fully compatible with those of Lotus 1-2-3. And aside from look and feel issues, Lotus has encouraged the use of a standard spreadsheet file format, which is used in its current version of the program.

Two file extensions are used for a Lotus 1-2-3 or compatible program: .WKS and .WK1.

> Note: .WKE is used in an educational version of Lotus 1-2-3. To import these files, they must be converted to either a .WKS or .WK1 format.

The .WKS format is the one used by the original version of Lotus 1-2-3, Version 1A. Version 2.0 and 2.1 of Lotus 1-2-3 use the .WK1 extension and a slightly different file structure.

dBASE IV is very compatible with the .WKS and .WK1 format, being able to import and export character and numeric fields, with the exception of Memo fields, for which there is no corresponding data type in Lotus 1-2-3.

Other spreadsheet programs, most notably Borland Quattro and Microsoft Excel, should have similar import and export capabilities with dBASE IV using dBASE IV's Lotus import and export utilities.

In some cases, the .WKS file format may also serve as a data bridge to the Macintosh or other computers. For networked systems, or for systems that can support both the Macintosh and IBM PC disk formats, Macintosh applications that can use or convert to .WKS format files can be used to import data from a dBASE IV file that was exported into that format and to export data in a .WKS format for import into dBASE IV.

The original version of Lotus 1-2-3 is supported as an appendable file; that is, from within the Modify Database screen you will be able to append from a Version 1A (.WKS) file (a non-dBASE file).

You will not be able to import such a file, however, unless you convert it from a .WKS to .WK1 format, using a conversion utility that may or may not be included in your current spreadsheet.

Lotus 1-2-3 Version 2.0 and 2.1 (.WK1) files cannot be directly appended to an existing dBASE IV data file. To append from a .WK1 database, you can import the file from the Tools Import menu, and then append from the dBASE-compatible file that is created when the file is imported.

dBASE IV exports to Lotus 1-2-3 in the .WKS format, the format used with the first release of Lotus. To use this data file in Version 2.0 or 2.1, or in another Lotus-compatible spreadsheet, it will probably require conversion to .WK1, or the import program in your spreadsheet should be told that the data file is in .WKS format.

VisiCalc (.DIF)

Before Lotus 1-2-3, there was VisiCalc. VisiCalc was the spreadsheet standard on the Apple II computer and, in fact, helped to create a market for personal computers. It was translated to run on the infant IBM PC and was successful until the much more capable Lotus 1-2-3 entered the market.

However, although VisiCalc is long gone, its file format with the extension .DIF has lived on. Again, as with Lotus 1-2-3, memo files are not supported by VisiCalc or other programs that use the .DIF format. As with all other spreadsheets, the format for date fields must conform to those that dBASE IV is expecting (MMDDYYYY) or imported files from your VisiCalc (or other .DIF) files will have incorrect date fields, which dBASE IV will be unable to use.

PFS:File, Professional File 2

PFS:File, PFS:Professional File 1.0, and Professional File 2 are all products of Software Publishing Corp. PFS:File and PFS:Professional File are both compatible with dBASE IV; the data files use no file extension. Professional File 2 files cannot be imported or appended to dBASE IV, because their format is different from that used for PFS:File and PFS:Professional File. Data can, however, be exported, with Professional File 2 converting from a PFS:File to Professional File 2 format.

dBASE IV will export to a file that uses the same name as the source data file, but without the data extension. Thus, if you exported PERSONEL.DBF, your PFS file would be called PERSONEL. The format for dBASE IV files and PFS files is very similar; in fact Professional File can read dBASE IV files without conversion.

Professional File 2 allows you to view or print an unconverted (not exported) dBASE IV file. Unfortunately, this is all you will be allowed to do, you will not be able to make any changes to the data in the file.

The file you export from dBASE IV is translated into a form that makes it usable by Professional File 2 with one exception: dBASE IV translates the file into a form that is compatible with Professional File 1 and PFS:File but not fully compatible with Professional File 2. When you first try to use such a file, you will get an error message as seen in Figure 6-10.

When you respond to the prompt provided by Professional File 2, the system will make the minor modification necessary to allow Professional File 2 to use the data. Once modified, however, the current version of dBASE IV will not recognize the Profession-

Figure 6-10

Professional File 2 error message.

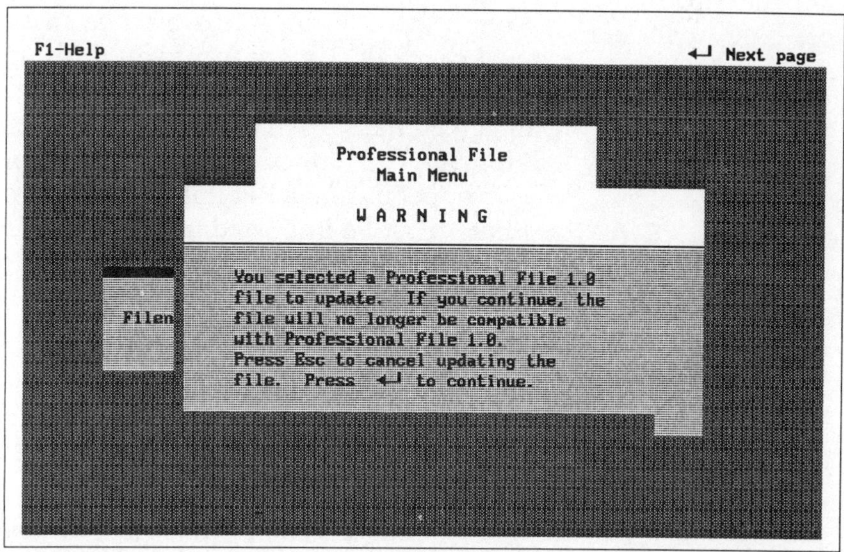

al File 2 file as a PFS file. Therefore, it is probably best *not* to attempt to use Professional File 2 files for import or export to dBASE IV.

When working with PFS:File and PFS:Professional File data files the export function is very straightforward. Importing is somewhat different, however. Because the file formats for dBASE IV and Professional File are so similar, to the system an imported PFS file will look like a dBASE IV file.

This poses some problems from within the Modify Data Structure menu. You will be unable to append from a PFS file because it is not supported as a non-dBASE format. Similarly, you will be unable to import the file as a dBASE IV file, because it has no file extension.

Simply adding the .DBF extension to your PFS file does not work; the PFS file contains information that also describes format and indexing settings for the file that makes sense only to PFS:File or PFS:Professional File. To bring the data into a dBASE IV application, it must first be imported from within the Tools menu in the Control Center (or from the dot prompt). PFS files that are imported by dBASE IV are given .VUE files and .FMT files, which tell the system how the data are to be viewed and formatted.

Care should be taken to give the PFS file a name that is different from that for a dBASE IV file. If you attempt to import a PFS:File file that has the same name as a dBASE IV file the system will prompt you to allow it to overwrite an existing dBASE IV file. In most cases this is *not* what you wish to do.

The file formats that are listed in the Import menu are imported and given the .DBF database extension. Similar care in avoiding duplicate file names is also required for these formats.

To append from a PFS:File and PFS:Professional File database, it must first be imported using the Tools menu from within the Control Center, or from within the dot prompt. (The command to do this is *Import filename type pfs.*)

SYLK-Multiplan

Multiplan is yet another spreadsheet that has its roots in the Apple II and Commodore 64 environment. It was also a contender under DOS, but is being phased out by most users. Its developer,

Microsoft Corp., has recently been selling the much more capable Excel. Thus, its future as a platform for spreadsheet users is certainly quite dim.

However, as with VisiCalc, its data format continues in some products. A file exported for Multiplan has no file extension. Thus, if you are attempting to export a dBASE IV file to both a PFS:File and a Multiplan application, you will run into a problem because dBASE IV will want to give the same file name to both exported files. Before it overwrites an earlier exported file, it will prompt you, asking if it should overwrite the file.

It is a good idea, once a file is exported, to move it to the directory that contains your other database or spreadsheet files. Alternatively, you can rename your exported file to avoid confusing the system.

When you have told the system that you wish to import a SYLK-Multiplan file, it will bring up a listing of the current directory, showing all files that are not clearly dBASE IV data or system files, program files, or other types of data files. Such files may or may not have extensions, and the list may appear quite lengthy. It is important that you know the exact name and extension of the file that you wish to import before trying to import a SYLK file.

SYLK-Multiplan files cannot be directly imported, because they lack a clearly identifiable file structure. They may, however, be appended to an existing database structure or one that you build to match the file order of your SYLK file.

Delimited Fields (.txt)

Delimited files are files that lack the structural rigidity of spreadsheets or other databases. In blank or character delimited fields, and in fixed-length text fields, the data in each field conform to a particular format determined by the user or applied by the system. Many word processing programs are quite capable of producing such fields, and many can use such delimited data files for mail merge printing of documents. In fact, one form or another of the delimited fields should be supported by almost any text editor, if not for merged printing, at least for simple data entry to export into dBASE IV or another database program.

Text Fixed-Length Fields (.txt)

The idea behind delimiters or fixed text-length files is simple: for the system to know when one field ends and the next begins, *something* must be done. In the case of text fixed-length fields, the length of each field is defined, usually in the first line of the data file. To provide a simple example, assume that you are working with a data file that lists only first and last name. If you give a 10 character length for first name and a 15 character length for last name, the system will automatically use the first 10 characters (no matter how many blanks appear following the actual first name) as the first name, and the next 15 characters (again, regardless of how many blank spaces appear) as the last name.

Text fixed-length fields are probably the least useful of the delimited fields, because the field data is not truncated. For example, if you wished to write letters to people in the database and the first name on the list was Bob Smith, your first letter may begin as follows:

> Mr. Bob   Smith
> Anystreet
> Anywhere, USA
>
> Do we have a special offer for you, Bob   Smith ! Yes, before long, the Smith   household may be proud owners of a mailbox with YOUR name, Bob   Smith   ,printed on it.

dBASE IV will automatically export data to such files, assigning data field widths that match the widths you defined when you set up your database file. Blank spaces will be added to fill in the fields. Such a file will be given the .txt extension (the same extension used for other delimited file formats).

A data file with fixed-length fields that was exported from PERSONEL.DBF is shown in Figure 6-11.

Text fixed-length field data can also be appended to an existing database file, from within the Modify structure/order window. Be careful, however, to ensure that the defined field sizes *exactly match* the sizes of your fields. If there is a mismatch, you will end up with data that are not in the correct fields.

Memo fields are ignored by dBASE IV, both at export and during append; that is, you should not leave spaces in your fixed-length file for memo fields; when dBASE IV exports to a fixed-length file, it skips the memo field. When it appends from a

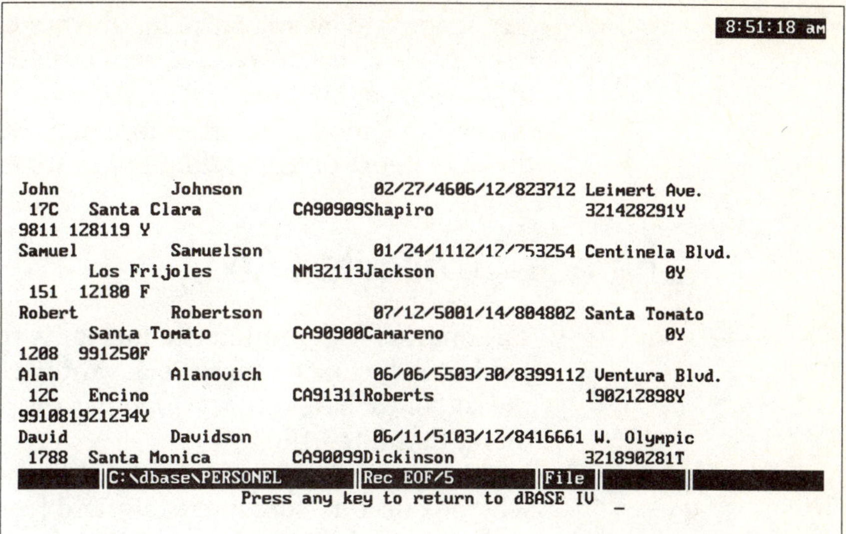

```
                                                                    8:51:18 am




John           Johnson              02/27/4606/12/823712 Leimert Ave.
 17C   Santa Clara          CA90909Shapiro                321428291Y
9811 128119 Y
Samuel         Samuelson            01/24/1112/17/?53254 Centinela Blvd.
       Los Frijoles         NM32113Jackson                       0Y
 151  12180 F
Robert         Robertson            07/12/5001/14/804802 Santa Tomato
       Santa Tomato         CA90900Camareno                      0Y
1208  991250F
Alan           Alanovich            06/06/5503/30/8399112 Ventura Blvd.
 12C   Encino               CA91311Roberts                190212898Y
991081921234Y
David          Davidson             06/11/5103/12/8416661 W. Olympic
 1788  Santa Monica         CA90099Dickinson              321890281T
        ||C:\dbase\PERSONEL        ||Rec EOF/5          ||File ||        ||
                      Press any key to return to dBASE IV  _
```

Figure 6-11

Fixed-length text file.

fixed-length file, it skips any memo fields in the database design and moves to the next valid field.

If you export to any of the three delimited fields, either fixed-length, blank delimited, or character delimited, the same file name will be given if you use the same database file. When overwriting an existing .TXT file, make sure that it has been moved into the appropriate directory for your word processor or other program that uses the delimited file.

Blank Delimited (txt)

A blank delimited file uses a blank space to indicate the end of a field. This is somewhat more efficient than the text fixed-length fields, because it resolves the problem of having many blanks complete a field in which only a small amount of text is actually used in the record. For example, the fixed-length first name field in the above example (Bob   ) will take only four characters in a blank delimited file (Bob). In mail merge applications, this is preferable.

There are, of course, limitations to this method, because the system recognizes *any blank* as the field delimiter. Street names like La Cienega or La Tijera would have to be truncated

(LaCienega) to avoid confusing the system. In addition, you will not be able to use a space within a field, unless you define each area that may include text.

Again, memo fields are completely passed over by dBASE IV during export or appending operations.

Character Delimited (.txt)

The character delimited file format is the most powerful of the delimited formats. It has the advantage of being able to indicate the end of each field, and overcomes the problems that occur with blank delimited files.

The actual delimiter used by this conversion is the comma, which is used to separate each field from the next. The use of a delimiter, in this case the quotation marks, tells the system which data are text. By enclosing your text entries with an ASCII character, you are telling the system that the enclosed data are a text field.

dBASE IV allows you to use any ASCII character (other than comma) as a delimiter. Practically, you would probably want to use a punctuation mark, or another symbol not commonly found in normal text.

When the system rebuilds a database from a character delimited file, it looks for the comma to indicate where one field ends and the next begins. It recognizes the quotation mark (in this example) as the begin and end marker for a text field. However, it ignores any text inside a text field (for example, the nickname "Davie" that was added to the Davidson record) that was exported from the original file.

The data file that is created by exporting **PERSONEL.DBF** to this type of delimited field is shown in Figure 6-12.

When working with a text field that contains a quotation mark, a second set of quotation marks must be used. For example, in Figure 6-13, David Davidson's nickname (Davie) was inserted into the data file before it was exported, and was dropped out when it was imported. One way to get around the problem of the lost "Davie" is to use a different delimiter, perhaps the exclamation mark (!). With this delimiter, all exclamation marks will be stripped out when the file is appended, but the quotation marks should remain entirely intact.

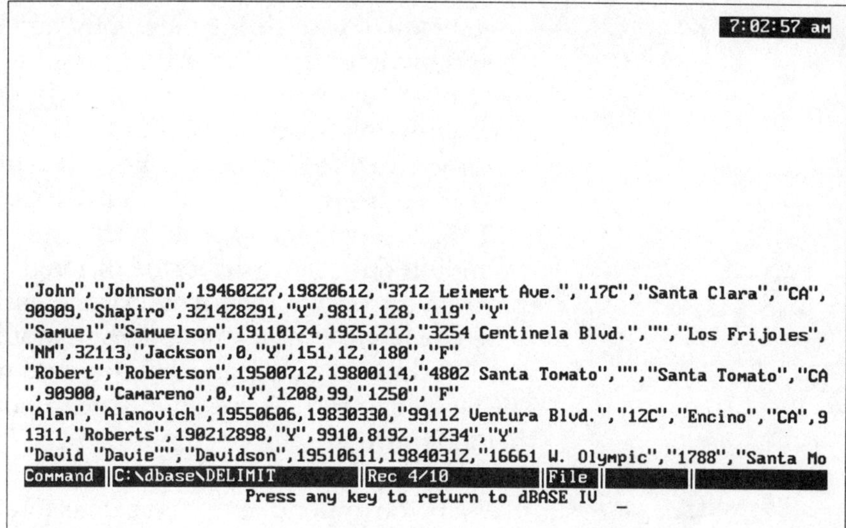

```
                                                                    7:02:57 am






"John","Johnson",19460227,19820612,"3712 Leimert Ave.","17C","Santa Clara","CA",
90909,"Shapiro",321428291,"Y",9811,128,"119","Y"
"Samuel","Samuelson",19110124,19251212,"3254 Centinela Blvd.","","Los Frijoles",
"NM",32113,"Jackson",0,"Y",151,12,"180","F"
"Robert","Robertson",19500712,19800114,"4802 Santa Tomato","","Santa Tomato","CA
",90900,"Camareno",0,"Y",1208,99,"1250","F"
"Alan","Alanovich",19550606,19830330,"99112 Ventura Blvd.","12C","Encino","CA",9
1311,"Roberts",190212898,"Y",9910,8192,"1234","Y"
"David "Davie"","Davidson",19510611,19840312,"16661 W. Olympic","1788","Santa Mo
Command ||C:\dbase\DELIMIT        ||Rec 4/10          ||File ||        ||
                    Press any key to return to dBASE IV _
```

Figure 6-12

Character delimited PERSONEL.txt file.

Again, as with the other delimited field types, the .txt extension is used. You should be careful, before exporting a file, that it will not overwrite another delimited file that has the same name. Also, remember that memo fields are neither appended from, nor exported by, dBASE IV's translation facilities for delimited files.

It is also important to remember that with any of the three dif-

Figure 6-13

Delimited file with field using quotation mark (Record 3).

Records   Fields   Go To   Exit   7:03:46 am

FIRST_NAME	LAST_NAME	BIRTH_DATE	HIRE_DATE	HOME_ADDR
John	Johnson	02/27/46	06/12/82	3712 Leimert Ave.
Samuel	Samuelson	01/24/11	12/12/25	3254 Centinela Blvd.
Robert	Robertson	07/12/50	01/14/80	4802 Santa Tomato
Alan	Alanovich	06/06/55	03/30/83	99112 Ventura Blvd.
David "Davie"	Davidson	06/11/51	03/12/84	16661 W. Olympic
John	Johnson	02/27/46	06/12/82	3712 Leimert Ave.
Samuel	Samuelson	01/24/11	12/12/25	3254 Centinela Blvd.
Robert	Robertson	07/12/50	01/14/80	4802 Santa Tomato
Alan	Alanovich	06/06/55	03/30/83	99112 Ventura Blvd.
David	Davidson	06/11/51	03/12/84	16661 W. Olympic

Browse || C:\dbase\DELIMIT || Rec 10/10 || File ||

View and edit fields

ferent types of text file formats, your word processor or other program may require a header line, or some other type of data line, describing the types of data and assigning field names. dBASE IV will not provide these header lines, because different applications require different header lines. It is also important to remove these lines from the file that you will be appending into dBASE IV. This is particularly true in the case of header lines that do not match data fields in terms of length or delimiters, because they may throw off the format of the entire appended database.

Before a file can be appended, it should be copied from your word processor or other program, and given the .txt extension. The header or format line should be removed, and the files should then be moved to the current dBASE IV directory so that it can be recognized and brought into your current database.

When you append or export a character delimited file, you will activate a screen that shows the ASCII characters. This is seen in Figure 6-14.

The default character, ", is usually popped onto the screen. The three columns represent the decimal and binary numbers for the symbol, and the symbol itself, in that order. By using the **UpArrow** or **DnArrow**, you can move the cursor to the delimiter with which you choose to work. The exported file or file to be appended from will then use the selected text delimiter character.

Figure 6-14

ASCII characters for export or appending from.

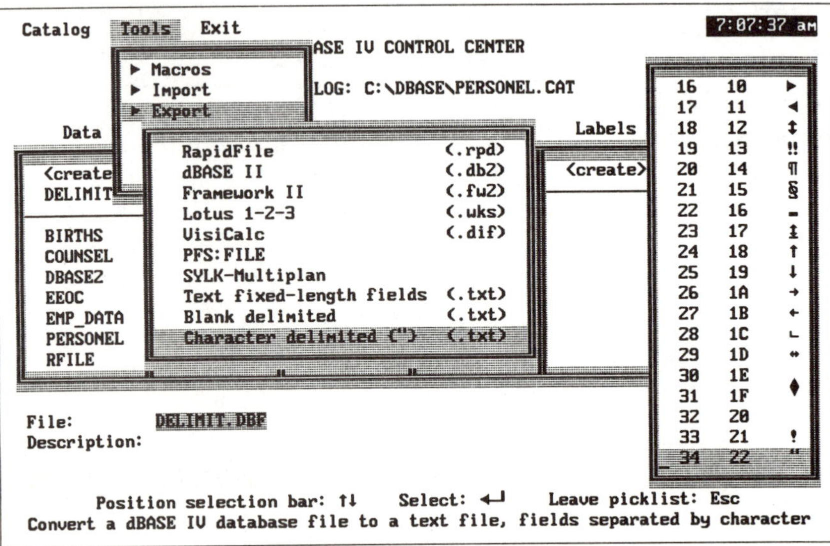

About Mail Merge

Mail Merge is a term that has become generic. It means the merging of variable data into a standard data document. For example, in the sample letter used to demonstrate fixed-length text fields, a basic letter was written, with the first name and last name inserted at the appropriate spot inside the text. This usage was a mail merge application.

Depending on the word processor you are using, certain forms of data selection can also be applied to the mail merged letter. An example of this type of functionality would be to print letters only to those people who had California addresses. Depending upon the difficulty of producing such a conditional list in your word processing program, you may prefer to make a specially tailored file with dBASE IV, and use that file as the source file for the mailing.

Some word processors, particularly MultiMate Advantage 2 and 3, also from Ashton-Tate, are said to be capable of directly importing data from a dBASE file. However, you may still want to prepare a file with the data already presorted and put into an order that most closely suits your mail merge tasks.

Again, depending on the word processor that is using your data files, you may have to physically go into the data files generated by dBASE IV and make modifications that would provide compatibility with the word processor that will be printing the data. Consult the manual that came with your word processor for the correct format for data files that will be mail merged.

The Query function, discussed in Chapter Ten, is very useful for making such preselected, presorted data files. Files can be built using data from many databases, if necessary. Once the file with the data in the correct order has been built, dBASE IV's export capabilities will allow you to move the file in the correct order and format for your word processor to work with.

From the Dot Prompt

Import, Export, and Append functions are all relatively simple and straightforward using the Control Center. However, if you wish to use program commands to accomplish the same functions, you can do this rather simply.

To import a file (again, remember that only Framework II and III files [.FW2], RapidFile [.rpd] files, dBASE II [.db2], Lotus 1-2-3 Version 2.0 and 2.1 files [.WK1] and PFS:FILE and PFS:Professional File files can be imported),

Type: *IMPORT FROM FILENAME type FILETYPE*

in which FILETYPE is the type of file that is being imported. For example, to import a dBASE II file called PERSONEL.DB2

Type: *IMPORT FROM PERSONEL TYPE DBASEII*

The file types for the other importable files are as follows:

RapidFile	TYPE RAPID
Framework II	TYPE FWII
Lotus 1-2-3 (.WK1)	TYPE WK1

Exporting files is done in a similar manner. However, the command Export works only for PFS, dBASE II, Framework II, and RapidFile. The currently active database is exported using this command. The syntax to export a file is as follows:

EXPORT TO FILENAME TYPE FILETYPE

in which FILETYPE is the file type designator used by dBASE IV. When you designate the target file, you may also include the path name.

For example, to export a file called PERSONEL to a RapidFile file,

Type: *EXPORT TO C:\DBASE\PERSONEL TYPE RPD*

File types for export are as follows:

RapidFile	TYPE RPD
dBASE II	TYPE dbaseII
Framework II	TYPE FW2
PFS:File	TYPE PFS

If you attach a view file to the data file (if a data form was attached in the Control Center or if you used the Set Format command from the dot prompt), a PFS view file will also be exported.

For the other supported file types, the Copy command is used instead of the Export command. With the exception of PFS:File, the other formats can also be exported using the Copy command. The currently active database will be copied using this command.

The syntax for copying a database file is as follows:

COPY TO FILENAME TYPE FILETYPE

in which FILENAME is the name that the file will be given, and FILETYPE is the type of file translation to be made.

Conditional statements can be used for the file definition but are beyond the scope of the current discussion.

In addition to the types listed above, the other data types are as follows:

Lotus 1-2-3 (.WKS)	TYPE WKS
VisiCalc (.DIF)	TYPE DIF
SYLK-Multiplan	TYPE SYLK
Fixed length	TYPE SDF
Delimited with blank	TYPE DELIMITED WITH BLANK
Character delimited	TYPE DELIMITED WITH <char> (where <char> is the delimiting character for text)

Appending from a foreign database or spreadsheet is very similar to copying the file. The file will be appended from the selected database and appended to the currently active file.

The syntax for the Append From command is almost the same as the Copy command. It is as follows:

APPEND FROM <FILENAME> TYPE <FILETYPE>

in which <FILENAME> is the name of the file to be appended from, and <FILETYPE> represents the file type as listed above.

In this chapter, you have seen how to work with the wide range of data files that are currently being used on personal computers. With the simple steps given, you should be able to share your data with other programs, in addition to bringing in and working with data from other software.

Index, Sort, and Text Edit

The design and entry of data into data files that were created by you are only the first steps in using dBASE IV. Once a database has been built, you still have to get at the data.

In addition to just viewing the data, you will most likely want to retrieve the data in a particular order. This is particularly important when printing forms, labels, cards, and reports. Because the Reports facility and Labels facility are designed for formatting and printing to paper, the screen, or a file on disk for later printing, any data that are to be printed using these functions must be put into the order in which you want the reports or labels output.

Fortunately, dBASE IV provides many tools for ordering your data files. In addition, memo fields are often used in dBASE IV files. The report and label processors are designed to print the contents of a memo field, but not to substantially change the appearance (aside from handling carriage returns when you merge text with data).

Learning the basics of editing text using dBASE IV's built-in text editor can aid in the entry of text, in writing text for reports, and in controlling the appearance of modified dBASE programs.

About Indexing

When a book is indexed, the indexer reads through the proof, highlights key points, and jots down the page or pages on which the points appear in the text. An index is then created for insertion at the back of the book. When readers want to find a particular topic, they go to the index (which is almost always in ascending alphabetic order) and find the topic and the page on which the discussion of that topic is located in the book. In effect, an index is a lookup table that allows you to find a desired string of text or other items.

An index prepared by dBASE IV is essentially the same. When you define an index in dBASE IV, the system goes through all the records in your file, puts them into the order that you specify, and then creates an index file that includes the record numbers in the desired order.

Your database does not change; only the order in which the records are displayed changes. And the indexed order is only temporary—record number 1 will always be record number 1, even if you have an alphabetically ordered file and the first record's name is Zeus.

When you include more than one expression for an index, for example, indexing by ZIP code, then last name, the system first indexes on the initial expression, then indexes *within each value* for the next expression. In an index by ZIP code and first name, all records with a ZIP code of 10000 will be placed at the front of the index order. Within this ZIP code, the records will be ordered alphabetically by last name. If, on the other hand, you selected an index on ZIP code only, the records for 10000 will still be at the beginning of the index, but the last names will be found in the same order as they naturally occur in the database.

dBASE IV handles index management in a much more efficient way than earlier versions of dBASE. Previous versions of the program allowed you to define an index structure, and then attach the index to a particular database. The index structure file used the .NDX file extension. With dBASE IV's new catalog management and index management capabilities, a new master index file is created that uses the extension .MDX (for master index).

And it truly *is* a master index. The master index file allows you to create many new indexes. You may also include the .NDX files created with earlier versions of dBASE into your master index. In addition, a master index may also contain .NDX structures that were designed for other catalogs or other databases. The master index allows you to select an index structure from within its library of indexes, as well as create an index statement of your own.

To see how the indexing functions work, go to the Control Center and tell the system that you want to Modify the structure of the Personnel file. To do this, move the highlight to the Data column and

Type: **PER**

The system should highlight the "PERSONEL" data file after the first letter or two that you type.

Press: **Shft-F2**

to bring you into the Data Design menu.

The Organize menu will pop up, with the file structure below it (Figure 7-1). The top half of the menu deals directly with indexing of your database. You will notice that there is a column on the right side of the database design box with Index as the column heading. Below that, a few fields are marked with a *Y*, with the majority of the fields filled in with an *N*.

When you designed your database, you told the system that you want it to create an index based on the fields marked with a *Y* in the Index column. To see how this works, let's browse your database file before and after applying your index to the file.

To remove the Organize menu,

Press: **Esc**

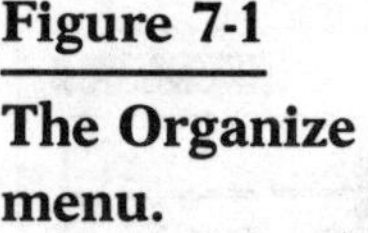

Figure 7-1

The Organize menu.

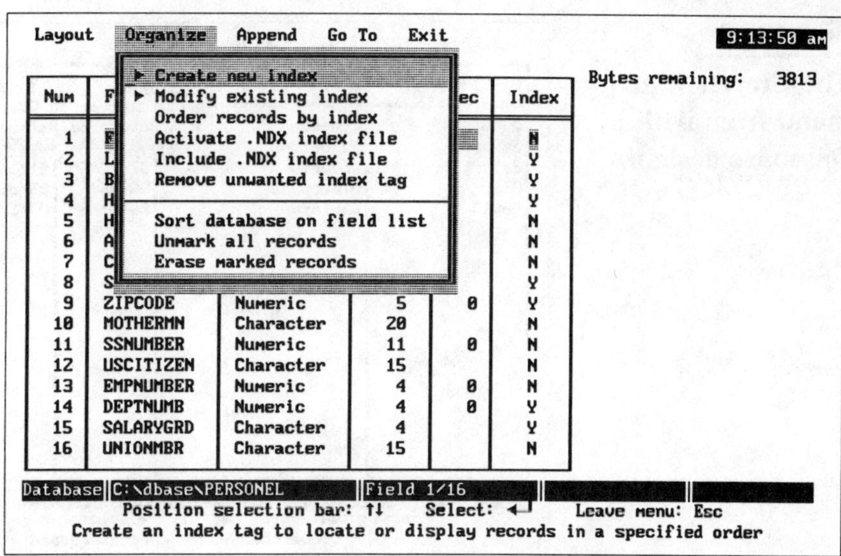

Records Fields Go To Exit 9:06:43 am

FIRSTNAME	LASTNAME	BIRTHDATE	HIREDATE	HOMEADDR
John	Johnson	02/27/46	06/12/82	3712 Leimert Ave.
Samuel	Samuelson	01/24/11	12/12/25	3254 Centinela Blvd.
Robert	Robertson	07/12/50	01/14/80	4802 Santa Tomato
Alan	Alanovich	06/06/55	03/30/83	99112 Ventura Blvd.
David	Davidson	06/11/51	03/12/84	16661 W. Olympic

Browse C:\dbase\PERSONEL Rec 1/5 File

View and edit fields

Figure 7-2

The Browse screen for unindexed data.

The Organize menu will be removed from the screen, and your Data Design screen will be active. To go into Browse/Edit,

Press: **F2**

Your system will bring up either the Browse screen, as seen in Figure 7-2, or the Edit screen, which contains only a single record.

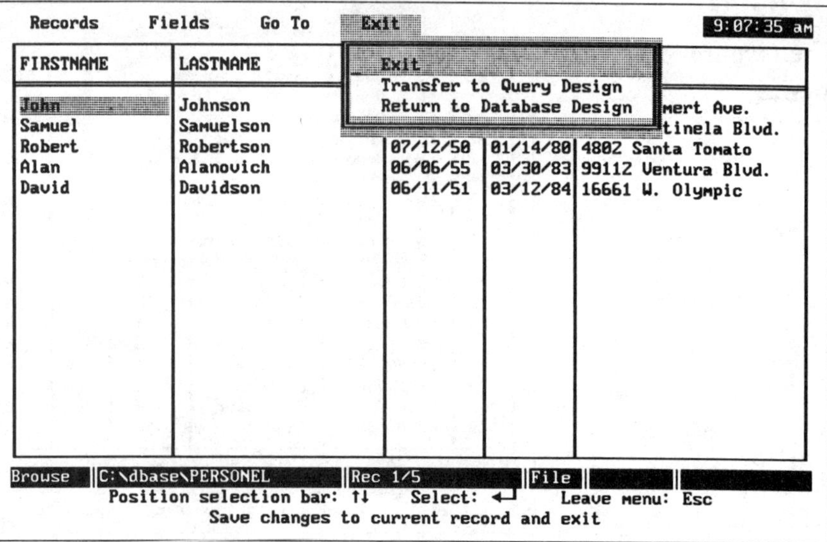

Figure 7-3

The Browse Exit menu from within Database design.

If the Edit screen is showing,

Press: **F2**

to toggle back to the Browse screen.

You will see that the names are in the order in which they were input into the database. If you use the **DnArrow** to scroll down, you will see that the record number (as seen in the information bar at the bottom of the screen) increases, going from 1 to 5.

Now, return to the Modify File Structure menu so that you can apply an index order to the database. To do this,

Press: **Alt-E**

to bring you to the **Exit** menu (Figure 7-3).

Select Return to Database Design. To do this,

Press: **R**

The system will return you to the Database design screen, with the Organize menu again active. Select Order records by index. To do this,

Type: *O*

The system will bring up a list of index names that are contained in the current database file's .MDX file. In this case, only the fields marked for indexing will be shown, as seen in Figure 7-4.

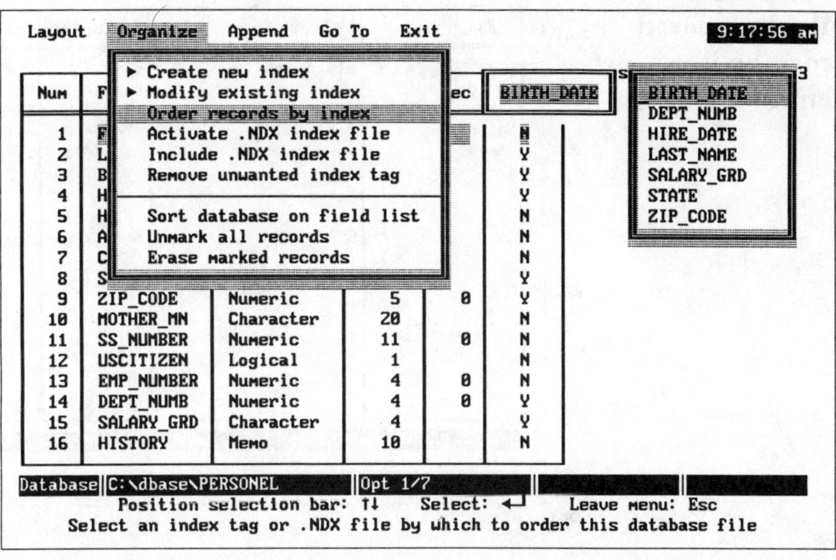

Figure 7-4

Pick list for index selection.

Select LAST__NAME

A window will appear briefly as the system reindexes the file. Now, to see how the index works, return to the Browse screen. To return,

Press: **F2**

The system will now show your files in LAST__NAME order, as seen in Figure 7-5.

> NOTE: In early versions of dBASE IV, including the last prerelease version, the index order was not applied. To apply the index, first use the Modify Index commands and accept the current index order setting by pressing **Ctrl-End**. The system will then index all files. At that point, you can Order the records by index order.

You should have noticed that the first displayed record is actually the fourth one that you entered into the database. Scrolling farther through the files (using **UpArrow** and **DnArrow**) will confirm that the record numbers are no longer in numerical order.

If, for some reason, the files were not in the correct order, it may be because the database structure has not as yet been saved. When you save a database design, the system automatically builds each index.

Figure 7-5

Files in indexed order, by last name.

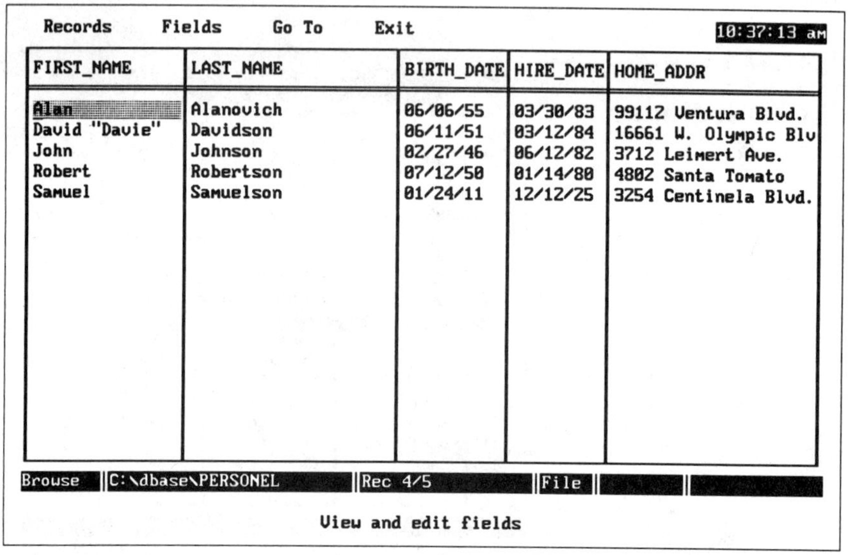

Records Fields Go To Exit 10:37:13 am

FIRST_NAME	LAST_NAME	BIRTH_DATE	HIRE_DATE	HOME_ADDR
Alan	Alanovich	06/06/55	03/30/83	99112 Ventura Blvd.
David "Davie"	Davidson	06/11/51	03/12/84	16661 W. Olympic Blv
John	Johnson	02/27/46	06/12/82	3712 Leimert Ave.
Robert	Robertson	07/12/50	01/14/80	4802 Santa Tomato
Samuel	Samuelson	01/24/11	12/12/25	3254 Centinela Blvd.

Browse ‖C:\dbase\PERSONEL ‖Rec 4/5 ‖File ‖

View and edit fields

If you Exit to the Control Center your data will appear in the currently indexed order. To see this,

Press: **Alt-E**

and select **Exit to Control Center**.

Making sure that "PERSONEL" is still highlighted,

Press: **F2**

to bring up the Browse screen. The files will still be in the index order.

It may be well to go to the Forms screen and tell the system that you want to Display your files. Again, the files will be shown in the indexed order, rather than in the order of entry.

It is important to remember, however, that the changes to the file are only temporary; these records will be in index order only until you use another database, apply another index, or turn the system off. However, an index is a handy tool for quickly organizing your data into an order that can be used for viewing or modifying, or for printing reports and forms in a particular order.

Now, return to the Modify Data Design window from within the Control Center by highlighting the "PERSONEL" database and pressing **Shft-F2**. When this window first pops up, the Organize menu will be open. This is no accident: the designers of dBASE IV realized that you will be accessing this menu most of the times that you go into Modify a Data Design. (Once a data design is made and saved, you probably will not want to make further changes to its structure; however, you may want to change the order of the files.)

To see how to work with an index file, we will go through the menu in roughly top-to-bottom order.

The first item on the menu, Create new index, is used to design a new index statement for defining a new type of index. When this option is selected, the system brings up an index design screen, as seen in Figure 7-6.

The top two options are opened using the **ENTER** key. Open the Name of index line and

Type: *CITYNAME* **ENTER**

to name an index that you will be creating to order your data by City and Last name, and move you to the Index expression line.

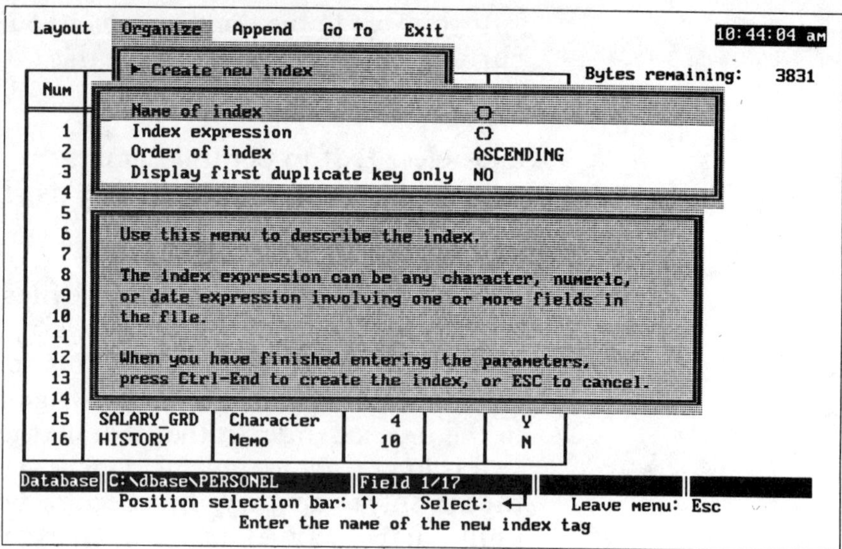

Figure 7-6

Index creation screen.

Press: **ENTER**

to open the Index expression line. To see available options for setting up your index,

Press: **Shft-F1**

A new screen will show all fields in the current data file and all available operators and functions. If you scroll through the list of fields, you will notice that logical fields are not highlighted in the menu. This indicates that they cannot be chosen as an index field.

The method for building expressions has been explained elsewhere in this book. To do a simple index on City and Last Name, use the + operator. The expression for the desired index is

CITY+LAST__NAME

You could also have put space between the fields and the logical operator. In this case, the + key is used to indicate sort order, and is not a mathematical expression. However, for numeric fields the situation is somewhat more ambiguous.

When your expression is completed,

Press: **ENTER**

to accept the expression and move you to the Order of Index item. Note that the system will check to determine whether or not your index expression is valid. If it is not, you will not be allowed to move to the next field unless it is corrected or the line is blanked.

The Order of index column allows you two options, toggled using the **Space Bar**. The first, Ascending, puts your data in order from *A* to *Z* then *0* to *9*; the second, Descending, puts your data in order from *Z* to *A* and *9* to *0*. Leave the order set to Ascending.

The final option, Display first duplicate key only, is also toggled using the **Space Bar** or **ENTER** key. This option tells the system what to do if it encounters more than one value for your index expression. For example, if you were indexing on LAST_NAME, and you have five people named Kozlowski, setting the option to *No* will display all five Kozlowski files. On the other hand, setting the option to *Yes* will put only the first Kozlowski into the index. This option is useful if you want to make a list of cities in which your employees reside, but not how many live in each city. Thus, if you made such an indexed file, and then set up a report to print only the city names, you would easily create an alphabetically sorted list of all cities in which employees live.

The current setup for the new index is shown in Figure 7-7.

To accept the new index, and have the system build the index,

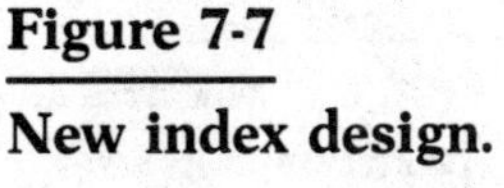

Figure 7-7

New index design.

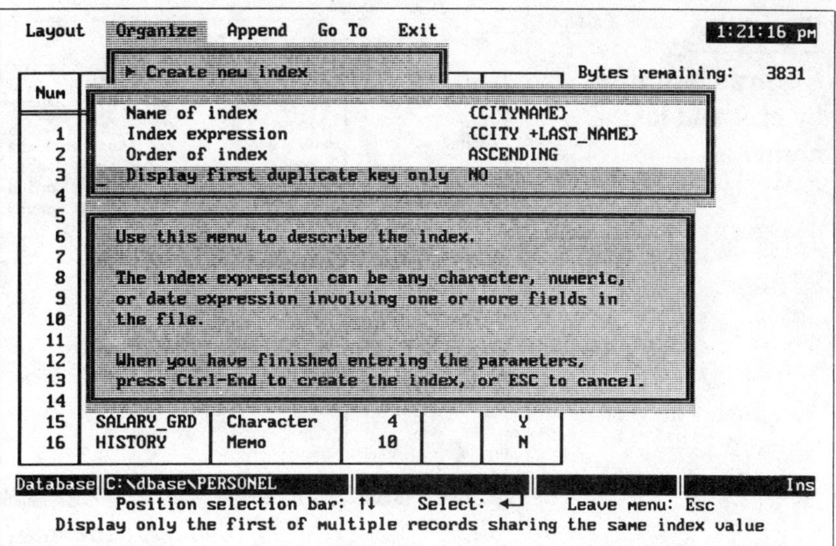

Press: **Ctrl-End**

The index expression will appear in the center of the screen, and the system will index the files, returning you to the Design menu. To see data set according to the new index,

Press: **F2**

Next, lock the first two fields, FIRST__NAME and LAST__NAME. To do this,

Press: **Alt-F2 ENTER**

Next, press the **Tab** key until the *City* field becomes visible. You will see that the records are, indeed, in order by city. The last names are also in order, based on the City field order. The names may appear to be out of order only because each record is in a unique city. However, if you had more than one employee who lived in the same city, the last names of those people in the same city will be shown in alphabetic order. The Browse screen with the files in order by City and Last Name is shown in Figure 7-8.

To return to the Database Design screen,

Press: **Alt-E** *R*

The next option in the Organize menu is Modify existing index.

Figure 7-8

Records in order by city and last name.

Records Fields Go To Exit 1:25:59 pm

FIRST_NAME	LAST_NAME	CITY	STATE	ZIP_CODE	MOTHE
Alan	Alanovich	Encino	CA	91311	Rober
Samuel	Samuelson	Los Frijoles	NM	32113	Jacks
John	Johnson	Santa Clara	CA	90909	Shapi
David "Davie"	Davidson	Santa Monica	CA	90099	Dicki
Robert	Robertson	Santa Tomato	CA	90900	Camar

Browse ‖C:\dbase\PERSONEL ‖Rec 4/5 ‖File ‖ ‖ Ins

View and edit fields

When this is selected, the screen will bring up a list of available indexes. The names of the indexes are displayed in the window to the right. A single index scrolls through a selection window as you move the cursor through the index list. The expression for CITYNAME and the index selection box are shown in Figure 7-9.

When you highlight an index and

Press: **ENTER**

the Index Creation screen (Figure 7-6) is brought up. If you decide not to change the index expression

Press: **Esc**

to return you to the Organize menu. If you change the name of an existing index, the system will reindex the database and apply a new name. You will not be able to copy an index expression by calling up the Modify menu, bringing up an index structure, and renaming the index, although this utility would be useful when complicated index expressions are to be used.

Order records by index has already been discussed. This option allows you to select an existing index and have the system put the records into index order. If the file has been previously indexed and not changed, the system may not bother reindexing

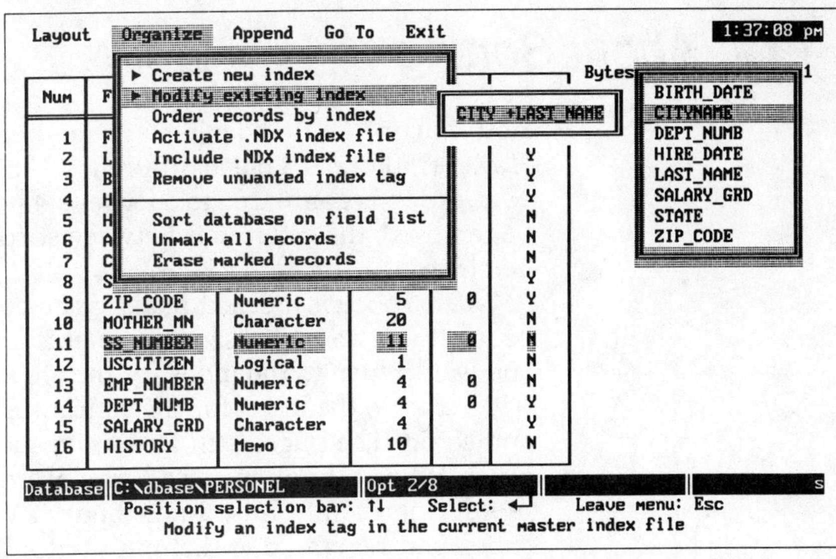

Figure 7-9

Index selection box, with CITYNAME highlighted.

the file; it will simply call up existing index pointers from the index table.

The next two options concern the .NDX index files created by earlier versions of dBASE. Include .NDX index file allows you to select a predefined .NDX file for incorporation into the current master index (.MDX) file. When you select this option, a listing of the .NDX files in the current disk subdirectory is displayed. To select an .NDX file, highlight it and press **ENTER**. If the desired .NDX file is not in your current directory, you may use this screen to navigate to other disks or directories.

Activate .NDX index file allows you to select an .NDX file that is already in your master index. This file will be updated as you make changes to your database. .NDX files that are not activated will be updated only when this option is selected.

Finally, Remove unwanted index tag allows you to select an index file to be removed from your current master index (.MDX). When you choose this option, two windows that are similar to those shown in Figure 7-9 will pop onto the screen. Once you select an index for removal, the system will remove the index from your .MDX file. The system will not prompt you to confirm that you want this done. Therefore, you must be careful before removing an index tag from your existing master index.

About Sorting

Both sorting and indexing are methods used to order data. However, there is a basic difference. If a bound book, with a set page order, is compared to a loose-leaf book, in which pages can be removed, the difference between sorting and indexing would be clear.

When a book is indexed, a table is created that refers to specific pages. If you wanted to see the contents of the book *in index order*, you would turn to the index for the page number of the first entry, return to the index for the page number of the second entry, and so on. The pages still remain in the book in their original order. When a book is sorted, you are removing the pages and reordering them. Thus, a new book is created, using the same pages, but rearranging them in sort order.

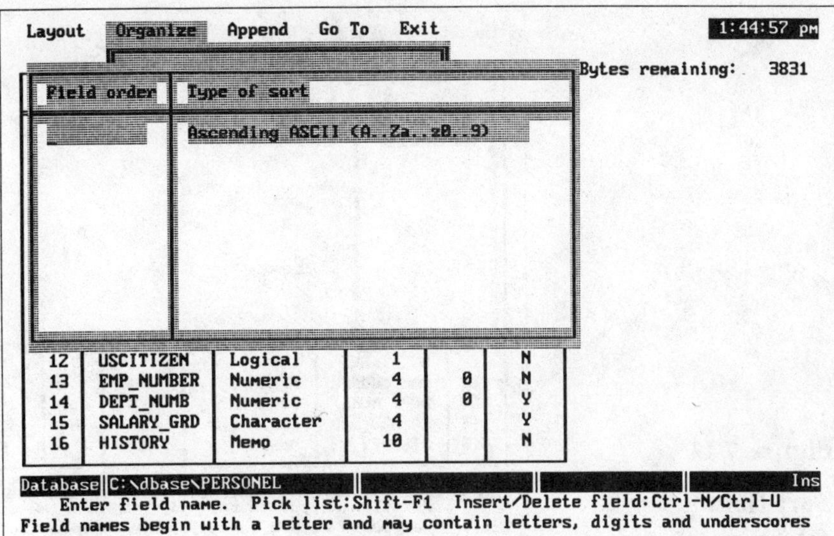

Figure 7-10

Sort order design window.

To see how this works, select Sort database on field list. The system will pop up a window for designing your sort specification (Figure 7-10). To see the available fields on which to sort,

Press: **Shft-F1**

This brings up a list of the fields in the current database (Figure 7-11). Those fields that cannot be sorted (memo fields) are shown in light rather than bold type. (Unfortunately, this difference in type cannot be seen in the figure.)

In this first example, you will build a new database in order by HIRE_DATE and LAST_NAME. Select HIRE_DATE from the pick list. The system will drop the field into the Field order column.

Press: **ENTER**

to move the cursor into the Type of sort column.

dBASE IV allows you to perform any of four different types of sorts. The **Space Bar** switches from one type of sort to the next. To see how each sort will work, assume that we have three records with the names Aaronson, adams, and Zeidler.

An Ascending ASCII sort sorts from uppercase *A* to *Z*, then lowercase *a* to *z*, and finally from *0* to *9*. Thus, an ascending sort

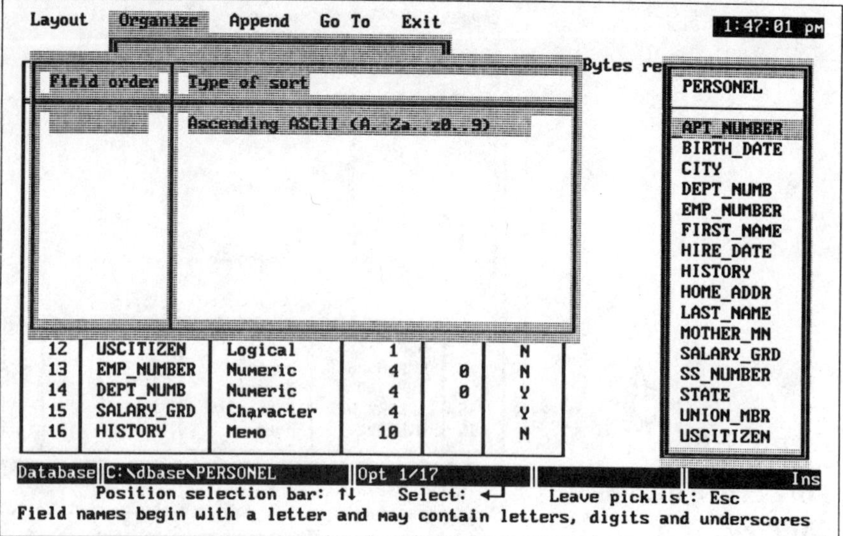

Figure 7-11

Sort field selection window.

of the above three names would yield a file in the following order: Aaronson, Zeidler, adams (because adams is lowercase and lowercase characters follow uppercase characters in a standard ASCII sort).

A Descending ASCII sort works in the opposite way, except that the numeric fields still follow the alphabetic fields. The order for a Descending ASCII sort is from lowercase *z* to *a*, then uppercase *Z* to A, and finally from *9* to *0*. Thus, in a descending sort the three names would appear in this order: adams, Zeidler, Aaronson.

The next two types of sorts, collectively referred to as Dictionary sorts, sort the data in order as a dictionary would; however, the case of the letters is not as important in setting the sort order. In an Ascending Dictionary sort the order for the three names would be Aaronson, adams, Zeidler, or pretty much what you expect from a standard sort. A Descending Dictionary sorts in the opposite direction, or from *zZ* to *aA* and from *9* to *0*. Therefore the order for the three names would be Zeidler, adams, Aaronson. It is interesting to note that if you had two entries, one for Smith, and the other for smith, the order in a descending sort for the two Smiths would be smith, Smith.

Select Ascending Dictionary for this sort by pressing the **Space Bar** until the desired sort method is shown and pressing **ENTER** to select the sort method.

One excellent addition to dBASE IV is its ability to correctly sort date fields. In earlier versions of dBASE, sorting dates was difficult and required special steps to convert a date to a numeric field, sort, and convert back to dates. dBASE IV now handles dates automatically.

You will add two additional sort fields, both of which will be ascending dictionary sorts. The first is LAST_NAME and the second is FIRST_NAME. For a large company, it is possible that more than one person with the same surname may be hired on the same date. By sorting on the first name after sorting on the last name, the first names will also be ordered within the sorted last name field.

After you add those fields, the system will bring up an empty bar for the next field order statement. Your sort selections will appear as shown in Figure 7-12. There are other options for editing a sort expression. To insert a blank line between two sort fields in order to position a new field onto your sort specification, move the cursor to the line in which you want to insert your new sort field, and

Press: **Ctrl-n**

To delete a sort field line, position the highlight on the line that you wish to delete and

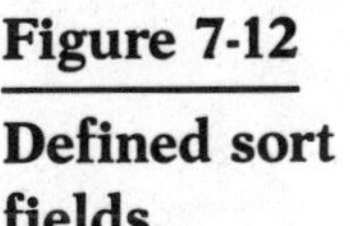

Figure 7-12

Defined sort fields.

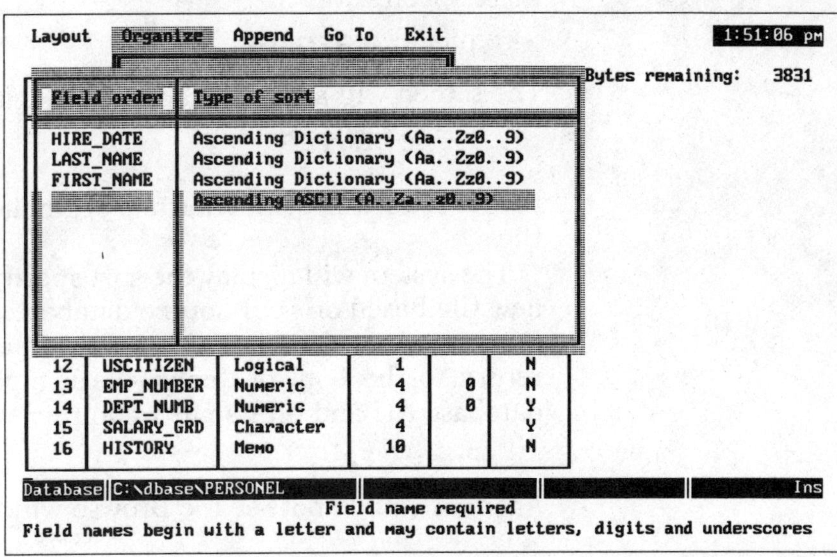

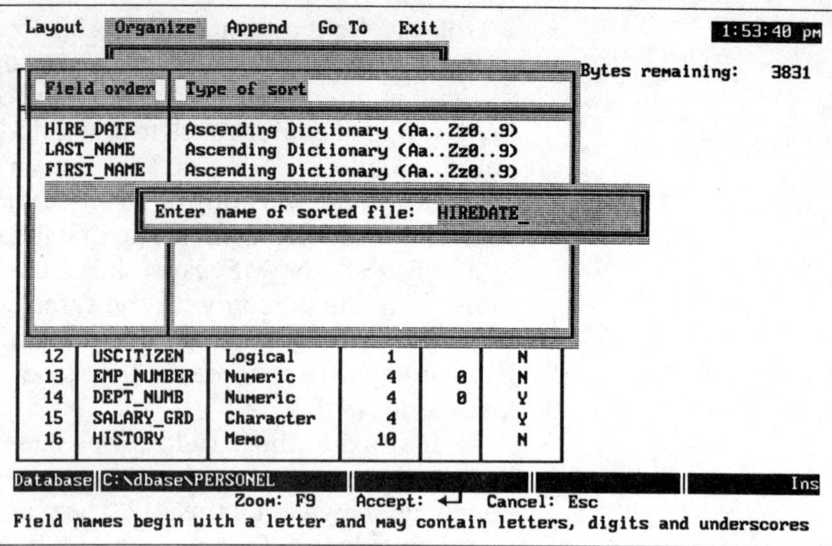

Figure 7-13

Naming a sorted file.

Press: **Ctrl-U**

Because, in this example, you have set up the sort order that you require,

Press: **ENTER**

The screen will ask for a name for your file that is sorted from these specifications.

Type: ***HIREDATE***

The screen will appear as shown in Figure 7-13.

Press: **ENTER**

to save the sort specification and begin the creation of the sorted file.

The system will display the sort specification, and produce a new file based on your source database and the sort specification. To see the new file, Exit from the Data Design menu file and return to the Control Center. Next, highlight the HIREDATE database file and browse it. To do this,

Press: **F2**

Again, if you do not see the Browse window press **F2** to switch

Records	Fields	Go To	Exit	1:56:10 pm

FIRST_NAME	LAST_NAME	BIRTH_DATE	HIRE_DATE	HOME_ADDR
Samuel	Samuelson	01/24/11	12/12/25	3254 Centinela Blvd.
Robert	Robertson	07/12/50	01/14/80	4802 Santa Tomato
John	Johnson	02/27/46	06/12/82	3712 Leimert Ave.
Alan	Alanovich	06/06/55	03/30/83	99112 Ventura Blvd.
David "Davie"	Davidson	06/11/51	03/12/84	16661 W. Olympic Blv

Browse | C:\dbase\HIREDATE | Rec 1/5 | File | Ins

View and edit fields

Figure 7-14

New file created by SORT options.

from Edit to Browse. The Browse screen for the new file will appear as shown in Figure 7-14.

You will notice that the files are now numbered in order by HIRE_DATE. A sort field is useful if you want to create a database file in a particular order, rather than using indexes to build an order for your files. If you are creating a database that will be used by others who may not know about or be comfortable with indexing, a sorted file may be the best solution, although a Query can do the same type of sorts and also create files from merged data using a variety of sorting variables.

Sort files take somewhat longer to produce than indexes because the system must first sort the data file based on your sort parameters, and then copy each file, in order, into a new file. More data need to be moved in creating a sort file than in creating a comparatively small indexing file.

If you wish, you may experiment with other types of sorts to see how files based on sort criteria are designed and generated by dBASE IV.

Sorting and indexing are also incorporated into the Query menu, and can be used to produce special data files based on query conditions and sort and index parameters that the user defines.

About Memo Fields and Text Editing

When you set up your form file for the PERSONEL database, you set up the form for the HISTORY field, a memo field, to show the word MEMO on your form. This type of display is shown in Figure 7-15. When you display data using this data entry form, the screen appears as shown in Figure 7-16.

The important thing to notice is that the Employee History section simply has the one word marker. When you update or view your files using this display, you can move the cursor into the marker. To get the memo window to open, however, you must move into it using the **F3** or **F4** keys, unless you move the cursor to the marker and press **Ctrl-Home** to open the Edit window.

If, on the other hand, you design a memo window onto your form, your data entry and view form will appear as shown in Figure 7-17, with the contents of the memo field displayed in a window on your form. The form design that produced the memo window is shown in Figure 7-18.

This type of window was set up from within the Fields menu. When a memo field is put onto the form, you are given a choice of Display options. When Marker is chosen, the word *MEMO* ap-

Figure 7-15

Form designed with MEMO marker.

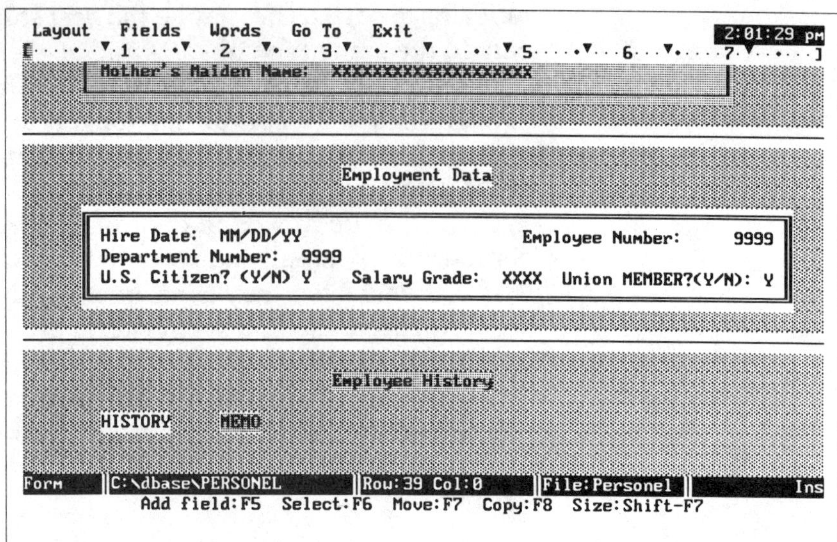

Layout Fields Words Go To Exit 2:01:29 pm

Mother's Maiden Name: XXXXXXXXXXXXXXXXXXX

Employment Data

Hire Date: MM/DD/YY Employee Number: 9999
Department Number: 9999
U.S. Citizen? (Y/N) Y Salary Grade: XXXX Union MEMBER?(Y/N): Y

Employee History

HISTORY MEMO

Form | C:\dbase\PERSONEL | Row:39 Col:0 | File:Personel | Ins
Add field:F5 Select:F6 Move:F7 Copy:F8 Size:Shift-F7

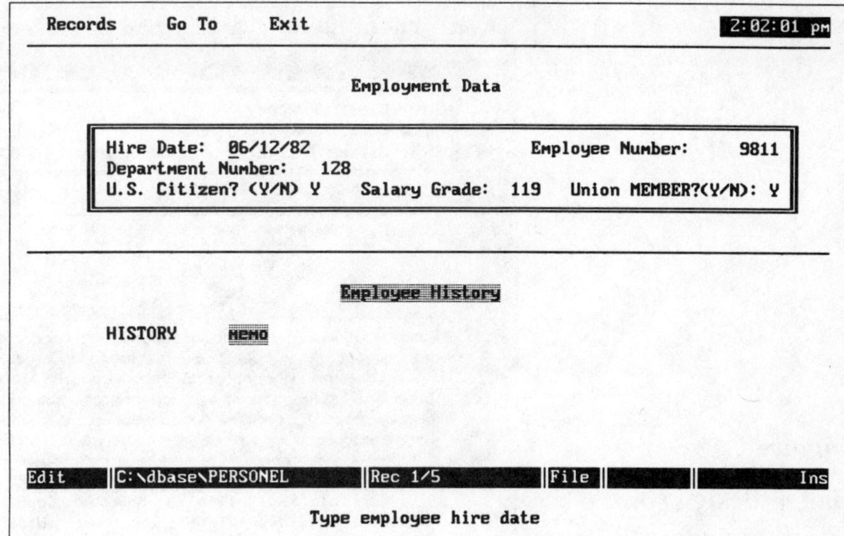

Figure 7-16

Data display, using marker for memo field.

pears on your form. Choosing Window allows you to define the size of the window and select the type of border for the window. When the form is used, the contents of the memo file will be displayed on the form.

It is useful to remember, however, that although the memo text

Figure 7-17

Memo display using memo window.

```
Records     Go To     Exit                                   2:08:08 pm

                          Employment Data

    Hire Date:  06/12/82                     Employee Number:     9811
    Department Number:    128
    U.S. Citizen? (Y/N) Y    Salary Grade:  119   Union MEMBER?(Y/N): Y

                          Employee History
    HISTORY

Edit  C:\dbase\PERSONEL        Rec 1/5       File

                         Type Employee Number
```

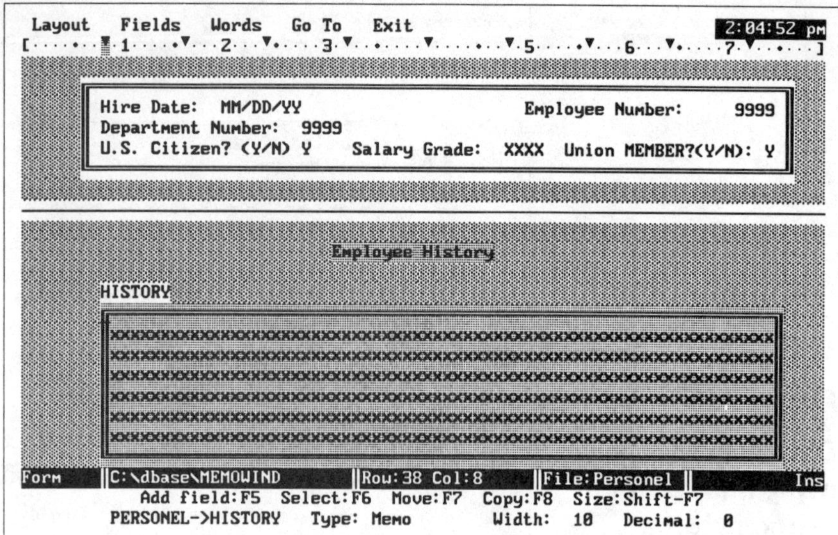

Figure 7-18

Form design for memo window.

is displayed in the window, it cannot be modified without opening the window in the same way as was done with a memo marker. A memo window is useful for viewing the first lines in your memo file for each record.

A memo field creates a text file that is viewed from within the form calling it. dBASE IV comes with a text processor that is suitable for most dBASE-related tasks. In addition to being used for data input and modification, the text editor is also accessible from within the Report Generator, which allows you to switch from the form design editor to the text editor, and in the Modify a Program feature of the Applications Generator. It is therefore helpful to know how the text editor works.

Reload PERSONEL from the Data column by highlighting "PERSONEL" and pressing **F2**. Next, cursor down to the SALARY_GRD field and press **F4** to move the cursor into the HISTORY field and open the Memo. You could also have used the **Tab** key or the **ENTER** key to move into the HISTORY field, but these would only have positioned the cursor in the field; they would not have opened the memo window. To open a memo window in which the cursor is positioned, press **Ctrl-Home.** If a Memo field is located anywhere but at the end of your data file, you may also back into and open the field by using the **F3** key.

Highlight the "PERSONEL" data file and

Press: **F2**

to load the Edit screen. The Browse screen can also come up. Next, using the **F4** key, advance through the fields until you get to the HISTORY field. If the window does not open when you move into it, use the **CTRL-HOME** key combination to open the Text edit window (Figure 7-19).

Type the text as displayed in Figure 7-19. You will notice that as you typed, the text automatically moved to the next line. This feature, called Word Wrap, is a part of the text edit mode. The form design mode, which allows you to design your forms, does not provide a word wrap capability at the end of each line. A carriage return is used to move to the next line.

The importance of word wrap is that the words automatically wrap from one line to the next without the use of returns. This is useful because you may often append text to memo fields, or insert text into a text-based document. In a file that is made using hard carriage returns at the end of each line, the system will treat each line as a separate paragraph, splitting the entire file into a series of paragraphs that are one line long. If you add to or remove text from such a file, the appearance of the text will change drastically, because instead of appearing to be one paragraph, your lines will wind up ending in places all over your screen. With

Figure 7-19

Text edit window.

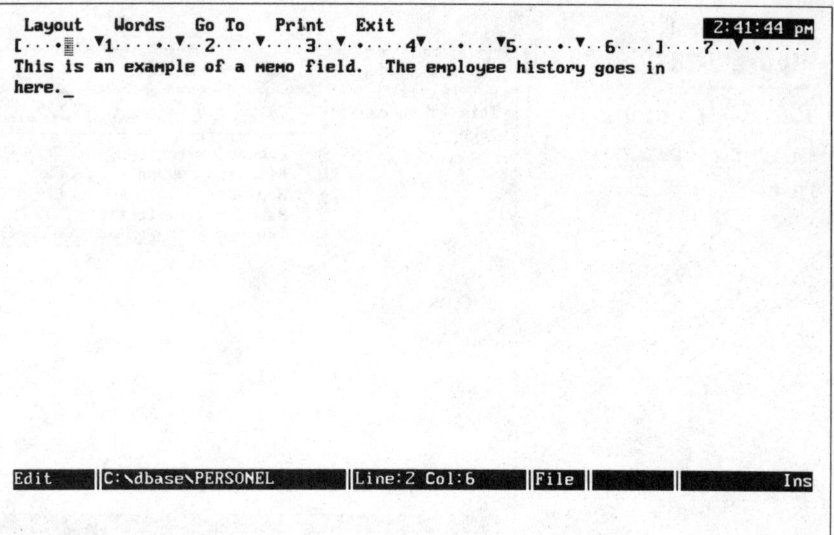

Word Wrap, you can add or remove text, and the system will automatically fit the text to fill the margins. The only time a carriage return is used in your text files is when you have pressed the **ENTER** key to indicate the end of the paragraph.

A quick look at the menus highlights a few differences from the layout design format. The Layout menu provides you with only one option: Save this memo field. You will recall that the layout editor provided you with the ability to perform a variety of forms layouts, and also allowed you to draw lines and boxes. The Draw and Layout functions are not supported by the text editor. (In the Report design form, however, you can switch between layout and Word Wrap editors, drawing a line or box, and then switching to text edit mode to create your text.)

The Words menu is very much like the one also used in the Reports design column. The options are explained in more detail in Chapter 9. Similarly, the Go To menu (Figure 7-20) allows you functionality similar to other Go To menus in the Forms, Label, and Report designer.

The Replace option is unique to the text editor. When selected, it will search for a selected text string. You next tell the system what the replacement text should be. The system then searches through the file and prompts to see if you want to make the replacement, skip the current occurrence of the word and go to the next, or replace all occurrences without asking. It also allows

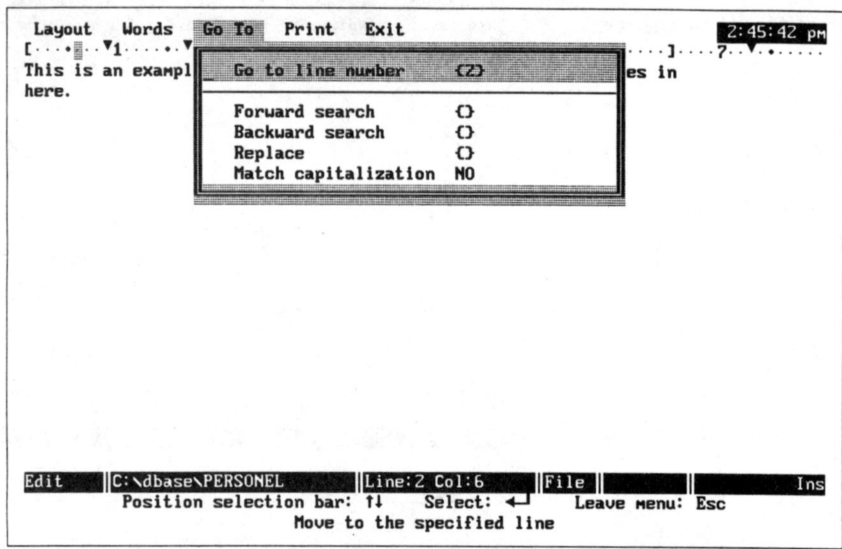

Figure 7-20

The Go To menu in word wrap mode.

you to quit the search process by pressing **Esc**. This capability is discussed further in later chapters.

The Print menu is also discussed further in Chapters Eight and Nine and will not be discussed here.

Finally, the Exit menu allows you to Save or Abandon your changes and exit to the point in your program that your cursor was in when the text editor was loaded.

The Save option in the Layout menu allows you to save your file without exiting.

Ruler line editing has already been discussed in Chapter 4. Ruler modification is not permitted when producing a memo field, although it is available from within Report design. It is probably a good idea not to make changes to the default settings, because text merged from files that use different margins may look wrong when combined with a text file using a different layout.

One other point needs mentioning: the text editor in dBASE IV cannot compete with today's full-featured, exceptionally functional word processing programs. It is not meant to. dBASE IV allows you to use other text editors. However, the editor used must be able to produce a plain ASCII file. Do not specify a new text editor instead of the one provided in dBASE IV because you may run into some compatibility problems with the new program, and the editor included in dBASE IV is, in most cases, more than adequate.

You can also create text files that can be imported into dBASE IV text files using your own word processor. However, before the text file can be read from your word processor into a text file, it must first be converted into straight ASCII. This type of file has no special text attributes or other special codes embedded into the file (most word processors put formatting and other codes in their files to tell the system how to display and print the special characters and formats).

Thus, although it may be easier or more convenient to have data entry operators type text fields using a familiar word processor, these files must be converted to ASCII to be correctly brought into a dBASE IV text field.

This chapter discussed indexing, sorting, and text editing. These capabilities allow you to modify the order in which your data are viewed and the actual record order of your files, and to create and modify text in your memos, labels, and reports.

8 Labels and Envelopes

dBASE IV provides you with a great deal of flexibility in producing text output. One of the areas that has been substantially improved is the design and printing of labels and envelopes. In this chapter, you will learn the techniques required to design and print labels and envelopes.

Preparing Data

When you design and print your labels, dBASE IV's label processor prints a label or envelope for each record in your database. There are no facilities within the Labels function for sorting, organizing, or deleting records in the database. You do, however, have the capability of selecting specific fields (or creating special fields) that will be included on your label. In many (probably most) cases, you will want to print your labels or envelopes in a particular order.

Mailing labels, for example, should probably be printed in ZIP code order to take advantage of special bulk rate mail rates offered by the U.S. Postal Service.

Using an example from this book, you may want to print updated employee data forms. You would probably want to print the forms in the order in which they will be filed, probably by last name and first name.

To produce labels in the desired order, the database file being used must first be in that order. The methods for sorting and indexing data in your file were discussed in depth in Chapter 7. For more sophisticated file creation, involving sorting and possibly also involving specific selection criteria and the use of data from more than one data file, the query function, covered in Chapter 10, can produce such a file from which to print.

It is important to make clear that the records in your database must be in the order in which you want the labels printed.

Designing Labels

Before loading the Labels processor, first select the file from which you wish to print labels or envelopes. Although you can change databases being used as the source of data for your labels from within the labels processor, it is best, when designing labels, to have the database that you wish to use as the source for your label data loaded into the system so that you can select the fields that you wish to print as you design the labels.

To select a file, move the cursor to the Data Bar and type the first letters of the file name, or move the cursor to the file name. In this case, we will still be using the PERSONEL data file that was created earlier.

With the "PERSONEL" file highlighted,

Press: **ENTER**

to bring up the Selection window. Tell the system that you want to USE the data file. To do this,

Press: **ENTER** (or *u*)

(You could also have pressed the **F2** key, which would have brought up the Browse or Edit screen, from which you would have had to **Esc** to get back to the Control Center. You will probably get into the habit of telling the system that you want to *use* a particular database by quickly pressing **ENTER** twice, without even bothering to read the screen asking what you want to do with the data file. This is faster than using the **F2** key, followed by **Esc**.)

If you wanted to use a file that was sorted by Index or created using the *sort* capabilities, you would have gone into the Modify Data Structure screen by pressing **Shft-F2** when the file was highlighted, and then put the file into order by index, or created a new file with data in sort order. You would then have returned to the Control Center . If you create a new file in the sort order,

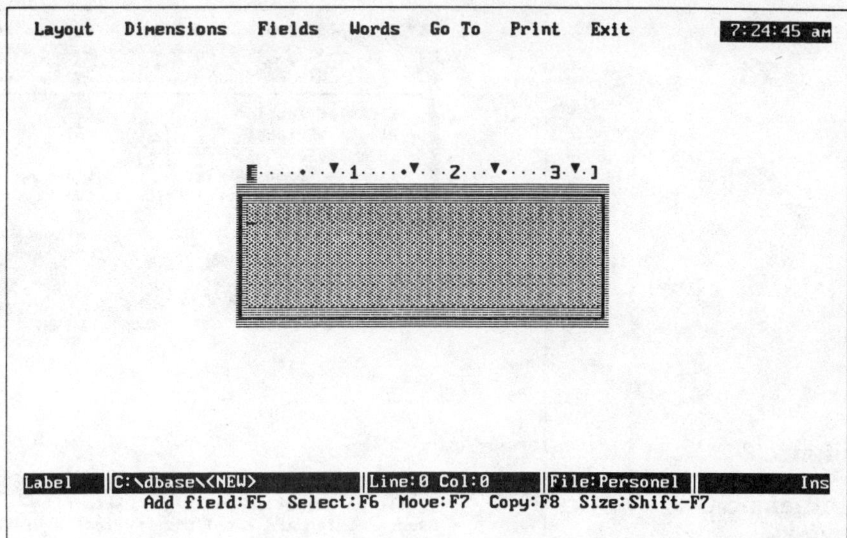

Figure 8-1

The Labels design screen.

you would then have to tell the system that you want to use the file that the sort created.

Next, to begin your label design, move the cursor to the Labels column and select <create>. You will notice that there is a small square area in the center of the screen (Figure 8-1). This is the area you will use to design your labels. Before doing so, the Menu options will reveal the numerous options available from within the Labels function. These will be looked at slightly out of order.

Dimensions

The Dimensions menu is seen in Figure 8-2. Note that a predefined size is displayed, highlighted on the top line of this window.

The Text editing window that appeared in the center of your screen when you first loaded Forms represented the design space for the selected label size. To see the available predefined sizes,

Press: **ENTER**

The screen, which displays the nine preset dimensions, is shown in Figure 8-3.

The first three options represent the size of standard labels. The first option is for a single column of labels, the second for a form

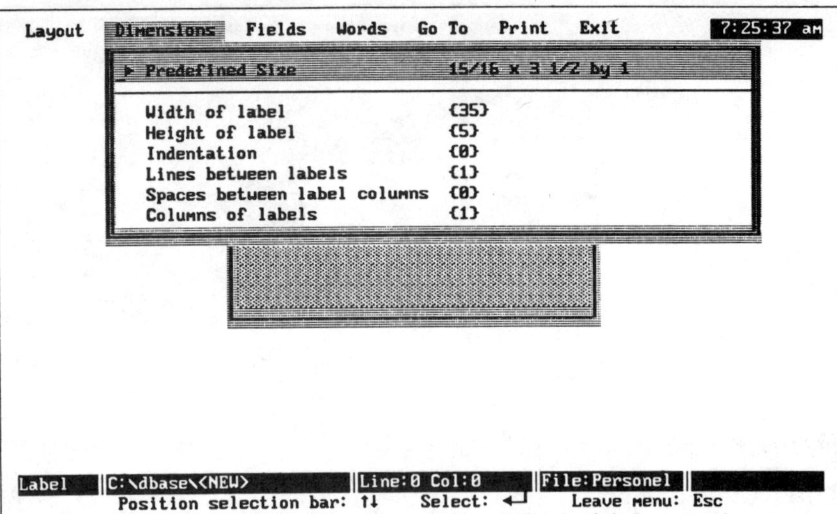

Figure 8-2

Dimensions window.

that prints two labels side by side, and the third for three labels side by side. When any of these options are selected, only one window will appear. At print time, the system will automatically print one, two, or three across, depending on the Label option selected.

The fourth option, Cheshire, is a label format used by mailing

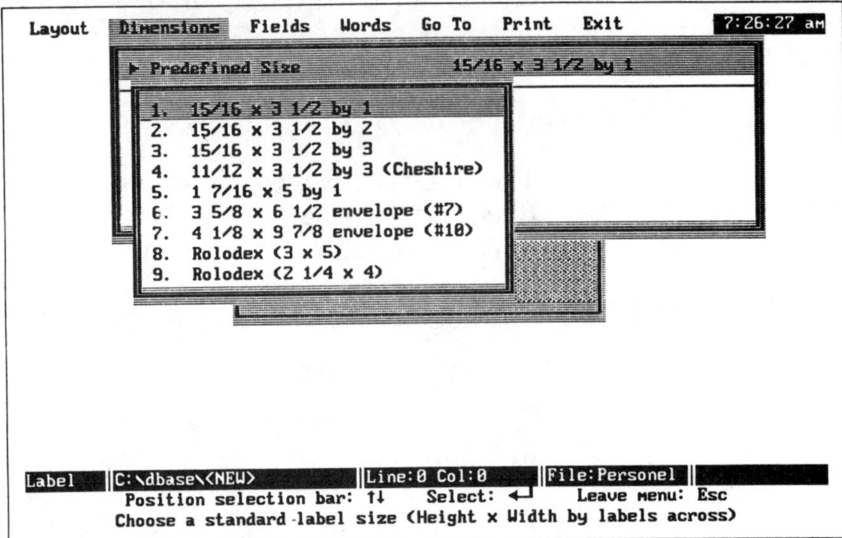

Figure 8-3

Predefined sizes.

list and mailing label companies. It is a format used by special machines to automatically place labels onto envelopes or printed forms.

The fifth option, $1^{7}/_{16} \times 5 \times 1$, prints a single column $1^{7}/_{16}$ by 5 inches. This is useful for printing the top of 3×5 index cards, and may also be used for labels that size, if such labels are available.

The sixth and seventh options, #7 and #10 envelopes, are designed for standard envelopes. It is important to remember, of course, that although you can fill in the entire front of an envelope, you should place your text in an appropriate position.

The last two options print Rolodex cards in either of two standard sizes. Depending on the type of printer you are using, you may be able to get tractor feed Rolodex labels, which will allow you to automatically print a continuous stream of labels without having to individually feed them.

For the purposes of this chapter, select 7, the #10 envelope (Figure 8-4).

Return to the Dimensions menu. The lines below the predefined size line indicate the width of the label, height, indentation, and other formatting features. Each of the options can be modified. The settings for the #10 envelope are shown in Figure 8-5.

The numbers provided in this screen assume that you will be

Figure 8-4

Number 10 envelope design screen.

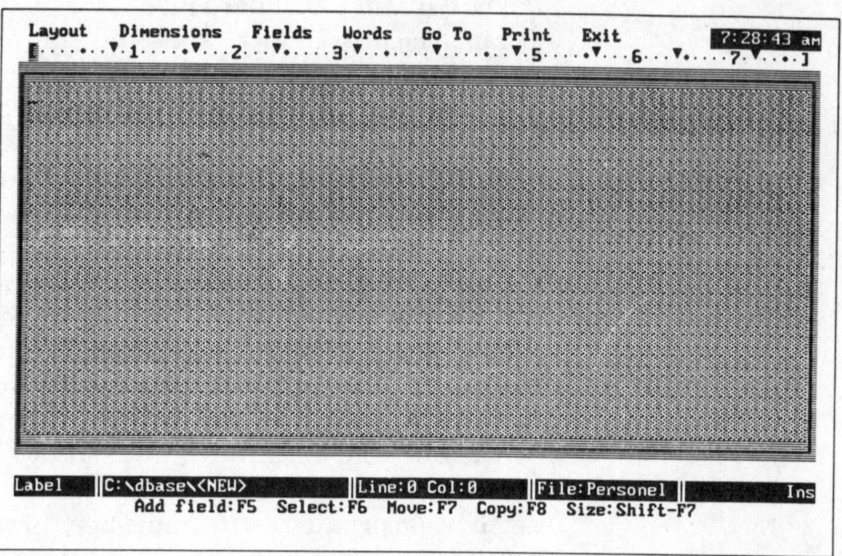

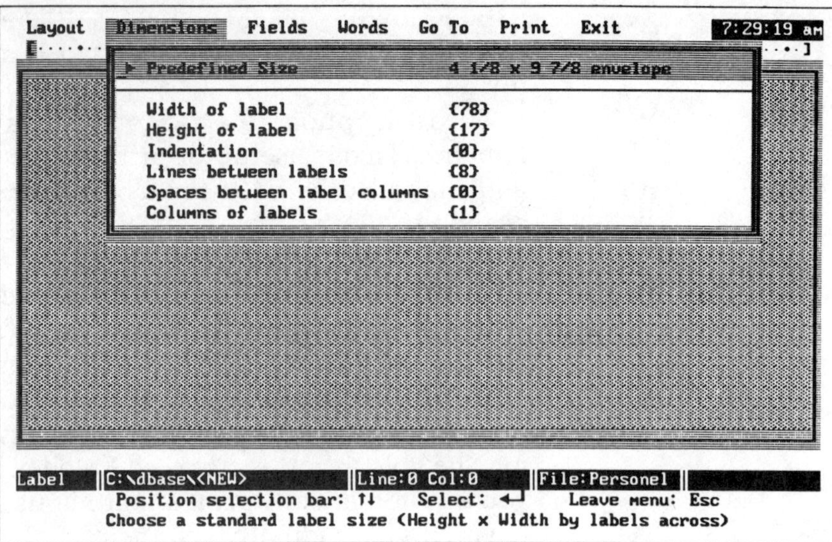

Figure 8-5

Settings for #10 envelope.

printing at 10 characters per inch (10 pitch) and 6 lines per inch. It should be clear from the settings that the system is allowing for margins during printing. Thus, the width of 9⅞ inches is larger than the 7.8 inches (78 characters divided by 10 characters per inch) that is specified for the envelope.

Depending on the type of form you are using, there may or may not be a margin. Standard labels, for instance, use 35 characters (3.5 inches) in a 3.5 inch label. You may also choose not to use a predefined form. In this case, you would indicate the desired size of your form by typing the appropriate line width and form height into the appropriate lines of the Dimensions box.

Most of the options are very straightforward. However, some further explanation would be useful. Height of label and Lines between labels work together to define the overall height of the form (be it envelope, label, or Rolodex card) being designed. In the case of the #10 envelope, although you are printing $2^5/_6$ inches of text (17 lines divided by 6 lines per inch), when you add the 8 lines between labels, you get a measurement that is as close as possible to the $4^1/_2$ inch height of the standard envelope.

Thus, if you were to begin printing at the top line of your envelope, the system would automatically load the next envelope, set to begin printing on the same line. (In actual practice, however, if you have envelopes connected, the difference between 25 lines and $4^1/_8$ inches may end up altering the actual position of the printing on the envelope. Some experimentation may be required to get the best performance from your printer.)

The Indentation setting tells the system how many spaces from the left margin to offset printing. For any forms (such as envelopes) that are not equal in width to the actual form (that is, are fewer characters wide than the form being printed onto), it may be well to do some sample prints to determine whether dBASE IV is already indenting.

Lines between labels is a setting that tells the system how many spaces to put between the bottom of one label and the top of the next. This normally assumes that you are using continuous forms or continuous envelopes. When doing envelopes on an impact printer (dot matrix or daisywheel) or an inkjet printer (actually this includes most nonlaser printers), one trick is to start printing your first envelope with the envelope positioned at the first line of print, and an empty envelope in the carriage behind the printer platen (assuming you are using a printer with a platen). As the printer finishes one envelope, it will automatically feed the next envelope to the correct starting position for printing. (An operator still has to be standing by to place envelopes behind the platen as each new envelope is printed.)

Spaces between label columns specifies how much space the printer should move between each column of labels. For multicolumn labels, this is already set.

Columns of labels tells the system how many labels are to be printed across the top of a label sheet or label forms. The total width of a printed form should not be less than the product of the number of columns times the width of the label, plus the number of spaces between columns. (For example, for a standard 8.5 inch sheet of label paper, you would have a maximum of 85 characters width. Printing 3 labels, each 27 characters wide, and with 4 character spaces between each column, would require 89 spaces, $[3\times27+2\times4]$ and you run out of space).

Although dBASE IV provides you with standard label sizes, you may modify the form size by changing the height and width settings. This is done by typing the first letter of each line, or by moving the highlight to the desired option and pressing **ENTER**. For the purposes of this chapter, you will be using a standard setting.

Layout

The Layout menu (Figure 8-6) differs somewhat from other menu screens in dBASE IV. You do not have any predesigned formats when working with labels, although you can make and save designs and then reload your standard designs whenever needed.

The options are as follows:

The Use different database file or view option allows you to select a different database file around which to build your label design. Although you could have gone into the Label Design menu without first telling the system that you were using a particular data file, it is always good practice to have loaded the data file that you wish to use to create labels.

On the other hand, you can load a label design and then select a different data file from which to create or print labels. For example, because PERSONEL and EMP__DATA both have many of the same fields, you may have designed a label or envelope using the fields in PERSONEL, and later decided to use the same fields from EMP__DATA. This can be done by loading the label design and then attaching EMP__DATA to it. You must remember to save the label form, using the new data file, with a new name.

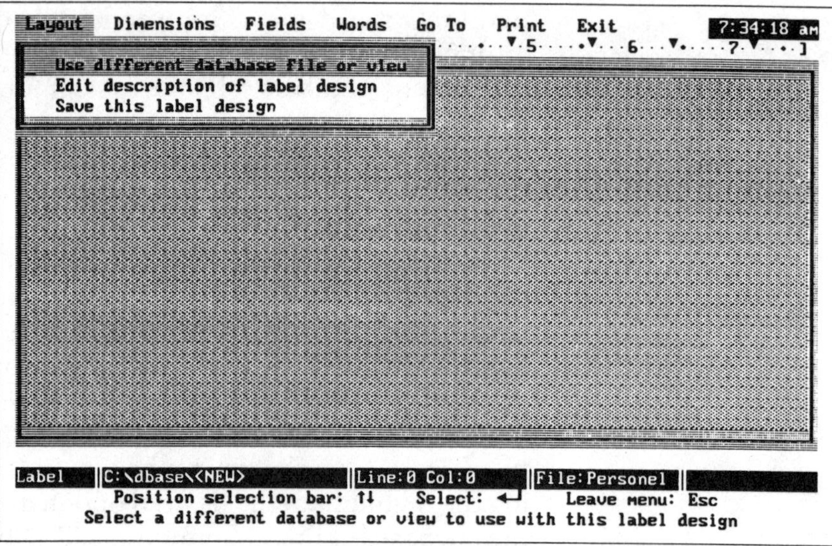

Figure 8-6

The Layout menu.

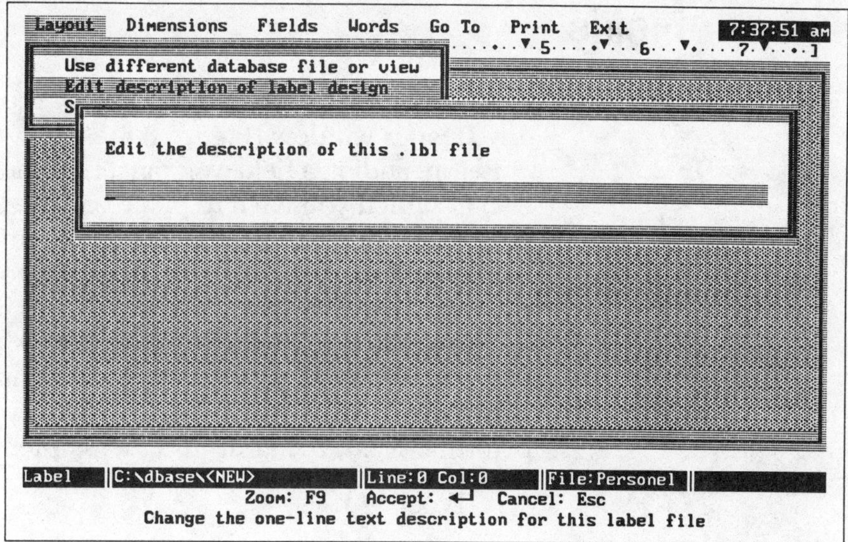

Figure 8-7

Edit line for label description.

Edit description of label design allows you to write a brief description of the label being designed. The Edit screen, once selected, appears as shown in Figure 8-7.

For the envelopes we are designing,

Type: *Envelope mailing address setup* **ENTER**

The screen will again appear as it did in Figure 8-7.

The next option in the Layout menu is Save this label design. This allows you to save the design, so that it can be reloaded at another time. A design is usually saved after all changes have been made.

In this case, you have done nothing other than specify a label size, save the design, naming it *#10perso* (#10 sized personnel envelope). The system will automatically give the label design the proper name extension. Although the system will allow you to type more than eight characters for the label name, it will accept only the first eight.

In actual use, you may load a predesigned form, modify it for use with a different database file or view (using the first Layout option), and save it, giving it a new name using the Save this label design option.

Fields

The Fields menu functions in much the same way as it does in any Design window (Figure 8-8).

Before adding a field, you must first move the cursor to the location at which you wish to place your field. Because in this case, you will be producing envelopes, the name line should be placed in a logical position on your envelope. You may begin printing at the top of the form, if you remember to place your envelope into the printer so that the first line you want printed is located under the printhead. Using the arrow keys, move the cursor so that it is at Line 1, Column 32. This is where your envelope will begin printing. Next, bring up the Fields menu. To do this,

Type: **Alt-F**

(or press the **F10** key and move the cursor to the Fields menu window). Next,

Press: **ENTER**

to tell the system that you want to add a field.

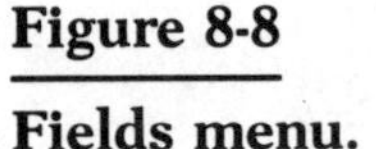

Figure 8-8

Fields menu.

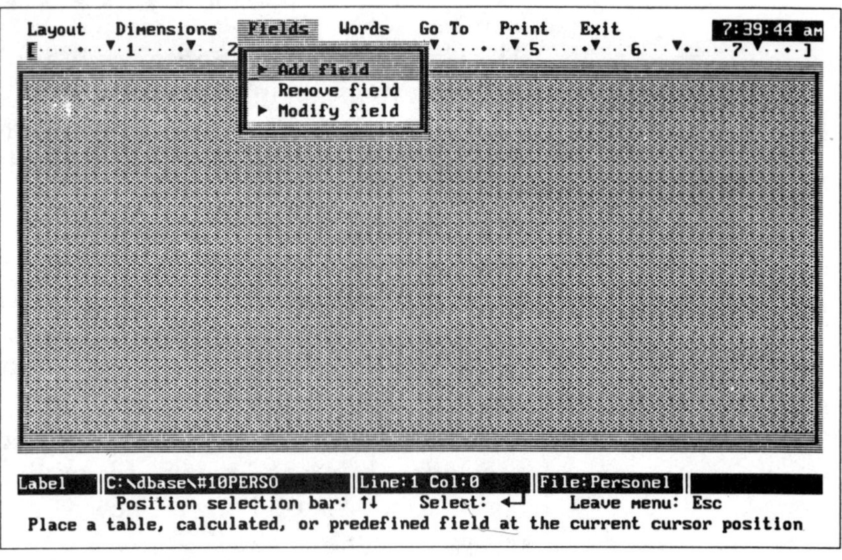

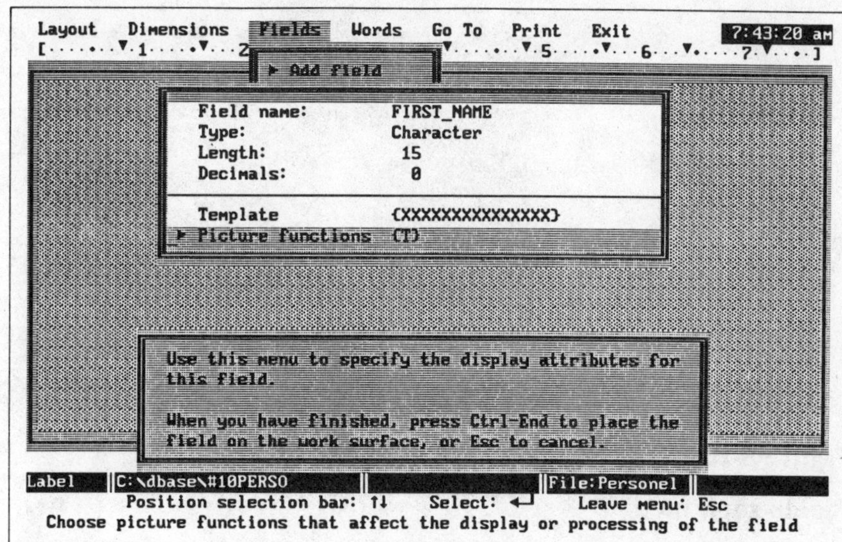

Figure 8-9

Settings for First_Name field.

NOTE: You could also have told the system that you wanted to add or edit a field by moving the cursor to the position of the field and pressing **F5**.

Select First_Name. This will bring up the Field modification window. The template and picture functions are essentially the same as those detailed in Chapter 4. You should set the trim function, from within the Picture functions menu, *On*. This will print the width of the characters actually typed into the field, and skip blanks in the field, as you will see later. Your settings for this field should match those in Figure 8-9.

To accept the settings,

Press: **Ctrl-End**

Touch the Space Bar once, and add the Last_Name field (try it using the **F5** key to bring up the Field selection window) using the standard default settings.

It is important to use a **Space**, rather than moving the cursor and leaving a blank between fields that you wish to be aligned next to each other. When you use a space, as seen in Figure 8-10, the first name will be truncated when it is printed, and will be

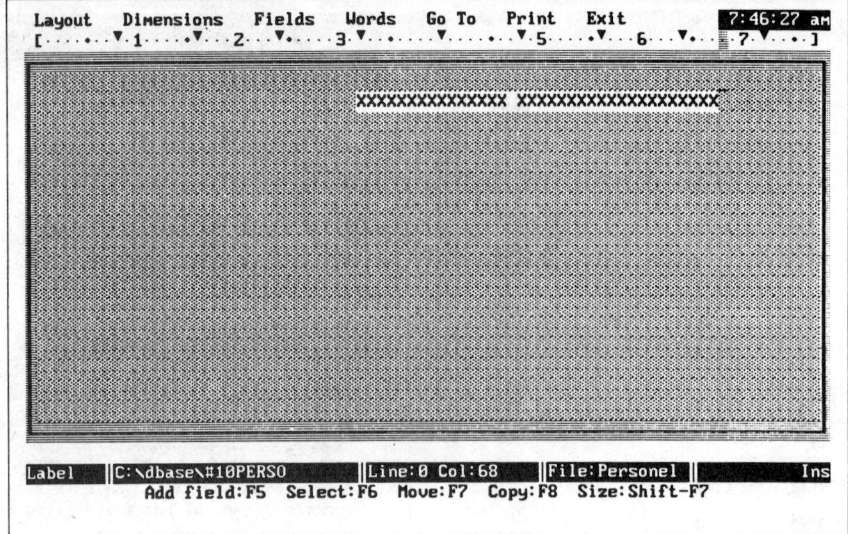

Figure 8-10

Fields separated by space.

typed as displayed in Figure 8-11. If you used a blank rather than a space, the first and last name will be printed as shown in Figure 8-12.

Next, add the HOME__ADDR and APT__NUMBER fields in the second line, with three spaces separating the two fields, and the

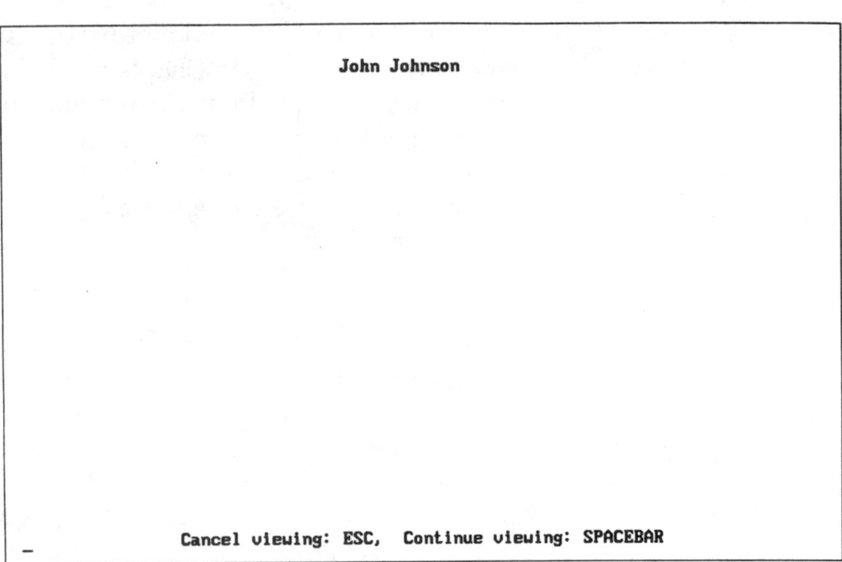

Figure 8-11

Truncated first name.

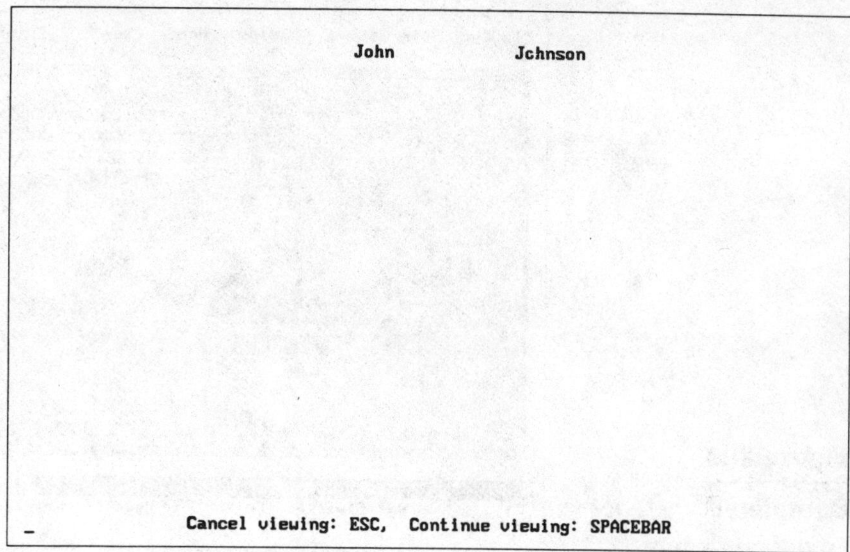

Figure 8-12

First and last name without truncation.

city, state, and ZIP codes on the third line. Be sure to type a comma and space between city and state, and provide two spaces between state and ZIP code.

> NOTE: You can select the picture functions and template design that are entered by the system when the field is selected by pressing the **RtArrow**, in addition to the **Ctrl-End** keys.

Your completed envelope design should appear as shown in Figure 8-13. The first envelope, when printed, will appear as shown in Figure 8-14.

The Add fields option allows you to generate calculated fields, and also uses predefined fields that you can place on your form and automatically print specific information. Although not appropriate for envelopes, the four fields, Date, Time, Recno (record number), and Pageno (page number), may be useful for labels and Rolodex cards.

Because you can print text, in addition to data, it is possible to use the Labels menu to design short letters that merge text and data, although it is not truly intended for such use. You could conceivably produce a letter using the fields already on the form to address the letter, the Date field to put a date on the form (although

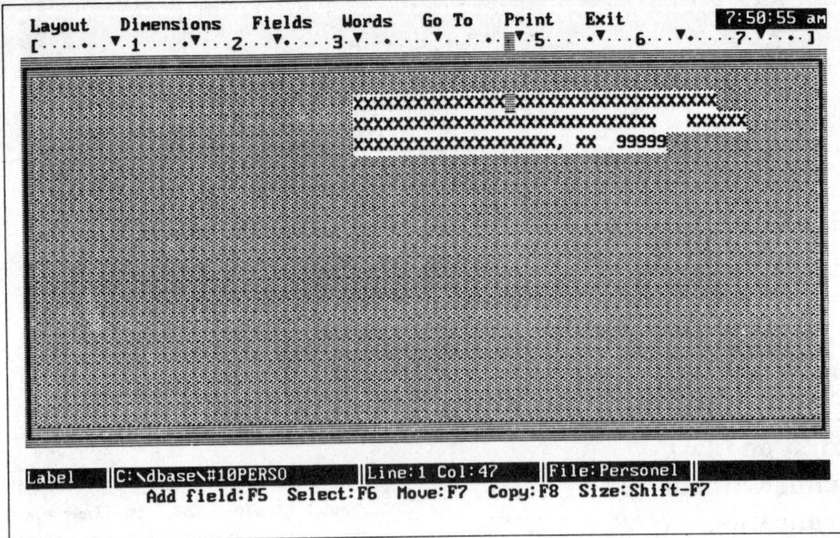

Figure 8-13

Completed envelope design.

it will not be in the normal format for correspondence), and whichever other data fields you wish to insert into your letter.

As with your Forms design, and as you will see in Reports design, you can place text on the form that will be printed or displayed every time the label (or report or form) is used. For ex-

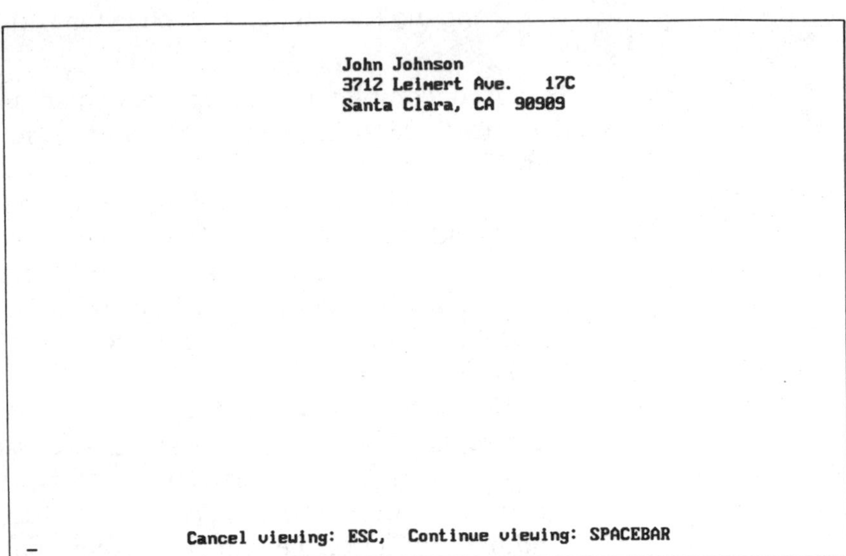

Figure 8-14

Appearance of printed address.

ample, you may place the text for a return address on your envelope form, or put a department and company name on the top of each label or card on which you are printing data. The only text character that has been added in the current example, the comma between city and state, prints whenever the label is printed, and shows up on screen when you view the Label form.

Words

The Words menu was discussed in detail in Chapter 4. However, character styles were not selectable from within that menu. When you select Style from within the Words menu, you are given the option of applying a number of predetermined attributes to your text (assuming your printer is capable of printing with the selected attributes). Only one of the options may be applied to any character or field.

To apply the character attributes to text, and not to fields, first select the text using the **F6** and **ENTER** keys. The bottom half of the Style is for printer control codes. From within this menu, you will be unable to enter such codes. These codes are set during installation or from within DBSETUP.

The Ruler is used to indicate margins and tabs. Instructions for modifying the Ruler have already been provided.

The Remove line option deletes the contents of a line. It does not, however, shorten the size of the window or the area available for entering text or data. (This contradicts the instructions on this text screen.)

The Write/read text file option allows you to write highlighted text into a file. It is useful if you are preparing many standard forms, based on similar information. When you highlight a block of text that you wish to write to a file, it can be saved to a specific file name (which you give it).

Next, when you are preparing another form, this "standard" text can be brought into your current label file. The ability to save text in one form design and recall and insert it into another can be a significant time saver. In addition, if you are using the Label menu to design boilerplate letters, you can easily prepare a library of standard paragraphs and "paste" them into your new form label (letter).

Go To

The Go To menu options are essentially the same as those in Chapter 4 with a few minor differences. In this menu, you cannot search for an indexed field. The search will not search through data in your database; rather, it will search through your form for the specific data that you are seeking.

The Replace option searches for a text string. When it finds the string, it replaces it with a different string. When it finds a match for your string, it prompts you to make a choice: Replace/Skip/All/Quit? (R/S/A/Esc). If you type *r*, the system will make the desired text replacement. If you type *s*, the system will not make the replacement, and will then seek the next instance of the selected text. Pressing *a* (for all) will make the replacement for this occurrence of the selected text, and all other instances too. You should be careful when using this global option because it will replace all instances of the text string. In some cases, the text may be part of a word. It is often good practice to include the spaces before and after a selected word to avoid this problem. In addition, turning Match capitalization on will select only exact matches of upper- and lowercase characters. The final option, *Q* (for quit), stops the search, does not make the replacement, and returns you to the Label design menu. If replacements have been made, the system will indicate how many occurrences of the indicated text have been replaced.

Match capitalization has already been briefly discussed. If you are searching for a particular text string and activate Match capitalization, the system will make an exact match, both for the characters and their case. Thus, if you wanted to search for the name *Brown*, the system will ignore all occurrences of the color *brown*. It will, however, match the color *Brown* if it is used to begin a sentence.

Print

The Print menu (Figure 8-15) was not a part of the Data design menus discussed earlier in this book. It is divided into three basic sections and provides a range of controls over your print operations.

When you have completed the design of your form, or if you

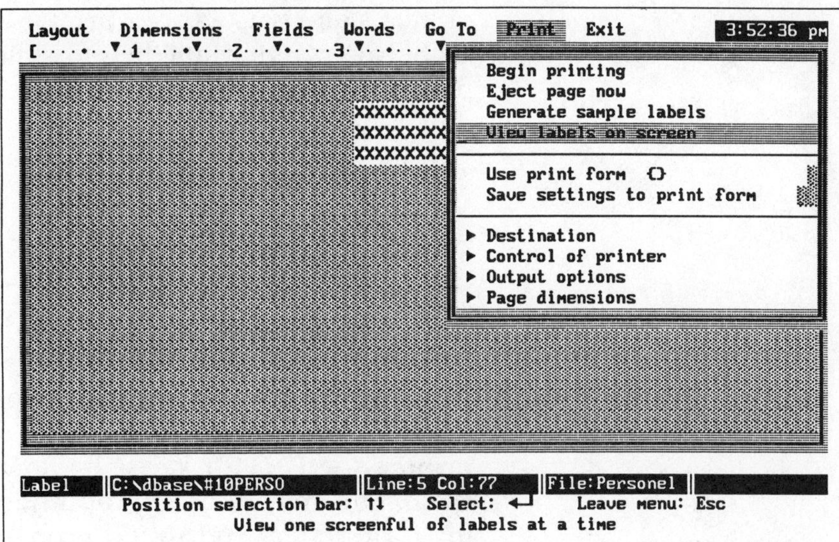

Figure 8-15

Print menu.

have loaded your print form, you should next make sure that the printer settings match those that you want implemented.

> NOTE: If you have already saved these parameters, or are satisfied with the system defaults, you usually will not need to use the options at the bottom of the menu box. For now, however, we will explore them to see what controls are available.

The printer setup and controls are as follows:

Destination: The Destination option allows you to print your labels to the printer, create a file with the data and printer control codes on your hard disk, or create a straight text file including the contents of each label on your hard disk. It is faster to print to a file, particularly if many labels are to be printed, because in outputting directly to the printer the system will eventually have to wait for the printer to catch up to the computer's data rate. In effect, the printer cannot print the characters as quickly as the computer can send the characters to the printer. At some point, the printer's memory buffer will be full, limiting the rate at which the computer can send the rest of the data to the printer.

If you print the labels to a file on disk, the system can print the file anytime. For example, if you were printing thousands of labels and trusted your printer and computer to run all night, you could print labels to a file during the day, set the printer on when you leave work, and have the labels printed during the off hour(s).

To toggle between Printer and DOS File as a printer destination,

Press: **ENTER** (or **Space Bar**)

When you toggle Write to DOS FILE, a file name will appear (or the system will ask for a name if one has not been assigned).

The third line, Printer model, normally shows the name of the default printer. If you have installed more than one printer, the **ENTER** key will allow you to toggle between them. This may be useful for different tasks. For example, for form letters you would probably want to use a laser printer because of its higher speed and letter quality output. For index cards or envelopes a dot matrix or formed character printer with a tractor feeder or envelope feeder would be preferable. The ability to switch printer types without having to go through any major reinstallation or initialization programs is an excellent feature of dBASE IV.

When a particular printer is selected and you are printing to a DOS file, the special printer control codes are also being sent to the DOS file. The file contains all the characters, including the printer controls, that would normally be sent to control the printer. To print such a file, you must return to DOS and use the PRINT command. For example, if you created a disk file called #10PERSO.PRF to print the file, you would

Type: *PRINT #10PERSO.PRF* **ENTER**

The system will ask which print device to print to, and once this is answered (usually with the response *LPT1*) the system will print the labels, exactly as if you had printed them directly from dBASE IV.

You will use the DOS PRINT command to print a print file produced by dBASE IV. If you want a straight character file, without the special printer-specific control codes, you may toggle the printer selection until "ASCII Text" is highlighted.

A straight ASCII file can be viewed on screen or merged into word processor or other types of files.

The Echo to screen selection in the Destination menu is an optional selection that toggles on and off. If you choose *Yes*, you will see the label on your screen at the same time it is being sent to the printer to print.

Control of Printer: This menu provides you with an additional set of printer controls (Figure 8-16).

The options are as follows:

The Text pitch option gives you four choices: default, pica, elite, and condensed. The default setting is the one with which your printer normally starts (usually 10 characters per inch). Pica, also known as 10 pitch, prints 10 characters to the inch, elite prints 12 characters to the inch, and condensed usually prints 15 characters to the inch. Condensed characters are the smallest of all those available; it is useful for printing lines of text that are longer than normal, for example, 120 condensed characters can be printed in the same space as 80 pica characters. If you wanted to print the entire contents of each record on a single line, condensed may be the only way to squeeze the maximum amount of characters onto your page.

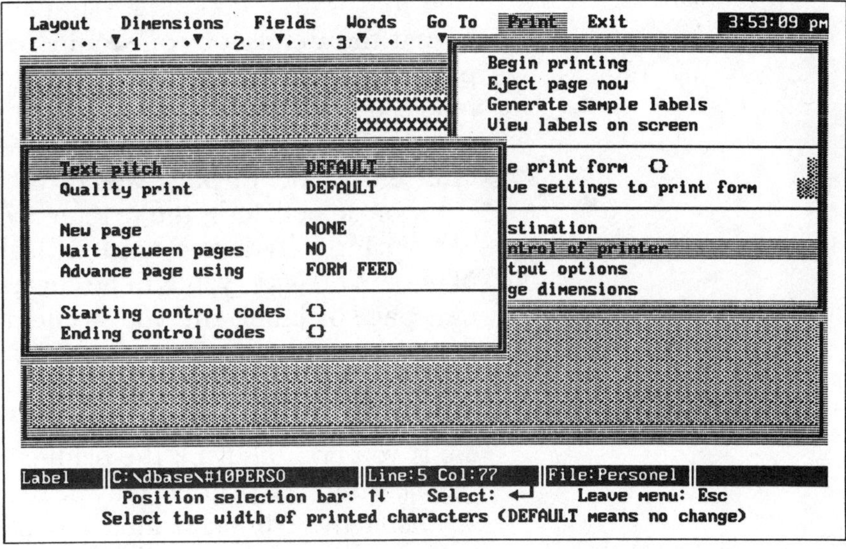

Figure 8-16

Printer control menu.

The Quality print line presents three options: default, on, or off. Although this usually applies to dot matrix printers, it could also affect laser printers. Quality print (often called near letter quality by dot matrix printer makers) usually takes longer to print than draft print because the print head deposits more dots for each character. This is done by making more than one pass on each line printed, or by activating more pins (or jets) in the print head. In either case, the printer takes longer to print quality print because it takes longer to calculate the controls to print each quality letter than it does to print a draft character. The print quality options are toggled by pressing the **ENTER** key.

The New page setting tells the system when you want it to start a new page. The options here are none, after, before, and both.

When none is selected, you are telling the system not to tell the printer to eject the page and start a new one. This option would probably be used if you were printing continuous form labels, and the total length of the label plus lines between labels equaled the label's total length. In this case, the print head will be at the top of each label whenever it completed printing the previous label. If you told the system to start a new page, either before or after a label was completed, every other label would be blank.

Before or After options are similar. The only real difference is that the Before option would eject the current sheet of paper or label in the printer before starting to print *any* labels. If After was selected, the printer would start printing on whatever was in the printer, and would insert a new sheet after each label or page was printed.

If you select Both, the printer will eject the page before your print job started, and will also eject the last page printed. This way, you will be certain to start printing on a new page or label, and you would also be assured that the last label on the last page is the last one printed. (Without activating the After option, part of your text, or the last label, may still be in the printer even after the print job is finished. If you do not check the printer, whatever is on the last page (still in the printer) may be discarded by the next person using the printer, printed with part of another document below the labels, or lost forever.

Wait between pages is designed for printers that cannot automatically feed the next page, envelope, or sheet of labels. The system stops at the end of each page and prompts you to load the next sheet and tell the system to start the next page printing. If you are using a sheet feeder or tractor feeder, and the system automatically loads the next sheet, this option should be *no*.

The next option, Advance page using, tells dBASE IV how it should tell the printer to load the next page. This also depends on your printer and its capabilities. The options are Form feeds and Line feeds, and they are selected using the **ENTER** key or **Space Bar** (as are most of the other options in this menu). Once the mode is selected, use the **DnArrow** or **UpArrow** or **F3** or **F4** keys to move to the next item in the menu. A form feed is a specific character that is sent to the printer and tells it to eject the current page and load the next. This is probably preferable for printers that can load single sheets. Using line feeds, the printer issues the line feed printer command to move the paper up until it is at the start of the next page. Some printers with tractor feed mechanisms require Line feeds to move to a new page. Again, the option selected depends on your printer's capabilities.

The final options in this menu, Starting control codes and Ending control codes, ask for specific printer codes required to set up the printer or reset it after the job is completed. For example, you may want to modify line spacing or page width, using special codes recognized by your printer. You may wish to print multiple copies of each form on a laser printer. To do this, you will send a special code telling the printer how many copies of each page to print. You will also want a code to reset the printer to 1 copy of each page after it has completed printing your labels. When you tell the system which codes to send, they will be sent to the printer before (in the case of Starting control codes) or after (in the case of Ending control codes) printing.

The codes for your printer should be listed in your printer manual. There are two ways to enter the codes. Most printers use what are known as Escape codes. These codes send the **Esc** character (ASCII Character 27) plus a letter or number. The command can be typed in using the word **Esc**, surrounded by curly braces, and followed by the control character or

ASCII code number. For example, to send **Esc A**, you would type *{ESC} A*. You can also send ASCII characters (using the ASCII character number from an ASCII number table). To send the code for **Esc**, type *CHR(28)*. For **Esc A**, type *CHR(27)+"A"*. (Letters are in quotation marks in this notation.)

Press the **ENTER** key to open the bar to allow you to type the options. If your control code extends beyond the space provided on this line,

Press: **F9**

to open a window at the bottom of the design area that is the width of the screen. Pressing **F9** closes the window. Once you have typed in the desired codes,

Press: **ENTER**

to close the line and accept the codes.

Any of the standard control keys (**Esc**, **Tab**, etc.) should be enclosed in curly braces if you choose to use the first method of entering codes.

Press **Esc** to return to the Print menu.

Output options provide you with some control over the pagination and page printing of the document. The four options, Begin on page, End after page, First page number, and Number of copies, are selected using the **ENTER** key. Typing in the appropriate number followed by **ENTER** will set that value.

The Number of copies setting may not do exactly what you want if you are using a laser printer. Laser printers can usually be set to print a number of copies of each page, storing the codes for the page in the printer's buffer, and quickly printing the image on the printer drum's surface. However, the laser printer will print multiple copies of *each page* when you use printer control codes to tell the printer to print more than one copy of each page. Thus, if you issue the printer control codes to print three copies, the system will print three of each page before going on to the next page. After the print job is completed, someone (probably you) will have to go through the pile of printed sheets and decollate them, separating them into three separate piles.

If you tell dBASE IV to print multiple copies, it will print one set of labels, go to the beginning, and then send the data to the printer to print another set. This takes considerably more time, but the sheets will not have to be separated later. A laser printer with a collator (currently a very hard item to find) would make the use of printer codes to print multiple copies the definite method of choice.

If you want extra copies of each page, you may want to set the printer control codes to tell the printer how many copies of each page you want *before* printing, and then reset the number of pages to 1 *after* printing.

Page dimensions tells the system about page length, line spacing, and indentation. The Length of page option tells the system how many lines can be printed on a page. The printer will usually be printing 6 lines per inch, although some printers can be set to print 8 lines per inch.

The page length is particularly important if you are using form feeds to indicate the end of a page, because the system will add enough form feeds to completely fill a page before it starts printing again. If you are printing labels, and have set the option to use form feeds at the end of each label, the system may print a 5-line label and scroll another 61 lines until it gets to what it thinks is the start of the next page. If you are using continuous form labels, about 9 out of 10 labels will be wasted. Thus, page length should probably be set to the actual length of your form, particularly if form feeds are not used to indicate the end of a page or label.

The Offset from left option indicates the left margin. In the example of the envelope, you could have entered a 40 character offset and prepared your form so that the fields were at the form's left margin. This option is primarily designed for smaller offsets. In one example, you may be producing a form with a laser printer. Most laser printers are unable to print all the way to the left or right margins; any characters sent to the printer for printing at the margin *will not print*. Thus, a 4 or 5 character offset may be necessary.

You should consider, of course, that the offset moves the rest of your labels. Thus, you may have to reduce a label's width if you are working with multiple columns, because the other labels will be similarly offset and may, as a result, end up printing into a wrong column.

Three choices are available for Spacing of lines: single,

double, or triple. These are straightforward and will not be elaborated on here.

The settings at the top of the menu have to do with actual production of the labels. The options are as follows:

Begin printing: Obviously, this starts the printing of your labels. Be sure that you have made the right printer and control selections and that your printer is on before selecting this option. The settings that you have just changed or those that are already applied to the form that you are using or the default printer settings will be applied to your current print job.

Eject page now: This command forces the printer to eject the current page. If your printer controls are not set to automatically eject a page before a print job starts, you may use this option to eject the page currently in the printer. If you are using a sheet feeder or tractor feed paper, the next sheet of paper or form will be loaded into the printer.

You may also use this command to eject the last page printed. This is useful if the printer has not been set to eject a page after it finishes printing. To use this, your printer must be turned on and must be on-line, that is, connected and ready to receive printer control commands.

Generate sample labels: The printer controls generated by your computer, the printer controls interpreted by the printer, and the commands generated by dBASE IV should, in ideal cases, function in accord. However, given the complexities of form design and printer control, this is not always the case. Therefore, before printing a large set of labels, envelopes, cards, or letters using dBASE IV, it is often a good idea to generate a few samples to make sure that your printed output is *indeed* what you expected it to be. Discovering errors on the sample check can prevent having to scrap an entire print job.

Although you can also print a few sample labels by telling the system to end after a small number of pages in the Output Options menu, you will have to change back to a larger number (the maximum is 32767) for larger print runs.

If your printer is on-line and ready to print,

Press: **ENTER**

to print sample labels. After sample labels have been printed, the system will ask if you want more printed or if you want to stop printing. Answer the system's prompts by responding as directed in the on-screen prompt line.

View labels on screen: This is also a useful option, because it can be used at any time during the design of your labels or reports. When activated, the system first produces a code specifying how the label or report will look, and then produces a sample form on your screen. The printer need not be on-line or even turned on to use the option. In fact, it can be used with no printer attached to the computer.

This option provides a relatively fast and easy way to see what your printed label or report will look like. It does not, however, display special text attributes such as bold or underline. But it is valuable in determining placement of the data onto your form or label and can provide fast verification of the appearance of your printed label or report. This option was used to produce Figures 8-11 and 8-12.

The final two options, Use print form and Save settings to print form, allow you to do form management. A print form contains all the instructions required to control the printer settings and produce your printed label or report. It is generally a good idea to save your form so that it can be reused, or used when building another, similar label or report.

When you select Save settings to print form by pressing **ENTER**, the system will prompt for a form name. The default name is the name of the current form, with the .prf (for print form) extension. In this case, with the form named #10perso, the system will suggest naming the form #10perso.prf, as seen in Figure 8-17.

Once a print form has been saved, the name of the form will appear in Use print form. When you call up Use print form, a window showing the directory structure and a list of print forms will be displayed on screen. To use another print form, simply highlight it (using the **UpArrow** and **DnArrow** keys, or by typing the first few characters in the form name) and

Press: **ENTER**

to load the print form.

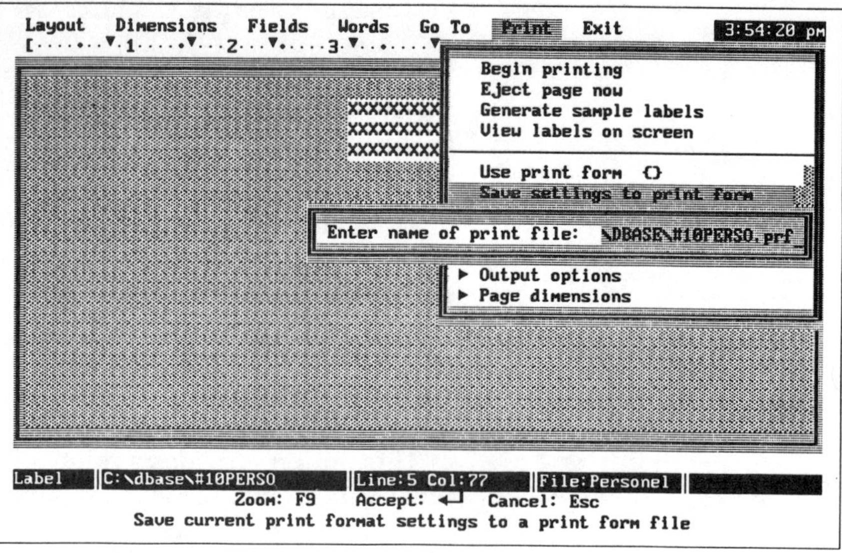

Figure 8-17

Saving a print form.

To escape from the Form Selection menu without changing print forms or loading a new print form,

Press: **Esc**

You should view a few labels on screen now to make sure that they are correct. Next, print a few sample labels. Once these are as you want them, you may proceed to print the entire database.

The final menu item, Exit, provides you with two options. If you choose to Save changes and exit, the system will recompile your label design and return you to the Control Center. If the file has not been named, you will be prompted for a label name. Remember that you can rename your form using the Layout menu. If you selected Save changes and edit, the system will save your file with the new name, and then return you to the Control Center.

The option Abandon changes and exit does basically that, not saving any changes made since the file was last saved, and bringing you to the Control Center. If you have renamed the file and saved it to a new name, the saved file will be unchanged.

You can also Browse/Edit your attached data file from within the Label design screen. To do this,

Press: **F2**

You will then be able to browse or edit your data. The Exit menu

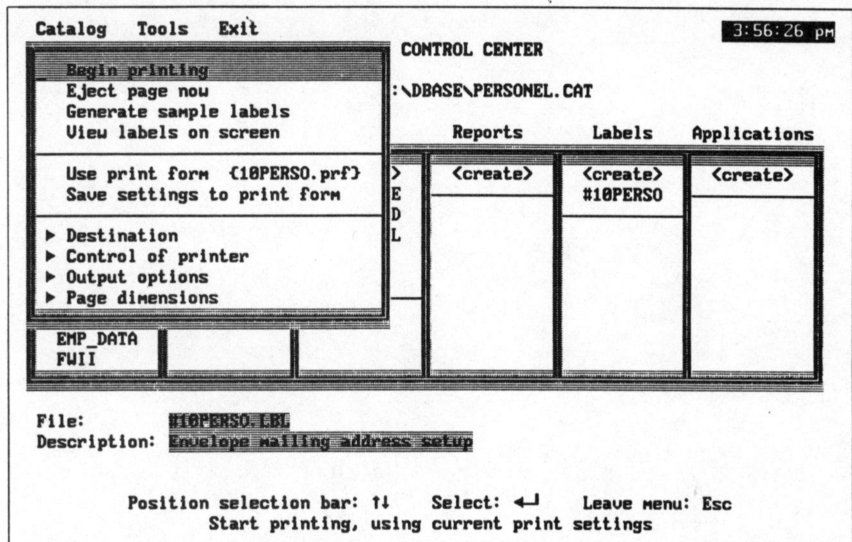

Figure 8-18

Printer control menu from the Control Center.

from within Browse/Edit will provide you with an option to return to Label design. If you have not completed designing your label or have not saved it, you should return to the Label design screen from the Browse/Edit Exit menu to complete the label design and should not return to the Control Center from within Browse or Edit.

From inside the Control Center, if you have selected a particular label design (by highlighting it and pressing **ENTER**), you will be asked if you want to Print label, Modify layout, or Display data. If you select Print label, the Printer Control menu will appear on your screen, as seen in Figure 8-18. The other options, Modify layout and Display data, can be selected either by bringing up the selection menu (by moving the highlight to the desired label design and pressing **ENTER**), or by pressing the **F2** (to Browse/Edit data) keys or the **Shift-F2** keys (to bring up the Label Design menu).

dBASE IV has been enhanced to provide you with a great deal of flexibility in designing labels, envelopes, cards, and even letters. The techniques discussed in this and earlier chapters give you full control over the design and printing of labels, envelopes, Rolodex cards, or other documents.

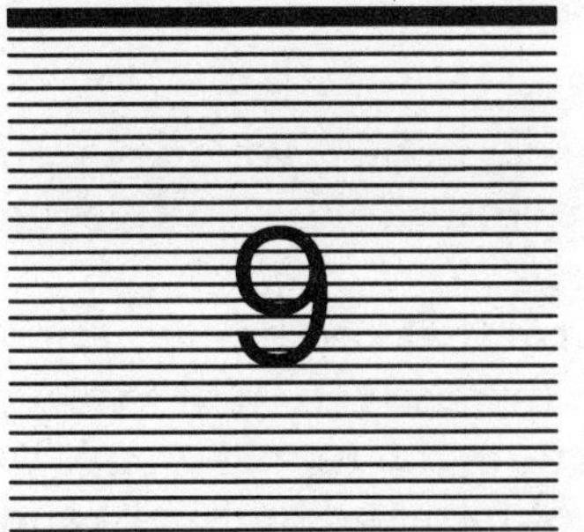

9 Report Design

Thus far, you have seen how to design a database, enter data, prepare printed labels, and manipulate some of the data. This is all useful, but unless you can get the data inside the computer out to some sort of useful document, you may find the program somewhat limiting.

The reporting capabilities built into dBASE IV allow you to rather easily design and produce printed reports based on the data that you have generated. Before selecting the Reports menu, however, you should first select a database file or query that will be used as the basis for your printed report.

In this case, again select the PERSONEL database file to demonstrate some of the abilities of the Report Generator. To do this move the highlight to the Data column,

Type: *PE*

to select PERSONEL, and

Press: **ENTER**

This brings up a prompt asking if you want to use the file, modify the file, or view the data. If PERSONEL is already the file in use, the system will ask if you want to close the file. If this prompt is presented,

Press: **Esc**

If not,

Type: *U*

to tell the system that you want to use the file. Because "Use file" is already highlighted, pressing **ENTER** a second time will also tell the system that you plan to use this file. In fact, you may well get into the habit of pressing **ENTER** twice, rapidly, to select a file and tell the system you wish to use it.

Next, it would be well to select the form that you have already designed for editing and viewing the data (in case you want to view, edit, or add records while you are designing the report form). To do this, move the cursor to the Forms column and highlight and select the desired form file.

Finally, move the highlight into the Report column. There should be no report forms showing in this column (unless you have already made some report forms). To create a new form and to see the various options available from inside this menu, highlight "<create>" and

Press: **ENTER**

The screen will come up with the Layout options window pulled down.

Press: **Esc**

to close the Layout window and see the initial Report form. The Report design screen appears as shown in Figure 9-1.

You should immediately notice that this form is strikingly different from the ones used to create labels or forms. This form has five different sections, referred to as *Bands.*

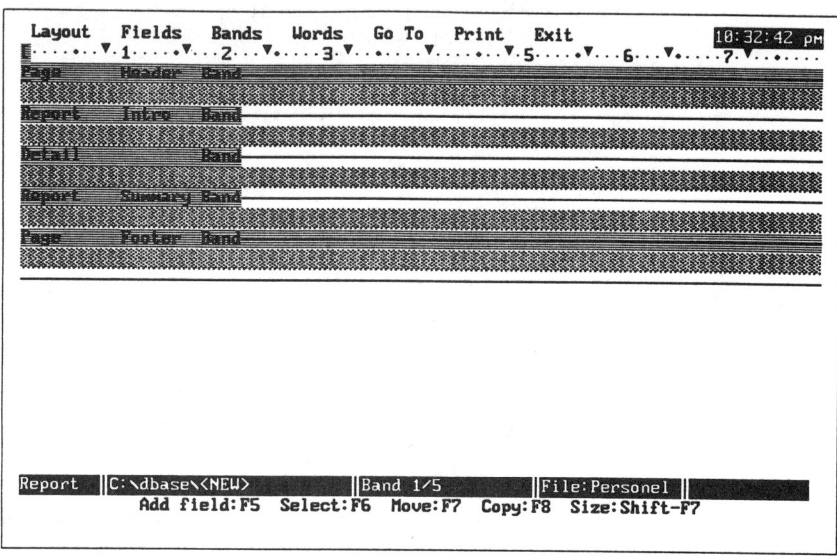

Figure 9-1

The Report design screen.

Bands

A *band* is a logical component of the printed report. You will see five different bands: a Page Header band, a Report Intro band, a Detail band, a Report Summary band, and a Page Footer band.

The Page Header band puts a line or lines of information at the top (header) of each printed page. These data often include the name of the report, date, time printed, and column titles, if columnar data are displayed in the body of the report. You will see what this does more clearly a little later.

The Report Intro band is designed to contain the text introduction (perhaps a cover letter) to the report. This band can contain formatted text and is useful for cover text or memoranda. Unlike the Page Header, the Report Intro text prints only at the beginning of a printed report, not on each page of the report.

The Detail band presents the data taken from the database. It may contain the contents of the data fields and may also use calculated fields or special predefined and summary fields. In addition, it may be used to contain the text and data fields necessary to produce mail merge letters, which combine standard text with field data.

The Report Summary band is designed to present summary data based on the numeric fields used to prepare the report. The summary report is printed after all the data in the Detail Band have been printed.

Finally, the Page Footer band prints the same footer text at the bottom of each page. When used in conjunction with the Page Header band, you have additional flexibility in modifying the appearance of your printed page. For example, the page header may contain the company name and title of the report, and the footer can show the page number and date of printing.

In addition to the standard bands provided by dBASE IV's Report function, you may also add new bands, referred to as Group bands. A Group band contains related information, for example, one group band may display the names and employee numbers for all employees in each department.

Bands provide interesting possibilities. As displayed in Figure 9-1, five blank lines will print if you tell the system to print the report, because all bands are open. The band must be opened for a band's contents to print.

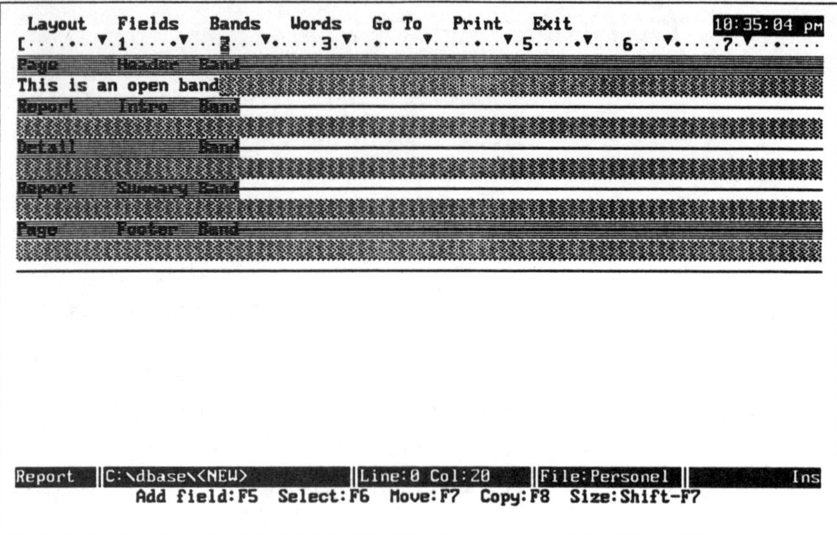

Figure 9-2

Open Page Header band.

To see what is meant by open and closed bands, move the cursor so that it is on Line 0 Column 0 (the first line in the Page Header band).

Type: *This is an open band*

The screen will appear as shown in Figure 9-2. Now, move the cursor up one line into the Page Header band, using the **UpArrow**.

Press: **ENTER**

to close the Page Header band. You will see, as in Figure 9-3, that the contents of the open band are not visible. Pressing **ENTER** again reopens the band.

The ability to open and close bands provides capabilities that may not be immediately apparent. Because you can also add Group bands, which combine various groups of data, you can, in effect, design specific types of groups for specific types of reports. In practice, you may be able to use the same form for a variety of different reports simply by closing those groups that you do not want and opening the groups that you wish to use.

Of course, the same applies for the five standard bands automatically provided by dBASE IV. For example, the Detail Band may be used to prepare both a summary report to the company's management department and a letter to the company's administrator. In one case, a basic report format with page headers,

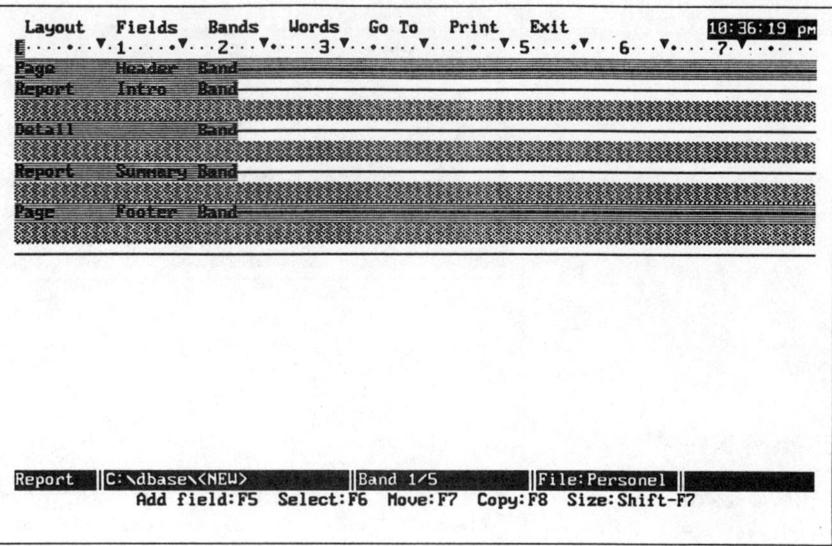

Figure 9-3

Closed Page Header band.

summary band, and details would be used. In the second instance, you may close the header and footer bands, and instead use a specially written Report Intro.

By putting all the possible types of information into the available bands (in addition to specially designed Group bands), you can tailor entirely different reports from the same basic report form just by opening and closing the required bands.

To edit the contents of a band, the band must first be opened. Once open, the standard techniques for placing text and fields onto your form can be used. These have already been discussed in other chapters. Some will again be demonstrated when you build a report in this chapter.

The Layout Menu

The Layout menu is similar to the menus provided in both the Forms and the Labels design screens. The Quick layouts, which were not available from within Labels, are very different from those available in the Forms design module.

Select the Layout menu by pressing **Alt-F**. Next, select Quick Layouts. Because this is the default selection when you choose Layout,

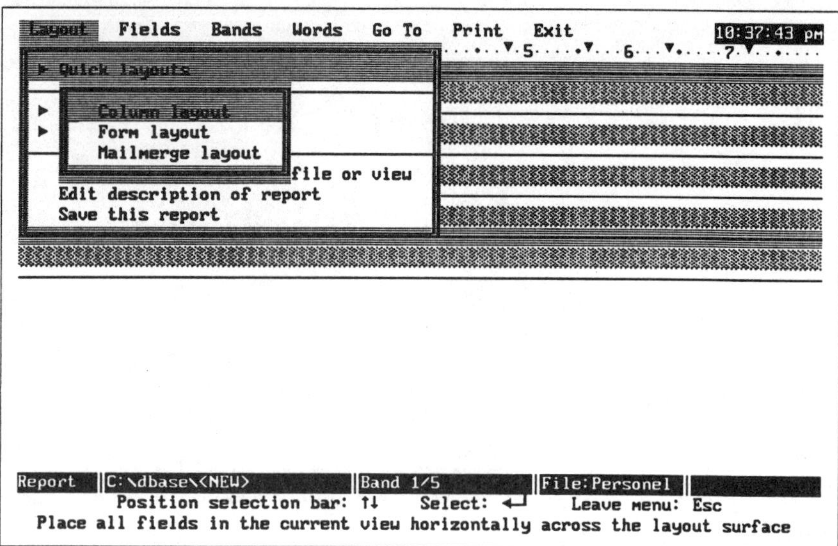

Figure 9-4

Quick layout options.

Press: **ENTER**

to bring up the Quick layout options. The three available layouts are shown in Figure 9-4.

> WARNING: Before selecting any new layout, you must first save your present design. When a quick layout is selected, the system automatically pulls fields from the data file in use and places them into appropriate bands. When it does this, however, it clears the existing report design that is currently in use. You must be careful, then, to save your report form *before* loading a quick layout, unless you want the system to discard your currently active design. (This option will not delete forms that have already been saved; only changes that have been made during the current editing session, or after the last Save was performed from within the Report design module, will be discarded).

Because what you have done to the current blank form is not really worth saving, feel free to accept the Column layout. To do this,

Press: **ENTER** (if "Column layout" is highlighted)

or

Type: *C*

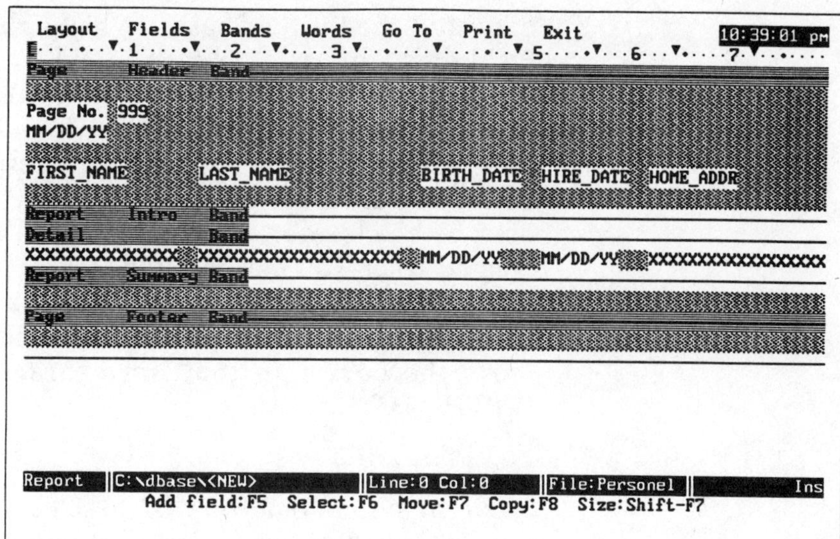

Figure 9-5

Column layout for PERSONEL data file.

The screen will appear as shown in Figure 9-5.

You will notice that the Page Header band shows the page number, date, and field names printed along a long column on the fourth line of the band. The Report Intro band is closed and the Detail Band is open. The detail band reveals the data template for the data corresponding to the field names directly above them in the Page Header band.

The Report Summary band and Page Footer band are open. The templates for two numeric fields are shown in the Report Summary band.

When this report is printed, it will in theory print the column heads (the names of each field), followed by the contents of each record. In the case of our current data file, this will not happen, however, because the width of the fields exceeds the width of the paper. If you try to print your extra-wide file, the system will send two or more lines to the printer corresponding to the text on a single line of your screen; that is, the system will cause the printer to scroll text that is beyond the print margin onto the next line. Thus, your columnar arrangement will not appear to make much sense. To solve this problem, you will have to delete many of the fields.

You have two options to delete a field. First, you may move the cursor to the field. When the cursor enters the field, it is highlighted by the system. Pressing **Del** removes the field. Alternatively, once the field has been highlighted, you can pop up the Field menu and select Remove field.

Note that the field name cannot be as easily deleted. You must delete it character by character or highlight the field name and then delete it. When a field or the corresponding field name has been deleted, the spaces on your line will not automatically close up. The block select and move keys allow you to fill the gaps created when you have deleted text or fields.

To see how to make the deletions and the effect they have on the layout and how to move files, first delete the Birth_Date field. Move the cursor to the first character in the field name, BIRTH_DATE.

Press: **F6**

to tell the system that you wish to select text (for moving or deletion). Once this is done, a highlight will appear at the cursor. Move the cursor until the entire field name is highlighted.

Press: **ENTER**

Next, to delete the text,

Press: **Del**

The text will have been deleted but no space gained, because the deleted text was replaced with blanks.

Move the cursor down to the line that corresponded to the Birth_Date field. When the field is highlighted,

Press: **F6 ENTER**

to tell the system that you want to select a field and that you want to select the entire field. Next,

Press: **Del**

to delete the field. Again, the spaces removed did not close up; instead, the area occupied by the data was replaced by blank space. (You could also have deleted the field by merely moving the highlight onto it and pressing **Del**.) The screen will now appear as shown in Figure 9-6.

To move the Hire_Date data band, move the cursor until the date area below the HIRE_DATE name field (inside the Detail band) is highlighted.

Press: **F6 ENTER**

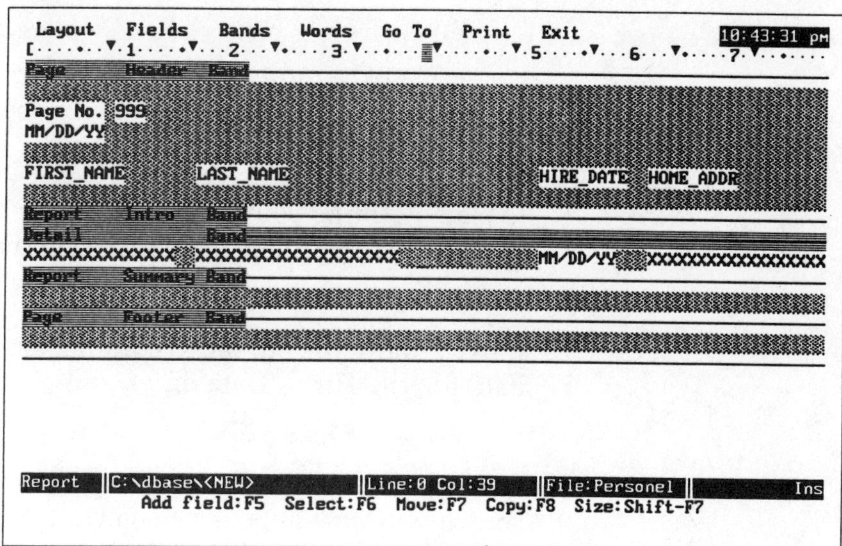

Figure 9-6

Screen with Birth_Date data field and field name deleted.

to highlight the field and select the entire field. Next, move the cursor to column 40 (the position of the tab stop, as seen on the ruler line) and

Press: **F7**

to indicate where the data field for Hire_Date is to be moved.

Figure 9-7

Data field for Hire_Date moved.

```
Layout   Fields   Bands   Words   Go To   Print   Exit          10:46:58 pm
Page      Header   Band
Page No. 999
MM/DD/YY
FIRST_NAME        LAST_NAME                         HIRE_DATE  HOME_ADDR
Report    Intro    Band
Detail             Band
XXXXXXXXXXXXXXX XXXXXXXXXXXXXXXXXXXX  MM/DD/YY              XXXXXXXXXXXXXXXXXX
Report    Summary  Band
Page      Footer   Band
Report  C:\dbase\<NEW>      Line:0 Col:40   File:Personel          Ins
        Add field:F5  Select:F6  Move:F7  Copy:F8  Size:Shift-F7
    PERSONEL->HIRE_DATE   Type: Date      Width:   8   Decimal:  0
```

Press: **ENTER**

to complete the move (Figure 9-7). Then move the cursor up to the *H* in Hire_Date in the Page Header band.

Press: **F6**

to start defining your block. Using the **RtArrow** key, extend the highlight to highlight the entire field name and

Press: **ENTER**

Finally, move the cursor to column 40 (the same position as the data for the Hire_Date data), and

Press: **F7 ENTER**

to move the field and place it at the new cursor position. The screen will now appear as shown in Figure 9-8.

Next, delete all fields and field names except SS_NUMBER and EMP_NUMBER and move the data fields and field names so that they are positioned as shown in Figure 9-9. Then move the EMP_NUMBER field in the Report Summary band under the field name, although a summary of this information makes little or no sense (and is being used purely for illustrative purposes). Finally, remove the template for DEPT_NUMBER, ZIP_CODE, and SS_NUMBER from the Report Summary band.

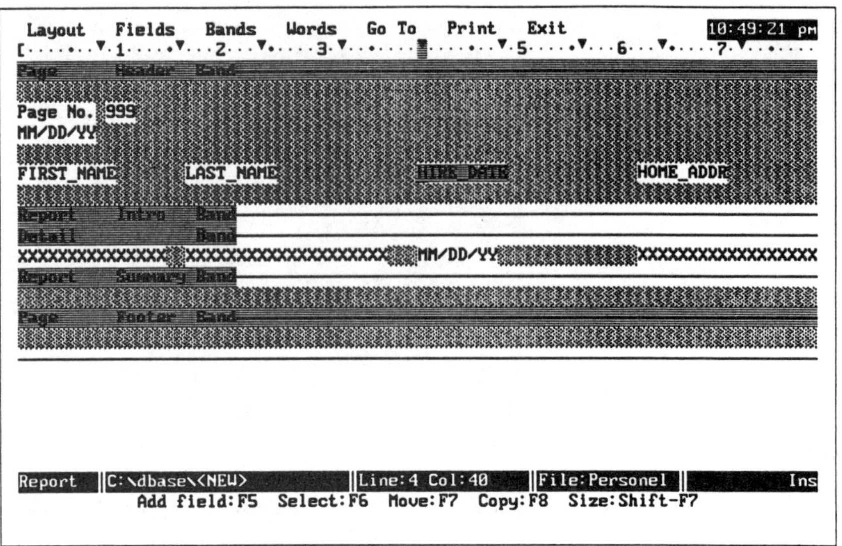

Figure 9-8

Birth_Date deleted and HIRE_DATE moved.

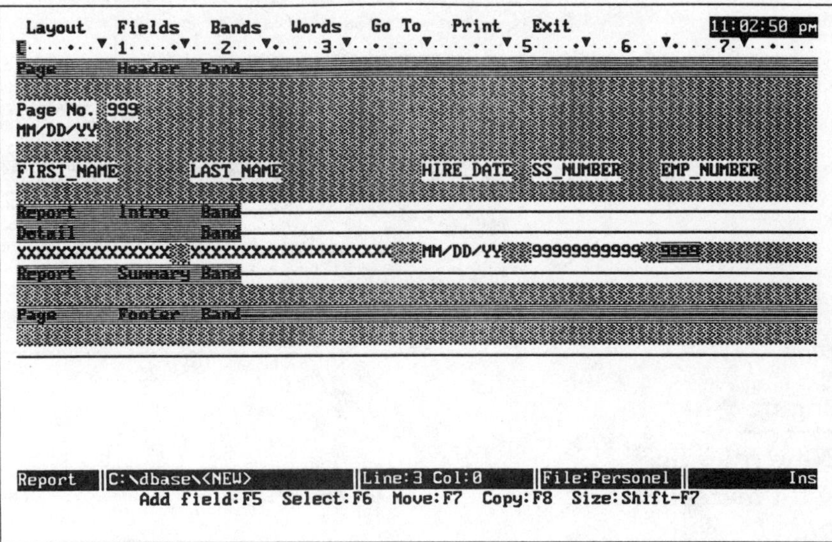

Figure 9-9

Layout of SS_NUMBER and EMP_NUMBER fields.

Although your columns are all consolidated, the width of your page is still the full available width of 256 characters.

Now, go into the Words menu and select Modify ruler. Set the right margin by moving to column 78 and typing *]*.

Press: **ENTER**

to finish modifying your ruler line. The screen, with the new ruler line, will appear as shown in Figure 9-10. Your screen will still display a width of 256 characters, but when you print the report, it will be only 78 characters wide.

The Column layout is obviously not well suited to displaying records that contain large amounts of data, because the line is limited in length. It would have been better to have modified the PERSONEL database so that it used only those fields that you wanted to display in your columnar report format.

Return to the Layout menu and select Save this report, naming it PERSCOLM (for Personnel Columnar). The system will generate a code to produce printed reports using the specification just defined.

The Quick layout for the columnar format, which is initially created by the system when you activate the Columnar format, is the same report that is prepared if you select Quick report by pressing **Shft-F9**.

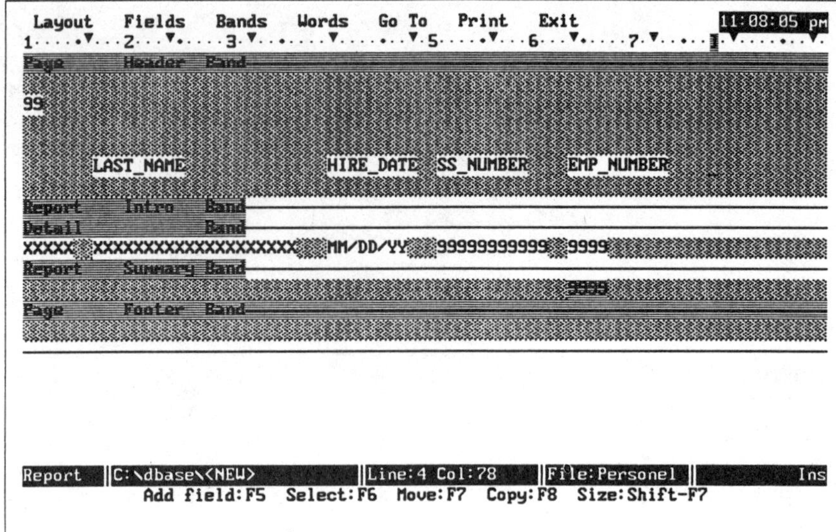

Figure 9-10

New ruler line with margin at 78.

You could, of course, have added boxes and other devices to the bands to enhance the appearance and readability of your form. Box and line drawing is done in the same way as in the Forms menu.

Next, from within the Layout menu, select Quick layouts and then select Form layout. The form that is created is very similar to the form created using Quick layout from within the Forms menu (Figure 9-11). This layout is not subject to the limits imposed on a Column layout. The only limitation is the width of your longest field, or the longest line you create if you have put more than one field on your form. This form is useful for printing Index forms or for other forms of printouts that list your entire database.

You can, of course, use the Box and Line options to draw lines and boxes to better organize your data. In addition, you can move data or fields, and type any text desired onto this form.

Specially formatted reports can be easily printed using this layout. As with the Forms menu, however, there may be times when it is easier and/or faster to add your fields using the Fields menu, rather than modifying, copying, or moving the fields in a standard form.

The third Quick layout, Mailmerge, is fundamentally different

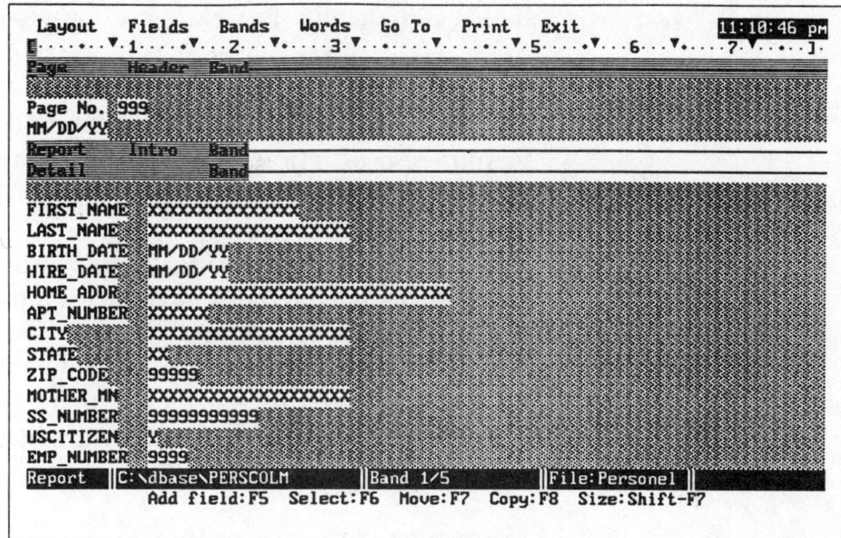

Figure 9-11

Report Forms Quick layout.

from the first two. It sets the system so that you can prepare form letters or other mail merge documents (Figure 9-12).

The editor in this mode functions much as it does within the text editor used for memo fields or within the Applications Generator, Modify dBASE Program function. The only open band

Figure 9-12

Report Mailmerge Quick layout.

```
Layout   Fields   Bands   Words   Go To   Print   Exit        11:12:41 pm
Page     Header   Band
Report   Intro    Band
Detail            Band
_

Report   Summary  Band
Page     Footer   Band

Report  C:\dbase\PERSCOLM   Line:0 Col:0   File:Personel
        Add field:F5  Select:F6  Move:F7  Copy:F8  Size:Shift-F7
```

in this setup is the Detail band, although you can add Group bands or open the other bands that are standard on the form.

To see how this editor works, you will prepare a letter to employees informing them that they will be receiving annual performance evaluations on the anniversary of their employment. The first thing you will do in this form is to define the margins for your printed menu.

To modify the ruler, bring up the Words menu and select Modify ruler. Next, set the left margin at 1 inch by moving the cursor to the *1* on the ruler line and typing *[*. The [that was originally at the left margin will now be located at the 1 inch marker. Next, set your right margin at 7 inches, using the] character to indicate the right margin. Once the margins have been set,

Press: **ENTER**

to accept the new ruler line.

Next, move the cursor to line 0 in the Detail band. The cursor will be placed at column 0, the first position on the line. The screen, with the new ruler and the cursor in proper position, will appear as shown in Figure 9-13.

If your company will be using preprinted letterhead, you will want to start your document 1.5 inches below the top of the printed form so that your data does not print on top of the letterhead.

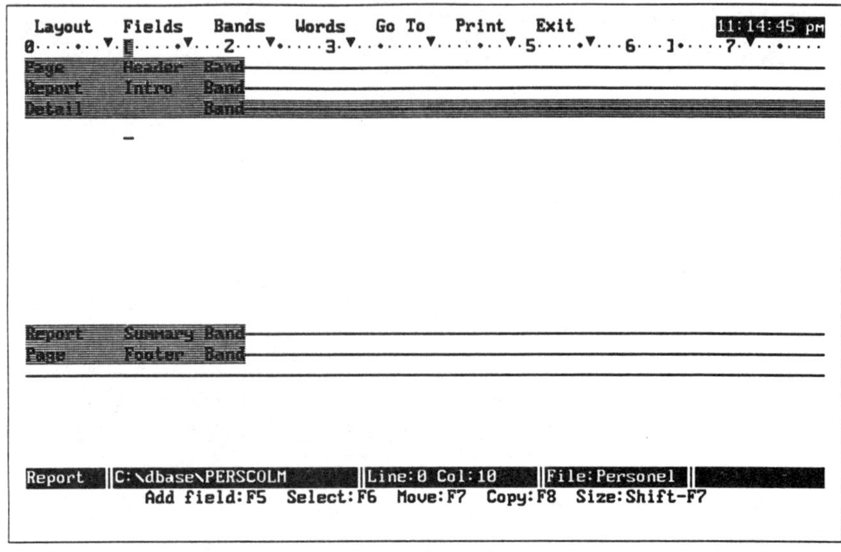

Figure 9-13

New margins, cursor at line 0, Column 10 in Detail band.

With **Insert** on (Insert is toggled on and off, using the **Ins** key) (the word *Ins* will be visible on the message line at the bottom right corner of your screen),

Press: **ENTER**

nine times to bring you to Line 9, column 10. The Insert cursor is larger than the standard Overtype cursor.

Now, go to the Fields menu and select Add field. (You can also add a field by pressing **F5**.) Select the predefined Date field, as seen in Figure 9-14. This will bring up a special Definition menu that will be examined in further detail later. For now, accept the current settings by pressing **Ctrl-End**.

The template for the data will be placed on line 9, beginning at column 10. Move the cursor to the end of the template and press **ENTER** two times to place a line below the date and move the cursor to a new line for the name line. Add the First_Name and Last_Name fields by selecting them from the Add fields option in the Fields menu (or by pressing **F5** and selecting the fields from the Pick menu). Separate first and last names by one space, and accept truncation for both fields.

Next, move the cursor to the end of the Last_Name template and again

Press: **ENTER**

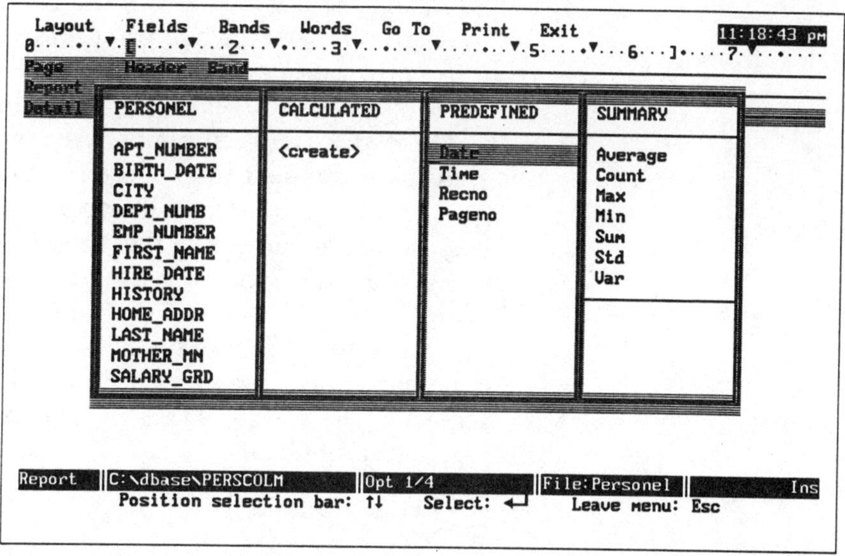

Figure 9-14

Predefined Date field highlighted, before selection.

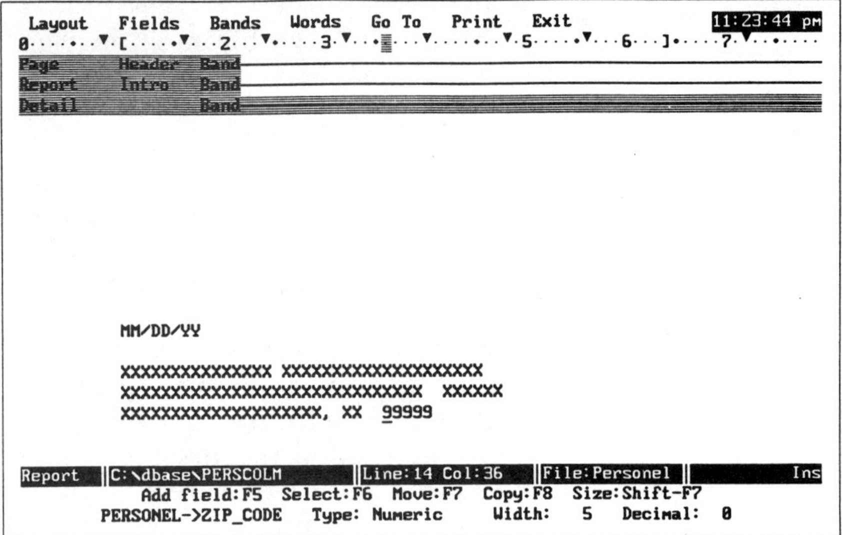

Figure 9-15

Date and address block for letters.

You will probably notice that if you try to use the lines below those you are currently editing (you can get to this line by pressing the **DnArrow**), the cursor will go to column 0. This is because the ruler line you have defined does not affect lines that already have a ruler applied to them (and the lines below your work area have the default ruler with a margin of 0 in effect). The format carries over from one paragraph to the next because you are in Insert mode and pressing the **ENTER** key at the end of each paragraph. The new paragraph started when you pressed **ENTER** uses the ruler from the previous paragraph.

In the second address line, add the HOME_ADDR and APT_NUMBER field templates, leaving a single space between the fields. On the next line, add city, state, and ZIP code. When completed, the templates will appear as shown in Figure 9-15.

Next, move the cursor to the end of the Zip_Code field and press **ENTER** twice to bring you to the salutation line. Because this is not a formal letter, you will not need to use a title (Mr., Mrs., or Ms.); the salutation will be Dear First_Name:. Type the word Dear, a space, then drop in the First_Name template, followed by a colon. Then press **ENTER** twice to bring you to the first line of your letter's body.

Press: **Space** (five times)

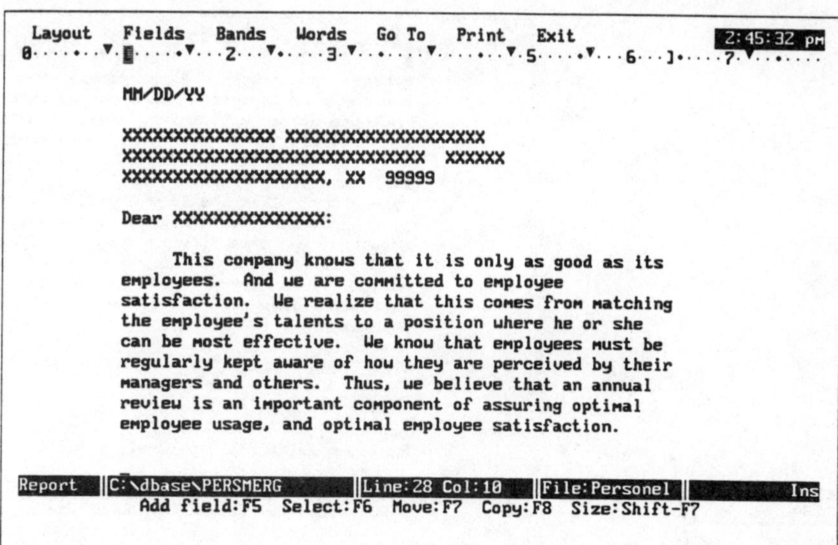

Figure 9-16

Header and first paragraph of letter.

to indent the text for the first paragraph. Type in the text as shown in Figure 9-16. Then type the following text:

> Shortly before your next anniversary with this company, you will receive an employee questionnaire, in addition to a performance evaluation from your supervisor. This should arrive within one month of your anniversary date with this company. Our records show that you were first employed on <Hire_Date>.

(where Hire_Date is the template for the Hire_Date field). Next, type the closing paragraphs of your letter. The last part of your letter will appear as shown in Figure 9-17. Finally, save the design, using the Layout menu and selecting Save this report. Name the form PERSMERG.

The system will create the report form for producing mail merged documents. Although not shown in this example, text that is entered into the documents from within a data field will properly fill the paragraph into which it is inserted; the lines of text will automatically word wrap so that the lines of text in which data have been added will not be any longer or shorter than the rest of the text in the paragraph.

Now that some of the basics of report layout have been seen, it is useful to go through some of the more important aspects of the menus provided by the report generator. Many of the options

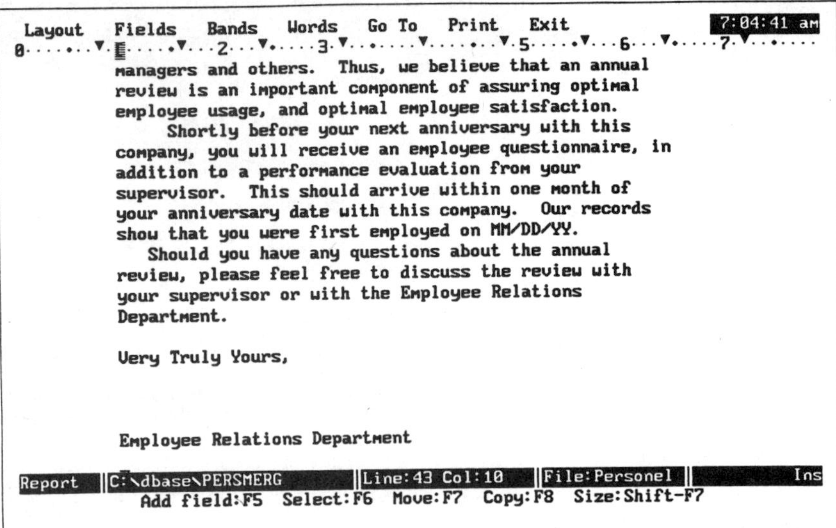
Layout Fields Bands Words Go To Print Exit 7:04:41 am

managers and others. Thus, we believe that an annual review is an important component of assuring optimal employee usage, and optimal employee satisfaction.

Shortly before your next anniversary with this company, you will receive an employee questionnaire, in addition to a performance evaluation from your supervisor. This should arrive within one month of your anniversary date with this company. Our records show that you were first employed on MM/DD/YY.

Should you have any questions about the annual review, please feel free to discuss the review with your supervisor or with the Employee Relations Department.

Very Truly Yours,

Employee Relations Department

Report | C:\dbase\PERSMERG | Line:43 Col:10 | File:Personel | Ins

Add field:F5 Select:F6 Move:F7 Copy:F8 Size:Shift-F7

Figure 9-17

Closing of letter.

are similar in operation to those available in previous chapters. Only differences or areas requiring further discussion are explored in this chapter.

The Fields menu is essentially the same as it appears in other menus. However, the available fields and types of fields go beyond those available in either Forms or Reports. In addition, fields can be *hidden* by the system.

Because the Report design screen is used to print reports rather than just printing out data, it has been designed to allow you to manipulate and calculate data. In some cases, you may want to perform calculations using fields that you do not want to print. For example, in designing a dunning letter to be mailed to past due creditors, you may want to prepare a boilerplate letter that states how much money is owed. This field may be calculated by taking an outstanding balance, adding new charges, and subtracting recent payments. The current balance will make use of the new charge totals and the last credited payments, neither of which is to be printed. Thus, the new charges and recent payments will be used to calculate the amount due but will be hidden from the system.

The Fields menu is shown in Figure 9-18.

To see the new Field options and more about the hidden fields, select Add field. Four columns will appear on screen, as seen in

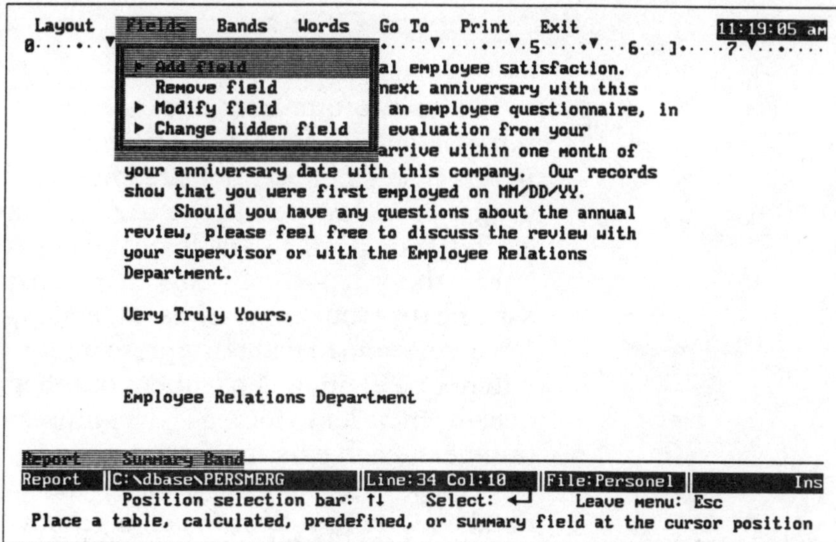

Figure 9-18

Fields menu.

Figure 9-19. The first column lists the fields in the data file currently in use. The column head is the name of the data file, in this case, PERSONEL. You may select any field by moving the highlight to the desired field or by typing the first letters of the field to move the highlight to it. Once a field is highlighted,

Figure 9-19

Add Field menu.

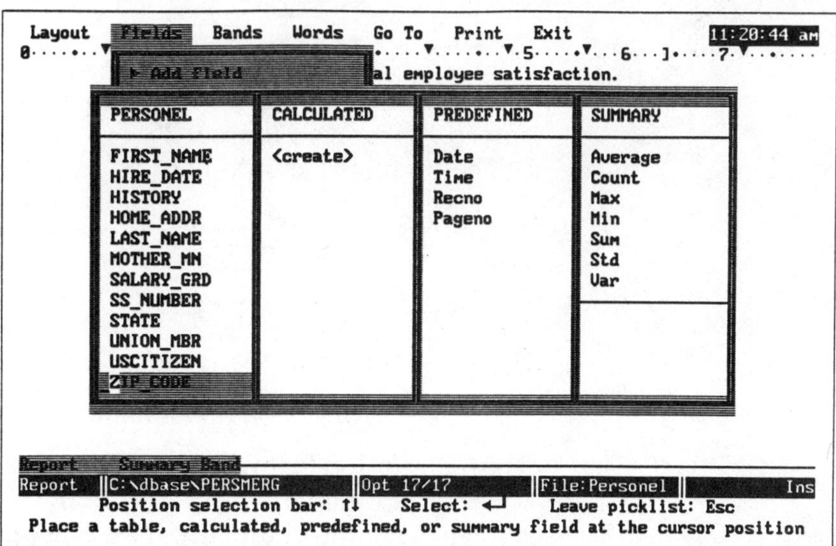

Press: **ENTER**

to complete selection.

The next column contains Calculated fields. To select a predefined Calculated field, move the highlight to it and press **ENTER**. In this case, since no calculated fields have been created, you will design one. However, in the current example none of the fields easily lends itself to any logical calculation.

For the purposes of this demonstration we will therefore assume that your company is undergoing a major reorganization. It has determined that if the present rate of growth continues there will not be enough department numbers to extend into the next decade. In order to increase the number of available department numbers, each existing department number will be multiplied by ten. In actual use, of course, you will have to modify your database file to reflect the change, but for the purposes of this demonstration, you'll be making the change using the Calculated field function in the current menu.

In addition, the calculated fields, quite logically, only work with numeric fields. While there is a method from within the dot prompt programming to convert character fields to numeric, they are beyond the scope of this book.

The options for creating a calculated field are straightforward. Move the cursor into the Calculated fields column. The highlight will be on "<create>".

Press: **ENTER**

The screen will bring up the calculated field design screen. This screen looks like Figure 9-20.

The highlight should now be on "Name."

Press: **ENTER**

and

Type: ***NEWDEPT*** **ENTER**

Move the highlight to "Description" and

Type: ***New department numbers*** **ENTER**

The description text will fill the window. If your description was longer than the width of the window, it would have scrolled in the window. You could also have pressed the **F9** key to *zoom* the text input line to the lower part of the screen, so that you could

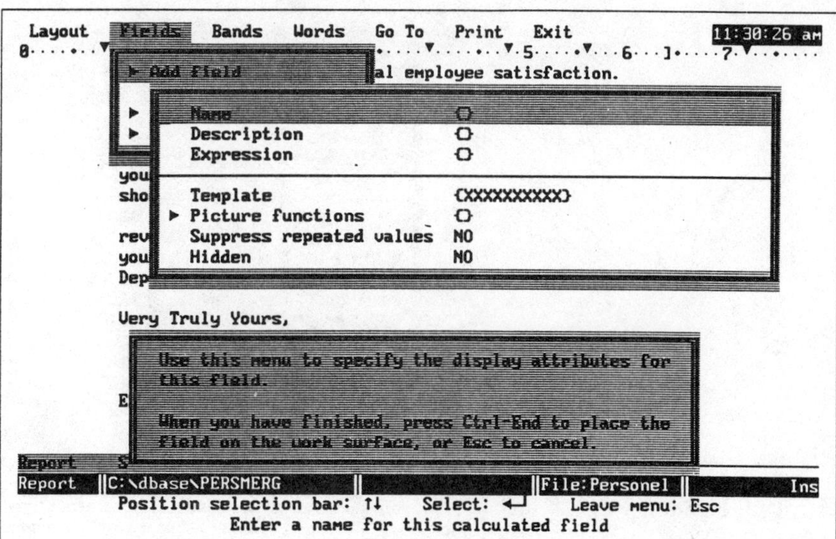

Figure 9-20

Calculated field design screen.

view the statement as you wrote it. Move the highlight to "Expression" and press **ENTER**.

The expression is the key to the calculated field. This statement tells the system how to calculate your field. You may type a mathematical expression or ask for assistance in designing the expression. The expression that you want to use is DEPT_NUMB * 10.

To see your options for designing the expression,

Type: **Shft-F1**

to pop up the Selection screen seen in Figure 9-21. With the Selection screen visible, highlight and select "DEPT_NUMB" as the first part of the expression. Next, press **Shft-F1** to select the mathematical operator. The system will again bring up the Selection menu.

Move the cursor to the Operator column and scroll through the operators. (It would have been easier just to enter the symbol for multiplication, *). The operators were discussed earlier in this book. However, it is useful to remind you that the ** operator means that you are squaring a number (multiplying it by itself) and that / is the symbol for division.

The third column allows you to select functions, which are expressions that can be used to evaluate your expression.

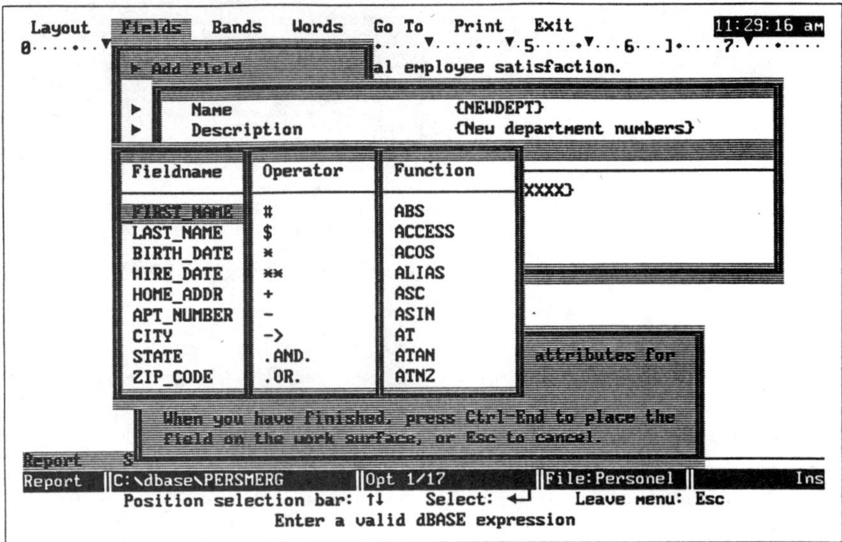

Figure 9-21

Expression selection screen.

In the present example, however, you are multiplying the DEPT_NUMB by a constant. To return to the expression line,

Press: **Esc**

Type: *10*

to put the constant into the expression. If the expression appears as shown in Figure 9-22,

Press: **ENTER**

The system will enclose the expression in curly braces and restore the highlight.

You will notice that the template uses two digits beyond the decimal point. The original numeric field used no decimal places. Thus, you should change the template to remove the two decimals. In addition, because the DEPT_NUMB field was only four characters wide, you should allow only a five-character width template. Change the template from its current values to 99999. You will not have to change any picture functions for this calculated field.

The last two items to appear on the Field Setup menu are Suppress repeated values and Hidden. Suppress repeated values tells the system whether to print only the first occurrence of a par-

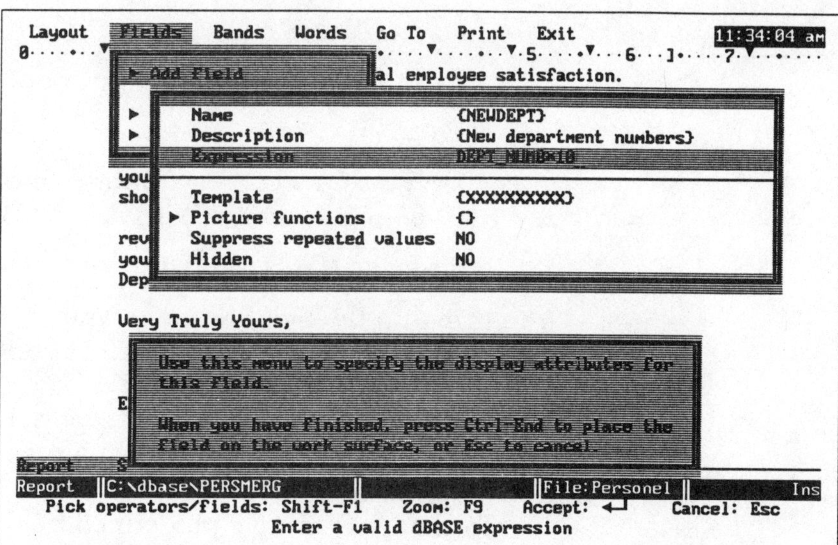

Figure 9-22

Design for calculated field.

ticular value in a field. For example, in the present database, you may be preparing a report that lists all departments. Each department would probably have many employees. Because the goal of your current report is to list only the departments, there is no need to print out the department number more than once. If you were using a database indexed by department number, the data file would thus have many listings for each department. When you set Suppress repeated values to *Yes*, you are telling the system that you want it to print a value only the *first* time it appears in the database. Leave this option set to *No*.

The final option, Hidden, asks whether you wish to hide the field. If you answer yes, the field is not printed in your report. Usually, a hidden field is one that is called into the report form and is used to calculate a field. For example, if you wanted to calculate a total price for items purchased, you would multiply the number of items ordered by the unit cost and then compute and add the applicable tax rate. If you were trying to create a new calculated field, Total_Cost, the intermediate field, which represented the product of unit cost and quantity ordered (itself a calculated field) may not be required. You may hide the field, referring to it when calculating the Total_Cost, but without making it part of your report. Leave this set to *No*. You will not be using the calculated field in this example, so

Press: **Esc**

to tell the system that you do not want to save the field, and

Type: *Y*

to answer the Cancel Procedure? prompt. The system will return you to the Fields menu. With the cursor on Add field,

Press: **ENTER** (or Type: *A)*

to bring up the Field Selection menu.

Predefined fields include Date, Time, Recno, and Pageno. When selected, these fields will print the date, time, record number, and page number onto your printed report. Each of these options has obvious utility. When you select a predefined field, a Selection menu pops up (Figure 9-23).

To change from one predefined field to another from within this screen, you may scroll through the list of predefined fields by pressing **ENTER** or the **Space Bar** until the field you wish is highlighted on the line. The options within this window change according to the type of predefined field you are selecting. You will notice the highlight, which indicates your options, changing as you scroll through the list of predefined fields. When the correct predefined field and values for the appropriate variables are on the screen, accept the settings using **Ctrl-End**. For now,

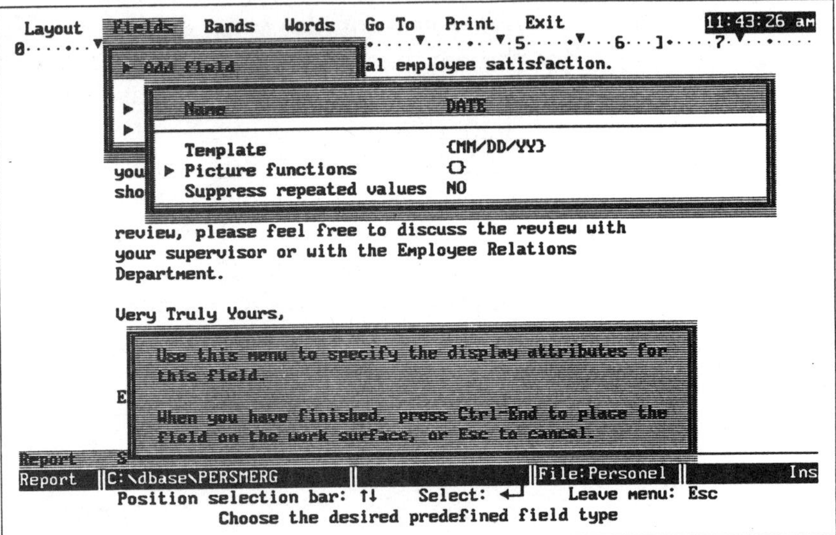

Figure 9-23

Predefined field selection window.

Press: **Esc**

and confirm that you want to cancel the procedure to return to the Fields menu. Again, select Add field to return to the Selection window.

Summary fields occupy the final column in the Fields menu. The functions in these fields perform specific actions on the data in a particular field. Average adds all data in the particular field and divides them by the number of records, resulting in an average value for a field. Count indicates the number of records in your database file. Max indicates the maximum value for data entered into a particular field. Min tells the system to find and display (or print) the minimum value for all the records in the selected field. Sum provides a total for all values in the field. Std provides a standard deviation for the data in the field. Standard deviation is a statistical expression that indicates how much a value deviates from the numerical mean. Using standard deviation, a user can evaluate the significance (or lack of significance) of a particular value. The Var function calculates variance, another statistical value related to dispersion of values within a particular field.

The summary fields are treated as calculated fields, which, of course, they are. When you select a summary field from the menu, a new Definition window pops onto the screen. This Summary selection window is seen in Figure 9-24.

Figure 9-24

Summary field definition window.

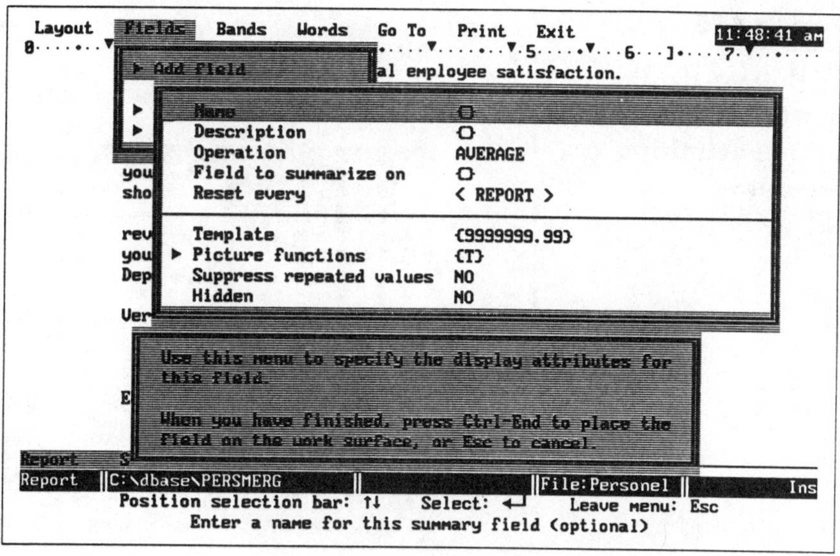

Many of the basic operations in this screen have been previously described. If you are defining a summary field and realize you wanted a different summary field, you need not **Esc** and reload the Add Field menu. To change summary options, move the highlight so that it is on "Operation," and

Press: **ENTER**

to toggle through the available Summary functions. The Selection window is shown in Figure 9-25.

To get a summary of a field, it is necessary to identify the field on which the Summary function is to be performed. To do this move the highlight to "Field to summarize on." The system will pop a new window onto the screen showing the calculated fields and the fields in your current database. The numeric fields, on which you can perform summaries, are highlighted, and are the only ones that you can select from within this menu. Only the Count function does not ask for a field to summarize on.

The system allows you two options for resetting the summary fields. The first is to reset every report. When this is selected, the system will keep running totals through your entire database, and will reset to zero only when you wish to produce another report. When you tell the system to reset every page, the system will print the summary for the current page, reset to zero, and then prepare

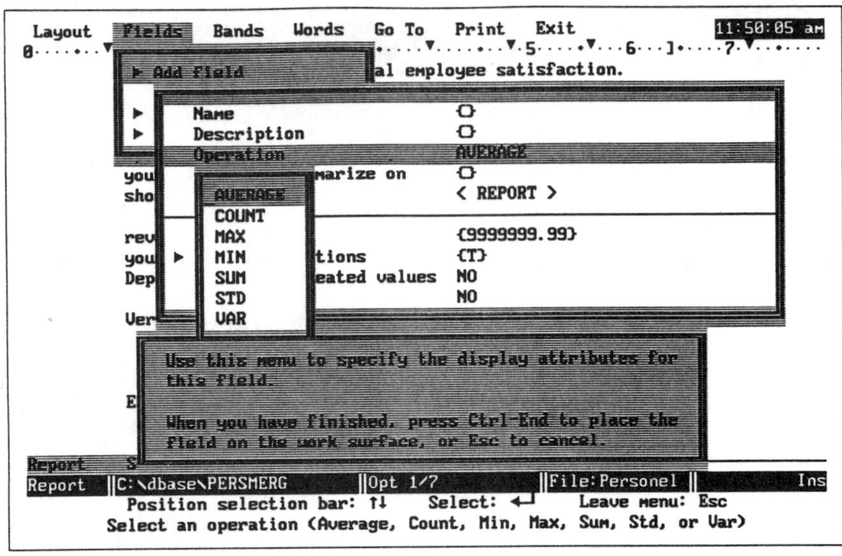

Figure 9-25

Summary field selection from within definition window.

a summary for the next page, resetting before going on to the next page.

Now, close the current window by pressing **Esc** and responding *Y* to the Cancel prompt.

The Bands Menu

You have already seen the basic bands that are built into the report form. Opening and closing bands, as previously mentioned, allows you to include, or exclude, the contents of the selected band. Bands toggle open or closed using the **ENTER** key.

In addition to the preset bands, dBASE IV allows you to define what it refers to as Group bands. A Group band includes related data or data fields. For example, you may have a group field that groups employees by salary grade. A Group band consists of two parts: a Group Intro band and a Group Summary band. Group bands may be added only in the areas above the Detail band (in the Page Header or the Report Intro areas).

To see how the bands work, **Esc** from the menus and move the cursor to the first line of the open Report Intro band. Now,

Press: **Alt-B**

to bring up the Bands menu (Figure 9-26).

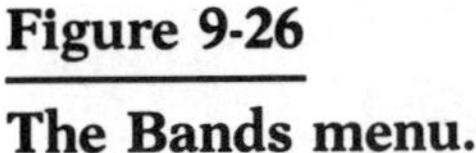

Figure 9-26

The Bands menu.

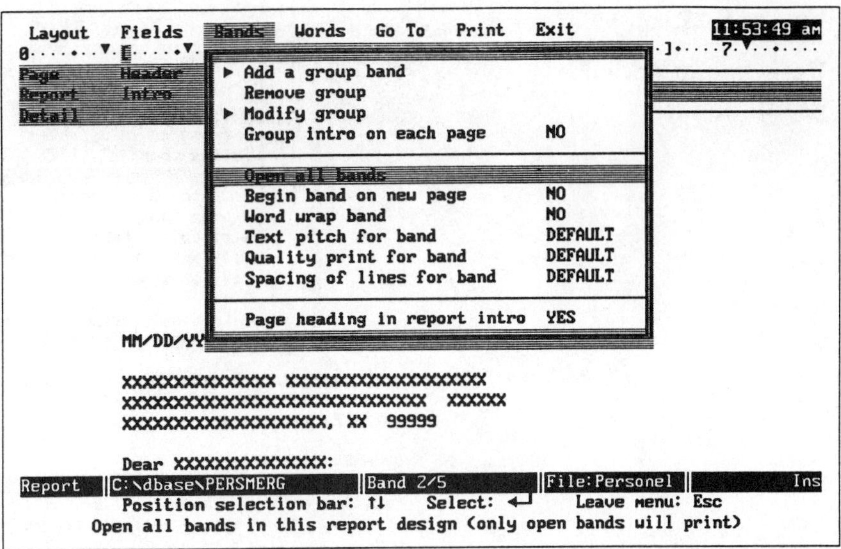

You will see what the various menu items do shortly. For now, select Add a group band. To do this,

Type: *A*

(or make sure the highlight is on "Add a group band" and

Press: **ENTER**

Once you select Add a group band, the system gives you three choices for defining how data will be grouped, as seen in Figure 9-27. The first choice, Field value, pops up a list of the data fields in the data file you are using. When this is selected, the system will start printing a new group each time the value of the selected field changes. For example, you will soon be defining one group by the Salary Grade field value. If you are making a report based on a sorted listing of salary grades, a new band will be printed when each salary grade changes.

The Expression value grouping allows you to define your group based on an expression. If you select this option, you may see your choices of fields, operators, and functions by pressing **Shft-F1**. This option allows you to report on records in which a particular parameter is met. For example, you may wish to report on all employees who are in departments 1000–3000.

The final choice is Record count. This option groups your data

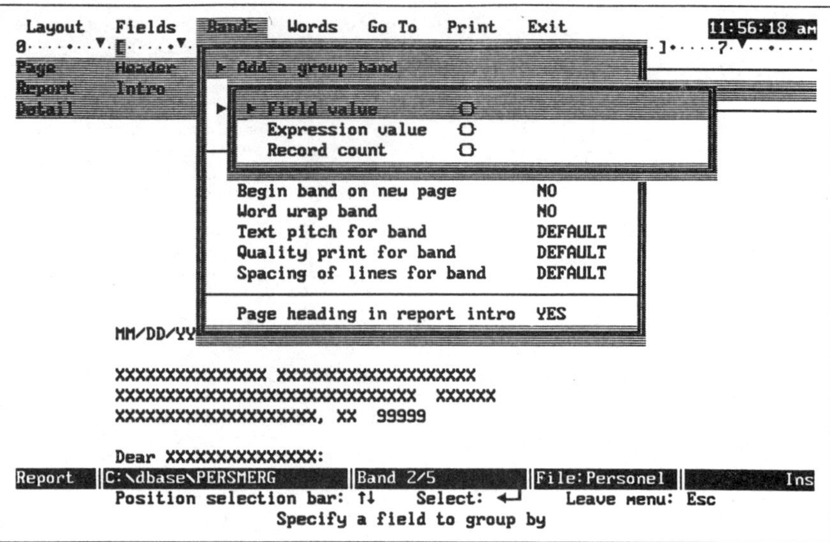

Figure 9-27

Defining an added group band.

into a number of predetermined records. For example, you may want to show your data with only 10 records per page. By selecting this option, and typing the desired number, you will tell the system to print only 10 records per page.

For now, select the Field value option and highlight and select the Salary_Grd field (highlight "Salary_Grd" and press **ENTER**). The system will add a Group 1 Intro band between the Report Intro band and the Detail band, and will place a Group 1 Summary band between the Detail band and the Report Summary band (Figure 9-28).

The Group 1 Intro band can be used for introductory text or column headings. Fields, expressions, and text may be added into the Group Intro and summary bands. In addition, Group bands may be nested; that is, one band can be put inside of another. To see how this works, move the cursor into the open Group 1 Intro band and bring up the Bands menu. Select Add a group band and define it as a Record count band. To do this, highlight the "Record count" line and press **ENTER** (or press *r* to select this option). Next, the system will pop up a window asking for an integer value. This value will tell the system the desired number of records into which the data are to be grouped.

Type: *15*

Figure 9-28

Group 1 Summary band.

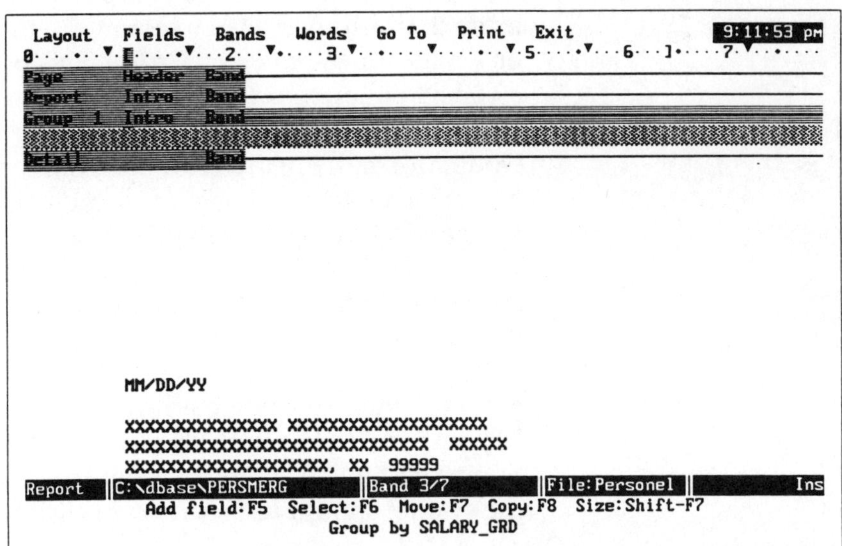

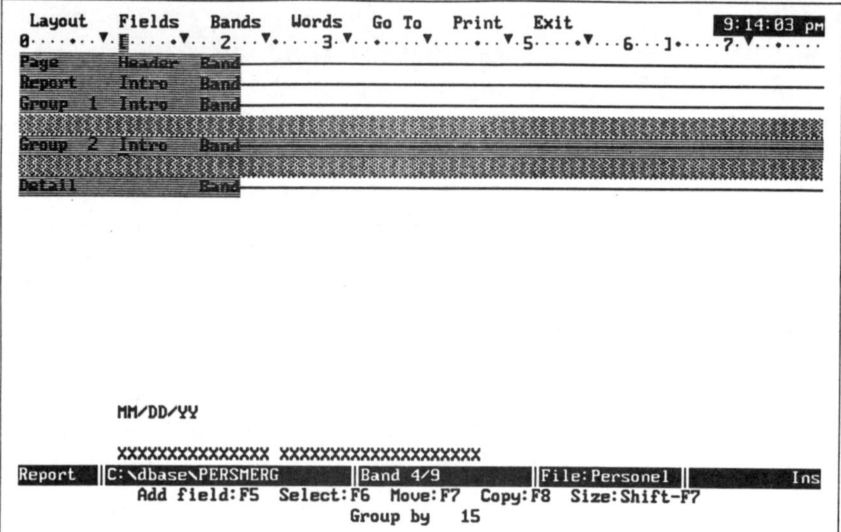

Figure 9-29

Group 2 band nested inside Group 1.

The Group 2 bands will now be added, and nested inside of the first Group bands (Figure 9-29).

You will notice that the Group 2 bands are placed inside the Group 1 band. If you added a third group, it will similarly be placed with the bands between the Group 2 bands and the Detail band.

The Record Count band (a group band that uses Record count as its definition) is used to count the number of records printed on a page for the selected Group. This band is useful in providing a consistent appearance to your printed output. If, for example, you were printing hundreds or thousands of records, the system would normally print a full page of records, go to the next page, and print another full page of records. Using a Record Count band, you can tell the system to print fewer records on a page. The advantage is that you can produce reports that allow more white space on the page, that is, more space above and below the printed data. This usually makes the data easier to read.

You can easily determine the type of band being used in your grouped bands by moving the cursor into the band selection line. When the cursor is in the band, the bands affected (the Intro and Summary bands) will be highlighted. At the bottom of the screen, the system should tell you how the highlighted band is grouped.

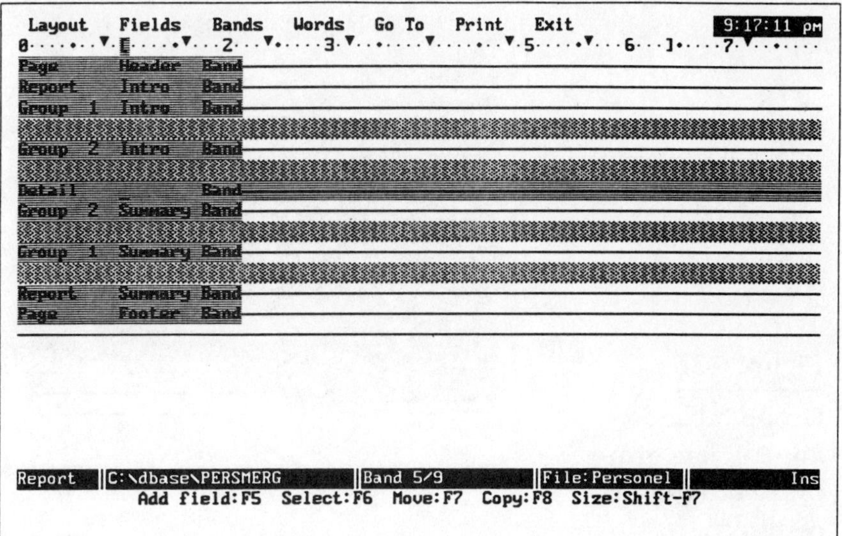

Figure 9-30

Another view of nested bands.

To see the band layout more clearly, move the cursor into the Detail band and

Press: **ENTER**

to close up the Detail band. The screen shows all the bands and illustrates the nesting of bands (Figure 9-30).

Return to the Bands menu. The next option after Add a group band is Remove group. Although the function this performs is obvious, the way it works may not be quite so obvious. When you remove a group band, the system removes the Intro and Summary bands for the selected group. In addition, it renumbers groups that were nested inside the band.

To see how the system renumbers the bands, move the highlight onto the Group 2 Intro band or in the open space below it and bring up the Bands menu. Select Add a group band and set a Record count band with the new count at 20. The system will add a Group 3 band. At the bottom of the screen, the system will confirm that Group 3 is grouped by 20, as seen in Figure 9-31. Now, move the cursor to highlight the "Group 2 Intro band" and bring up the Bands menu. Before doing so, you should again notice that the band is grouped by 15. Select Remove group.

The system will ask you to confirm that you want to delete the Intro and Summary bands, as seen in Figure 9-32.

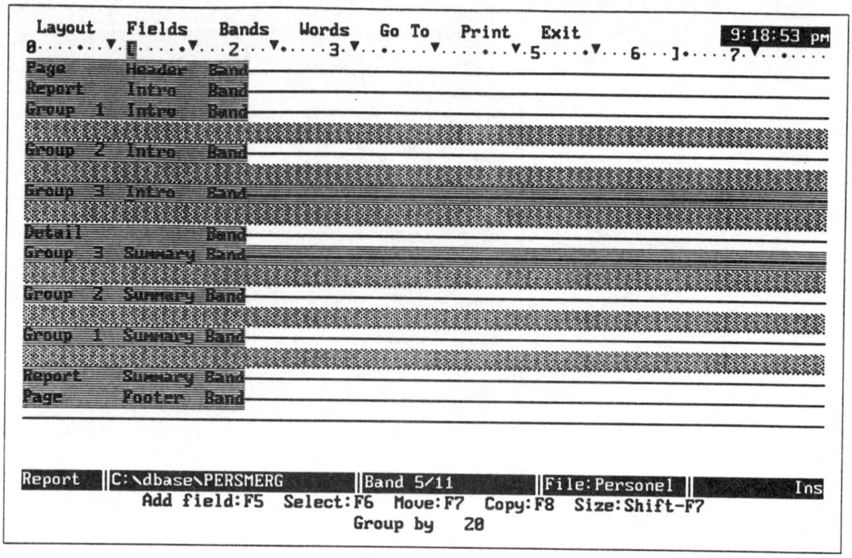

Figure 9-31

Group 3 band added, note group by 20 at bottom of screen.

Press: *Y*

You could also have removed the band by positioning the cursor on the Intro or Summary band for the selected group and pressing **Del**. The system would again have asked if you wanted to delete

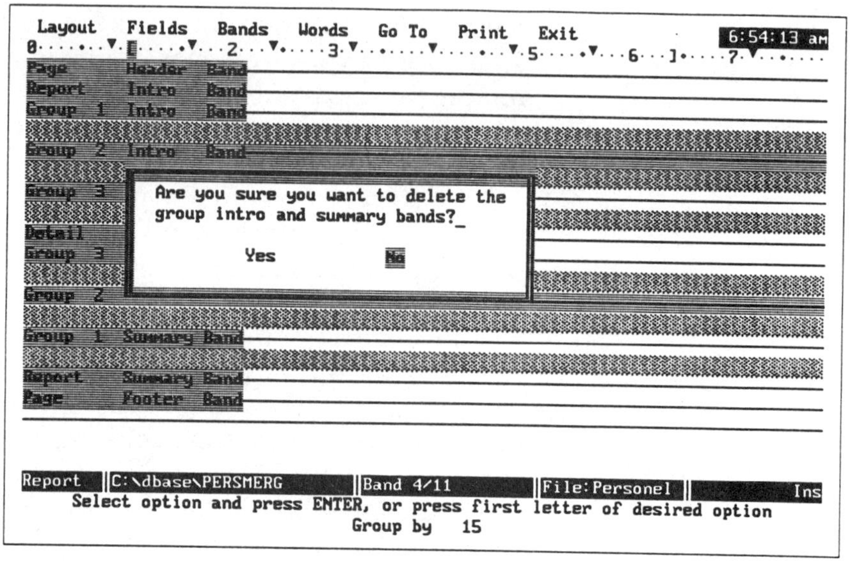

Figure 9-32

Confirmation prompt for removing a group band.

the Intro and Summary bands. Confirming by pressing *Y* would then have removed the band.

With the original Group 2 band removed, the display will now show two group bands. The highlight will be on "Group 2 Intro band." At the bottom of the screen, the system shows that the band is now grouped by 20, as seen in Figure 9-33. Thus, when you remove a band, all lower numbered (parent) bands (such as Band 1 in this example) remain unchanged. Higher numbered (child) bands (such as Band 3 in this example) are renumbered to reflect their new order, as Band 3 was in this example.

The next option from the Bands menu, Modify Group, is used to modify the type of grouping. In selecting this option, the modifications affect the group on which the cursor is currently located. This option can be selected with the cursor positioned in the editing area of the band or on the band highlight. When this option is selected, the same menu used to define the type of grouping when you first add a band is brought onto the screen. You may then change the Field value, Expression value, or Record count for the selected group.

The next option from the Bands menu is Group Intro on each page. When this is set to *Yes*, the system will print the Group Intro on every new page of the report. This is particularly useful

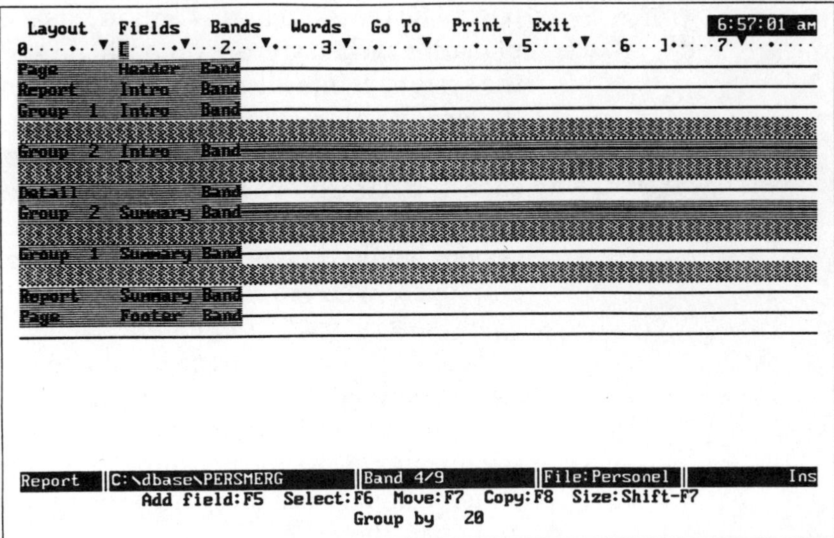

Figure 9-33

The new Group 2 (formerly Group 3).

if you have bands that contain multiple columns of data and have many records to print. The intro can be used as the header line for each page of columnar printouts. This would indicate to what the data in each column refer.

In effect, the Group Intro will function much like a page header. By allowing the intro to print on each page, you would, in effect, be printing a header for each page on which group data are printed.

The default for this option is *No*. For noncolumnar data or other types of data, you may not want the intro to print on each page. Experimenting with the printout of your particular data files should help you determine whether or not this capability is required.

In some cases, one group will begin printing on one page and end on the next. It is useful to be able to transfer the heading to the next page(s). This option allows you to tell the system to carry the heading from one page to the next.

The rest of the options in this menu apply to all bands in your report, not just the Group bands. They will allow you to control how and, to some extent, when the data are printed.

Open all bands is a fast way to tell the system to print the contents of all the bands in a report form. For report forms with numerous bands, the ability to open all bands can save some time.

Begin band on new page obviously begins a new band on a new page. The reason that this option exists deserves some further explanation. When you are preparing reports based on group bands, the system prints all data that relate to a particular group. When the group value changes, a new group printout is started.

For example, if you were printing a report on salary grades for each department, you would create a salary grade field. Using a data file that was already sorted or indexed on salary grades, the system would then print a band that included information on all employees who are classified in a particular salary grade. When a new salary grade is encountered, the previous band would be closed, the Summary band would be printed, and the Intro band for the new salary grade would print. Next, the data for the new salary grade would begin printing. In terms of nested group bands, the group closest to the center of the design (that is, the group with the highest number) would be printed first, followed by bands higher in the order.

For example, if you wanted the report on salary grades to be prepared by department, a second group band, based on department number, could be nested inside the Salary Grade band. Assuming that you had two salary grades in the database (salary grades A and B) and two department numbers (Department 1 and 2), the bands would be printed in the following order:

Salary Grade A Department 1, Salary Grade A Department 2, Salary Grade B Department 1, Salary Grade B Department 2

The system will print the groups in the lowest nested level (highest group band number) first. A new group will be printed as the group value changes. Once all records in the highest numbered group print, the next lower numbered group data will be allowed to change its value, with the highest numbered group again printing all appropriate values.

Let us return to the option Begin band on new page. This option asks you to tell the system how to handle the printing of a group band when the previous band is completed. When used in conjunction with a band that is grouped by number, the system will then start the display of the data on a new page.

The relationship between grouping a grouped band by number and beginning a band on a new page is important. For example, if you are grouping by 10 records and your page will actually hold 20 records, with the Begin band on new page set to *No* a group of 10 records will be printed and summarized. A new band *on the same page as the previous band* will then be started and begin printing. You would thus have two groups of 10 printed on each page (perhaps slightly less if you have a group intro on the beginning of each printed group). Thus, selecting a grouping by number of records and leaving Begin band on new page set to *No* will often produce printed output that you do not really want. When you have any grouping by numbers, make sure that Begin band on new page is set to *Yes*. It should be clear that this option also applies to standard, nongrouped bands.

In a Word Wrap band the text is treated as text that is to be printed, rather than data that must occupy a fixed format. One main difference between Word Wrap bands and standard bands is that in the Word Wrap mode the system will automatically position text that goes beyond the end of a line onto a new line, whereas in the design mode, your text will go to the end of the line or screen and bump into the edge, requiring a return to be placed at the end of each line. In addition, Word Wrap bands do not support the placement of lines and boxes. (From within a band, using the Band menu, you can switch between Word Wrap and design modes by turning the Word Wrap band on or off.) Word Wrap bands are used primarily for letters and other types of correspondence, for example, a form letter that uses standard text and that merges in field values or a report in which you are merging the contents of one or more memo fields. If the report was done in standard layout mode, the text, after merging data, may not look right on the printed page and, indeed, may print beyond the page's right margin.

The final three options, Text pitch for band, Quality print for band, and Spacing of lines for band, are all printer control functions. These functions are self-explanatory and have been discussed in Chapter 8, in reference to print options.

The final option, Page heading in report intro, asks if you want it to print header and footer information when it prints the report intro. If you do not want the header and footer to print on the same page as the intro, set this option to *No*. To change the setting for this option, move the cursor to highlight "Page heading in report intro" and

Press: **ENTER**

The Bands menu will close. You should notice that the positions of the Page Header band and the Report Intro band as well as the Report Summary band and Report Footer band are reversed. This is useful if you want the report intro to be on a separate page of your report. This page (or pages) will be printed without a Header or Footer. Of course, you could close the Header and Footer bands, disabling them. But if you wanted headers and footers on all pages other than your intro or summary, setting this option to *No* would be preferable.

The Words menu (Figure 9-34) has been discussed in other chapters. However, there are some points that should be mentioned here.

Insert page break places the code to end a page and begin a new page. If, for example, you are using the report processor to prepare a letter, you may wish to tell the system to force a page break at a particular point. Your letter may be designed to be sent to many different groups and may have text merged from fields of widely different sizes. Such a letter could conceivably range

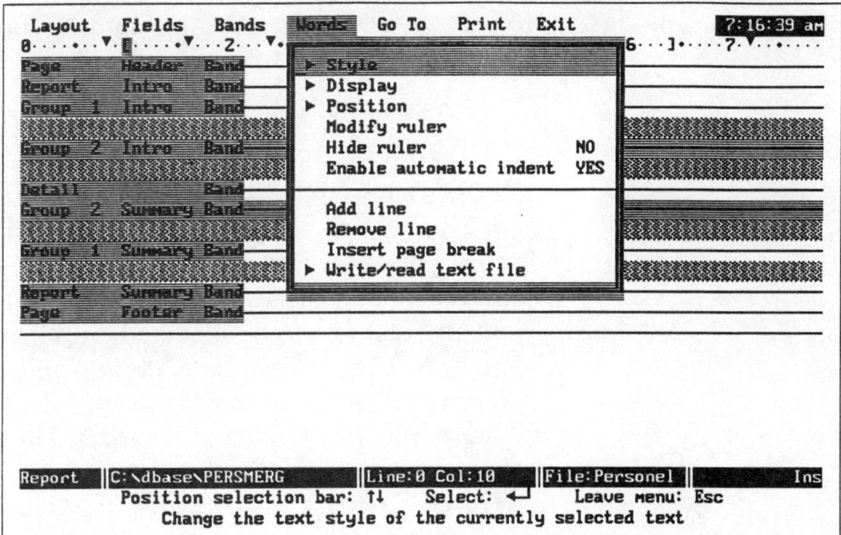

Figure 9-34

The Words menu for report design.

from 35 to 50 lines long (in this example, at least). Although there may be no problem with allowing the system to automatically break the page at 50 lines, the system may not automatically make the break at 35. Your page two is designed to start at the top of page two, and not be folded into the text on page one. Forcing a page break at the end of your page one, regardless of the length of the page, would ensure that page two begins printing in the right spot every time.

Write/Read text file is designed as a time saver. If you were designing a boilerplate letter (that is, a letter that uses text that has already been typed, merging the data into your letter at the appropriate locations), you would be able to tell the system which file to read and where to place it in your letter. Similarly, if you are preparing such a letter, you may highlight a block of text and save it to a text file so that it can be copied into, and printed in, other reports.

To write a text file, make sure that you have set the Word Wrap option in the Bands menu to *Yes*. Next, move your cursor to the beginning (or end) of the block of text that you want to copy into a text file, and

Press: **F6**

to tell the system that you want to select a block of text. Using the cursor keys, move the highlight to include the entire block of text that you want to copy, and

Press: **ENTER**

Next, bring up the Words menu, select Write/read text file, and tell the system that you want to Write a text file. Next, name the file. The system will automatically assign a file extension and record your selected text to the file.

To read a text file, move the cursor to the position at which you want the text file to be inserted, and bring up the Words menu. Next, select Write/read text file, and select Read. The system will prompt you for the name of the text file. Type the name of the file or press **Shft-F1** for a list of text files. The text will then be merged into your report form.

The Go To menu has been discussed in earlier chapters and will not be further discussed here.

The Print menu, shown in Figure 9-35, has similarly been explored, with some minor exceptions. The Page dimensions option allows you to tell the system about the size of your page (length, usually in lines per inch, at 6 lines per inch; with 14-inch legal sized paper, you will change this setting from 66 to 84). This setting helps the system know when to send a form feed at the end of a page, or how many line feeds to send to bring it to the begin-

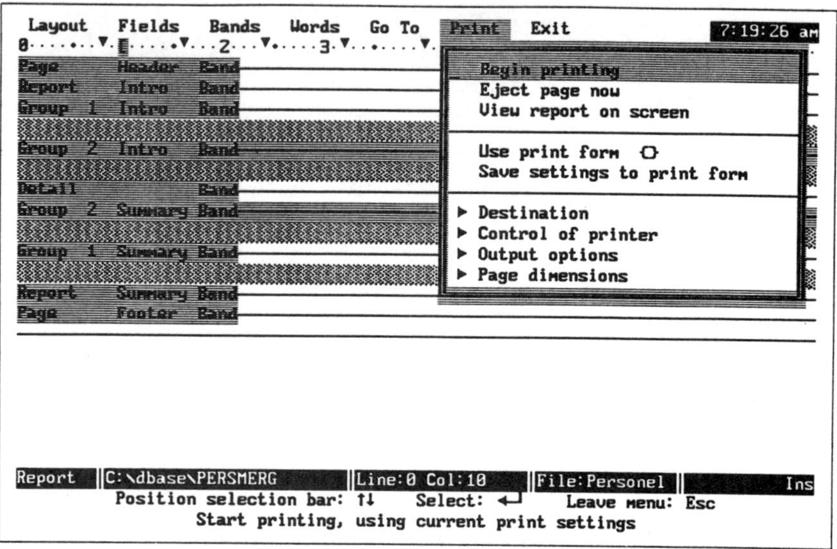

Figure 9-35

The Print menu for reports.

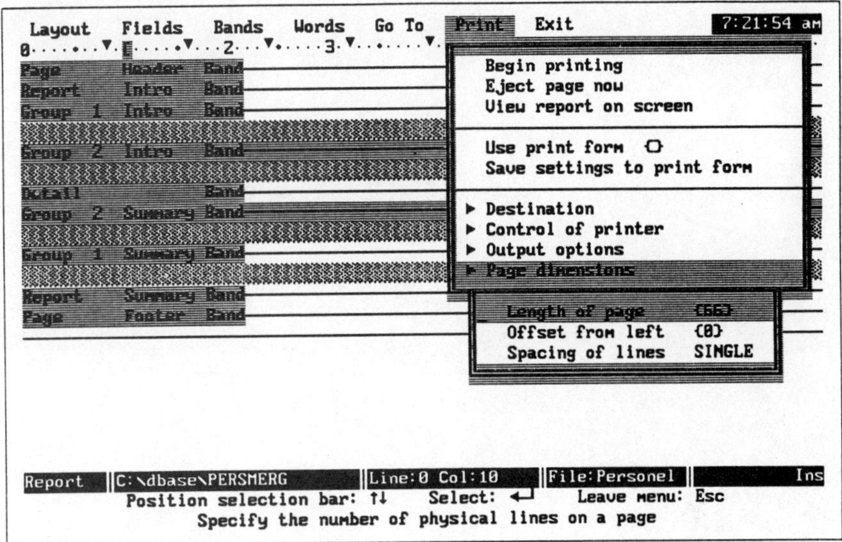

Figure 9-36

The Page dimensions option window.

ning of a new page, if your printer requires form feeds or carriage returns for page endings. The Page dimensions option window is shown in Figure 9-36.

The Offset from left option asks for an overall left indent. You should experiment with your printer to see if it already has a page offset before changing this setting. Finally, Spacing of lines allows you to select single, double, or triple spacing for the lines in your report. To switch from one setting to another,

Press: **Space Bar**

The final option, Exit, is pretty much the same as all other Exit menus. You may either save your changes and exit or abandon your changes and exit. If you abandon your changes, anything you have done since you last saved your report form will be lost. Pressing the **Esc** key and confirming that you really do want to leave the form without saving your changes does basically the same thing as selecting Abandon changes and exit. You should also recall that you can save the form, or different versions of the form, using the Save this report option in the Layout menu.

The Report menu option allows you to design custom reports. With the tools discussed in this and earlier chapters, reports based on your data, as well as letters and other correspondence, can be easily produced.

Queries (Getting the Data You Need Out of Your Database)

This book has provided you with instruction in designing your database, designing the various forms, reports, and labels that can be produced with dBASE IV, and organizing your data. Chapter 7 demonstrated how an index allows you to display the data from your database in a particular order. You also saw how setting up a sort created a new data file with the records put into the sort order.

Although these capabilities serve as basic tools for organizing your data, they probably do not provide all the capabilities that you sought when you decided to use dBASE IV. In fact, if all you need is to sort and index your data, dBASE IV is probably the wrong choice; for basic file management tasks, a less expensive flat file manager would probably do just as well, and save you substantial amounts of money.

The real power of dBASE IV resides in its ability to analyze multiple data files, relating the data in one file to those in one or more other files. For example, in our personnel system, you may want to see which employees have not received a probation review. This information is in the COUNSEL.DBF database. In addition to just finding the employees who were not reviewed, you want to create a database file of those employees, including their name, address, and office phone number. The name and address data are in the PERSONEL database. Thus, you will have to retrieve data from the two databases and produce yet a third.

dBASE IV's Query utility allows you to do this, and considerably more. If, for example, you wanted to find a particular record in a very large database, you could define a query that matches the individual record you seek, and the system will find the unique record for you.

Database updating can also be accomplished using the query function. For example, if you have a large personnel database, and you do not want data entry operators to have access to it, you can create a data entry database file into which new employee data are entered, and then use the query function to append the new records to your PERSONEL database. Not only will this save a lot of system overhead by reducing the size of the file(s) being edited, it also allows numerous data entry operators to be performing data entry concurrently, and prevents any changes from being made to the PERSONEL database.

The ability to append records may be particularly useful for order entry applications. Each order entry clerk will work on a separate entry file. At the end of the day, or at various times during the day, the orders received can be appended by the system to the master order database or to a master daily database.

In this chapter, you will see how to use many features of the dBASE IV query facility. First, however, you will have to add records to the COUNSEL file so that you can work through the design of a few queries. Make the changes and additions to the COUNSEL file as indicated below. You will probably also have to delete the first record for Jack Jackson. The easiest way to do this is to load the Edit menu (by pressing **F2**) and, going into the Records menu, select Blank Record to blank out the record. Jack Jackson was deleted from the Personel system in earlier chapters.

dBASE IV's Query by example facility allows you to handle different files containing varying numbers of records. However, for the purposes of the current example, we will work with two databases that contain records for the same number of employees.

Edit the COUNSEL database so that the records match those in the following list:

FIRST NAME: John
Last Name: Johnson
Hire Date: 06/12/82
Mother MN: Shapiro
SS Number: 321-42-8291
US Citizen: T
EMP NUMBER: 9811
DEPT NUMB: 128
Salary grade: 119

Union Mbr:	y
Office Phone:	3211
HISTORY	MEMO
Probation RVW:	F
Annual Rvw:	F
RVW 1989	F
RVW 1990	F

FIRST NAME:	Samuel
Last Name:	Samuelson
Hire Date:	12-12-25
Mother MN:	Jackson
SS Number:	111-11-1111
US Citizen:	T
EMP NUMBER:	151
DEPT NUMB:	12
Salary grade:	180
Union Mbr:	n
Office Phone:	5210
HISTORY	MEMO
Probation RVW:	F
Annual Rvw:	T
RVW 1989	F
RVW 1990	F

FIRST NAME:	David
Last Name:	Davidson
Hire Date:	03/12/84
Mother MN:	Dickinson
SS Number:	321-89-0281
US Citizen:	Y
EMP NUMBER:	8910
DEPT NUMB:	12
Salary grade:	122
Union Mbr:	T
Office Phone:	5799
HISTORY	MEMO
Probation RVW:	N
Annual Rvw:	Y
RVW 1989	N
RVW 1990	N

FIRST NAME:	Alan
Last Name:	Alanovich
Hire Date:	03/30/83
Mother MN:	Roberts
SS Number:	190-21-2898
US Citizen:	T
EMP NUMBER:	9910
DEPT NUMB:	8192
Salary grade:	1234
Union Mbr:	Y
Office Phone:	1988
HISTORY	MEMO
Probation RVW:	Y
Annual Rvw:	Y
RVW 1989	Y
RVW 1990	N

FIRST NAME:	Robert
Last Name:	Robertson
Hire Date:	01/14/80
Mother MN:	Dickinson
SS Number:	123-45-6789
US Citizen:	Y
EMP NUMBER:	1208
DEPT NUMB:	99
Salary grade:	1250
Union Mbr:	N
Office Phone:	4712
HISTORY	MEMO
Probation RVW:	Y
Annual Rvw:	Y
RVW 1989	N
RVW 1990	N

Once the COUNSEL database has been updated, bring up the Exit menu. The menu will ask you whether you want to Exit or Transfer to Query design. In most cases, when you want to design a query, you would select this option by pressing *T*. For now, however, you will access the Query design screen from the Queries menu. Move the cursor into the Queries menu column. The highlight should be on "<create>".

Press: **ENTER**

to bring up the Query design screen (Figure 10-1). The screen that comes up is ready to build a query for the COUNSEL database, because that is the database in use. You may also design a query with no database files in use, although you must specify files to use, from within Query design, to run or design a query.

This screen displays many of the capabilities of the Query by example system that you are about to use. The top line of this screen, as with all dBASE IV screens, contains a menu line. Below the menu line is an area called the File Skeleton. This shows the name of the database in the left-most box and the field names along the rest of the skeleton. At the bottom border of the skeleton box an arrow points to the right. This indicates that there are more fields in the file on the side of the screen at which the arrow is pointing.

When you scroll through the skeleton, you will see that the field names scroll, while the database name remains in the left-most box. To further differentiate between the database name and the fields, the fields are printed in uppercase characters and lack a file extension, whereas the database name is in upper- and lowercase letters and includes a file extension, in this example, .dbf.

The next line is used to enter the query argument or arguments. The area between this line and the view skeleton, located lower

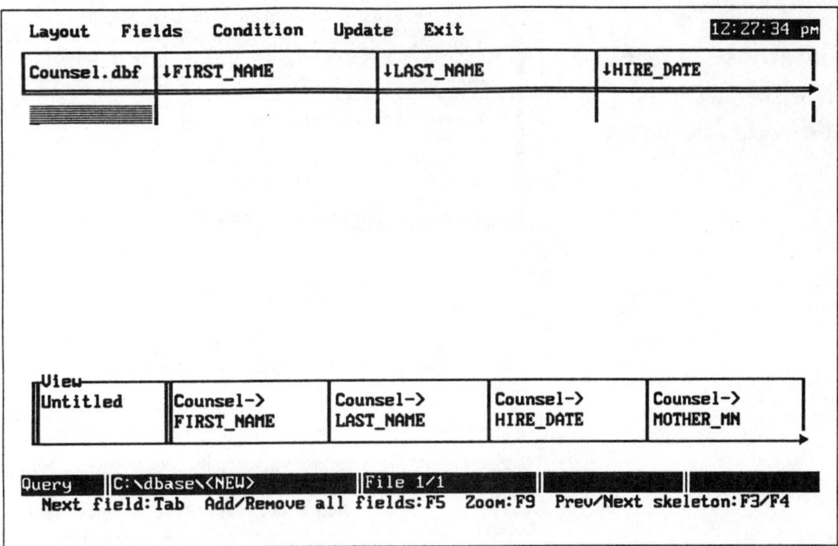

Figure 10-1

The Query design screen.

on the screen, is used to design your query. However, you are not limited to only this space. If you enter more arguments than there is space on the query design form, the argument screen will scroll down to allow you to add query arguments. To see how query statements fill the screen, press and hold the **PgDn** key. Additional lines will be added to the form, and the form will stop scrolling when the cursor hits the View line.

However, if you add a database file to the query, you will be able to scroll farther down the screen. To add a database file, select the Layout menu and the Add file to query option. The system will bring up a list of the database files in the current catalog (Figure 10-2). Select Personel by moving the cursor to that item or typing *P*.

Press: **ENTER**

If your screen was filled with query lines for COUNSEL.DBF, PERSONEL will be in its own window. Pressing **F3** moves you back from file to file; if you were in PERSONEL, pressing **F3** will move you to COUNSEL.DBF, pressing **F3** again brings you to the View skeleton, and finally pressing **F3** brings you back to the Personel skeleton.

The **F4** key moves you forward through the query, in the reverse order of the **F3** key. Use the **F3** key to bring the cursor back to the Counsel file skeleton. If lines have been added to the Counsel

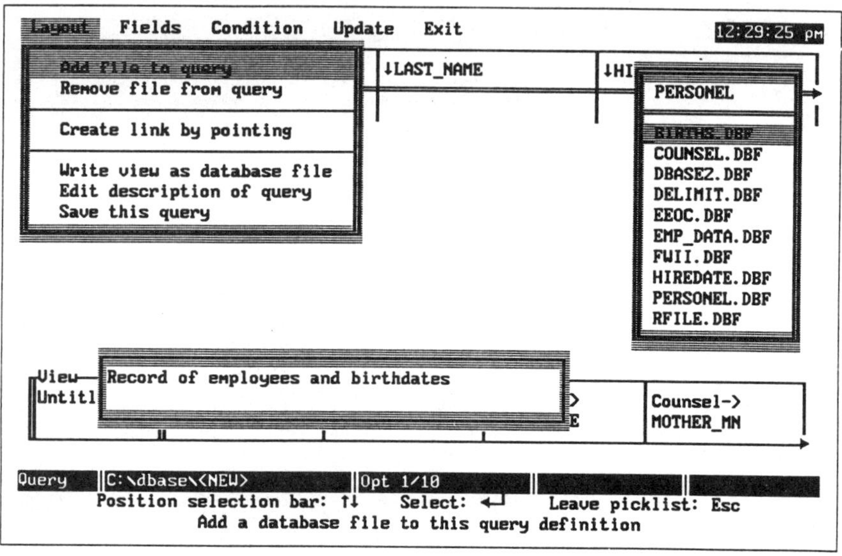

Figure 10-2

The file selection window for adding a file to a query.

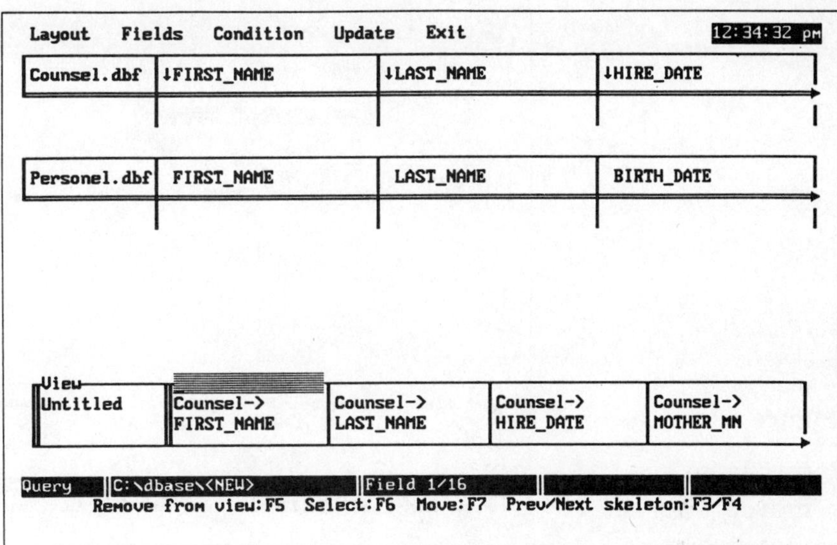

Figure 10-3

Query window with two data files attached.

skeleton, remove them using the **PgUp** key. As you do, the Personel skeleton will scroll back onto the page. The screen with both database skeletons will appear as shown in Figure 10-3.

You will see how to write queries shortly. At the bottom of the screen, the last skeleton is the View skeleton. This is the design for the database view that will be generated by the query facility. If you start the query function with a file in use, the system will put all the fields into the View skeleton.

To move from one field to the next, use the **Tab** or **Shft-Tab** key combinations. The **Tab** key moves the highlight from left to right and the **Shft-Tab** combination from right to left across the skeleton.

A field can be added to, or removed from, the file skeleton using the **F5** key. If you look at the View skeleton, you will notice that FIRST_NAME is the first field. Using the **Tab** key, move the highlight in the Counsel skeleton to "FIRST_NAME" and press **F5**. The system will appear to reach down and grab the FIRST_NAME field from the View skeleton and pull it back to the Counsel skeleton. You will notice that the field was removed from the View skeleton, with LAST_NAME now the first field in the view. The View skeleton with the FIRST_NAME field removed is shown in Figure 10-4.

To place the field back into the View skeleton,

Press: **F5**

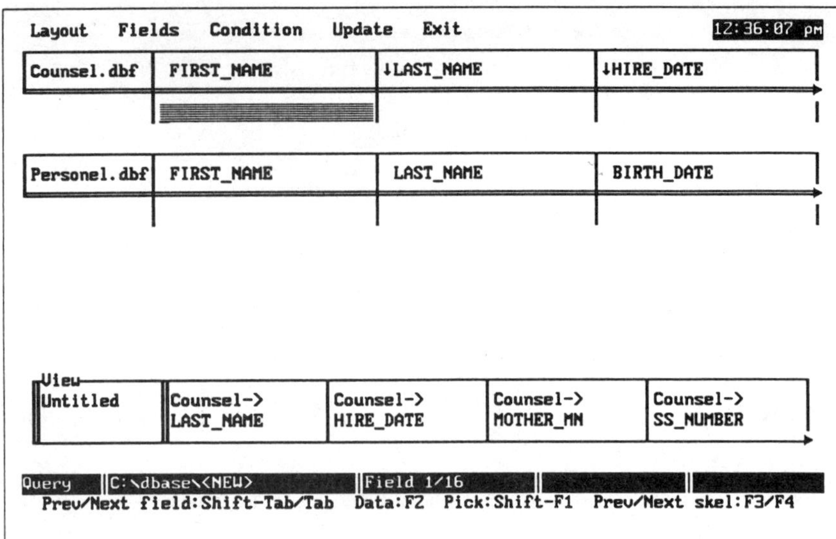

Figure 10-4

First Name removed from file skeleton.

The system will appear to grab the FIRST_NAME field and move it down to the View skeleton. However, it does not put it back in its previous position.

When a field is added to the view skeleton, it is appended to, that is, placed at the end of, the skeleton. To move the field back to the front (or, for that matter, to move any field or block of fields on the skeleton), move the highlight to the field you wish to move. If you want to move more than one field, move it to one of the fields on either end of the block of fields to be moved so that you can extend the selection highlight from one end to the other.

In this case, using the **Tab** (or **End**) key, move the highlight to the "FIRST_NAME" field (Figure 10-5). To move a field in the View skeleton, highlight the field and

Press: **F6**

A box will form around the highlighted field, and the system will prompt you to **Tab** or **Backtab** (**Shift-Tab**) to mark the fields involved in the move. The **LtArrow** and **RtArrow** keys also work to mark the fields to be moved. You may want to use these keys to see how the system marks fields that you want moved. The screen, with the selected fields marked, is shown in Figure 10-6.

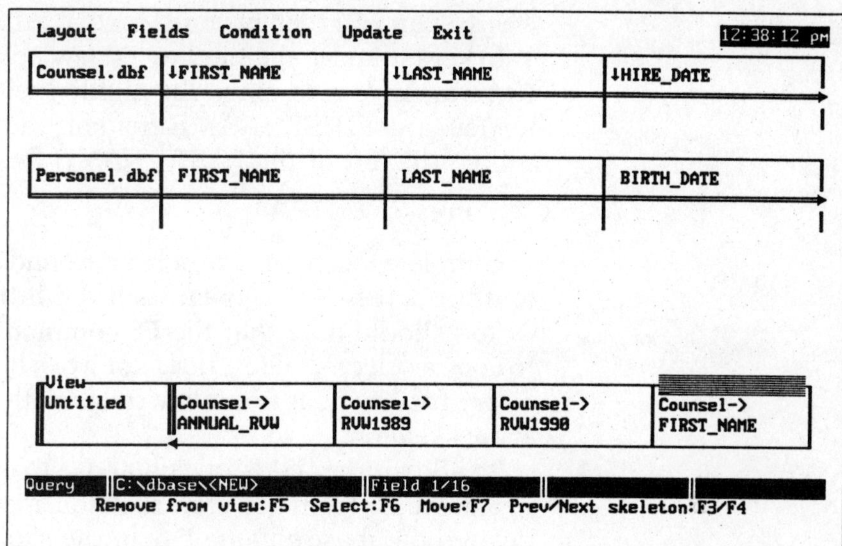

Figure 10-5

First Name field appended to file skeleton.

When the field(s) you want to move are selected,

Press: **ENTER**

to set the field for movement. To move the field(s),

Press: **F7**

Figure 10-6

First Name field highlighted for moving.

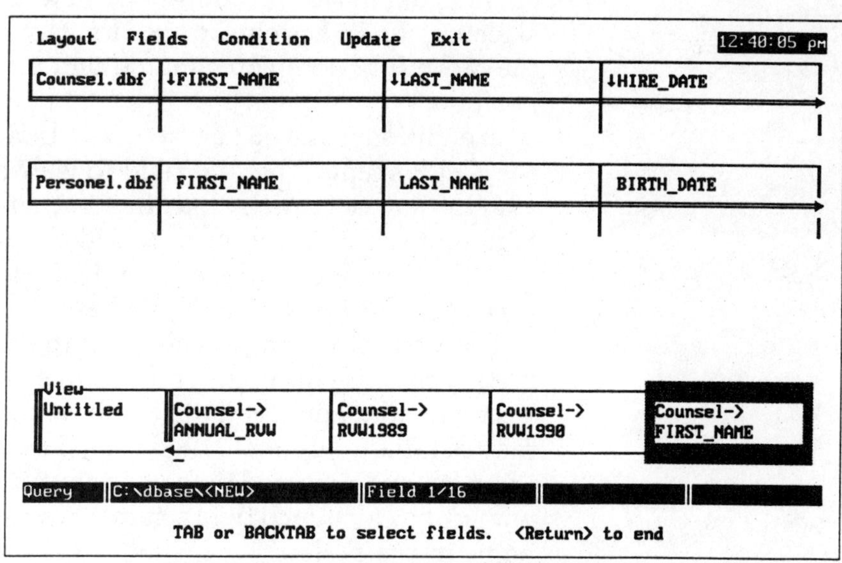

The system will then prompt you to use the **Tab** or **BackTab** (**Shft-Tab**) keys to move the field to its new position. The **LtArrow** and **RtArrow** keys also move the highlighted field or fields.

Move the FIRST_NAME field all the way to the left, so that it is to the left of the LAST_NAME field, and

Press: **ENTER**

to complete the move. The border around the box will be removed, and the screen will appear as it did in Figure 10-3.

You should note that the **F8** command, used in other menus to copy a selected block, does not work here, because dBASE IV's query facility does not allow fields with duplicate names in the View skeleton.

To add all the fields in a database to or to remove all the files in a database from the View skeleton, move the highlight into the desired database's name bar in the skeleton and

Press: **F5**

The question of duplicate field names is one you may encounter. If you attempted to add all the fields in PERSONEL to the skeleton, the system will prompt you to rename each duplicated field. The system does not have the ability to look through your database field structure and add only those fields that are unique to the current database. To add only a few unique fields to a View skeleton, the **F5** key can be used for each highlighted field. Using the Move function, you can add and move them to the desired position.

In addition to the **F5** key, fields can be added and removed from the Fields menu. The Add field to view and Remove field from view options act exactly like the **F5** add/remove toggle. You must highlight the field you want added or removed before selecting the add or remove options from the Fields menu. In most cases, it is much easier to use the **F5** keys.

The View skeleton provides you the field name in the center of each box with the name of the source database file (the file from which the data are read) listed above it. In some instances, you may rename a duplicate field or add a calculated field (more on these later). A renamed field or a calculated field will have its new name (or a calculated field's name) inserted above the actual file's name in the skeleton.

When you use the View skeleton and define your query, you

may then use Browse/Edit by pressing **F2**. When you do this, the system will create the query instructions, search through the database or databases that are involved in the query, and bring you into the Browse/Edit screen. The records that match the query instructions will be displayed on this screen and the field order will match that in the View skeleton.

To see a simple example of how the View skeleton works, create a View skeleton that shows only the employee First Name, Last Name, and Hire Date. To do this,

Press: **F4**

until the highlight is in the "Counsel.dbf" skeleton.

Press: **Tab**

until the MOTHER_MN field bar is highlighted. Next,

Press: **F5**

The system will remove the field from the View skeleton.

Press: **Tab**

to move the cursor to the SS_NUMBER field, and

Press: **F5**

to remove the next field, and repeat this for all remaining fields.

You could have gone into the View skeleton to remove the fields. However, when you delete a field on the View skeleton, the highlight returns to the first field in the skeleton. To move to the next field to be removed, you must press the **Tab** key many times. From within the database skeleton, you can simply **Tab** from one field to another.

In this example, when you are deleting most of the fields from a view skeleton, it may have been even easier to remove all the fields from the skeleton by moving the highlight into the file name bar and pressing **F5**, and then selecting and moving the few fields that you want added to the skeleton. The View skeleton with only three fields selected appears as shown in Figure 10-7.

Because you want to view the contents of only one file, remove the PERSONEL.DBF file (for now) from the query. To do this,

Press: **F4**

to highlight the "PERSONEL.DBF" file.

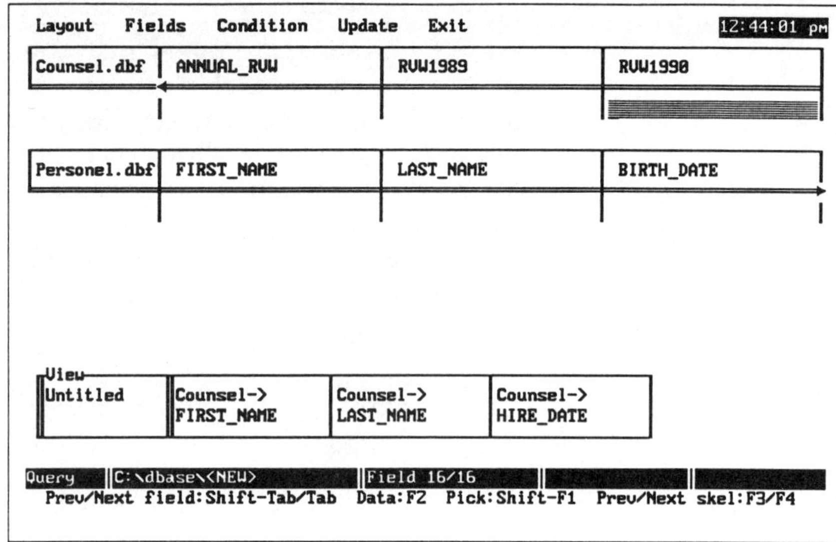

Figure 10-7

View skeleton with three fields selected.

Press: **Alt-L**

to bring up the Layout menu, and

Press: *R*

to remove the file from the query.

To view the results of this simplest of queries,

Figure 10-8

Browse screen with results of query.

Records Fields Go To Exit 12:45:00 pm

FIRST_NAME	LAST_NAME	HIRE_DATE
Samuel	Samuelson	01/24/11
John	Johnson	06/12/82
David	Davidson	03/12/84
Alan	Alanovich	06/06/55
Robert	Robertson	01/14/80

Browse C:\dbase\COUNSEL Rec 1/5 File Del

View and edit fields

Press: **F2**

The system will perform your query, and bring up a Browse or Edit screen. If the Edit screen is brought up, press **F2** to bring up the Browse screen (Figure 10-8).

To return to the Query design screen,

Press: **Alt-E**

to bring up the Exit menu.

Press: *t*

to select Transfer to Query design.

Creating a Query

The query capabilities in dBASE IV's query processor are quite extensive. First, you may search your file for specific matches or values. For example, to find *one particular record* in a file with hundreds or thousands of records, you could define a query that includes as much unique information as possible about the record.

Let us assume, for example, that you want to find an employee named *Robert Robertson.* You do not have a department number or department phone, only Robertson's name. To set up a query on a text field, type the contents of the field in the appropriate spot in the database skeleton. The name or value in a text field that you are attempting to match must be enclosed in quotation marks. The query to find Robert Robertson will appear as shown in Figure 10-9. When you select that query and press **F2**, the system will go through the database and present all records that match the query specifications. The results of this query are seen in Figure 10-10.

You can also make an equality statement inside a field to select records that match your selection criterion. For example, assume that you want a list of all employees who work in departments with numbers higher than 50. To make this query, first delete the contents of the first name and last name query fields (by moving the cursor into the fields and pressing **Del** to delete the contents of the field) and move the highlight to the "Dept_Numb" field.

```
Layout   Fields   Condition   Update   Exit                     12:49:10 pm

Counsel.dbf | ↓FIRST_NAME  | ↓LAST_NAME   | ↓HIRE_DATE
            | "Robert"     | "Robertson"  |

View
Untitled | Counsel->   | Counsel->  | Counsel->
         | FIRST_NAME  | LAST_NAME  | HIRE_DATE

Query  C:\dbase\<NEW>   Field 2/16
 Prev/Next field:Shift-Tab/Tab  Data:F2  Pick:Shift-F1  Prev/Next skel:F3/F4
```

Figure 10-9

Query to find all Robert Robertsons.

Type: *>50* **ENTER**

The system will review your syntax and return the highlight to the field.

To view the records that match the field condition,

Press: **F2**

```
Records    Fields    Go To    Exit                              12:50:25 pm

FIRST_NAME | LAST_NAME  | HIRE_DATE
Robert     | Robertson  | 01/14/80

Browse  C:\dbase\COUNSEL   Rec 5/5   File

                        View and edit fields
```

Figure 10-10

Files that match query parameters.

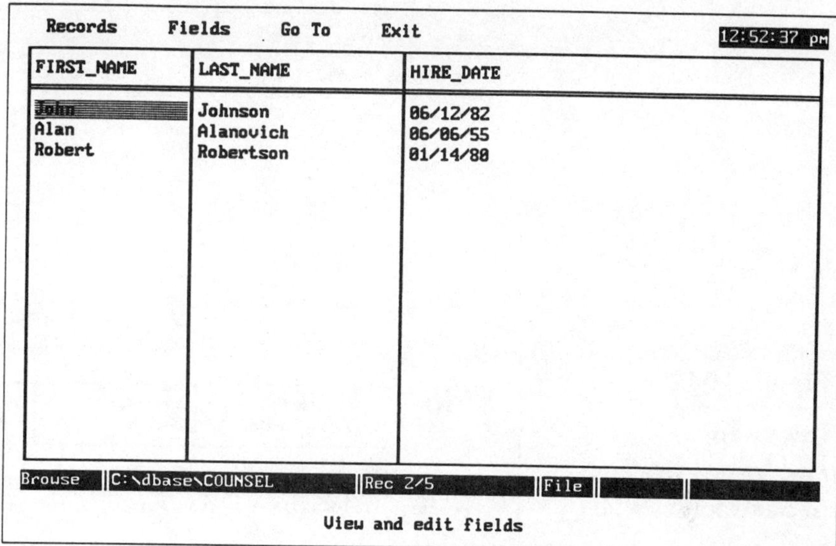

Figure 10-11

Result of query for employees in departments above 50.

The Browse screen created by the system, in response to your query condition, is shown in Figure 10-11.

Next, return to query design using the Exit menu. To see the actual department number, with the highlight in the "DEPT_NUMB" field,

Press: **F5**

The system will move this field down to the View skeleton.

Next, create another condition: you do not want to view employees in departments with numbers higher than 200. The proper way to assign multiple conditions is to put a comma between each condition statement. You may also use the standard operators available from within dBASE IV. These may be popped up using the **Shft-F1** key. The query to show all employees in departments numbered higher than 50 and lower than 200 is seen in Figure 10-12. The Browse screen produced by this query is shown in Figure 10-13.

You may also ask that more than one field condition be satisfied before a data file is selected. For example, assume you want a list of all employees with the last name Robertson who are employeed in departments 51 through 199. You already have the query for the department number written. In the LAST_NAME field

Type: *"Robertson"*

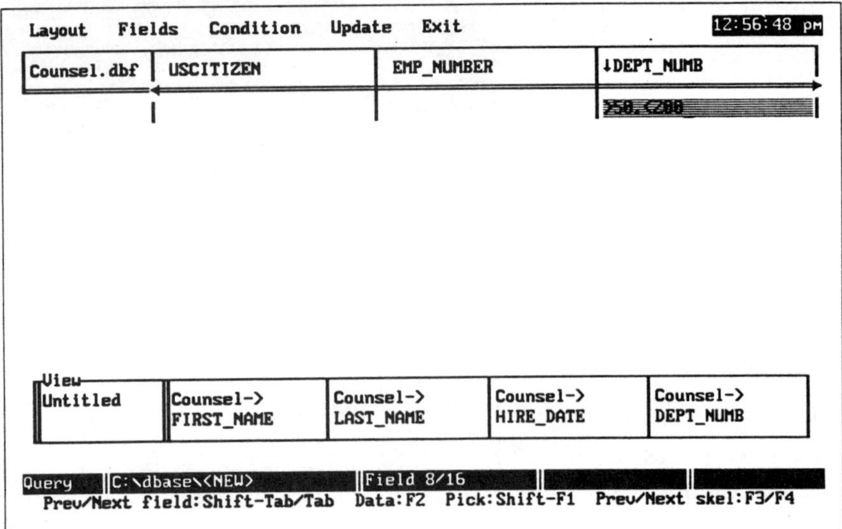

Figure 10-12

Query for employees in departments >50 and <200.

Putting more than one field query on the same skeleton line indicates that you want all files listed in which *all* conditions in the query line match the data conditions. In this example, you are asking for all employees in Departments 51 through 199 *and* who are named Robertson. The Browse screen generated by this query is

Figure 10-13

Browse screen showing results of query in Figure 10-12.

Records Fields Go To Exit 12:57:18 pm

FIRST_NAME	LAST_NAME	HIRE_DATE	DEPT_NUMB
John	Johnson	06/12/82	128
Robert	Robertson	01/14/80	99

Browse C:\dbase\COUNSEL Rec 2/5 File

View and edit fields

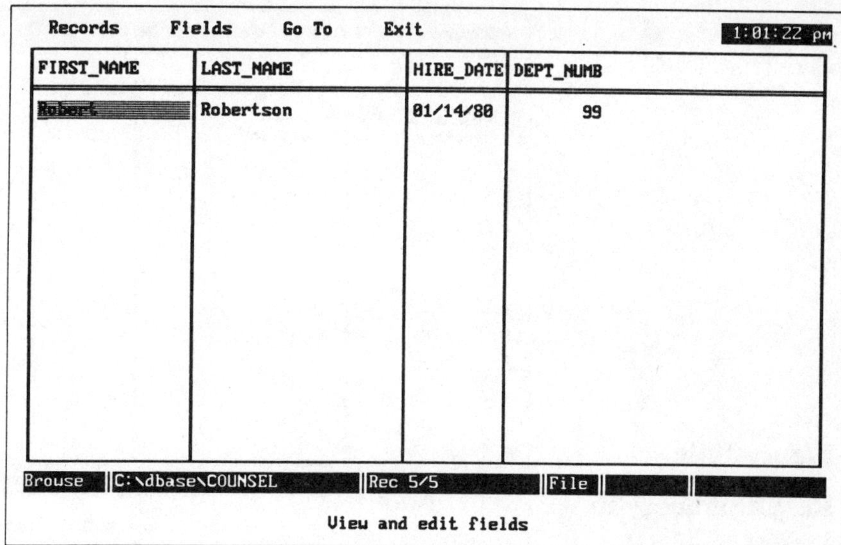

Figure 10-14

Browse screen, all Robertsons, departments >50 and <200.

shown in Figure 10-14. As you can see, only one record matched both conditions.

When you put each part of a query on a separate line, the system sees this as an *or* query. In this case, if you add a second line to the query and set the system to find anyone named Davidson, as shown in Figure 10-15, you are asking the system to find all records

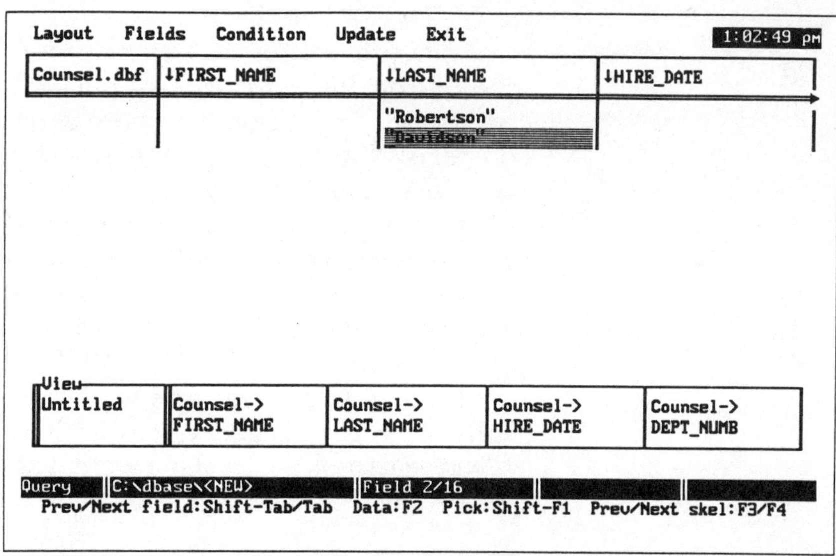

Figure 10-15

Query showing *or* processing.

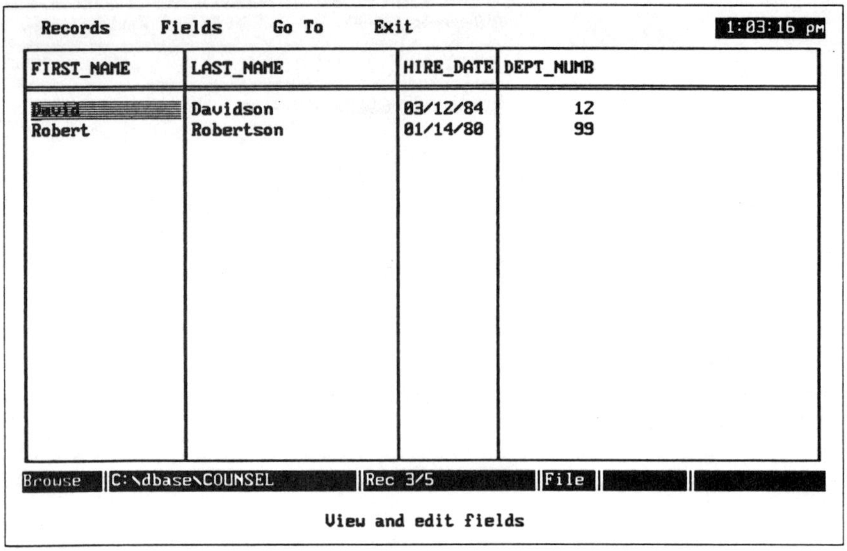

Records Fields Go To Exit 1:03:16 pm

FIRST_NAME	LAST_NAME	HIRE_DATE	DEPT_NUMB
David	Davidson	03/12/84	12
Robert	Robertson	01/14/80	99

Browse | C:\dbase\COUNSEL | Rec 3/5 | File

View and edit fields

Figure 10-16

Result of query in Figure 10-15.

in which the condition in one line *or* the condition in the next line (and so on) is met. The result of this query is seen in Figure 10-16. You should note that the department number for Davidson is 12, a number below 50. This value would not have been included in the query condition on the top line, and appears because it meets the condition of the one line *or* another in the query statement.

Another type of query compares the values of two or more fields. For example, if you have an order processing system, you may want to check for customers whose orders exceed their credit limits. To do this, you must first put a tag (which is a marker used strictly for comparison purposes) into the field representing the comparison value, and an equality statement that refers to the tag in the field being checked.

For example, in a field called C_LIMIT (for credit limit), you may use the tag *CL*. In the T_DUE (total amount due) field, you may use the expression >CL. When processing this query, the system first checks CL, the credit limit, and then compares that limit to the contents of the T_DUE field. The equality statement is evaluated, and if true (the total due is larger than the credit limit), the record is added to the View skeleton.

Aggregate fields can also be created through the use of your query statements. The aggregate fields, which can be selected from the pick list, are MAX (for maximum), MIN (for minimum), SUM (a total of all values in a field), AVG (an average for all values in the field), and CNT (a count of all records that meet query conditions). The sum and average values are for those records that are included in the query, and not necessarily for all the records in your database.

Assume that you want to find the hire date of the employee who has been with the company the longest time. To do this, first clear the existing query conditions, then move the highlight into the "HIRE_DATE" box and

Type: *min*

When you press **F2** to bring up the Browse menu, the system will go through all the records in your database to find the earliest hire data. When you use a single line command for an aggregate process, only the contents of the aggregate field will be displayed (the rest of the fields are blank), as can be seen in Figure 10-17.

If you use a *Group By* command in other fields, the system will find the aggregate value for each unique field value. For example, you may find the earliest hired employee in each department by using the command Group By in the DEPT_NUMB field. To do

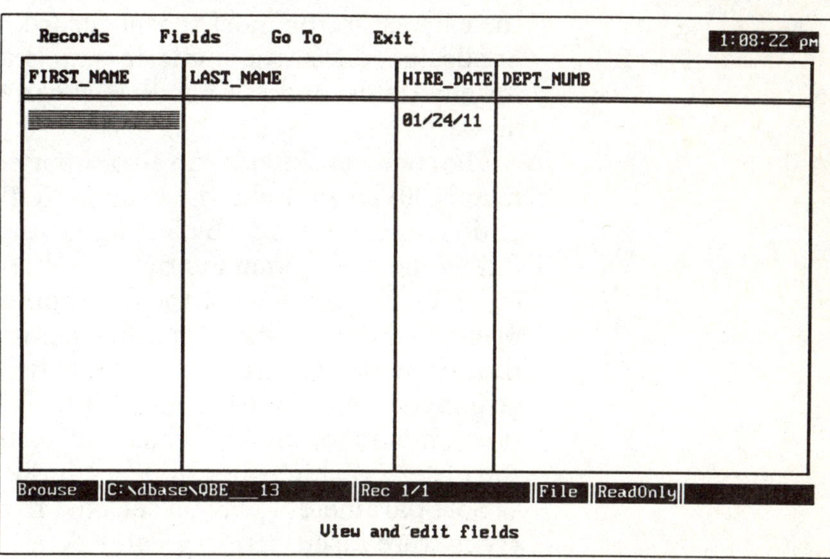

Figure 10-17

Display of value for MIN hire date.

```
Records    Fields    Go To    Exit                                  1:13:52 pm

FIRST_NAME | LAST_NAME | HIRE_DATE | DEPT_NUMB
           |           | 01/24/11  |     12
           |           | 01/14/80  |     99
           |           | 06/12/82  |    128
           |           | 06/06/55  |   8192

Browse  |C:\dbase\QBE___14   |Rec 1/4   |File |ReadOnly|

                         View and edit fields
```

Figure 10-18

Minimum hire dates for each department, in order by department.

this, leave the MIN operator in HIRE__DATE, and type *Group By* in the DEPT__NUMB fields. The Browse screen created from this query, which shows the earliest hire date for each department, is seen in Figure 10-18.

However, for a date field, the use of an ASCII sort will also yield similar results. If you sort on a date, you may elect to sort from the earliest to the most recent record. The aggregate functions are designed for true numeric data, although CNT can be used for any fields, and MAX and MIN can be applied to date fields as well.

The contents of fields can also be sorted through the Query commands. To sort a field, the command ASC is used. For example, to do a multilevel sort by last name, then first name, you would follow the ASC command by a number that indicates the order in which the contents of the file should be sorted. Thus, to sort by last name, then first name, the command ASC1 would go into the instruction for LAST__NAME, and the command ASC2 would go into the instruction box for the FIRST__NAME field. If you omit the numbers for an ASCII sort, the system sorts the numbers in the order in which they appear on the file skeleton.

Sort parameters may be selected from the Fields menu. Sort types were discussed in greater detail in Chapter 7.

Linking Files

In many cases, the data needed to produce a report or new database reside in different databases. Some database programs are unable to use data in multiple files. However, dBASE IV provides the relational capabilities required, and it is relatively easy to do the file linking with dBASE IV's query processor. Assume, for the next example, that your company is trying to implement a car pooling plan to reduce parking problems and to help conserve energy.

The report that you are attempting to produce will include the names and addresses of all employees, sorted by zip code (to establish reasonable proximity of a group of workers' homes), plus the office phone number, in case you need to call employees at their offices to coordinate the car pools. The problem is that the employee addresses are listed in the PERSONEL database, while the office phone numbers are in the COUNSEL database. You want to somehow combine both files to extract the information required to prepare your list.

The first thing to do is to add the PERSONEL file to your query list. This has been done earlier in this chapter using the Layout menu. Again, select the Layout menu (type **Alt-L**)

Press: **ENTER**

and select the PERSONEL file. A file skeleton for Personel.dbf will be placed on the screen below the Counsel.dbf file.

To use the data in two or more files, the data in the files have to be linked. This is done by asking, "How do I know which record in one database should be matched with another record in a second (or third, or fourth, etc.) database?" The answer is to find a field on which to match for a common value. In the case of the personnel files used here, the EMP_NUMBER field is probably best. In creating a link, you always look for a field that is unique for a particular record.

In a small database, you could probably link on last name or zip code; however, in a larger database you run the risk of having more than one record with the same zip code or last name. Because each employee receives only one unique number, a match on this field should avoid any problems with more than one record in one file matching more than one record in a second file. Social Security number or driver's license number (if in the database) are also good unique identifiers. However, keep in mind that input operators sometimes make errors in entering long numbers, so there may be cases in which links that should be made are not because the unique numbers in multiple files are incorrectly entered in one of the files.

To create a link between two files type any text in the first linking field. (For example, you could type LINK1, or an alphabetic character or string. You could also type any other character that is not a function or aggregate operator.) In this example, the letter *X* was used to identify the linking fields. The field linking is shown in Figure 10-19.

Once this is set up, the system will link the PERSONEL.dbf record with the COUNSEL.dbf record for each record in which the employee number is the same in both. This will not link any records for employees who have not been put into both databases or for employees whose employee number was erroneously entered into one of the databases.

Now that the two database files are linked, the View skeleton and query can be built. Because the goal of this query is to match it is first necessary to sort the records by ZIP code. From the Fields menu, you may select Sort on this field and select the type of sort

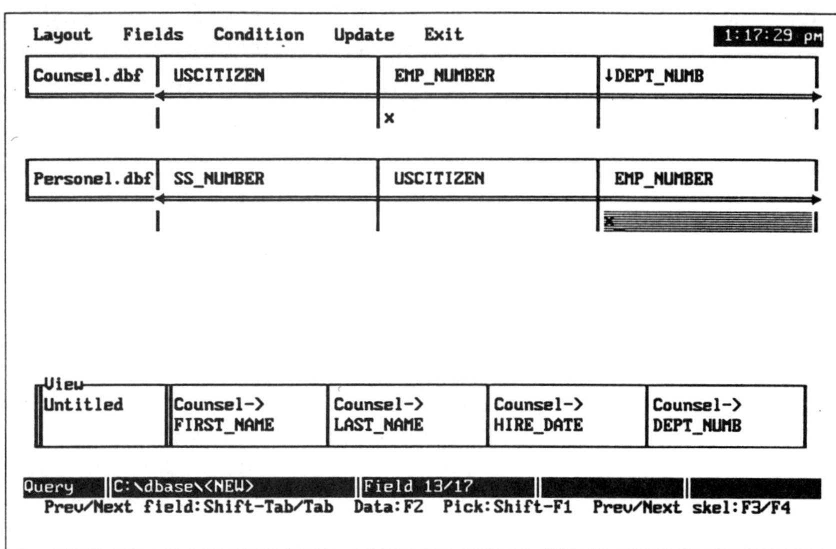

Figure 10-19

Linking records in two files based on unique number.

menu, you may select Sort on this field and select the type of sort desired. In this case, you want an ascending sort. For numeric fields, either a dictionary or standard ASCII sort can be used.

The sort just set up will be the primary sort in this query. You should check that the number 1 follows the ASC command in the ZIP_CODE field to establish the sort order. You will also want to sort the report by last name and first name (assuming that there are enough employees in your database to require further sorting of the names in each ZIP Code). Apply an ASCII Dictionary sort to LAST_NAME, and an ASCII Dictionary sort to FIRST_NAME, making LAST_NAME a priority 2 and FIRST_NAME a priority 3 sort.

Now that the sorts and the subsequent query are defined, you should set up the View skeleton so that the proper information is produced. The system should have the FIRST_NAME, LAST_NAME, HIRE_DATE, and DEPT_NUMB fields in the skeleton. Delete the HIRE_DATE and DEPT_NUMB fields from the skeleton by moving the highlight to those fields (from either the Counsel.dbf skeleton line or the View skeleton line) and

Press: **F5**

Next, move the cursor into the Personel.dbf skeleton line and move the following fields into the View skeleton, in the following order (again, using the **F5** key):

HOME_ADDR, APT_NUMBER, CITY, STATE, ZIP_CODE

Finally, add the OFF_PHONE field from the Counsel.dbf skeleton. Your query should now be ready to run. The last four fields of the view design appear as shown in Figure 10-20. To process the query,

Press: **F2**

The Browse menu (with the left two fields locked, to show the first and last name, and to allow the city, state, ZIP code, and office phone to be displayed on one screen) appears in Figure 10-21.

Linked fields do not require identical field names in both records. For example, one database file may use the field name FIRST_NAME, and the other F_NAME.

Other, more esoteric links can be created. For example, if you wanted to mail a letter (rather than sending interdepartmental mail) to each employee at his or her work location, you could

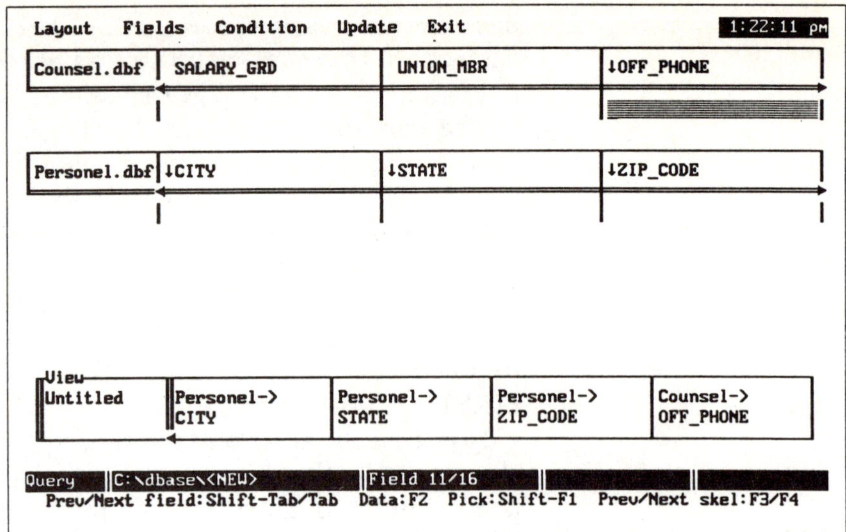

Figure 10-20

Last four fields of linked query.

match an employee's department to a list of department locations. The PERSONEL and COUNSEL databases both include the DEPT_NUMB fields. A second database may contain the address for each department. An example of this kind of link, using more than one copy of the same file, is seen in Figure 10-22. Linking

Figure 10-21

Browse data showing merged query from Figure 10-20.

Records Fields Go To Exit 1:23:17 pm

FIRST_NAME	LAST_NAME	CITY	STATE	ZIP_CODE	OFF_P
Samuel	Samuelson	Los Frijoles	NM	[illegible]	5210
John	Johnson	Santa Clara	CA	90909	3211
David	Davidson	Santa Monica	CA	90099	5799
Alan	Alanovich	Encino	CA	91311	1988
Robert	Robertson	Santa Tomato	CA	90900	4712

Browse | C:\dbase\COUNSEL | Rec 1/5 | File | ReadOnly | Del

View and edit fields

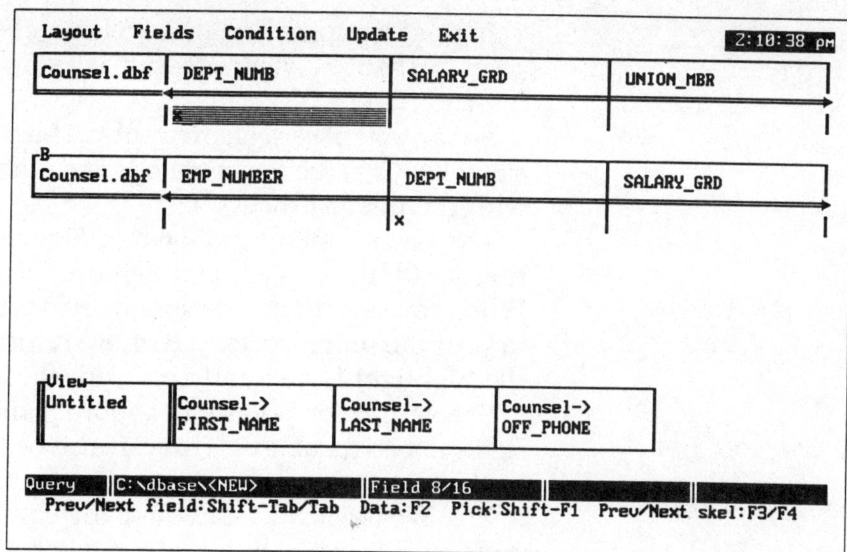

Figure 10-22

Query using two copies of same data file.

the DEPT_NUMB field for an employee with the DEPT_NUMB field in the address database will allow you to mail letters to the employees at work.

In some types of queries, for example, in a list in which you want to match employees in a work group with other employees in the group, you could link to a second copy of the database file. In this example, you could add a data file from the Layout menu. The system treats the second copy of the file as a new file. You can then link the DEPT_NUMBER fields, and produce a matched list of employees in a department.

By designing a link between two skeletons for the same file, you can match on employee number, for example, and print the names and numbers of records that are duplicated in the file. You can also have the system purge duplicate records.

In the rare case in which the link fields do not find a match (this should not happen if you use the same file, because there should be no duplicates), dBASE IV provides a mechanism for listing and identifying the mismatched records. If we return to the car pool example, using the argument *every x* (instead of *x*) in the EMP_NUMB field prints every record. However, for records that are not matched in both files, only those fields that are taken from the Counsel.dbf database for use in the View skeleton will print.

In this example, then, those mismatches in Counsel.dbf will appear in the new view file, but without displaying the address information.

So far, you have seen many of the basics of query design. Now, a quick look at the menu options and other things that can be done with the query processor.

The Layout menu is shown in Figure 10-23. The first two options, Add file to query and Remove file from query, do just that. When you select Add, the system brings up a list of database files in your current directory. Remove removes the file skeleton that the highlight is currently on from the query.

Create link by pointing is another method of linking unique fields in two databases. This can also be done as described earlier in this chapter.

The Write view as database file can be used to create a new database file using the query and database files already developed. This is extremely useful, because the only other methods of creating new files involve sorts (which are limited to single files) or complicated dot prompt programming. When you select Write view as database file, the system asks for a name for the database file, generates a code for the query, and then produces a database file, based on the output of the query (the data from the selected files from which the query is built).

Figure 10-23

Query Layout menu.

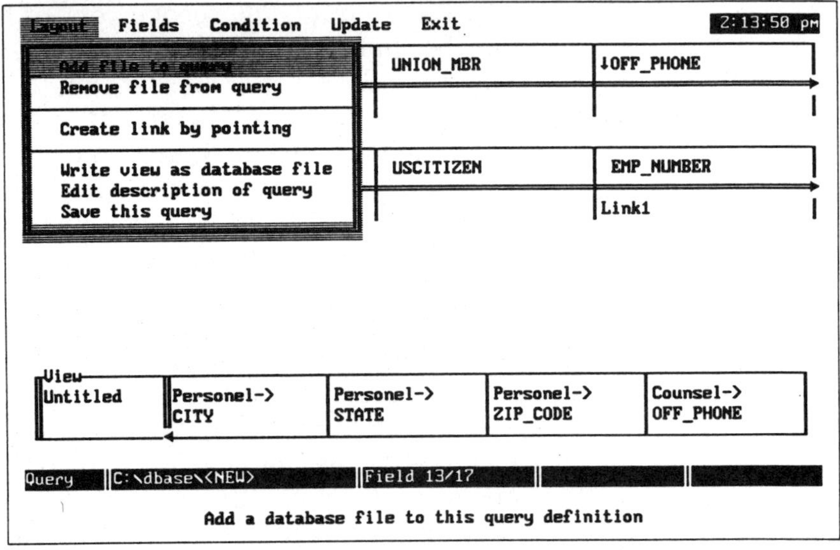

Edit description of query allows you to write a description for the query, which appears in the Control Center when you move the cursor into the query file.

Save this query saves the query file. This is different from writing the view as a database file, which creates a new file based on the query written. When you save a query, it can be called up when you want to perform the same query on your data files. For complex queries, the ability to save and reload queries can save considerable time, and can provide consistent analysis from session to session. This can be quite useful in the order entry example when you use one query design to perform regular updates from input files, or for other repetitive analyses.

The Fields menu (Figure 10-24) provides some field manipulation functions. Add field to view adds the field that the highlight is on to the View skeleton. This is the same function as pressing the **F5** key when a file is highlighted (**F5** is a toggle, alternately adding and removing a field from the View skeleton). Remove field from view is the reverse of Add field to view. It is available only when the highlight is on a field that is included in the view. Again, **Alt-5** performs this function. Edit field name allows you to change the name of a field in the View skeleton or the name of a calculated field. This may be necessary when you are using two fields with the same name in your View skeleton.

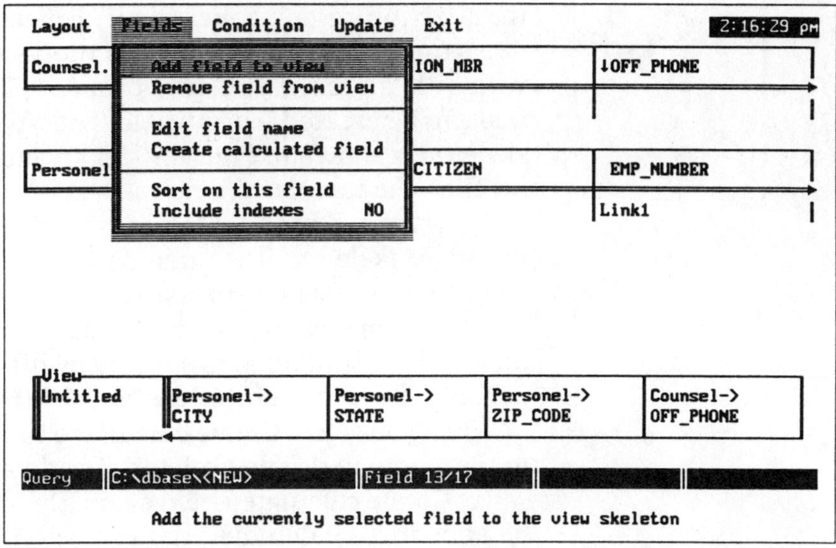

Figure 10-24

Query Fields menu.

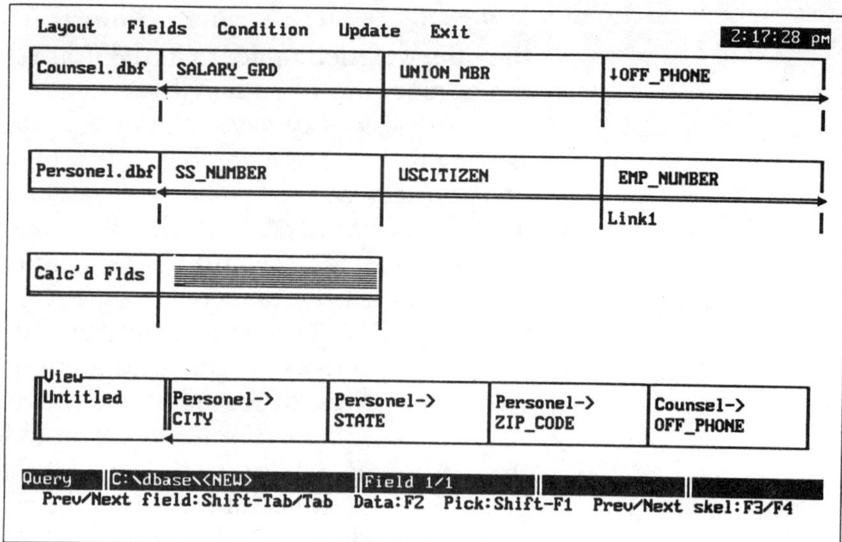

Figure 10-25

Calculated field skeleton.

Calculated fields may be used as part of the file selection criteria and are not necessarily used in the View skeleton. If they are used in the View skeleton, they must be given a name. The Edit field name option allows the user to give a calculated field a name.

A calculated field is a special type of field that is used as a filter for selecting files that are to be included in a file generated by the query processor. For example, a query for an accounts payable department may be designed to produce a list of all customers with bills more than 60 days past due. The number of days past due can be created using a calculated field. The calculated field skeleton is shown in Figure 10-25. In addition to its use in selecting files, the calculated field can be included in the View skeleton. When it is used in the calculated field skeleton, but not put into the View skeleton, it is unnamed.

A calculated field expression can consist of an expression that uses mathematical functions that are permitted by dBASE IV, and may include functions supported by dBASE IV. For a pick list of permitted expressions, press **Shft-F1** (Figure 10-26).

When you select Create calculated field, a single field is added to the calculated field skeleton. To add another calculated field, select Create calculated field again. Up to 20 calculated fields can be added to a calculated field skeleton.

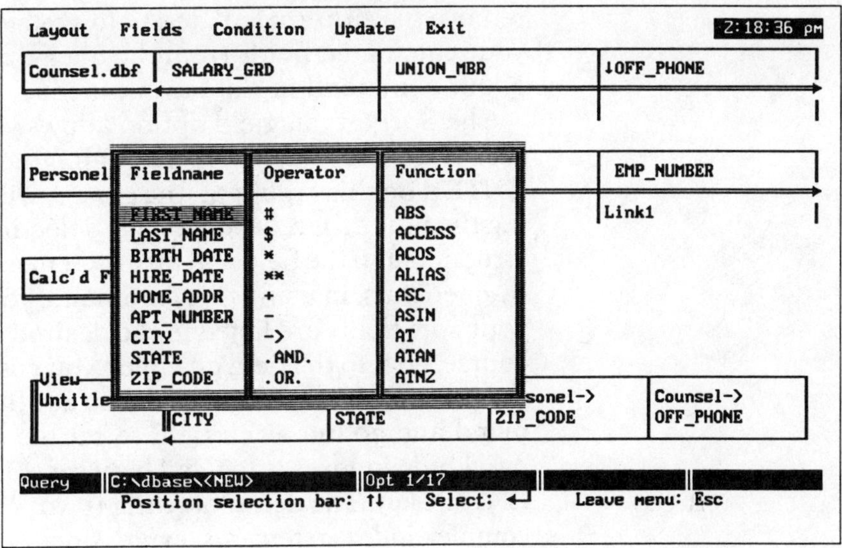

Figure 10-26

Calculated field pick list.

An expression that is longer than the box for typing the expression scrolls through the expression window. You are not limited to the 21 characters shown in the window. To enlarge the window for entry of, or viewing, the calculated field,

Press: **F9**

A large window will fill most of the screen. To close the window, again press **F9**. The lines below the expression are for query statements. You cannot link to or sort a calculated field, however. Otherwise, you have the capabilities that are available in the other skeletons.

An example of a calculated expression (for an accounting application) could be PAY=COMMRATE*SALES, in which COMMRATE is a salesperson's commission rate. An argument for the field could be >5000, to produce a list of sales people who have earned more than $5000 commission in a given time period. In this particular example, you may not want to print the actual pay for employees, just a list of names and divisions for a Sales All Stars list. Thus, although you have created the calculated field, and used it to select records that fit the criteria, you are not including the value in your new database file or any reports.

Once a calculated field is added to the skeleton, it can be blanked out or not used, but it cannot be physically removed. To remove the *entire* calculated field skeleton, which will remove all your calculated fields from the query, use the Remove file from query command in the Layout menu.

The Sort on this field option allows you to specify the type of sort you want to apply to the highlighted field. When you press **ENTER** on this highlight, the system will bring up a menu showing the four different sort types. Selecting one places the sort instruction into the field and also increments the sort order number by one. Thus, in using this command, you should be careful that your sort fields are listed in the desired sort order. You could, of course, go into the field on which you wish to use a sort and enter the sort command. You could also use the Sort on this field command and go into each field to set the sort order.

Include indexes is toggled between *Yes* and *No* by pressing the **ENTER** key. The default setting is *No*. When this is selected, any complex index statements (expressions other than merely the field name) that are used in your database are listed in the field selection bar on your file skeleton. Each index is given a # prefix, which identifies it as a pseudofield. A pseudofield is not really a field but is treated by the system as if it were.

In the field line, the index expression appears in the field name window. This is useful if you already have a complex index for your database file. For example, if you have an index for *last name* by *ZIP code* (that is, an index ordered by ZIP codes, followed by an alphabetic list of last names in each ZIP code), you can retype the expression in the value line, and the system will use the already created index to arrange your records.

This provides a few advantages. First, it is faster than defining a sort that accomplishes the same function but requires entry of the sort expression in two or more fields, because the index is already created, and a sort would necessitate going through all the records in the database file. Second, a link can be developed between two files that do not have a unique shared field. In this case, if you use the same index expression for each data file, you can structure your index to select unique records. For example, a search by first name, last name, and ZIP code will probably return unique records. If you have this same index expression in both files that you wish to link, you can create a link between the two expressions, and thus write a query based on the two databases.

To see how index fields are added, move the highlight into the

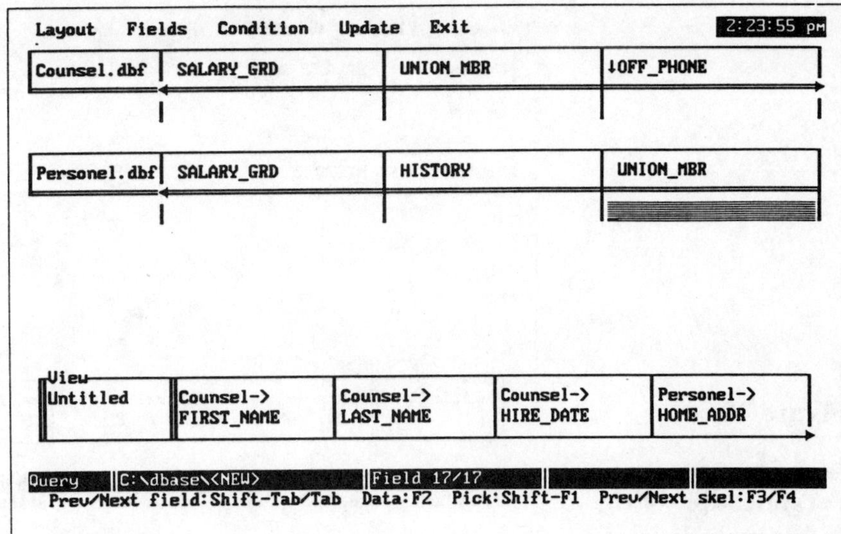

Figure 10-27

End of Personel.dbf, without index added.

Personel.dbf skeleton, and **Tab** to the last field (or press **End** to jump there) (Figure 10-27). Now go into the Fields menu and highlight the "Include indexes" prompt.

Press: **ENTER**

(You could also have brought up the Fields index and typed *i*.) The Fields box will close and the one complex index field you have created will pop up to the right of the last field in the skeleton. Now move the cursor to the right to see that the field is in the new skeleton, as seen in Figure 10-28.

If the index statement is not in the skeleton,

Press: **F10 ENTER**

to bring up the Fields menu with the Include indexes prompt already highlighted and accept the setting. The index pseudofield should now be in the Personel.dbf skeleton. If not, it is possible that the complex index was not created or could not be read from Personel.dbf. If it is not there, you can save the query, go to the Modify Database screen from within the Control Center, and add the complex index. The screen, with the added pseudofield index, is shown in Figure 10-28. Next, you can reload the saved query by highlighting it and pressing **Shft-F2**, and then include the index in your Personel.dbf skeleton.

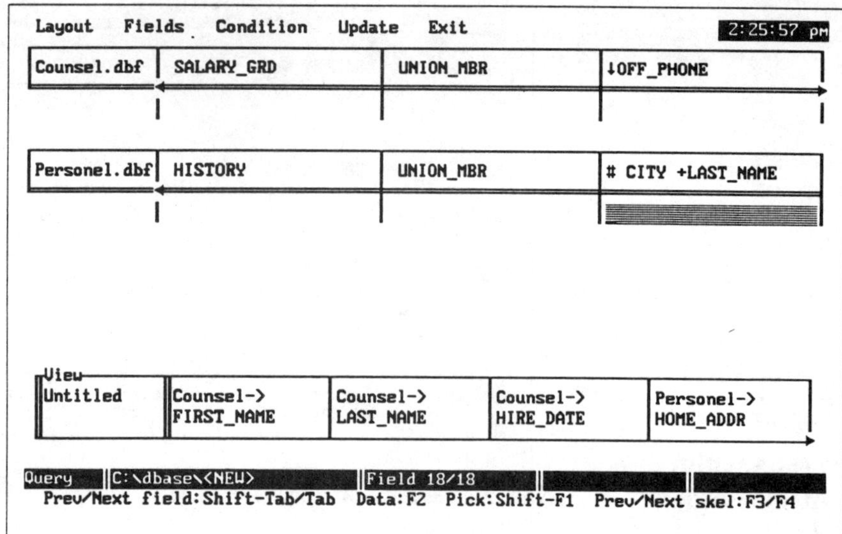

Figure 10-28

End of Personel.dbf, with index included.

The Condition menu allows you to use, delete, or hide a Condition Box. A condition box (Figure 10-29) specifies a condition that must be satisfied before a record is used by the query. The condition may contain multiple expressions.

For example, you may want to prepare a query on employees who do not live in California and who have not yet had a proba-

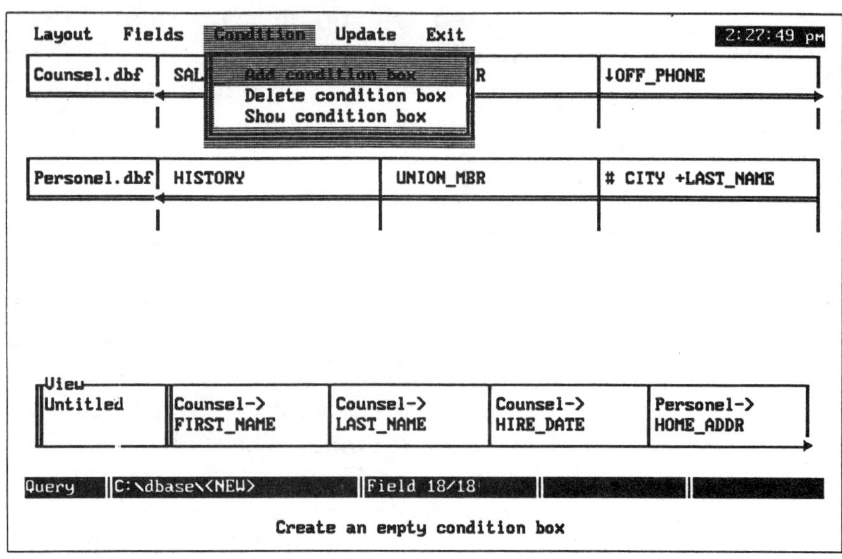

Figure 10-29

The condition box.

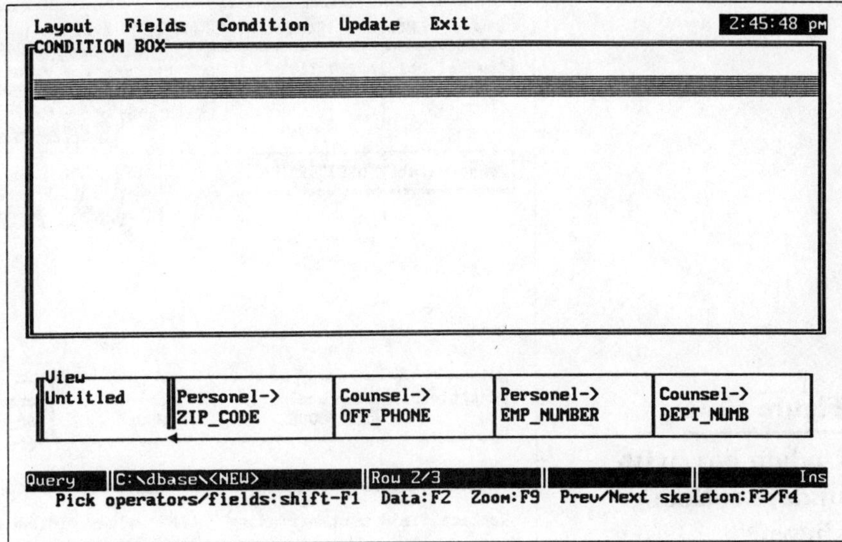

Figure 10-30

Condition box enlarged, using F9 key.

tion review, but only in departments numbered higher than 800. If you create a condition box with the following two line equation:

STATE # "CA" .and. (the # used here means not equal to)

DEPT_NUMB >800

the query process will be applied only to the records that satisfy the condition.

To add a condition box, choose Add condition box from the Condition menu. If the condition box is too small to enter (or view) the condition, **F9** allows you to toggle zoom (to enlarge the window) on and off. The enlarged condition box is shown in Figure 10-30. The Delete condition box prompt removes the condition box from the query. Show condition box is toggled on and off using the **ENTER** key. When the toggle is set to *No,* the condition box should be closed and replaced with CB marking the position of the condition box.

The Update menu allows you to modify records in your database files. The Update menu, with Specify update operation selected, is shown in Figure 10-31. Examples of what each option does follow.

An update that uses the Replace values argument is a special type of update that locates records that meet a certain condition and replaces the field value with a new value. For example, your

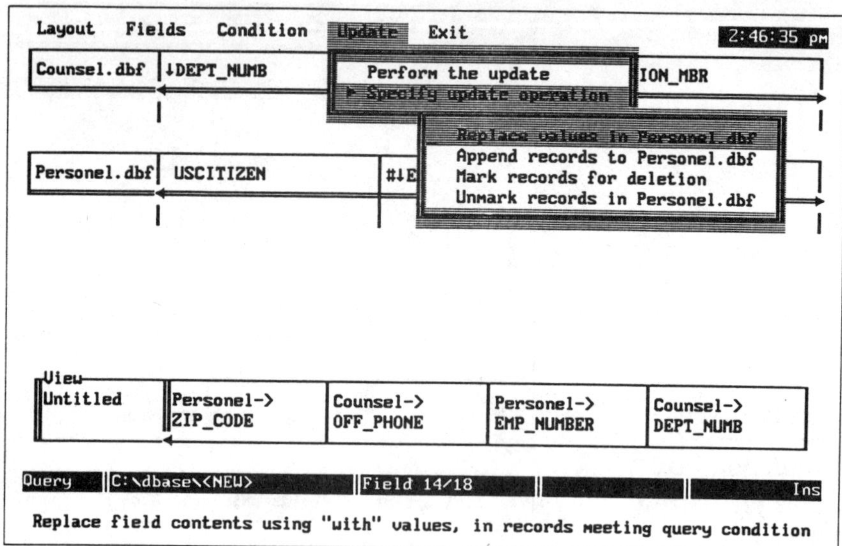

Figure 10-31

Update box, with update options shown.

employees have just voted to go 100% union. This will make all employees at all levels of the company union members. The logical field, UNION_MBR, can be changed using a replace query. When you are performing a replace update, you must type the word *Replace* in the box under the data file name. If you are working with a query that uses a View skeleton, the system will warn you that the update query will delete the View skeleton from the query. After the word *Replace* has been placed in the database file box, the word Target will appear at the top of the box. This shows that you are going to make the update on the selected database.

Next, you must go into the field in which the replacement is being made. When you are in this field,

Type: *With*

followed by the replacement expression. In the example in Figure 10-32, you will be replacing whatever value is entered in the UNION_MBR field in each record with the logical value *Y* (for yes, or true).

Depending on the type of file on which you are working, you may do multiple replacements in a single data file. For example, you may be able to use an adjustment for inflation to update your price list. Assuming the price for each item is in a field called PRICE, and the inflation rate is 4%, the replacement expression

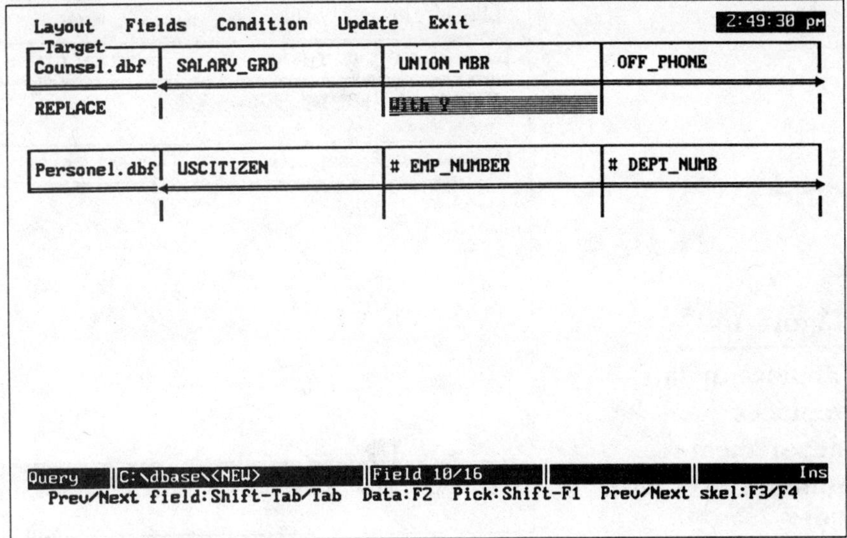

Figure 10-32

Replace update, replaces contents of field with *Y*.

*With price * 1.04* would quickly increase the price of all items in the database by 4%. Similarly salary increases and department number changes can be made in the same query argument.

Assume, for example, that department #8911 was being combined with department #8912. To perform this replacement the syntax will involve the value being replaced, followed by a comma, the word *With*, and the replacement value. In this case, the argument would be *8911, With 8912*, as seen in Figure 10-33.

Replacements can be made to only one data file at a time. To make replacements for multiple data files in your skeleton, the system allows you to switch from file to file from within the query screen. When you select the replacement update, the system knows that you want to make the update from the currently highlighted data file.

Append records to places records in a generated data file to another database. For example, you can design a special update file that has the same fields as your master PERSONEL file. By opening file skeletons for the PERSONEL file and the UPDATE file, you can set the append instruction to add all files in the UPDATE file to the PERSONEL file. To set the instruction, type *Append* in the box under the name of the target file. Next, go to the file and type the name of the field in the Source file to be appended into your target file.

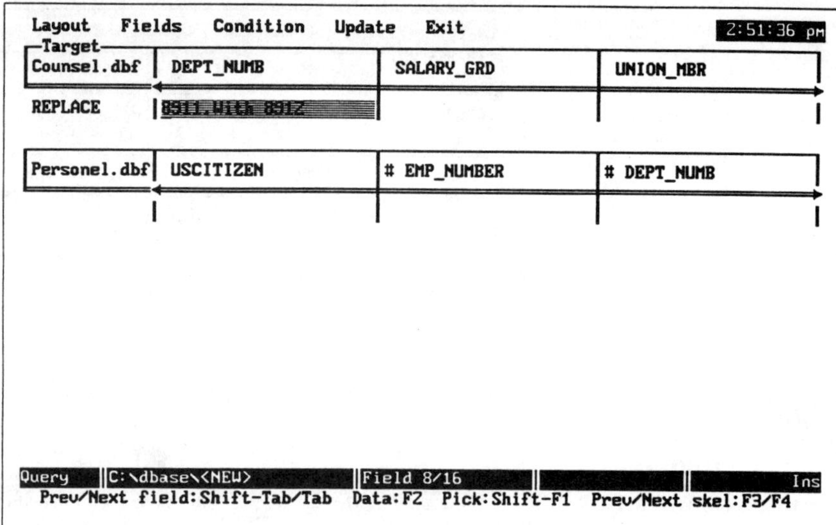

Figure 10-33

Replace update, replaces department number 8911 with 8912.

When you select Append records to your target file, the system will copy the contents of those designated fields from the source file to your target file. In addition to straight data transfers, however, you may also set conditions for the data to be transferred. For example, you may be appending order information from a daily order entry database into a master order system. There may be no need to provide a *total order* field in your daily entries, but you would want to know the amount of the order for your summary file. An expression to append the UNIT_PRICE times UNIT_ORDER fields into a TOTAL_ORD field will place the total order, calculated while the file was appended, into the TOTAL_ORD field.

Mark records for deletion is a rapid way to select records that you want removed from your database. In one instance, an accounts payable system's *dunning* database requires regular updates to remove those customers with zero balances from the dunning list. To do this you can mark those records indicating BALANCE <= 0 for deletion. A subsequent file pack operation (using the Erase Marked Files from within the Data Design menu) will rewrite the file, removing marked records.

To mark records for deletion, position the highlight in the box under the file name and

Type: *Mark*

Next, set the selection conditions for those files that you want to delete, in this case, moving to highlight the "BALANCE" column, and typing (in the field box) that you want the data appended into <=0. The system will then find all customers with zero balances and mark those records for deletion.

Of course, you may use complicated query commands to select the files to mark for deletion. Marks for deletion may also be simple. You may wish to delete all records for a particular person or customer. Typing the name of the customer, enclosed in quotation marks, on a separate line in the skeleton will tell the system to mark that particular record (or all records for that customer) for deletion.

The final update option is Unmark records. This option allows the system to quickly remove all deletion marks from your data file. To use this option, type the word *Unmark* in the box beneath the file name that you wish to unmark, and select Unmark records in the Update option box.

This option can be run globally, or for records that meet a certain condition. For example, if your dunning list has not yet been packed, that is, if the list of customers to be deleted from the list has not yet been deleted, you may want to do a final check to compare balances owing. If there is a positive balance for the customers in this database, the files will be unmarked, and will not be deleted when you pack your database. To quickly mark every record in the database, use the command *every* in one of the fields. This tells the system to accept all records in the database. The command works both in the Update and View queries, which produce new views or databases based on your query design.

The final menu is the Exit menu, which gives you two choices. You can save the query, using its current file name (if the query is unnamed, the system will prompt for a file name) or you can abandon your changes and exit from the Query menu. Any changes you made since you last saved the query will be lost when you select this option.

There is another way to exit. You may jump over to the Browse/Edit menu screen, which will display the file that the query produces, and exit from that screen. If the query has not been saved, however, exiting this way may result in the query's disappearance from the system.

This chapter has concentrated on using dBASE IV's query by example processor, a very powerful way of telling the system, without complicated codes, how to display your data, how to retrieve data using relations among multiple databases, how to update existing databases, and how you want new databases created, among other functions. A minimum of programming is required to achieve this substantial functionality. Additional query examples are provided in the documentation that is shipped with your copy of dBASE IV. The query function is one of the primary advantages of dBASE IV.

The Applications Generator

The first nine chapters of this book discussed how to install dBASE IV, design the database, set up the entry and reporting forms that you will be using, produce reports, and sort and index your data. For many users, these skills may provide enough power to manage a data system. Chapter 10 provided some very powerful query tools that allow you to link files, organize your data, make new database files using data from one or more data files, in any order, update existing files, and perform other data management tasks. The query capabilities, when combined with the basic data creation and reporting capabilities of dBASE IV, form a system that can meet the needs of a wide range of users.

dBASE IV's Applications Generator provides additional capability. It allows you to create complete applications that provide all the capabilities you have already seen but shield the user from any of the design processes involved in creating the database system. With the Applications Generator, you can build a database system that is almost entirely menu driven. To perform a function, you simply have to select a desired action from a list of options, and the action would be executed.

Although the Applications Generator is primarily aimed at developers who wish to create complex or intricate applications (and some features are beyond the scope of this book), many of the features are equally useful to most dBASE IV users.

By the end of this chapter, you should be able to generate a quick application, produce and modify menu screens, and begin to understand many of the key features of the Applications Generator.

To start the Applications Generator, move the cursor to the Applications column. If you wish to modify an application that has

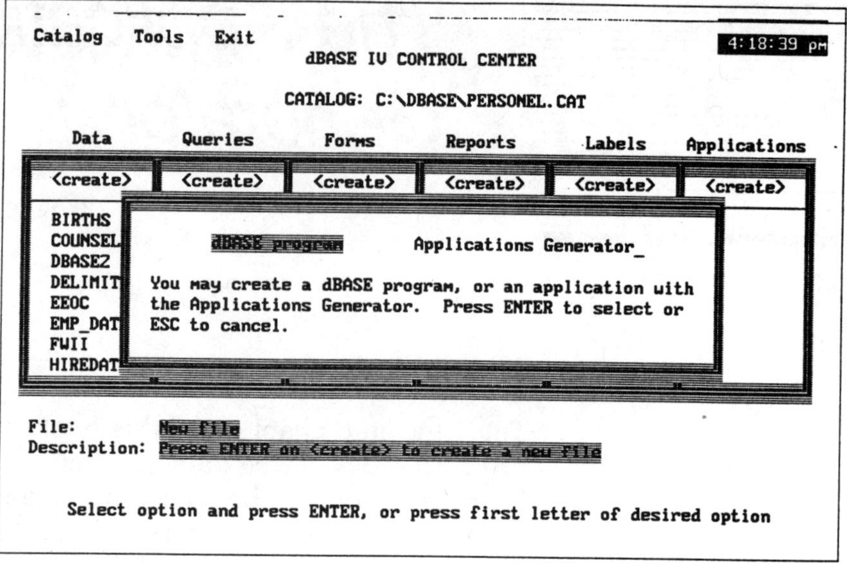

Figure 11-1

Applications Generator selection screen.

already been written, you may highlight the application that you want to change and press **Shft-F2** to bring up the Applications Generator design surface. Because you probably have not created any applications using the Applications Generator, make sure that the highlight is on "<create>" and

Press: **ENTER**

The screen will give you two options, as shown in Figure 11-1.

The Applications column is the only one that allows you to choose between applications. In this case, you want to choose the Applications Generator as the task you want to perform. If you had selected dBASE program, the system would have activated a text editing screen that allows you to write, and run, a program for dBASE. For now, however, select the Applications Generator by pressing **A**. The system will bring up the Application Definition screen. In this screen, seen in Figure 11-2, you tell the system the name of the application, describe the application, and tell it which menus and database files to use.

The Application name line asks for the name that you want to give your application. This is the name that the end user—data input operator, update operator, or even you—will use to call up and run the application. Name this application PERSONEL, to keep it consistent with the rest of your database.

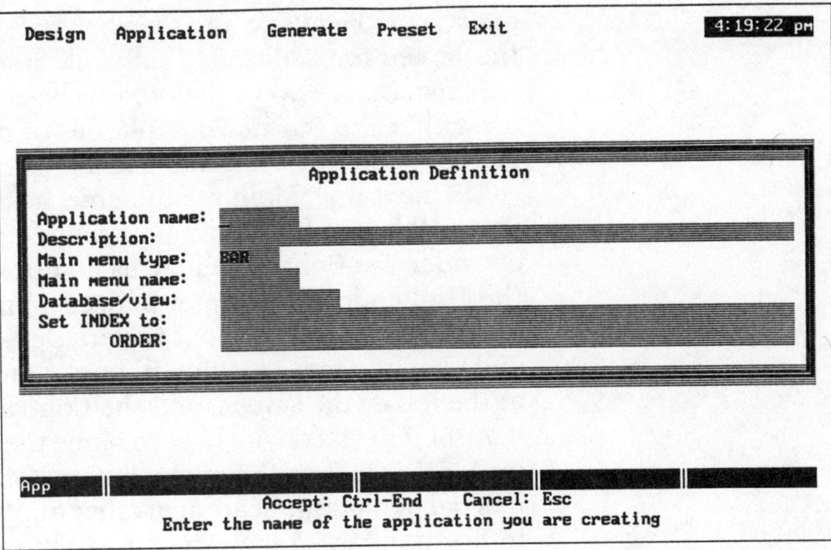

Figure 11-2

Application Definition screen.

The next line, Description, asks you to describe the application that you are building. This description is displayed from inside the Control Center when the application is highlighted.

Type: *This is a sample personnel management application*

The next option, Menu, asks you which type of main menu you wish to use in your application. The three options are Bar, Pop-up, and Batch. A Bar menu is the same type of menu used by dBASE IV for its menu lines. The top line of your screen is a bar, with menu options located along the bar.

A Pop-Up menu is similar to the ones that are popped onto the screen when you select a menu item. With the Applications Generator, you can modify the size and location of the Pop-up menus. A Pop-up main menu consists of a box that pops onto the screen, giving the user a list of options that can be highlighted and selected, either by moving the cursor or by typing the first letter(s) of the option. You can also include informational lines that can be read but that do not call up any files or functions.

The third option for main menu type is Batch, which calls up a batch program that executes certain functions. A batch program uses commands that have been prewritten and that automatically perform the batch functions. For example, one batch may select a query that updates a data file; this batch mode will load the query, run the query, and then bring the edit screen display onto the screen for addition of data, all automatically.

In most cases, you will probably be designing applications that use either the Bar or Pop-up types of menus. For the purposes of this chapter, select Bar by highlighting it and pressing **ENTER**.

The next line, Main menu name, asks you to name the menu that will be the first, or main, menu for your application. If you consider the Control Center as an application developed using the Applications Generator (it uses many of the capabilities and features of the Applications Generator, and has a very similar look and feel), the main menu will be the one that brings up the bar at the top of the screen, and the Control Center columns below it. Although you do not have to name the main menu, it is usually well to do so. If you plan to use some of the menus designed for this particular application in other applications, you will be able to use the named main menu as the main menu for the other application(s).

For a list of the main menus available, press **Shft-F1**. The system will show all the menus of the particular type that you are using. (That is, if you have selected a Bar or a Pop-up menu, the system will show all Bar or Pop-up menus in the directory. If the menus selected are not loaded, the system will prompt you that there were no such menus in the system.)

A main menu may have a name that uses up to eight characters. The system automatically assigns an extension to the name. For the present example,

Type: *PERSMAIN*

Database/view: asks you to tell the system which database or query view file is to be used as the main database for the application. To see a list of those that are currently available, press **Shft-F1**. Select the PERSONEL.DBF database.

Following Database/view:, the system asks you to select an *index* to be used with the database file. Again, you can view the applicable index(es) by pressing **Shft-F1**. The index that you select is the master index (.MDX), which includes the indexes that you have created for use with your data file. Chapter Seven discusses the master index in further detail. In the case of the PERSONEL.DBF database, you have only one index file, PERSONEL.MDX. Select that one now. To select a database or view

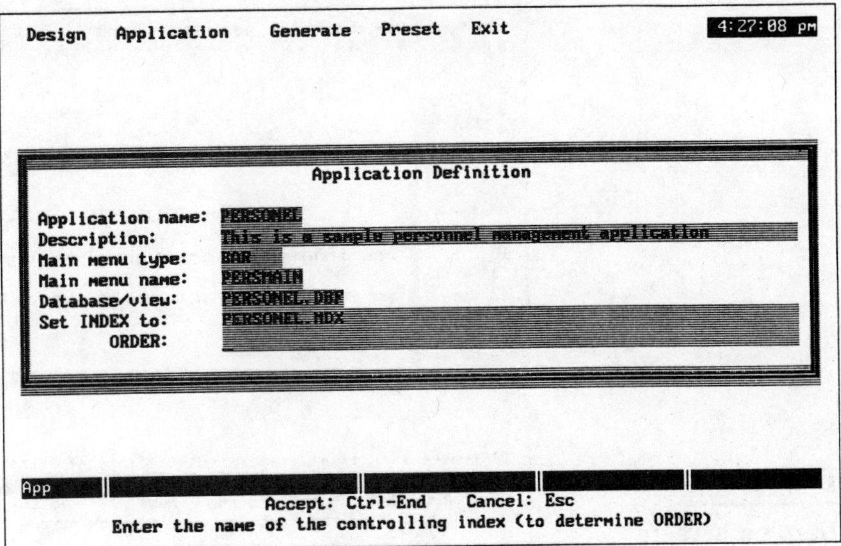

Figure 11-3

Application Definition screen, completed.

from within the pop-up, highlight the database or view that you wish to use and

Press: **Ctrl-End**

The final item, ORDER:, asks which index in the master index selected is to be in effect when you start your application. When you indicate a particular index, the records will appear in the order of that selected index. Because dBASE IV does not provide a list of the indexes in the master index, you will have to know the name of the index that you want to be the controlling index. This can be changed from within the actual Applications design screen. For now, leave this option blank. Your settings should appear as shown in Figure 11-3.

Once the applications have been set as you want them, accept them. To do this,

Press: **Ctrl-End**

The system will bring up the design window. In the center is a box that serves as the sign-on screen for your application. As dBASE IV is shipped, the applications generator sign-on screen will appear as shown in Figure 11-4.

The design screen is the display surface that you use to design

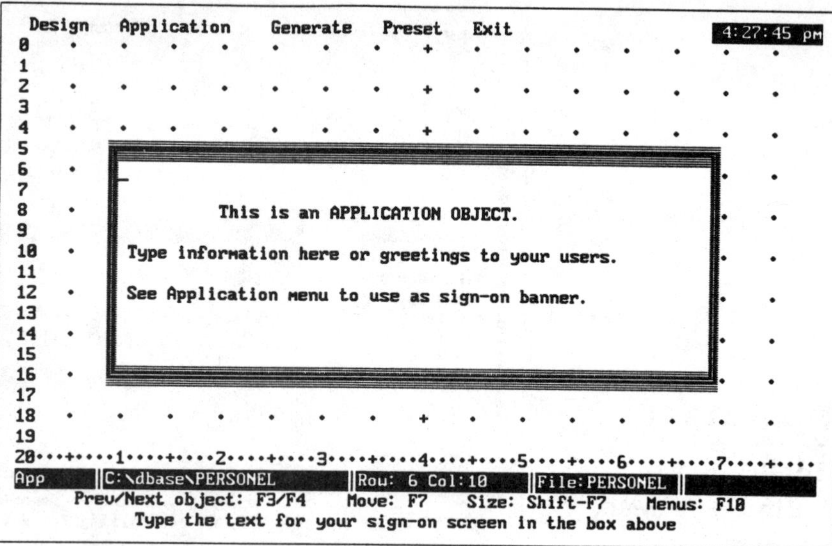

Figure 11-4

Sign-on screen.

the appearance and structure of your application. As displayed here, it contains a fair amount of clutter—particularly at the bottom of the screen. To open your screen farther,

Press: **F9**

The menu bars and information lines will disappear, and the screen will appear as shown in Figure 11-5.

The ability to toggle the menus on and off is particularly useful if you have designed screens and wish to view them without having the Applications Generator screens interfere with your view. The **F9** key is a toggling key, so to return to the full menu,

Press: **F9**

The sign-on screen is shown when the application is first started. The display on the screen is called an Application object. It will remain on the desktop (the screen area) when an application is run. The screen can be used as a sign-on screen (Welcome to the personnel manager), or as the initial menu screen for the application. To be used as a sign-on display, an option in the Application is used.

If you plan to use this as a sign-on screen, you may retype the text for this screen, making a change to this screen for the purposes of this application. To do this, move the cursor to the posi-

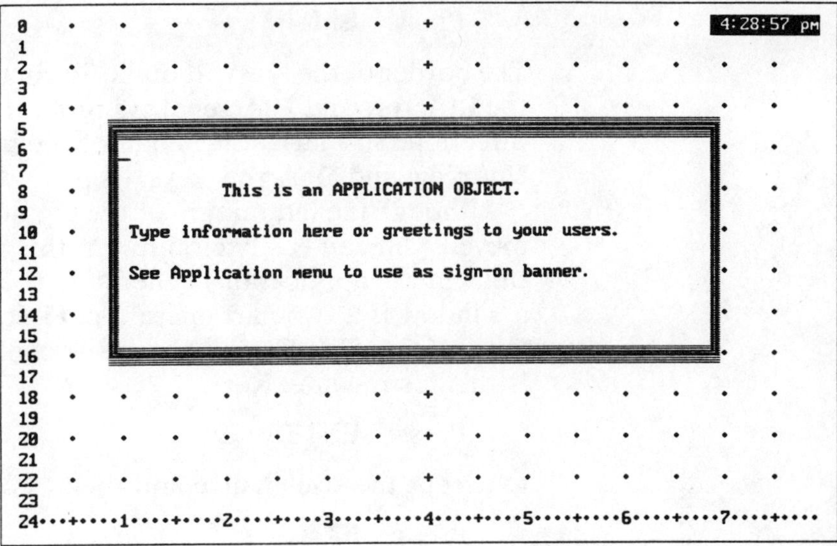

Figure 11-5

Screen with menus removed, using the F9 key.

tion at which you wish to make the change and type the new sign-on text, as shown on Figure 11-6.

You may prefer to change the sizing of this screen, which is somewhat larger than the text that it encloses. To change the size of a screen,

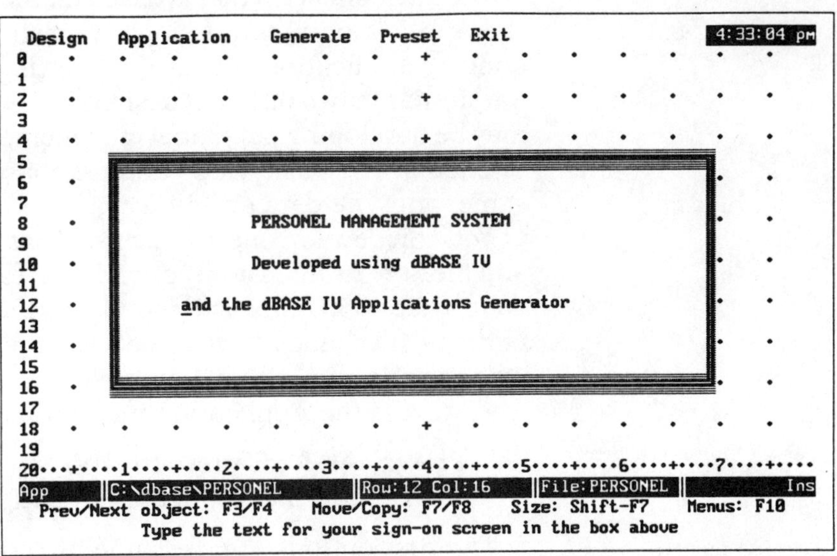

Figure 11-6

Revised sign-on text.

Press: **Shft-F7**

The border of the box will blink. To change the width of the box, the **LtArrow** and **RtArrow** keys move the border in the desired direction. Similarly, the height of the box is changed using the **UpArrow** and **DnArrow** keys.

Although the left margin or the top line of your box cannot be moved, you can easily circumvent this by using the move functions in the applications generator. The resizing and moving of a window is a two-part operation. First, use the resize function (by pressing **Shft-F7**) and expand or contract the window until it is the desired size. Next,

Press: **ENTER**

to accept the size change and then

Press: **F7**

to tell the system that you want to move or copy the newly resized box. Again, the borders of the box will blink. Using the cursor arrow keys, move the box to the position at which you want it, and press **ENTER**. The box will be repositioned in the location you desire. A screen can usually be resized and moved with little trouble. Boxes can also be copied to multiple locations on the screen.

If you want to change the setup of your current application or create an application that is based on the current application, use the Application menu. Using an existing application to create another application is useful when the basic menus and setup are similar in two different desired applications. For example, you may be developing personnel management systems for a number of clients. The basic views and database file structures are the same; only the data are different.

You can develop one application that applies to all the clients and then create a "custom" application for a new client by loading your basic application and modifying the name, description, and, perhaps, file names. Saving the new application with a new name will provide you with a new, custom application.

To access the Application menu (Figure 11-7),

Press: **Alt-A** (or press the **F10** key, and use the arrow keys to bring up the Application menu)

The first options are the same as those used to create a new

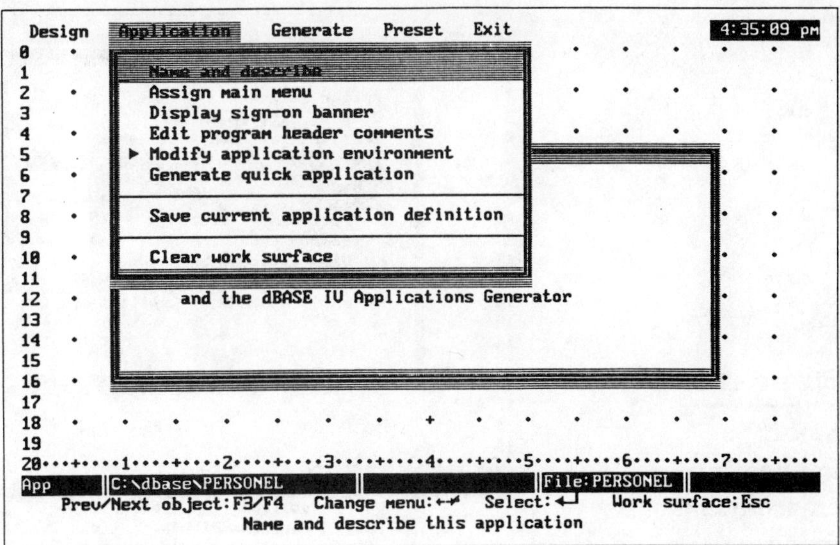

Figure 11-7

Application menu.

application. Selecting Assign main menu enables you to create a new menu by assigning a new name. When this is done, the named menu must be designed (or already exist) for the application to run properly.

The Display sign-on banner prompt allows you to decide whether the initial screen (the application object mentioned earlier) is popped up when the user first starts the program. The options for this item are *Yes* or *No*. *Yes* displays the sign-on screen and *No* tells the system not to display it.

Edit program header comments allows you to change the text that appears when the application begins running. When the application program is generated by dBASE IV, the contents of this screen are set to display when the user starts the application. Actually, the text of the sign-on screen, shown earlier, must be typed in this screen for the application sign-on to be displayed as you want it. The contents of the current window will be displayed as the sign-on text for any applications generated by the Applications Generator.

Type the text displayed in Figure 11-6. To accept the new text,

Press: **Ctrl-End**

Modify application environment brings up another menu that

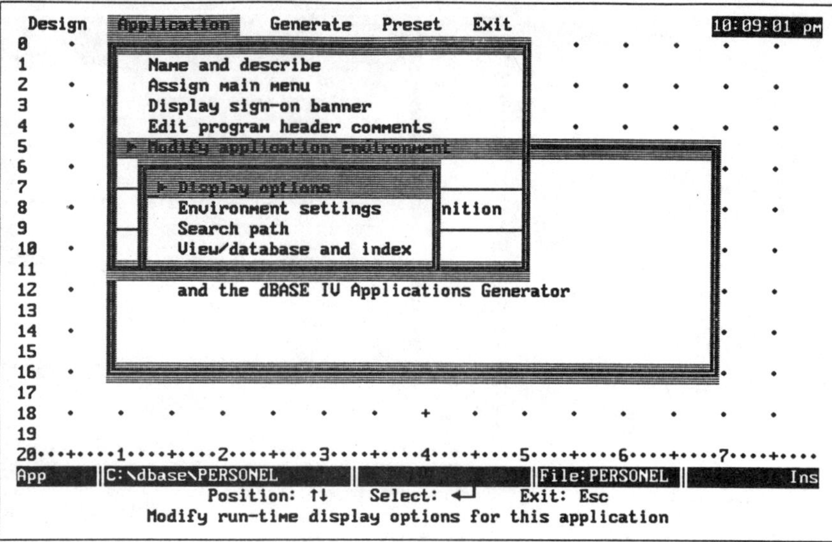

Figure 11-8

Modify application environment menu.

allows you to check and, if necessary, change a variety of options in the current application. This menu appears as shown in Figure 11-8.

The Display Options menu is very similar to the display options menus available in the setup and configuration screens for dBASE IV. Selection of colors for text are made in the same way as in the other menus. You are also givenn a choice of display formats for the screen perimeter: Double (for double line), Single (for single line), Panel (for a wide frame), or None (for no border), which are toggled using the **Space Bar.** Once you have selected your display options,

Press: **Ctrl-End**

to select the options. If you prefer not to make changes to the current options,

Press: **Esc**

to return to the Modify application environment screen.

The Environment Settings option allows you to set a number of performance variables for the application. Because the current settings are appropriate for most applications, these will not be discussed further here.

Search Path allows you to define a path for the system to search your hard or floppy disk drive for files. The search path screen

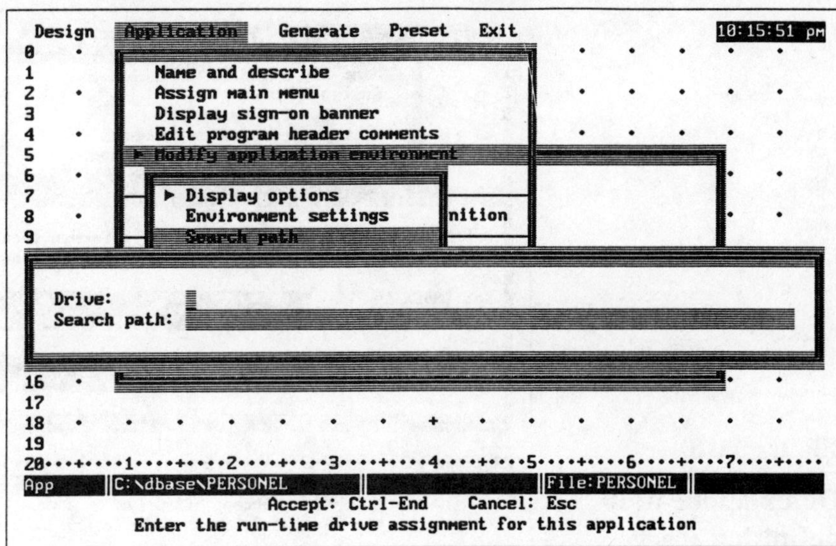

Figure 11-9

Search path definition screen.

appears as shown in Figure 11-9. The search path setting is the default path that loads at runtime. If your personnel files are on a directory called PERSONEL on your hard drive, the path would be \personel.

Finally, the View/database and index settings match the same option in the screen used in creating your new application. In this screen, you tell the system the default database to use, the default master index (.mdx), and the desired index to apply to your database. To accept changes to this screen,

Press: **Ctrl-End**

If you prefer not to save your changes,

Press: **Esc**

The next option is Generate quick application. This allows you to produce an application without extensive knowledge, or use, of the features in the Applications Generator. When this is selected, the screen will appear as shown in Figure 11-10.

The menu will ask you to specify the database file you wish to use in the application, the screen format file (designed using the Forms design screens), the report format file (designed using the Reports processor), and the label file format (designed using the Label processor). If the current database is acceptable,

```
Design  Application  Generate  Preset  Exit                      10:16:58 pm
0
1            Name and describe
2            Assign main menu
3            Display sign-on banner
4            Edit program header comments
5          ▶ Modify application environment
6            Generate quick application

  Database file:      PERSONEL.DBF        Screen format file:
  Report format file:                     Label format file:

  Set INDEX to:      PERSONEL.MDX
        ORDER:

  Application author:             PERSONNEL MANAGEMENT SYSTEM
  Application menu heading:

19
20····+····1····+····2····+····3····+····4····+····5····+····6····+····7····+····
App      ║C:\dbase\PERSONEL          ║            ║File:PERSONEL║
                Accept: Ctrl-End    Cancel: Esc
      Enter the name of database file to use with the quick application
```

Figure 11-10

Quick application definition sceen.

Press: **ENTER**

to move to the next option.

To see the designs that are available from the current catalog,

Press: **Shft-F1**

You may highlight the file that you wish to use as the format for each of the format files. To select the highlighted files as part of your database application,

Press: **ENTER**

After each format file is selected, the cursor jumps to the next type of format file. If you do not see the format you wish to use, you may <create> a new one. When you select <create>, the system moves to the appropriate format design processor (i.e., the Forms design, the Reports design, or the Labels design process) and allows you to design the format for the desired report, data input form, or labels. You can **Esc** back to the Application menu at any time during the description of your quick application. To return to the Applications Generator from the design screen, use the Exit menu, and select Save changes and exit.

After specifying the data file and the format files for your application, the system asks you to select the index and index order. These settings default to the settings that were in effect when you last saved your application design, or when you started the Applications Generator.

The system allows you to select from indexes in your selected data file. The ORDER prompt asks for the name of the index that you want to use to determine the order in which your records will be displayed. dBASE IV is not able to provide a list of the indexes in the selected .MDX file. Thus, you must already know the name of the controlling index to set up this option. If you leave this field blank, the system will display your records in the order in which they were added to your system (or in the order in which a sorted file has been saved). For the current application, tell the system that you wish to order the records by LAST__NAME.

The last two lines of the quick application specification screen allow you to provide information on the author and an Application menu. The Application Author line allows you to put your name or comments into the application. Although this information will not appear on the application screens, it will be included as a comment in the program code that the system generates to produce the application.

One possible response would include your name and the version date of this revision of the application. To see how this works,

Type: *My Application, Version 1.0*

then delete the rest of the text on the line. The next line asks for the text of the menu heading. The menu heading appears at the top of the application screen. For this line,

Type: *Personnel Management Application, 1.0*

and delete any characters that may remain on the line. Enter the data in Figure 11-11.

Finally, to accept the application just designed,

Press: **Ctrl-End**

The system will ask if you wish to generate a quick application, based on the files and information you just entered onto the screen. This is your last chance to stop generation of the quick application. The word "YES" should be highlighted by the system. If it is,

Press: **ENTER**

If not,

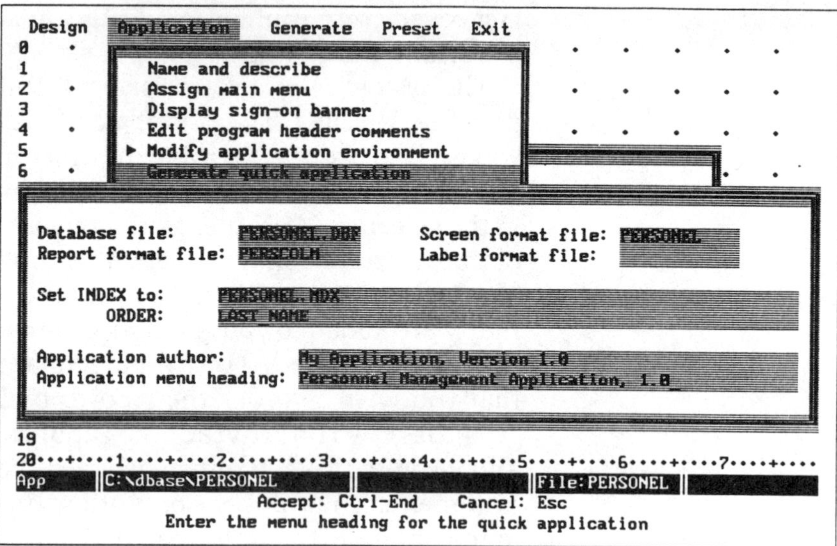

Figure 11-11

Quick application definition screen, with definitions.

Type: *Y*

to tell the system to generate the application.

The system will clear the Application Specification menu and begin generating code to produce your quick application. When the application is generated, the system will ask you to press any key to continue using the Applications Generator. Press any key, and the system will bring you back into the Application menu.

The next option, Save current application definition, stores the description, main menu, program header, and sign-on status just defined for your application (or the changes made since the last time you saved the definition). This is implemented by touching the **ENTER** key.

The final Application menu item is Clear work surface. In the Applications Generator, you are able to define Bar menus, Pop-up menus, and Batch processes. The displays that are associated with each type of menu or process are placed on the screen allowing you to see what your application will look like. However, displaying the menus and submenus takes up memory, and displaying too many menus will easily decrease the somewhat limited memory available when you use dBASE IV. In addition, the screen can get quite cluttered when you have more than a few menus or pop-ups on the screen. When you invoke the Clear work surface command (by pressing **ENTER**) with the command highlighted, the system removes all but the initial sign-on banner from the screen, asking if you want to save each screen before it is removed from the work surface.

We will return to the Applications Generator shortly, but for now, we will look at the application that the system automatically generated. To do this, exit from the Applications Generator, saving your changes before exiting. (Press **Alt-E**, then press *S*.) Next, highlight "PERSONEL" in the Applications Generator column and

Press: **ENTER**

The system will ask if you want to modify or run the application.

Type: *R*

to tell the system that you want to run the application. The system will again ask if you want to run the application,

Type: *Y*

The system will load and run the Personel application, bringing up a menu like the one in Figure 11-12.

This simple application provides many of the options needed to manage this system using the single database file, and without the use of special queries. The first option, Add Information, loads the form for PERSONEL and brings you to an empty menu screen.

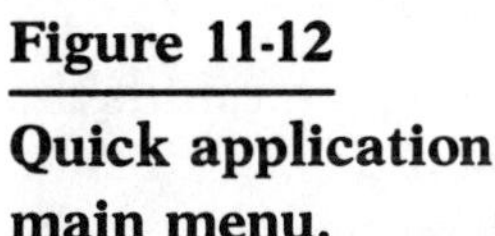

Figure 11-12

Quick application main menu.

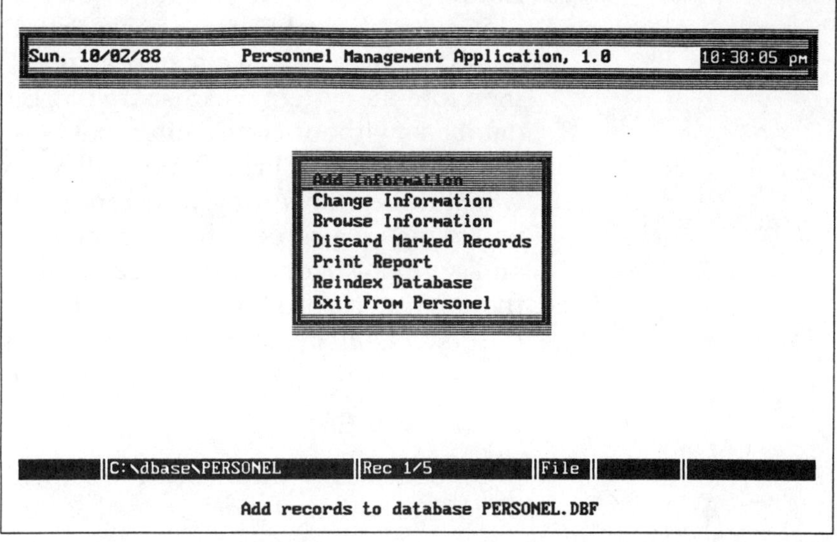

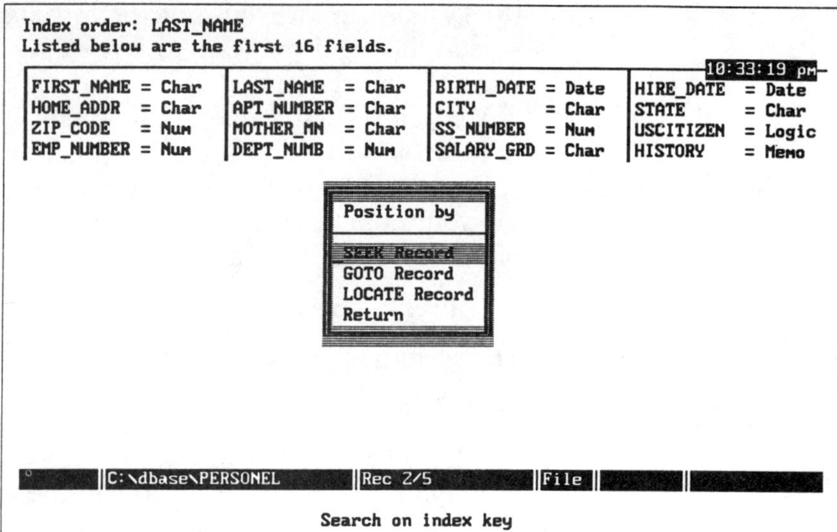

Figure 11-13

Print menu from PERSONEL application.

The second option, Change Information, loads the same screen and brings the system into a current database record. Using the GoTo function, you may bring the cursor to the file that you wish to update. The **F2** key will still work as a toggle between Browse and Edit.

Browse Information brings up the Browse screen. From within this screen the **F2** key can be used to toggle between Browse and Edit.

Discard Marked Records packs your database and rebuilds the database index(es). This option does not include a fail-safe; therefore the system will discard marked records and reindex the database without confirming that you really want it done.

The next option, Print Report, allows you to select a record from which to begin printing your report. When selected, the system will bring up a screen showing the index order, the field names, and a window from which to select the functions needed to find the starting record (Figure 11-13). Once the cursor is positioned, the system will begin preparing your report. If you wish to begin printing the report from the first record on,

Press: **Esc**

to go to the destination selection screen (Figure 11-14). Only those options to which a form has been assigned can be selected. In the

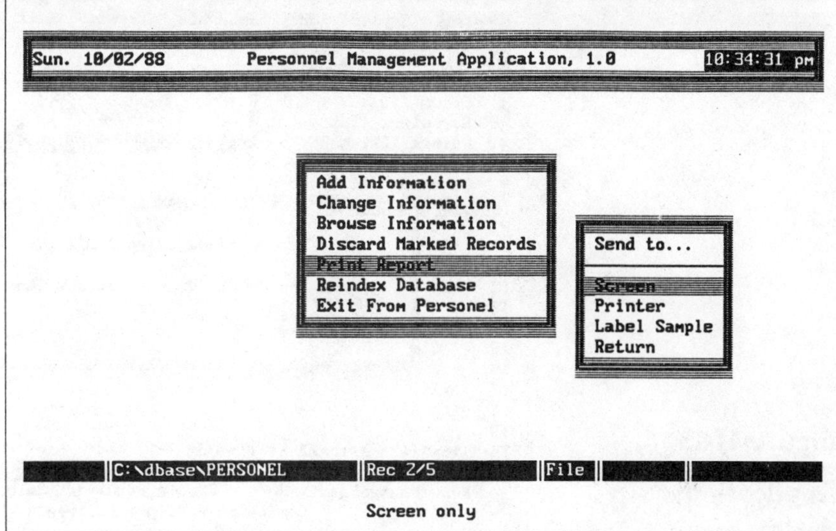

Figure 11-14

Print destination definition screen.

current example, because a label format was not included in the specification for the application, you will be unable to select Label Sample. A printed report will use the form you designed using the Reports generator in the Control Center.

The next option, Reindex Database, automatically goes into the database and rebuilds the indexes that you originally created. This is similar to what happens in Delete marked records, with the obvious exception that no records are deleted. The reindex capabilities are useful if records have been added to the database.

Finally, Exit from Personel allows the user to leave the application and return to the Control Center. The application that was generated using the Quick Applications Generator does not prompt for confirmation that you want to leave the application. In addition, the system does not reset memory variables, the addresses in memory at which the contents of various portions of your data are stored. The use of a memory variable speeds up the execution of a program written for dBASE IV (such as the application that the system generated), and is commonly used by dBASE programmers. In the version of dBASE IV that was used during the writing of this book, the memory variables were not cleared.

This means that the memory occupied by these memory variables is still in use, even after you exit the program. This reduces the memory available for running dBASE IV, and in some

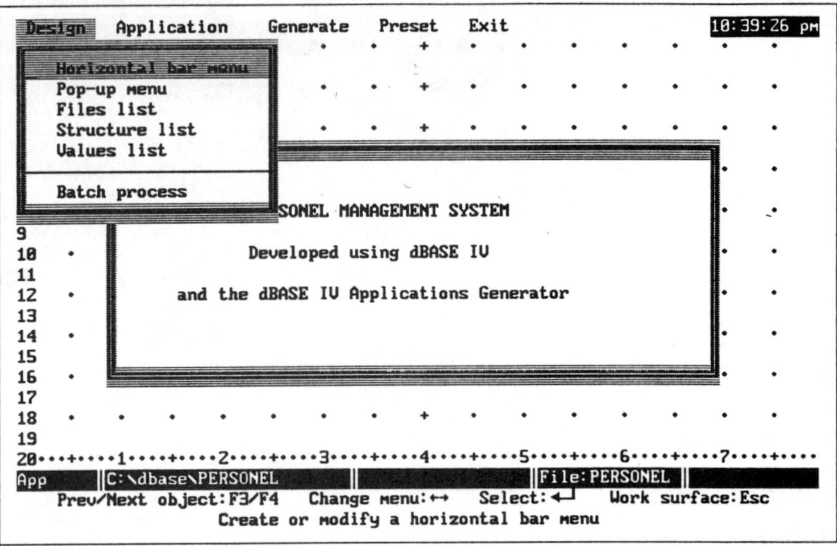

Figure 11-15
Application design menu.

cases will reduce the memory to the point at which you will not be able to load the Applications Generator, and possibly some other processing modules in dBASE IV. If you run out of memory, you may have to Exit to DOS and reload dBASE IV.

Obviously, the application generated using the Quick Applications Generator is limited. It allows the user to use only a small series of forms and lacks some of the fail-safe features you may want to use to prevent exiting without an Are you sure? prompt or deleting marked files without a similar prompt.

The Applications Generator allows you to design applications that use a variety of forms; you can design your own prompts and you can run queries. It can also be used to design elaborate systems. The intricacies of working with the Applications Generator can easily take up a major portion of an advanced user's book. For current purposes, a quick look at many of the features available in the Applications Generator will be useful.

Reload the Applications Generator by selecting PERSONEL and pressing **Shft-F2**. The system will bring you back into the Applications Generator design screen. Now, to see how the system works, activate the Design window (Figure 11-15). This menu allows you to select and design the various menus and submenus (or actions) that will be used in your application. Select Horizontal Bar menu, and the system will bring up a list of menus that have already been created by this application. With "<create>" highlighted,

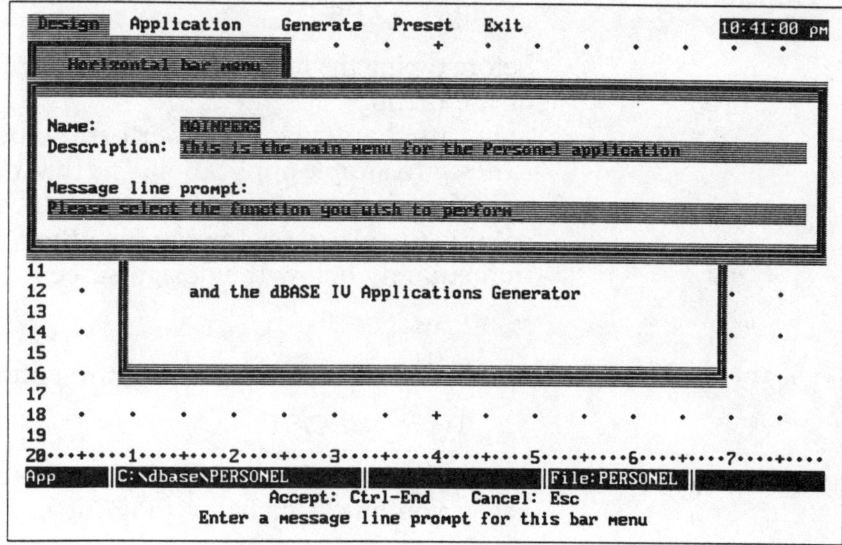

Figure 11-16

Horizontal bar definition (MAINPERS menu).

Press: **ENTER**

to create a new menu. Once selected, the system asks for a name of the menu, a description, and a message line. The message line prompt is a line of information or instructions that is displayed at the bottom of the screen when the menu is activated.

Name this menu MAINPERS. The description line tells what this menu is.

Type: ***This is the main menu for the Personel application* ENTER**

The system will bring the cursor into the Message line prompt line.

Type: ***Please select the function you wish to perform***

The screen will appear as shown in Figure 11-16.

To save the menu definition

Press: **Ctrl-End**

The system will bring up a Horizontal menu that appears at the top of the screen. The cursor will allow you to move from left to right across the screen.

If you define a menu item with the Applications Generator, the items will call up other menus. To define text on the menu line as a menu, move the cursor to the place at which you want the menu item to begin, and

Press: **F5**

before typing the name of the menu and after completing the name of the menu.

In this chapter, you will perform some of the basic steps used to design a simple application. The first menu item you will create is UPDATE, used to update your database. Move the cursor to column 6 (you can see the column number on the information line immediately below the design screen), and

Press: **F5**

to tell the system that you want to enter a menu name here.

Type: *UPDATE*

As you type, the system will display your text in highlighted video. When you have finished typing the menu name,

Press: **F5**

and the menu item will be located on the menu bar. You can add other menu items to the main menu bar, depending on the types of items you wish to guide the user through. Add an item called EXIT starting at column 55. Again, remember to press the **F5** key before and after typing the name of the menu item. The horizontal menu bar is shown in Figure 11-17.

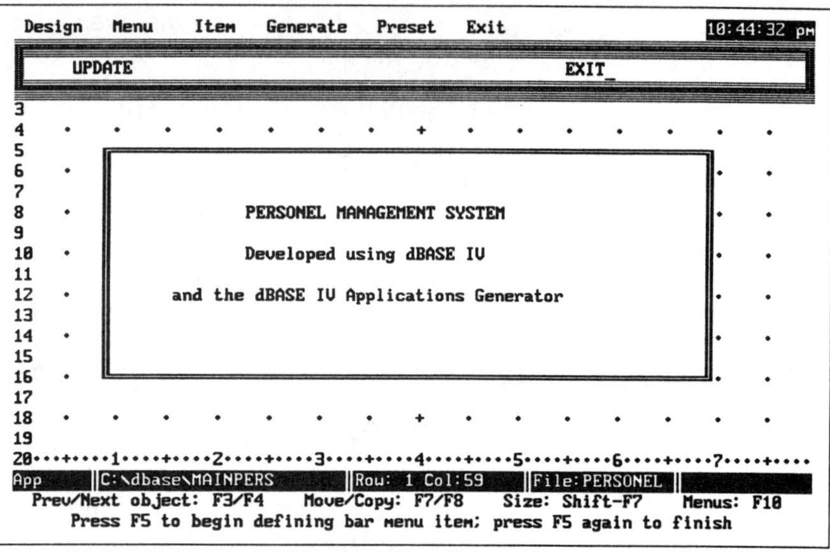

Figure 11-17

Horizontal menu bar with fields added.

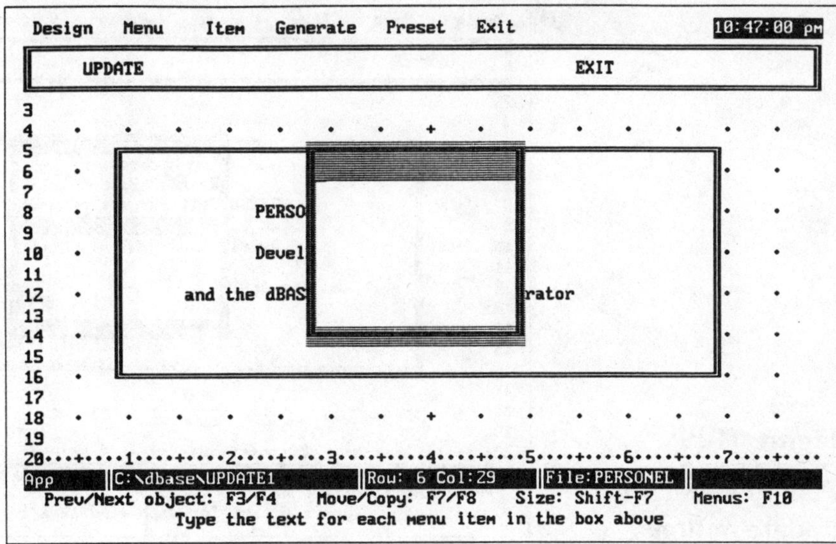

Figure 11-18

Pop-up menu window.

Now, you will design a Pop-up menu that is activated when Update is selected from the menu. Move the cursor so that it is inside the Update item. Next, select the Design menu, so that you can design the submenus or functions that this menu selection brings onto the screen.

Press: **Alt-D**

to bring up the Design menu, and select Pop-up menu from the list of options. A list of Pop-up menus will appear in a window at the right side of the screen. Select <create>. Name the new menu UPDATE1. Give it the description: Update menu, and the following message line: Select update function desired. Save your settings by pressing **Ctrl-End**.

The system will bring a Pop-up menu onto the middle of the screen. Using the **UpArrow** and **DnArrow** keys, you may move the highlight to any line on the Pop-up menu screen. The menu screen can be moved and its size can be changed. The pop-up screen appears as shown in Figure 11-18.

Add a few menu items, using one line for each item in the Pop-up menu. The following items will be added: Add Records, Reindex file, Edit current records, Run Query. Other update options could also have been added to this menu, which should now appear as shown in Figure 11-19.

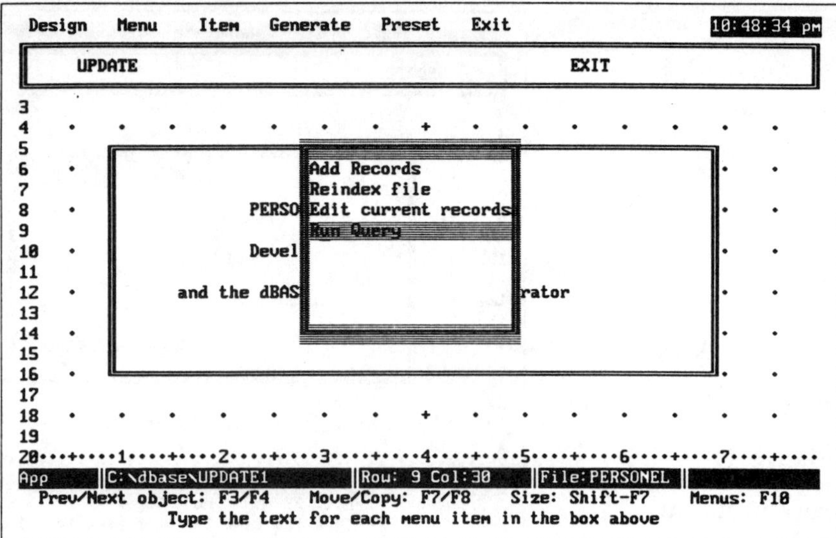

Figure 11-19

Pop-up menu with update options.

After typing the options, resize the window, bringing up the bottom of the box. To do this,

Press: **Shft-F7**

The borders of the Pop-up menu will be highlighted and may also blink, indicating that the box is being resized. If you were planning to use text that is larger than the box width, you may resize the box and then retype the text. The resize operation uses the arrow keys. Only the right margin and the bottom margin can be resized; the box margins cannot be brought in far enough to delete text already typed into the box. Move the bottom margin up to the last line of the menu text.

Press: **ENTER**

to indicate that you have completed resizing the window.

The new, smaller window will appear on the screen. Next, you may move the window so that it is located under the Update menu option. To do this,

Press: **F7**

to select the box to be moved. The system will bring up a box, as seen in Figure 11-20, that asks whether you want to move the en-

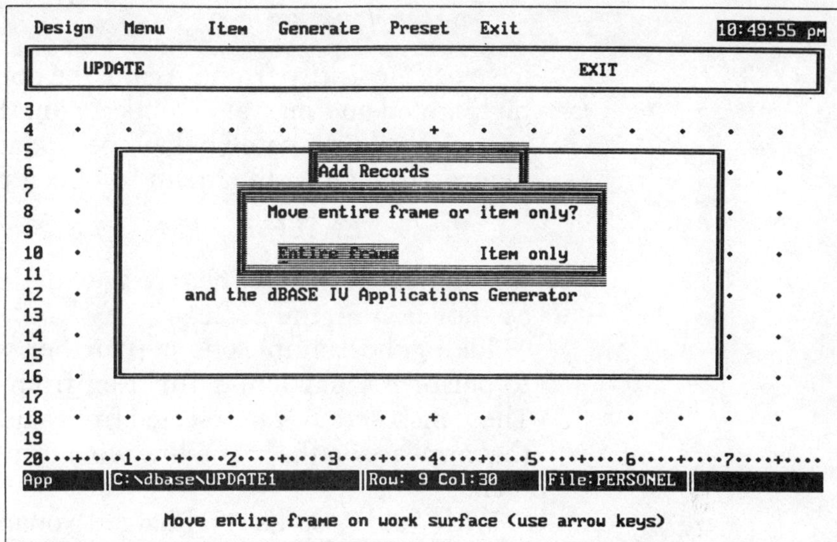

Figure 11-20

Move entire frame? or item only? prompt.

tire frame or a single item. If you choose to move an item, the item currently highlighted can be moved to another position inside the Pop-up menu. Selecting Entire frame allows you to move the Pop-up menu and all text inside the menu. Make sure the highlight is on "Entire frame," and

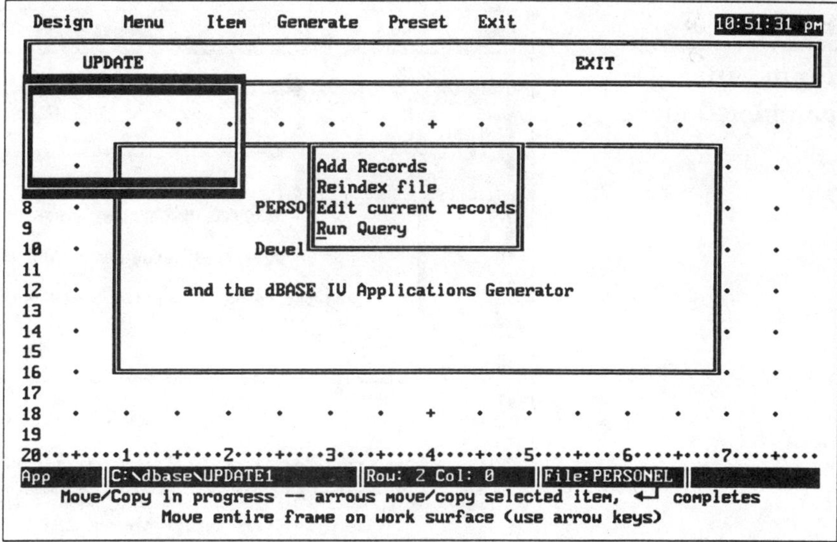

Figure 11-21

Marker for entire frame located under Update menu item.

Press: **ENTER**

to select the Entire frame. Again, the border of the frame will be highlighted and may also blink. Using the arrow keys, move the box so that it is located below the Update menu item, as seen in Figure 11-21. Once the menu has been positioned,

Press: **ENTER**

to complete the move. The screen, with the moved pop-up, appears as shown in Figure 11-22.

Taking the example one step further, you can add instructions to perform a particular function from within the application. These instructions are selected from a new menu, the Item menu, that appears on the menu line when you have activated a Pop-up menu.

With "Add Records" highlighted, you may wish to invoke a command to load the Personel file and to bring up the Edit screen. To do this, bring up the Item menu (by pressing **Alt-I**). The Item menu (Figure 11-23) offers many options that can be performed at this point. It also branches to a number of additional submenus, which can be used to further define the action you want to take when the currently highlighted option is selected.

Select Change Action to bring up the Change action menu,

Figure 11-22

Frame after completed move.

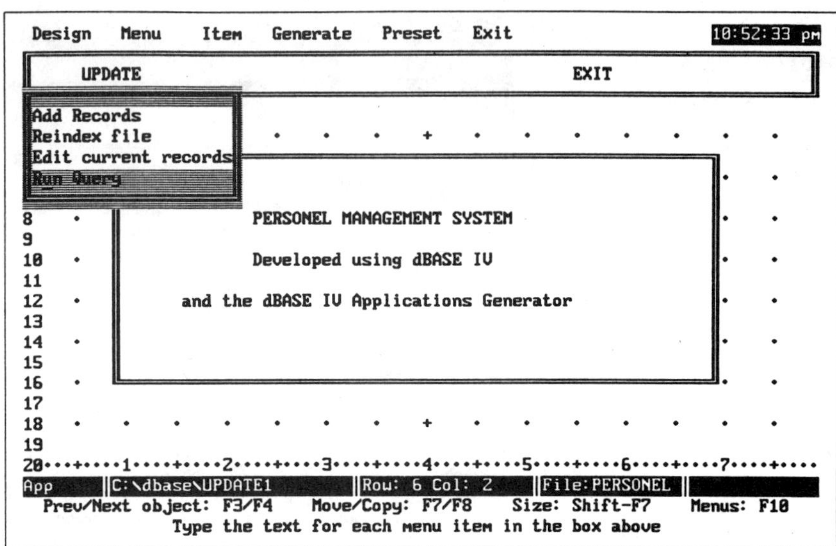

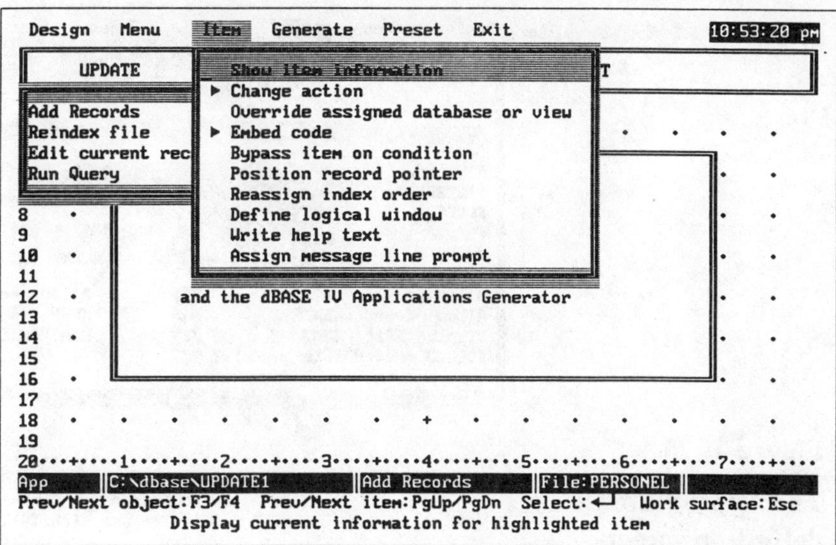

Figure 11-23

The Item menu.

shown in Figure 11-24. This menu provides you with additional options. The one you wish to select is Edit form. When this is selected, another definition screen is popped up. The Append/Edit definition screen is seen in Figure 11-25.

The FORMAT file you will be using is PERSONEL. You may

Figure 11-24

The Change action menu.

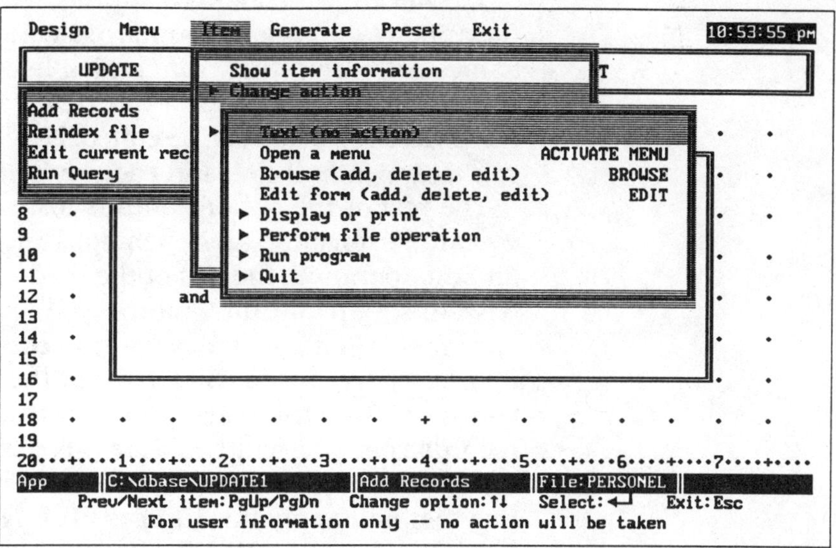

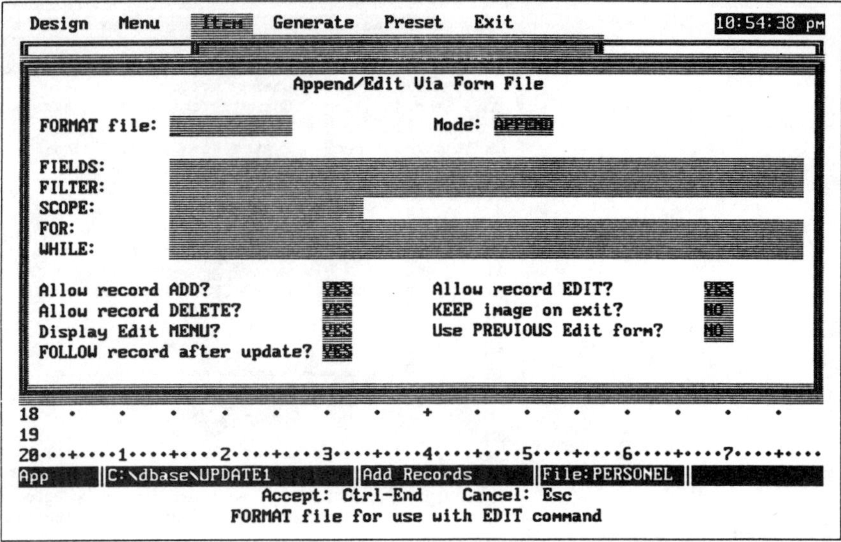

Figure 11-25

The Append/Edit definition screen.

type in the name of the file, or press **Shft-F1** to pop the list of forms files in the catalog onto the screen, and select the file by highlighting it and pressing **ENTER**.

The system will next offer a choice of modes, toggled by pressing the **Space Bar**. These choices are Edit and Append. Accept "Append" by highlighting it and pressing **ENTER**.

The next line, Fields, asks for the fields you want to include in the append operation. You may select fields by typing the field names or by selecting from a pick list that is brought onto the screen using the **Shft-F1** key. If fields are put on this line, only those fields selected can be edited. Leaving this line blank allows you to append all fields in each record. Leave this line blank.

The rest of the options on this form are not accessible when you are performing an Append operation. If you were to set up an Edit operation, the rest of the fields could be accessed. If you wish to set up an Edit window (you will probably do this for a later menu item), you may want to complete some of the other items. Briefly, this is what some of the options do. Filter allows you to specify a file, usually a query file, that is used to select the records that you will be editing. For example, you may have a query that selects all new employees. The command in the Filter line that will apply this filter is FILE NEWEMP (assuming that the query is called NEWEMP).

SCOPE, FOR, and WHILE allow you to specify how many files (for example, under *scope*, you may enter *all*) or conditions under *for* and *while* must be met for a record to be edited.

Allow record ADD tells the system whether files can be added to the database (or if the database can be edited, but not appended). Allow record DELETE lets you tell the system whether the user can mark records for deletion from the database. Both these options, and the ones that follow, are toggled between *Yes* and *No* by touching the **Space Bar**.

Display Edit menu tells the system whether to put the standard File Edit menu onto the screen. This menu is the one that is normally brought onto the screen when you Edit a file.

FOLLOW record after update, when set to *Yes*, places each new record into its correct position according to the active index. If, for example, you were adding records that were indexed on LAST__NAME and changed (or added) a record with a new last name (perhaps an employee just got married), the system would position the record in the correct alphabetic order. The next record to be viewed or edited would then be the record that is next in the alphabetic sort of last names in the database.

Allow record EDIT will allow the user to make changes to the database, as opposed to simply viewing but not modifying records.

KEEP image on exit sets the system to retain the image of the last Edit or Browse screen when the user leaves the Browse/Edit/Append function.

Finally, Use PREVIOUS Browse table tells the system whether to use the table that was designed or implemented in the previous Browse operation.

Although you can go into Edit mode and make changes to the other options, and then return to Append, the parameters in the bottom half of the screen will not be implemented unless you are in Edit mode.

To save the form,

Press: **Ctrl-End**

Additional options can be selected by highlighting the desired action (and possibly stepping through submenus) and completing the appropriate forms (if a form is required). To save the setting for this menu item,

Press: **Esc**

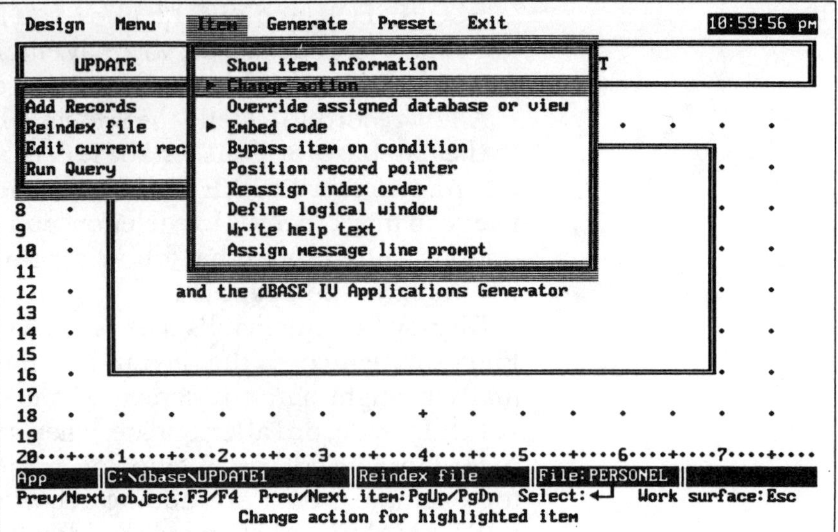

Figure 11-26

Change Action for Reindex file menu selection.

This will return you to the menu item to which you just assigned an action. Use the arrow keys to select the next menu item to be edited.

If you want to apply actions to other menu items from within the Item menu,

Press: **PgUp** (or **PgDn**)

You should notice the menu item name change in the bar in the middle of the information bar below the design screen. **PgUp** moves toward the first item in the menu currently being edited; **PgDn** moves toward the last item in the menu to which you are assigning actions.

To see how this works,

Press: **PgDn**

The menu item active should now be Reindex file. Select Change action. This will bring up the menu seen in Figure 11-26. Next, select Perform file operation to bring up the File operation menu, seen in Figure 11-27.

Highlight and select "Reindex." This will reindex all active index files for the current database. The system will also prompt you to acknowledge that this is OK.

Next, close the Item menu by pressing **Esc**. Then tell the system

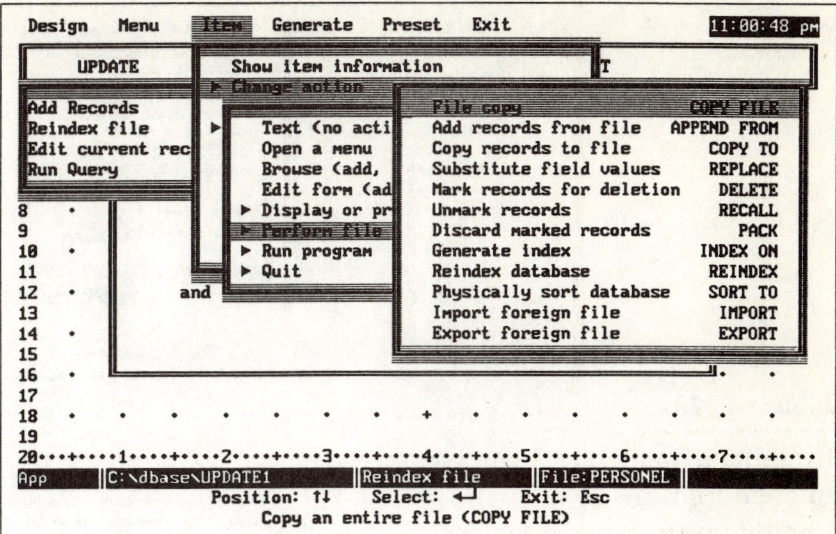

Figure 11-27

File operation menu.

to open the Update menu when the UPDATE item is selected by the user. To do this, press the **F3** or **F4** key until the main menu is brought to the front of the screen. Activate the Item menu and select Change action. Select Open a menu. This will bring up a menu selection window.

The menu you want to use is a Pop-up.

Press: **Space Bar**

until Pop-up is active on the screen. Next, tell the system which menu to activate by typing UPDATES in this line, or by pressing **Shft-F1** to bring up a pick list of all available Pop-up menus, from which you can select the appropriate one by highlighting and pressing **ENTER** (Figure 11-28).

To select this setting,

Press: **Ctrl-End**

Now that a minimal system that will pop up an Update menu and allow the user to append or reindex a file has been set up, you can generate the code to create this application. Bring up the Generate menu (Figure 11-29). The options available are Begin generating, Select template, and Display during generation. Display during generation tells the system whether to allow you to see the code on screen as it is generated.

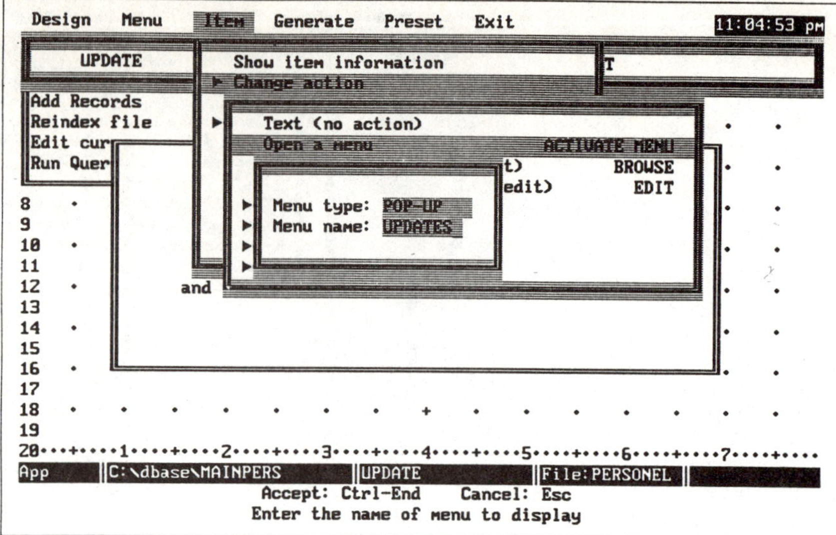

Figure 11-28

Defining a menu to open from the Update menu.

Select template is of most concern to developers and programmers (and may be available only in the Developer's Edition of dBASE IV). A template is a program that is used to generate code. In most cases, you will not want to change the template being used. If you are a programmer, you may have created your own custom

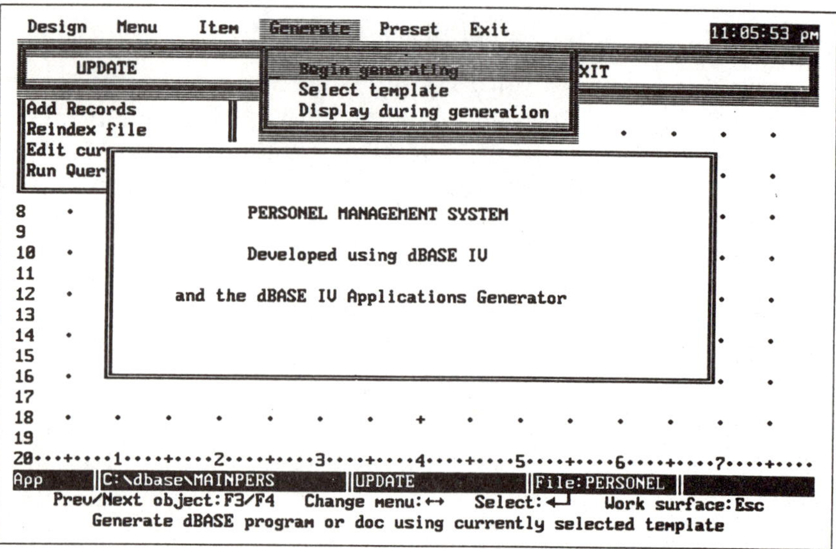

Figure 11-29

The Generate menu.

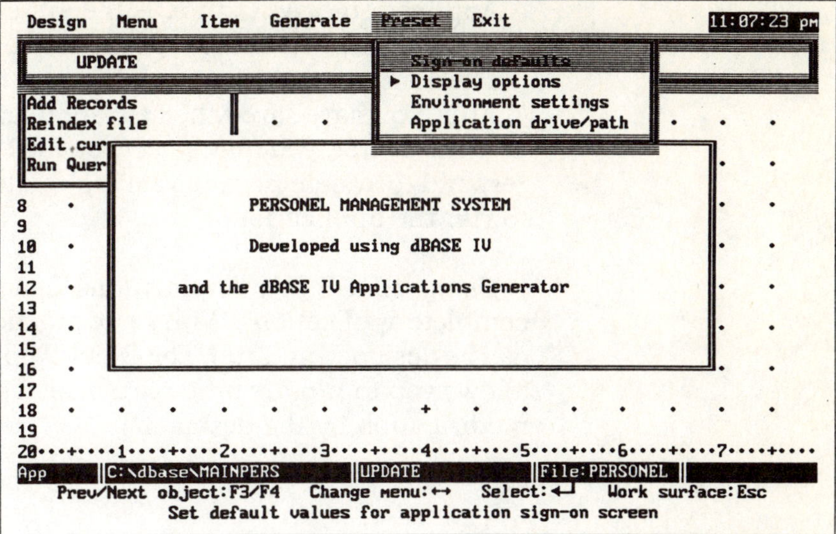

Figure 11-30

The Preset menu.

template for code generation. This option allows you to select another template for generating your application.

Finally, Begin generating tells the system to generate a program code for your application. The system will prompt you to respond *Yes* or *No* to begin generating the application.

By now, you have gone through most of the main menus in the Applications Generator. The final two, Exit and Preset, remain to be explained. The Preset menu is shown in Figure 11-30.

The Sign-on defaults allow you to edit the text of the sign-on screen that is displayed when the Application is first started.

Display options allow you to specify the colors for the text, boxes, messages, and fields. You are also able to select the border style for applications objects. (Typically, this refers to menus that are displayed on the screen during the application.) The border styles can be cycled using the **Space Bar**.

Once you have set your display options,

Press: **Ctrl-End**

to save the settings.

Environment settings tell the system how to handle certain options in running the program. These are explained in further detail in the appendix on SET options.

Application drive/path tells the system where to look for the application and the associated files to be used by the Application.

The Exit options have been discussed in previous chapters.

After you have saved the new application and returned to the Control Center, you may select the PERSONEL application and respond to system prompts asking you to confirm that you want to run the application.

Using dBASE IV's Applications Generator, you can generate complete applications. With some practice, complex applications can be designed and run. The Quick Applications Generator also allows you to rapidly produce a basic application with minimal modification by the designer.

Programming and Structured Query Language (SQL)

The focus of this book has been on making effective use of dBASE IV. We hope that the approach taken, exploring the use of the program through the Control Center, has been effective and has provided enough capability so that you can design, manage, and report on your data using only those tools available from within the Control Center.

Chapter 11 discussed the basics of application design. Through the use of the Quick Applications Generator, you developed a running, usable application. The relationship between menus and actions was explored and, we hope, made clear enough to enable you to develop your own applications.

Most of what you need to know to do useful work with dBASE IV has been covered thus far in this book. And most of what you need to do can be done through the Control Center.

On Programming

dBASE IV is the first version of dBASE that truly lets you design, build, and run database applications without being a database expert. The previous versions, including the much improved dBASE III+, still required a fair degree of programming knowledge and ability. Earlier versions of dBASE spawned an entire industry of add-on software products that automated or simplified many of the functions that can easily be performed from within the Control Center, in addition to creating a market for dBASE experts who had the fortitude and aptitude to learn and produce dBASE program code.

In dBASE IV, as well as earlier versions of dBASE, program instructions told the system how to do the things that you wanted to do to manage a database. With dBASE IV, program instructions are still used to control the design and operation of databases—special program templates that are part of the Control Center interpret the designs that you produce from within the individual design processors and generate code that the system uses to create your structures, reports, queries, and other components of your database.

Thus, although the Control Center can be considered a replacement for programming, it is not. Instead of having to write and debug a program, the system writes code for you, which (usually) needs no debugging. In some cases, the system goes one step further, producing machine code that talks directly to the dBASE IV database engine and provides faster performance than earlier versions of dBASE.

In earlier versions of dBASE, the most commonly used user interface was the Dot Prompt. Basically, this is a blank screen, with a dot in the lower left corner. As you write or edit lines of program code, the system scrolls the old text up the screen and adds new program instructions at the bottom.

Each of the forms that you designed—the Report form, the Label form, the Query form, and even the Forms form—produced program routines that the system used to create code that dBASE IV uses to quickly implement your instructions. In an application, these routines are often linked together, with each specific program routine called up and loaded into the system when the particular routine is required by the application.

When a program is written, it used specific functions and commands that tell the system to do specific things. By stringing together the commands, function calls, and other components of a program, dBASE IV is instructed to carry out specific operations.

There are a number of ways to write a program or to see how a program is written. To see how a program is written, and to see two of the ways to access a program that was already generated by a forms generator in the Control Center, you will be looking at the program file called PERSONEL.FMT.

The first way to view and edit the program is to access it through the Control Center. To do this, move the cursor to the Applications column and select <create>. A window asking whether you want

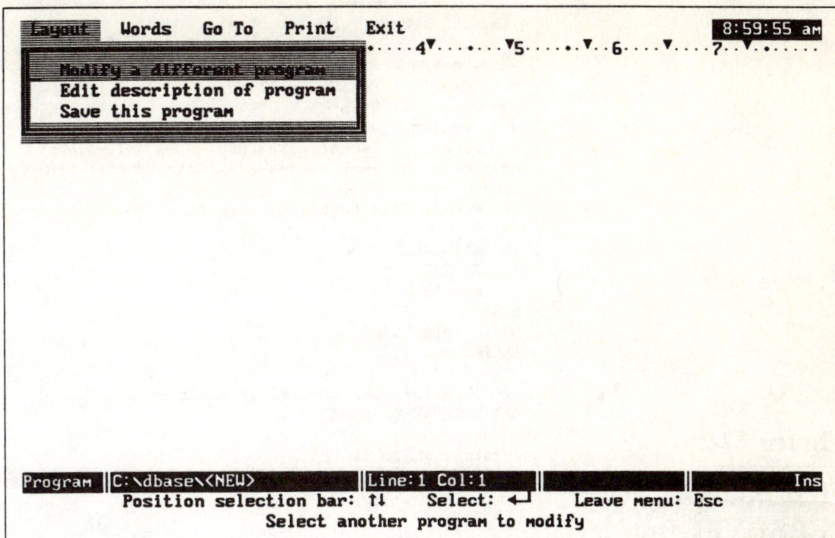

Figure 12-1

The Layout menu for dBASE programs.

a dBASE program or the Applications Generator will pop onto the screen. Select dBASE program. The system will bring up a blank editing screen. To load a program for viewing or editing, activate the Layout menu. To do this,

Press: **Alt-l**

The blank editing screen and the Layout menu are shown in Figure 12-1.

Select Modify a different program. The system will prompt for the name of a program to modify. If you press **Shft-F1**, the system will bring up only .PRG (program) files. You can, however, load other files and certain text files. For example, if you wanted to modify your CONFIG.DB file (which tells the system about some of the default setups used when you load dBASE IV), you can type in the name of the file that you want to modify, and the system will load it.

In this case,

Type: ***personel.fmt*** **ENTER**

The system will bring up the first 20 lines of PERSONEL.FMT (Figure 12-2). You will notice commented information at the top of the program. Lines preceded by the asterisk are treated by the system as comments, rather than program instructions.

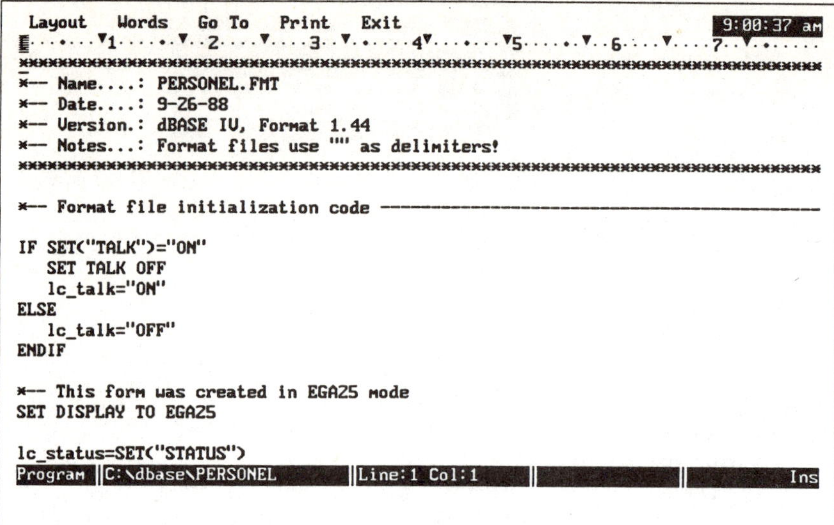


```
********************************************************************
*-- Name....: PERSONEL.FMT
*-- Date....: 9-26-88
*-- Version.: dBASE IV, Format 1.44
*-- Notes...: Format files use "" as delimiters!
********************************************************************

*-- Format file initialization code ---------------------------------

IF SET("TALK")="ON"
   SET TALK OFF
   lc_talk="ON"
ELSE
   lc_talk="OFF"
ENDIF

*-- This form was created in EGA25 mode
SET DISPLAY TO EGA25

lc_status=SET("STATUS")
```


Figure 12-2

First lines of PERSONEL.fmt.

Although the actual steps involved in writing a program are thoroughly discussed in numerous books, and the new Control Center allows you to design the features that the system automatically converts to programs, it is useful to point out some of the components of this and many, typical programs.

The first lines are the program header. Although this is optional, it is a good practice to put this information at the top of your file so that you can identify it if you ever wanted to review or debug the program.

The next line, and many places throughout the program, have comment lines describing the process that follows. For example, the line with the comment Format file initialization code tells you (or anyone else viewing this program file) that the following routine will initialize the format file.

The next set of instructions does just that. It also points out a common structure used in many dBASE programs, IF.. ELSE..ENDIF. This logical expression actually means this: If the conditions that follow the *IF* expression are *true*, perform the operation in the following line(s). If they are not true (*ELSE*), perform the function(s) in the subsequent lines. Whichever function is being performed, the conditional statement is concluded by the *ENDIF* statement.

In this example, if the TALK option is set to *on*, the system will reset this option to *off*. It will also set lc_talk to *on*. If the TALK is not set to *on* (the *ELSE* condition), lc_talk will be set to *off*. Clearly, a different setting for lc_talk is made, depending on whether TALK was on when the expression was evaluated. This is because lc_talk is a memory variable set by the program and is used to store the value (*on* or *off*) of TALK. For the program to run properly, TALK must be *off*. However, the program is designed so that it restores TALK to its original state (*on* or *off*) when the program is concluded. When the program finishes executing, it checks the value of lc_talk to see if it is *on* or *off*. This variable (lc_talk) stored the value of TALK, and the value for this variable is used to reset TALK at the end of program execution, as you will see a little later.

A more basic logical operator is IF..ENDIF, seen below the TALK logical expression. The STATUS operator is set to *on* regardless of whether it was preset to *on*. The IF statement works as follows. IF the logical argument is true (in this case, if STATUS [or lc_status, a function that reads the STATUS setting] is *off*), the next line (which sets STATUS *on*) will be implemented. If STATUS is already *on*, the next line (which sets STATUS *on*) is skipped, because there is no need to change this setting. The ENDIF command ends the logical operation.

Note that IF..ELSE..ENDIF and IF..ENDIF arguments can be nested inside other arguments. The innermost arguments are evaluated first, followed by the next argument in order, until the entire expression is evaluated.

A little farther down, the windows and input formats are developed, as seen in Figure 12-3. In the first line of the setup, @ 1,0 SAY " ______________________ (to the end of the line)," the @ 1,0 expression tells the system *where* in the window to perform the following function. SAY tells the system to print the contents of the data that follow, in this case, the part enclosed by quotation marks (a solid line is painted on the screen). This corresponds to the top line of the PERSONEL form previously designed.

The next line, @ 2,30 SAY "Employee Data Form" COLOR n/w, tells the system to print the words Employee Data Form at column 30 to line 2. In addition to displaying the words, the COLOR n/w tells the system what *color* to give to the characters. The argument n/w tells the system to use *black* (with dBASE IV, *n* means black) letters on a white (*w*) background.

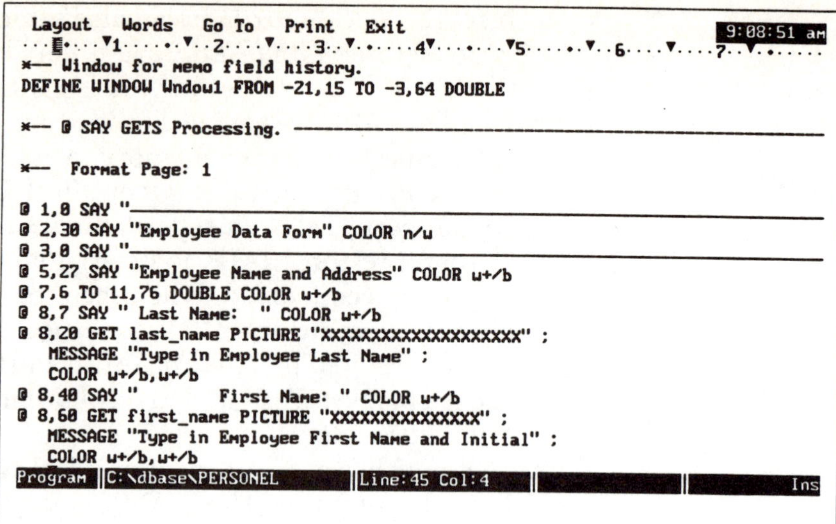

```
Layout   Words   Go To   Print   Exit                                9:08:51 am
*— Window for memo field history.
DEFINE WINDOW Wndow1 FROM -21,15 TO -3,64 DOUBLE

*— @ SAY GETS Processing. ——————————————————————————————

*—  Format Page: 1

@ 1,0 SAY "————————————————————————————————————
@ 2,30 SAY "Employee Data Form" COLOR n/w
@ 3,0 SAY "————————————————————————————————————
@ 5,27 SAY "Employee Name and Address" COLOR w+/b
@ 7,6 TO 11,76 DOUBLE COLOR w+/b
@ 8,7 SAY " Last Name:  " COLOR w+/b
@ 8,20 GET last_name PICTURE "XXXXXXXXXXXXXXXXXXXX" ;
   MESSAGE "Type in Employee Last Name" ;
   COLOR w+/b,w+/b
@ 8,40 SAY "         First Name: " COLOR w+/b
@ 8,60 GET first_name PICTURE "XXXXXXXXXXXXXXX" ;
   MESSAGE "Type in Employee First Name and Initial" ;
   COLOR w+/b,w+/b
Program  C:\dbase\PERSONEL       Line:45 Col:4                          Ins
```

Figure 12-3

Beginning of code defining Window and Input formats.

Still farther down the form, the system begins to specify the lines of a box. The statement @7,6 to 11,76 DOUBLE COLOR w+/b says to draw a box with double lines, beginning at row 7, column 6, and ending at row 11, column 76. Further, the lines will be bright white (*w*+) against a blue (*b*) background.

In the next two lines, note that "Last Name" is enclosed by quotes. This tells the system to print the text enclosed by the quotes onto the screen. The next line says to GET LAST_NAME, telling it to insert the contents of the field LAST_NAME (or to put what is typed into that field into the current record) for the record being viewed (or edited) at row 8, column 20. The PICTURE function provides a template for the input of a response.

Altogether, five lines of instructions are used to prompt for and fill in the contents of this line, in addition to specifying the colors of the text and background.

This form is composed mainly of screen painting instructions. By scanning through this file, you can fairly easily get a feel for the instructions used to design the form. At the end of the file, you will see the Format file exit code, shown in Figure 12-4. This code will show why the lc_status settings were different, depending on the original STATUS setting when the form was first loaded.

lc_status was a memory variable created when the form was

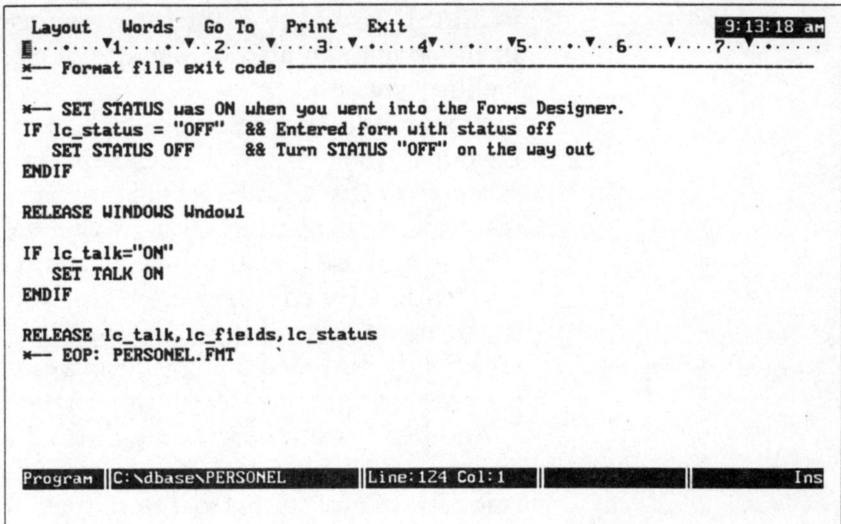

```
Layout   Words   Go To   Print   Exit                                    9:13:18 am
*— Format file exit code ————————————————————————————————————

*— SET STATUS was ON when you went into the Forms Designer.
IF lc_status = "OFF"   && Entered form with status off
   SET STATUS OFF      && Turn STATUS "OFF" on the way out
ENDIF

RELEASE WINDOWS Wndow1

IF lc_talk="ON"
   SET TALK ON
ENDIF

RELEASE lc_talk, lc_fields, lc_status
*— EOP: PERSONEL.FMT

Program ||C:\dbase\PERSONEL        ||Line:124 Col:1 ||          ||          Ins
```

Figure 12-4

Format file exit code, code to end program.

loaded, the purpose of which was to remember the original setting of STATUS. The setting of the lc_status had no impact on the way the code was generated, or on the code generated. However, when you quit the procedure, you want to reset STATUS as it was before the screen was activated. This is done using an IF expression. You will recall that the STATUS was set on after it was tested and lc_status set. Until the system gets to this IF, the STATUS is on.

When the system encounters IF lc_status = "OFF," the next line turns STATUS back off. If lc_status was *on*, the system jumps to the ENDIF line and proceeds without changing the STATUS (which was, and still is, *on*). Finally, the system resets the windows, releases the temporary memory variables (lc_talk, lc_fields, and lc_status) from memory, and stops operating.

From this example and others that you can easily call up and examine, you can see the steps and commands involved in programming in dBASE IV, although we hope you seldom have to. The Control Center is designed to assist in developing applications without the necessity of dot prompt programming.

By studying the examples that you have created, in addition those shipped with dBASE IV, and possibly programs already used by your company, you should gain some insight into programming in dBASE. In addition, the functions and *set* commands included in this book can also be used to design applications that work well for you.

From within the program editing window, you may also use the Layout window to edit the description of the program, as well as save the program, under its current name or a new name. You may want to take a routine, such as the one already loaded into the system, and use it as the basis of a similar procedure in another application. By editing the existing form, changing the name of the form, and possibly modifying some fields or colors, you can rename the form, add a new description, and easily create a new program (or procedure) for your other applications.

Another advantage to using this editor is the ability to import or export text files, to automatically indent (this is required inside certain procedures to differentiate them from commands that call the procedure—see the second and later lines of any IF command sequence), and to quickly move to desired lines or text in your program. Further, your program can be directed to a printer to be reviewed, studied, and, if needed, debugged. In addition, the program can be saved on exit and quickly loaded back into the editor for modification. The Exit menu allows you two options in addition to the standard Save and Abandon, as can be seen in Figure 12-5.

The two new options are Run program and Debug program. When you select Run program, the system converts the instructions into code that dBASE IV can execute, and the program is run. In doing this make sure that all necessary files are already activated or the program will not run. For example, if you tried to run PERSONEL.FMT with no data file active, the system will not be able to run PERSONEL.FMT, because it does not know which database file to display. Debug program is used primarily by developers and those familiar with dBASE programming. When this option is selected, the system prompts for debug parameters. Debugging of dBASE programs is beyond the scope of this book.

A second way to write or modify a program is from within the dot prompt. To get to the dot prompt from within the Control Center,

Press: **Alt-E**

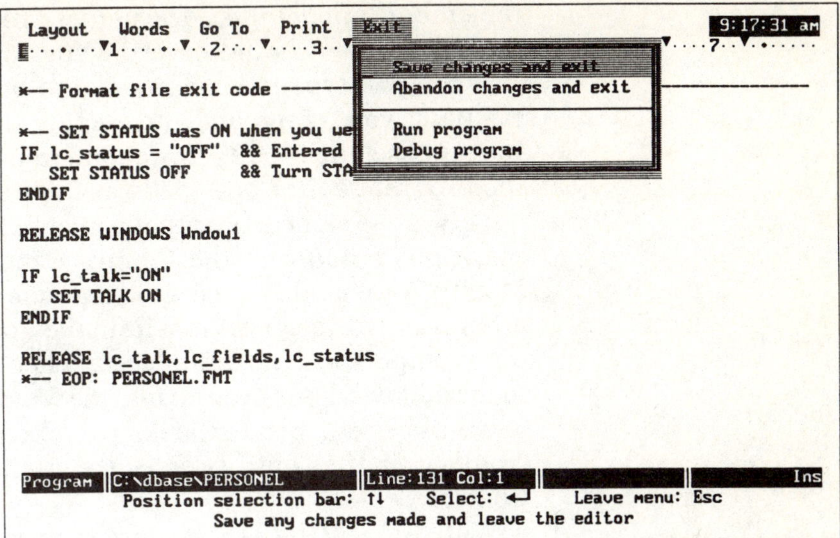

Figure 12-5

Program design Exit window.

to bring up the Exit menu, and select Exit to dot prompt. The system will then bring you out of the Control Center and into the dot prompt. Although you can also get to the dot prompt by pressing **Esc** and confirming that you want to abandon your operation, this method may bring you into the dot prompt, but without the data file that you loaded in the Control Center being active. Thus, if you wanted to work on a file that you made active in the Control Center, you must use the proper form of exit (from the Exit menu) to go to the dot prompt.

To edit or create a new program from within the dot prompt, use the command MODI COMM (or MODIFY COMMAND), followed by the name of the file that you want to edit or create. For example, to edit the file called PERSONEL.FMT,

Type: *MODI COMM PERSONEL.FMT*

The case of the letters (upper, lower, or mixed) does not matter when typing a dBASE IV instruction. In addition, MODI COMM and MODIFY COMMAND are equivalent in dBASE IV, because the program's command interpreter recognizes only the first four characters of a command and ignores the rest of the command word. Experienced programmers quickly learn to drop any character beyond the fourth in a command to the system. (Also remember that *complete* file names are used by the system, and that file names should never be cut down to four characters.)

When you type the command and press **ENTER**, the system evaluates your command and executes the function you request. In this case, the Modify Command (modi comm) function loads the program editor and loads in the file Personel.fmt.

This is the same editor that you activated from within the Applications column in the Control Center. Thus, in the case of Modify Command, there is little difference in actual function from attempting to design from within the Control Center or from the dot prompt. The main difference is when you complete the editing in the edit window. If you go into the window from the dot prompt, you will be returned to the dot prompt. If the window is opened from within the Control Center, the cursor will be returned to the Control Center.

With dBASE IV, dBASE programmers will have much less need to do programming from within the dot prompt. In fact, they may not be able to easily design (or use) special routines that were available to them in earlier versions of dBASE. For example, to design screen displays (forms design), the programmer may now use a command called CREATE SCREEN. This brings up the screen design module that is part of dBASE IV's new forms design module. Other *create* options load the label, query, application, report, and View modules.

In earlier versions of dBASE, programmers may have designed their own modules that allowed them to design screens or forms. In dBASE IV, the system automatically loads the new design modules that are included as part of the program. Experienced programmers, or those users who do not want to use the Control Center, may load the modules using the *create* or *modify* commands.

From within the dot prompt, a number of functions are preassigned to the function keys. These were briefly discussed earlier in this book, and are repeated here.

The **F1** key brings up the HELP menu. In dBASE IV, the help functions are very extensive and should prove to be an excellent resource (in addition to programming manuals and programming guides) for the operation of dBASE IV from within the dot prompt. The **F1** key also works from within the Control Center. Function keys other than **F1** may perform differently in the Control Center than in dot prompt programming. This section covers the functions from within the dot prompt.

The **F2** key issues the command Assist, followed by **ENTER**. This command loads the Control Center.

F3 lists the contents of your active database. To see how this works,

Type: *use personel* **ENTER**

The system will load PERSONEL as the active database. Now,

Press: **F3**

The system will list the field names, then record number and field contents, as seen in Figure 12-6. If you used a smaller data design, perhaps one with only first name, last name, and employee number, the screen would have a much more readable table of data.

F4 provides you with a directory of database files. You may also type the command DIR, followed by the parameters that you want to look for. Without specifying directory parameters (for example, *.*), the system will show only database files. When directory parameters are provided, the DIR function acts as it would if this were a DOS command.

Figure 12-6

F3 used to display contents of active database.

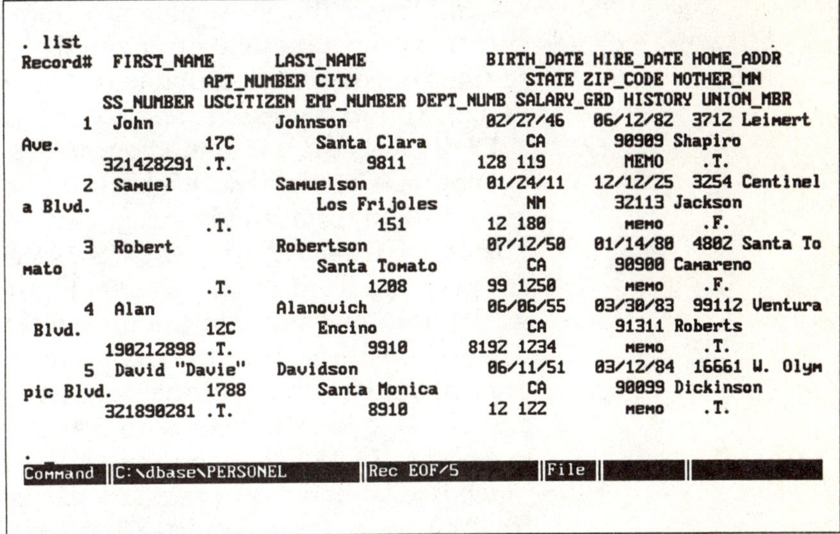

```
. list
Record#  FIRST_NAME       LAST_NAME              BIRTH_DATE HIRE_DATE HOME_ADDR
                APT_NUMBER CITY                    STATE ZIP_CODE MOTHER_MN
        SS_NUMBER USCITIZEN EMP_NUMBER DEPT_NUMB SALARY_GRD HISTORY UNION_MBR
      1  John             Johnson                02/27/46   06/12/82  3712 Leimert
Ave.            17C        Santa Clara             CA       90909 Shapiro
        321428291 .T.               9811       128 119       MEMO    .T.
      2  Samuel           Samuelson              01/24/11   12/12/25  3254 Centinel
a Blvd.                    Los Frijoles            NM       32113 Jackson
                  .T.               151        12 180        memo    .F.
      3  Robert           Robertson              07/12/50   01/14/80  4802 Santa To
mato                       Santa Tomato            CA       90900 Camareno
                  .T.               1208       99 1250       memo    .F.
      4  Alan             Alanovich              06/06/55   03/30/83  99112 Ventura
 Blvd.          12C        Encino                  CA       91311 Roberts
        190212898 .T.               9910     8192 1234       memo    .T.
      5  David "Davie"    Davidson               06/11/51   03/12/84  16661 W. Olym
pic Blvd.       1788       Santa Monica            CA       90099 Dickinson
        321890281 .T.               8910       12 122        memo    .T.

.
Command  C:\dbase\PERSONEL     Rec EOF/5     File
```

```
Structure for database: C:\DBASE\PERSONEL.DBF
Number of data records:       5
Date of last update    : 10/02/88
Field  Field Name  Type        Width    Dec    Index
    1  FIRST_NAME  Character      15               N
    2  LAST_NAME   Character      20               Y
    3  BIRTH_DATE  Date            8               Y
    4  HIRE_DATE   Date            8               Y
    5  HOME_ADDR   Character      30               N
    6  APT_NUMBER  Character       6               N
    7  CITY        Character      20               N
    8  STATE       Character       2               Y
    9  ZIP_CODE    Numeric         5               Y
   10  MOTHER_MN   Character      20               N
   11  SS_NUMBER   Numeric        11               N
   12  USCITIZEN   Logical         1               N
   13  EMP_NUMBER  Numeric         4               Y
   14  DEPT_NUMB   Numeric         4               Y
   15  SALARY_GRD  Character       4               Y
   16  HISTORY     Memo           10               N
   17  UNION_MBR   Logical         1               N
Press any key to continue..._
Command ||C:\dbase\PERSONEL        ||Rec EOF/5        ||File ||
```

Figure 12-7

Active database structure, retrieved with F5 key.

F5 displays the structure of your database file. It also tells how many records the file contains and when it was last updated. The first screen of output for PERSONEL.DBF is seen in Figure 12-7. As with the other preprogrammed keys, you could have obtained the same result if you had typed *DISPLAY STRUCTURE* **ENTER**.

F6 enters the command DISPLAY STATUS **ENTER**. This causes the system to display multiple screens of information about the system. It lists the active database, index tags, and a number of system parameters that are currently in use. It also displays the settings for the programmable function keys (one of which, the **F6** key, you just pressed), as seen in Figure 12-8.

F7 displays the use of memory in the current system. This information is primarily useful to programmers who must be concerned about the use and management of limited system memory. This is particularly true with DOS versions of dBASE IV, because the program itself takes up so much memory to run. Although Ashton-Tate insisted that the program's memory requirements would drop by the time the final product was released, a very late preproduction version of the program still had trouble loading and running on a system with 640 kilobytes of memory. This makes it difficult to develop any extensive applications that make much use of memory or memory variables. It is hoped that the final, shipped version of dBASE IV provides adequate available memory to run useful applications. (This can be quickly checked

```
Number of files open =     6
Current work area =    1

ALTERNATE  - OFF  DELIMITERS - OFF  FULLPATH   - OFF  SAFETY     - ON
AUTOSAVE   - OFF  DESIGN     - ON   HEADING    - ON   SCOREBOARD - ON
BELL       - ON   DEVELOP    - ON   HELP       - ON   SPACE      - ON
CARRY      - OFF  DEVICE     - SCRN HISTORY    - ON   SQL        - OFF
CATALOG    - OFF  ECHO       - OFF  INSTRUCT   - ON   STATUS     - ON
CENTURY    - OFF  ENCRYPTION - ON   INTENSITY  - ON   STEP       - OFF
CONFIRM    - OFF  ESCAPE     - ON   LOCK       - ON   TALK       - ON
CONSOLE    - ON   EXACT      - OFF  NEAR       - OFF  TITLE      - ON
DEBUG      - OFF  EXCLUSIVE  - OFF  PAUSE      - OFF  TRAP       - OFF
DELETED    - OFF  FIELDS     - OFF  PRINT      - OFF  UNIQUE     - OFF

Programmable function keys:
F2        - assist;
F3        - list;
F4        - dir;
F5        - display structure;
F6        - display status;
F7        - display memory;
Press any key to continue..._
Command  ||C:\dbase\PERSONEL         ||Rec EOF/5        ||File ||
```

Figure 12-8

Programmable function keys, system settings, using F6.

from within the dot prompt programming area by pressing **F7**, in addition to some other tests not included here.)

The **F8** key enters the command DISPLAY **ENTER**. This command displays the structure of the active data file and the first record in that file. It is similar to LIST, except that it displays only a single file, while LIST displays all files in a database.

F9 brings up the Append menu. If you have a database that is already active, pressing the **F9** key brings up the Edit screen, and brings the user to a blank file at the end of the database.

F10 loads the Edit menu. This menu brings up the Edit screen and positions the cursor into an existing record in the database. Pressing **F2** toggles between Browse and Edit. The **F2** key toggle also works when Append is selected.

It should be clear from the examples provided that much of the functionality available from within the Control Center has migrated down into the programming environment. Conversely, many of the programming functions (and, indeed, many of the more time-consuming design aspects of programming) have found their way into the Control Center.

The approach of this book takes advantage of the functionality of the Control Center without having to do dot prompt programming. Although some functions and procedures are available only within the dot prompt, for most users' needs the Control Center should be more than adequate.

On Structured Query Language (SQL)

Structured Query Language is a method of relational database management originally developed in the last decade by IBM. The language is used on mainframe computers and many minicomputers. By using the language on compatible systems, the user can rapidly retrieve the needed information from the system.

Elements of SQL have been incorporated into a few microcomputer software products, with SQL an announced feature of future products as well. For example, Paradox, a database program from Borland International, includes (or will soon include) a version that works with SQL. Microsoft, Sybase, and Ashton-Tate are jointly developing a product called SQL Server that will work with networked versions of OS/2. Additional software companies have also announced that they will support SQL in future products. SQL will probably have an impact on microcomputers in two areas.

First, as a universal method of designing and retrieving data from different databases, SQL could prove extremely useful. This capability would be somewhat analogous to the current import and export functions in dBASE IV and most available database and spreadsheet software.

With a relatively uniform structure built using SQL rules, it is conceivable that a query written using one database or other program could retrieve data from another database program that supports SQL queries. Thus, in theory at least, a query written using SQL on dBASE IV could retrieve data from a database running under Paradox, and vice versa. A problem arises from assuming that this approach will always work. In addition, the initial implementation of SQL in dBASE IV is not SQL at all—rather, it uses an interpreter that converts SQL commands into dBASE commands (and the two do not always exactly correlate).

In addition to the use of SQL as a data bridge between microcomputer databases, one of the primary perceived uses of SQL is to allow microcomputers access to large databases that reside on mainframe computers. To this end, the implementation of SQL in dBASE IV is claimed to be fully compatible with the IBM mainframe database language, DB2.

In networked versions of dBASE IV, this will allow much of the data querying and analysis to be done on the microcomputer running dBASE IV, rather than on the mainframe running DB2. To explain further, consider the situation before dBASE IV, with its ability to develop compatible SQL queries. A user would be connected to the mainframe, running DB2, via a computer terminal. Typically, the mainframe computer is serving dozens or, in many cases, hundreds of users. Each user is vying for time on the computer. The data analyst who is hooked into such a network must design the queries and all other data management-related operations while connected on-line (either directly connected or via a bridge or other mechanism for communicating with the mainframe). Each time a line of code is written, each instruction sent to the computer is competing for time on the mainframe.

After a query is designed and the mainframe generates the data asked for by the terminal, the data operator must continue to use mainframe time analyzing the data. Much of the query design and data analysis can be done on a microcomputer. With dBASE IV and other SQL-generating products, a query can be designed and refined using dBASE IV and, once the query is completed, can (in theory, at least) be sent over the network to the mainframe. The mainframe in this instance is able to manage an extremely large database and can retrieve the desired data more rapidly than can a microcomputer with its slower processing speed and smaller disk capacities.

Once the data are retrieved and sent back to the terminal that made the query (in this case, a microcomputer on the network, running SQL), the data can be stored in that computer. Further analysis of the data retrieved from the mainframe can be done on the microcomputer using dBASE IV.

Thus, the process of developing a query and the later stages of evaluating the data retrieved from the mainframe's database can be done entirely on the microcomputer. This gives more power to the microcomputer user, frees the mainframe for other tasks, and maintains the integrity of the mainframe database, because data are retrieved but not necessarily modified by the microcomputer user.

As a method for data entry, a system can be designed to allow the user to do data entry and updates on a PC, and then append the new data to the mainframe. SQL compatibility allows for data entry and transfer to DB2 or other SQL-compatible databases.

As a platform for future links between the increasingly capable microcomputers and mainframes, SQL appears to offer a great deal of promise. However, in Ashton-Tate's initial implementation of SQL, the actual connections are much more limited. In fact, in the initial release of dBASE IV, there were no connections between the program and an SQL server. The SQL implementation was primarily for practice developing SQL queries, or to make dBASE IV more accessible to experienced SQL programmers.

dBASE IV includes a special mode for running SQL. This is accessed from the dot prompt. To start dBASE IV's SQL processor, Exit to dot prompt and

Type: *SET SQL ON* **ENTER**

The dot prompt will be replaced by an SQL. prompt that indicates that the SQL mode is active (Figure 12-9).

When SQL is active, you will be able to perform all data management functions that standard SQL allows. In addition, dBASE IV allows the use of specific dBASE commands for use within the SQL processing mode.

Before further discussion of SQL, however, it is important to detail a conceptual difference in terminology in dBASE IV and SQL. dBASE IV database files are made up of fields and records. SQL databases are made up of tables. An SQL table is equivalent to a dBASE data file. An SQL database is roughly equivalent to

Figure 12-9

SQL processor activated.

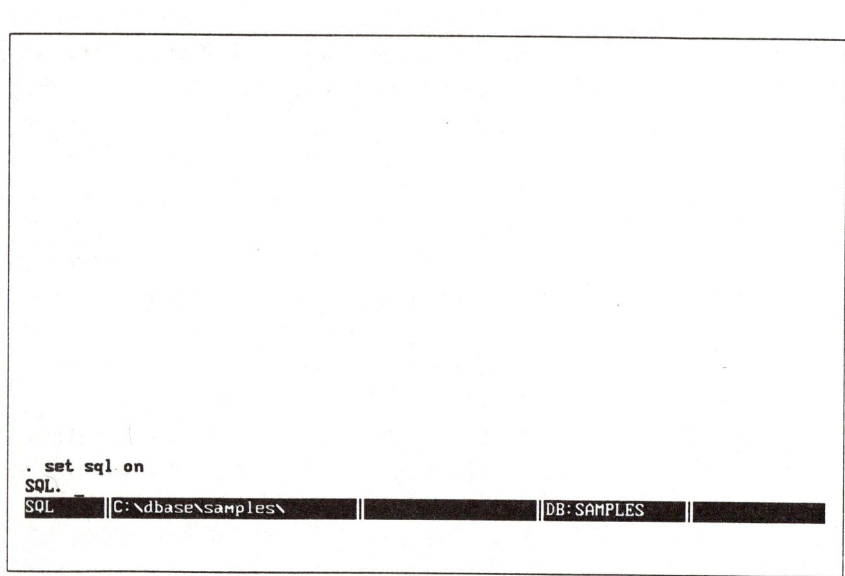

a dBASE catalog, being made up of related database files. Each SQL table consists of rows and columns. An SQL row correlates to a *record*, whereas a column represents what, in dBASE IV, would be called a field. Conceptualizing an SQL table, we could easily see a dBASE IV browse table, with the row and column labels substituting for records and fields.

When an SQL query is designed, the system looks through its tables of data and creates a new, temporary table that contains the data that meet the conditions of the query. This is similar to what happens when you write a query to show information that matches the query criteria.

Compared with dBASE IV, SQL uses fewer commands, yet provides more relational power. One example is SQL's ability to reflect changes in one table in other related tables. For example, in an accounting system, you may have a data table that contained parts on hand and another table that contained customer orders. The customer order table would relate to the parts on hand table to make sure that there were enough parts to fill the order. Until each part in the customer's order is shipped, it is listed on the table as a back-ordered item. A third table would track parts shipped. Once the parts of an order are shipped, the number of parts back ordered is reduced by the number shipped; the number shipped to the customer is updated, and the number of parts available is reduced by the number of parts shipped. All this is done automatically in SQL. Multiple steps would be required to achieve similar functionality in dBASE IV.

To stop the SQL processor,

Type: *Set SQL off* **ENTER**

Structured Query Language truly is a structured language. It consists of a substantially smaller number of commands than those used to program dBASE IV.

Microcomputer database experts and analysts agree, however, that SQL will probably *not* become a significant factor in microcomputer databases. The belief is that the end user or developer should not have to learn SQL to retrieve data from a mainframe or other computer that uses SQL commands.

An approach taken by Borland, International in future releases of its database products will probably have some impact on the future path of dBASE IV. Borland is taking an approach that provides a series of processors that can take a query written using the Paradox (or other) query facilities and write a series of SQL commands that will let the system talk to the computer that runs SQL. The process of SQL code generation is done automatically by the system (in much the same way that the Control Center writes dBASE code). It will not be necessary to learn SQL—in fact, the user may not even know that SQL is being used to communicate with the other computer.

This seems like a very sensible approach. The use of SQL, then, will probably be fairly limited. In addition, Ashton-Tate may also have to develop some similar SQL code generator if the Borland approach encroaches on dBASE IV's market share.

Because SQL is well covered by the HELP system inside dBASE IV and the focus of this book is on building and running systems without programming, the commands and actual programming of SQL will not be discussed further.

When future versions of dBASE IV actually provide bidirectional support for structured query language, allowing the system to recognize and operate on SQL commands produced by other systems, as well as generating code that can be sent to other systems, the elements of SQL programming may be added to revisions of this book. No such capabilities were designed in initial versions of dBASE IV.

APPENDIX

Fine-Tuning and Other Goodies

Throughout this book, you have been shown how to use dBASE IV. Little was done to automate the program or to match it more closely to your needs. This Appendix explores some of the tricks that can be used to more closely match dBASE IV to your particular needs or work style.

Optimizing Your Screen Display

The examples shown throughout the book were created using EGA in 25-line mode. This mode was used because its appearance more closely approximates that of most other display adapters (CGA, MDA, HERCULES) than the 43-line EGA mode. However, if you are using an EGA adapter and monitor, you may prefer to use the 43-line display option. The 43-line screen provides more information than the standard 25-line display and is shown in Figure A-1. This may be the display mode of choice, if you have an EGA or VGA display system.

There are a few ways that you can get the 43-line display to work within dBASE IV. If you're using a 25-line display and want to temporarily use the 43-line mode, activate the Tools menu (by pressing **Alt-T**). Next select Settings.

The Settings menu allows you to modify options that are in effect during your work session. From within this menu, you can also change the Display parameters. If you use an EGA display, you may toggle between 25- and 43-line modes using the **Space Bar** or **ENTER** key.

Settings can be saved using the Exit menu, which returns you to the Control Center.

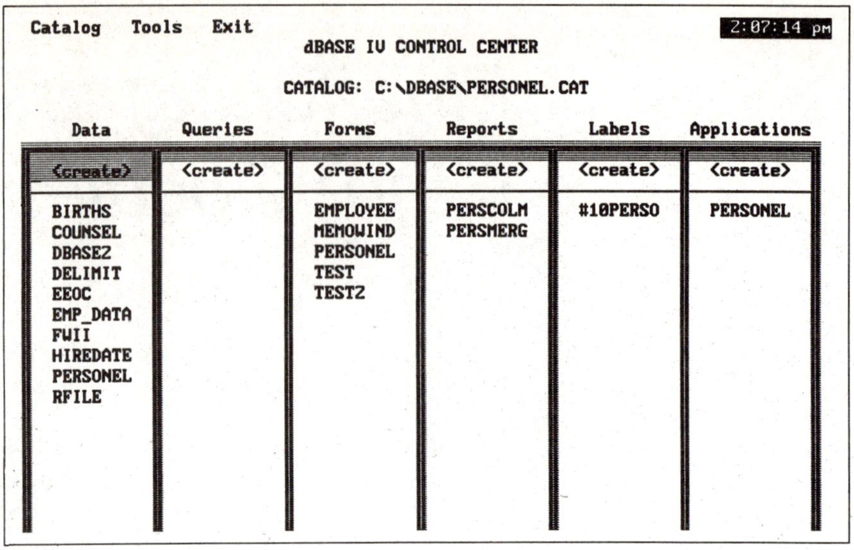

```
Catalog   Tools   Exit                                          2:07:14 pm
                          dBASE IV CONTROL CENTER

                       CATALOG: C:\DBASE\PERSONEL.CAT

   Data        Queries      Forms       Reports      Labels     Applications
 <create>     <create>     <create>    <create>     <create>     <create>

 BIRTHS                    EMPLOYEE    PERSCOLM     #10PERSO     PERSONEL
 COUNSEL                   MEMOWIND    PERSMERG
 DBASE2                    PERSONEL
 DELIMIT                   TEST
 EEOC                      TEST2
 EMP_DATA
 FWII
 HIREDATE
 PERSONEL
 RFILE
```

Figure A-1

You can also make your changes by modifying the CONFIG.DB file from within the DBSETUP program, or by editing the CONFIG.DB file, using the program editor (discussed in Chapter 12) or a text editor. The CONFIG.DB file contains the configuration information that dBASE IV reads when it first loads the program and that tells it how to set up the program on your system.

Modifying CONFIG.DB

As mentioned above, CONFIG.DB can be modified from within dBASE IV using the Applications function's dBASE Program editor (or with the same editor loaded using Modify Command and the DOS prompt). More on this in Chapter 12.

CONFIG.DB, as set up by the Install program you used when you installed dBASE IV, should look something like Figure A-2. There will be differences in a number of areas, including the printer names and printer drivers, unless you are using the same printers as those specified during setup. And the setup date will be the date that you installed dBASE IV or modified CONFIG.DB, and *not* the date shown in this sample screen.

You may use a text editor to modify the contents of any line in the file, but you should be careful if taking this approach that

```
 Layout   Words   Go To   Print   Exit                                    2:36:23 pm
[.....▼1.....▼..2....▼....3..▼......4▼.......▼5......▼..6....▼....7..▼......

*
*       dBASE IV Configuration File
*       Friday September 16, 1988
*

COLOR OF NORMAL       = W+/B
COLOR OF HIGHLIGHT    = GR+/BG
COLOR OF MESSAGES     = W/N
COLOR OF TITLES       = W/B
COLOR OF BOX          = GR+/BG
COLOR OF INFORMATION  = B/W
COLOR OF FIELDS       = N/BG
COMMAND               = ASSIST
DISPLAY               = EGA25
PDRIVER               = HPLAS100.PR2
PRINTER 1             = HPLAS100.PR2 NAME "Hewlett-Packard LaserJet 100 dpi graph
PRINTER 2             = IBMGP.PR2 NAME "IBM Graphics Printer" DEVICE LPT1
SQLDATABASE           = SAMPLES
SQLHOME               = C:\DBASE\SQLHOME
STATUS                = ON
```

Figure A-2

you enter values that make sense to the system. For example, changing the Display line from EGA25 to EGA30 confuses the system, because it supports only 25- and 43-line EGA display modes.

If you prefer assistance in making the modifications, it is probably best to use the DBSETUP program from DOS level. This program, which is loaded from DOS by typing *DBSETUP* **ENTER**, brings up the menu seen in Figure A-3 (shown in 43-line EGA mode).

Select CONFIG.DB, and you will have the choice of creating a new CONFIG.DB file or modifying an existing one. In most cases, it's best to use the existing CONFIG.DB file on your disk.

When you tell the system that you want to modify or create a new CONFIG.DB file, the system brings up a menu like that in Figure A-4. You may move from menu item to menu item using the cursor keys or the **Alt** key plus the first letter of each option.

Although most of the options are beyond the scope of this book, it should be clear that you can easily modify the display, add or change printers, and define (or redefine) the action of the function keys. Instructions at the bottom of the screen will aid you in making changes to the CONFIG.DB file.

Most options either toggle (using the **Space Bar** or **ENTER** key) or require some form of parameter entry or completion when

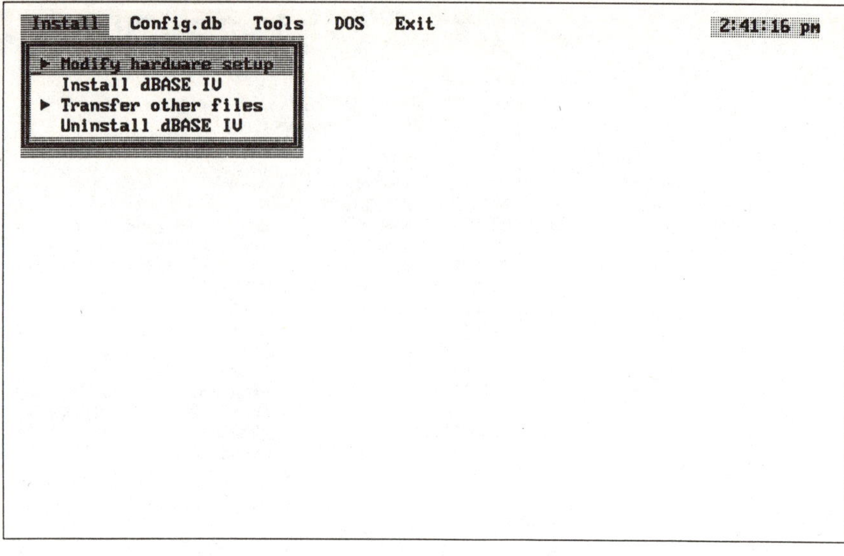

Figure A-3

selected. In some cases, the **Shft-F1** combination may provide a pick list for selecting values for the option.

When finished with the modifications, the Exit menu allows you to save your changes and return to the SETUPDB menu, or abandon the changes and return to the menu.

Figure A-4

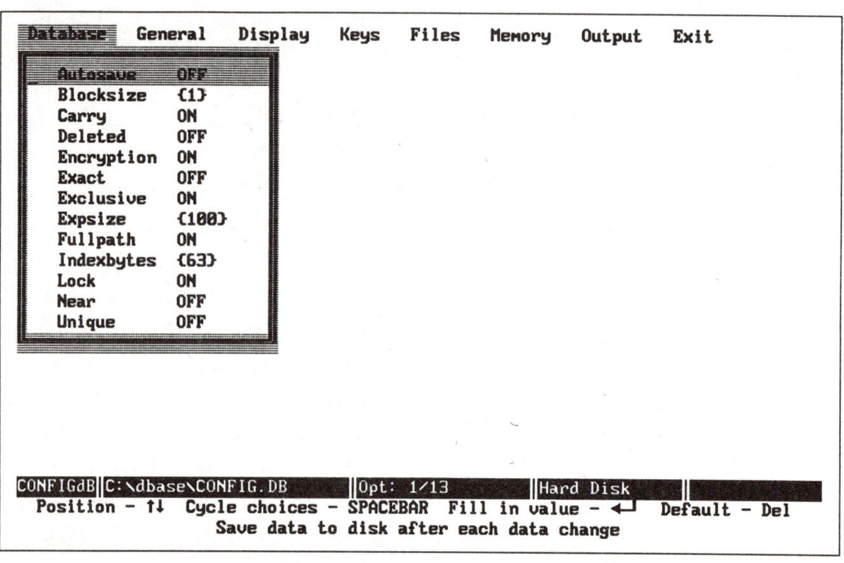

One aspect of the CONFIG.DB file that is not changed by this menu and that must be added or modified using a text editor is the Command= line. This line automatically issues a system command when the program is loaded. As seen earlier, the line Command=Assist in the CONFIG.DB screen tells the system to automatically issue the Assist command, which loads the Control Center when you start dBASE. If you prefer to go directly into dot prompt programming, deleting this line allows you to do this.

Fast Loading of dBASE

If you don't need to see the startup screens, you can quickly load dBASE IV by issuing the command DBASE/T. This command tells the system to load the program and not display the startup screen.

To load even faster, you can create a batch file that automatically loads the program, yet requires fewer keystrokes. Such a file was discussed in Chapter 2. Using a basic text editor, create a batch program called DB.BAT that uses the following command:

DBASE/T

When you type *DB* **ENTER**, the system loads DBASE/T and the program quickly comes onto the screen, ready for work.

File Protection

The Protect data option in the Tools menu assigns a password to your database structure and data files. Once set, the utility requires use of the password to gain access to your data structure and data files.

You should exercise extreme vigilance in remembering the password used to protect files. If you forget or lose the password, you will be unable to use the data files if they are password-protected.

Index